The Intext Series in

FOUNDATIONS OF EDUCATION

Consulting Editor

HERBERT M. KLIEBARD

University of Wisconsin

CULTURE AND SCHOOL
Socio-Cultural Significances

CULTURE AND SCHOOL
Socio-Cultural Significances

RONALD SHINN

Sacramento State College

INTEXT EDUCATIONAL PUBLISHERS

College Division of Intext

Scranton   San Francisco   Toronto   London

ISBN 0-7002-2394-0

COPYRIGHT © , 1972, BY INTERNATIONAL TEXTBOOK COMPANY

This book is dedicated to my mother
VIOLET LUM
for her thoughtfulness and inspiration
throughout my educational career.

Foreword

Our *schools* must change. On this most people agree. Here are some changes for "el-hi" schools to which I would give first priority:

From	*To*
Offering curriculums *about* life	Curriculums that *are* life
Providing teacher *imposed* content	Student composed *content*
Being teacher directed	Pupil inner and self-directed
Concentrating on *book*-centered learning	*Community*-centered learning
Emphasizing a *credential*-concerned society	*Competence*-concerned society
Having the goal to make a difference in the *minds* of children	The goal is to make a difference in the *minds* and *hearts* of children
Being *depersonalized, dehumanized*-oriented schools	*Person-to-person, humanistic*-oriented schools

But before changes in these directions can become widespread—or even implemented at all—*teachers* themselves must change . . .

From	*To*
Using the model "T" teacher (who believes teaching is *talking,* usually from up front and on high)	The model "A" teacher (who believes teaching is *action*—being *a*round and *a*bout the classroom, listening to students—emphasizing inquiry, social sensitivity and self-direction, guiding, probing, feeling, encouraging)
Being *learned*	Life-long *learners*
Being *self-contained*	*Organizers* of multiple teaching resources—human and technological
Offering whole-class teaching	Individual, small group, family-size teaching
Having concerns for what and who	Concerns for why and how
Emphasizing answer-centered instruction	Answer-asking instruction
Centering on product learning	Process learning

For these reforms to occur we need to recruit a new breed of teachers who

ix

see their role as change agent rather than conservators of the cultural heritage. We need to initially prepare these new teachers and at the same time retrain thousands of our present staff of teachers on a totally new and different set of assumptions about teacher education. Such a new set of assumptions about the education of teachers includes:

> that learning to teach is essentially being engaged in a process of personal growth;

> that learning to teach is best accomplished through direct experience and intensive involvement in the act of teaching, given also the concurrent opportunity to reflect on these experiences by sharing in the established body of principles and theories of education and by simultaneously testing their applicability to concrete situations;

> that the development of personal skill, style, and integrity in teaching can best be accomplished by a focused examination of both the issues and their relationship to one's self from several different (or as many as possible) perspectives and points of view; that this process of examination be continuous and on-going; that closure on these issues be regarded as tentative;

> that through this process the teacher clarifies and expands his alternatives for behaving in significant and honest ways with his students;

> that teaching, therefore, is not to be considered only a set of skills that one developes through some sequential process, but that it is a way of *being*—a way of developing one's personal and professional resources in order to relate to other human beings in a certain purposeful way (i.e., teaching/learning);

> that teacher education is therefore not something that necessarily submits to a highly structured format but is rather a highly personal phenomenon which amalgamates theory and practice, teaching and learning, content and process, behavior and attitudes, acting and contemplating, the concrete and abstract, the affective and cognitive—all reciprocal, confluent relationships, not polarities or entities as they generally and traditionally are described.

Dr. Shinn's book, *Culture and School,* will be an important resource in this new training and retraining to which I've referred. His is a humanistic approach to problems of education and it succinctly yet adequately identifies the crucial problems in dealing with culturally unique children and youth. The focus is the development of a new cultural awareness that comes from understanding the origin and causes of cultural conflict in the classroom and between the school and the community, and a cognizance of the importance of the social-cultural determinants that affect learning and behavior.

If ever the schools are to achieve some greater degree of equal opportunity for all, there must be a dramatic upgrading of teachers' knowledge about and empathy for those who bring to school a cultural background that is unique. Much of that which we have assumed to be a part of America's melting pot hasn't melted. Some are saying now it won't melt—that the answer is an apartheid society. Dr. Shinn's book is an eloquent plea for the melting to continue at a rapid and increased pace. It is significant that this plea comes from an author who himself was once a high school dropout. I am proud Dr. Shinn has asked me to write these introductory remarks for his first major publication.

James C. Stone
Professor of Higher Education
University of California, Berkeley

Preface

Schools cannot operate in a vacuum. Often school curricula are rendered ineffectual due to myths and misconceptions about the lifestyles of ethnic minorities and youth sub-cultures. Consequently, the expectations and constraints placed upon children from diverse sub-cultures adversely affect their self-concept and augment alienation. Unaware of this phenomenon, the school is negatively reinforcing student rebellions as well as social maladjustment of youth by identifying and grouping children according to low achievers, slow learners, mentally retarded, and emotionally handicapped on the basis of their nonaffinity to the dominant culture.

Teachers should be cognizant that their middle-class values might preclude their acceptance of students who hold a different set of values stemming from their heritage and peer group associations. The notion of acceptance based on the concepts of culture can facilitate the ability of teachers to relate to children from diverse sub-cultures. Education, in its fullest sense, cannot be realized unless school personnel come to grips with the socio-cultural determinants of the learning and socialization processes of youngsters in the public schools.

Hopefully, the reader will experience a "mirrors of man" effect which transcends test scores and achievement records of students in order to appreciate the socio-cultural dimensions involved in the learning processes. Also, the thrust of the book prescribes open communication and interaction between the school and community subsequently leading to a joint venture in the educating of youngsters.

R. Shinn

Sacramento State College
September, 1971

Acknowledgments

Many have contributed tirelessly to assist me with this project. My heart-felt appreciation goes to the faculty of Sacramento State College. Dr. Fannie Canson was a constant source of inspiration and help. Leda Cotton worked diligently in the clerical and correspondence aspects necessary to get the project well on its way. Linda Tugade was instrumental in helping the project in its terminal stages.

Special thanks and appreciation go to my wife. She not only adjusted well to the demands and rigors of this project but actively participated throughout the varying phases of the book.

R.S.

Contents

CULTURE AND SCHOOL
Socio-Cultural Significances

I / THE NOTION OF CULTURE

Leslie A. White*
University of Michigan

1 / The Concept of Culture †

Virtually all cultural anthropologists take it for granted, no doubt, that *culture* is the basic and central concept of their science. There is, however, a disturbing lack of agreement as to what they mean by this term. To some, culture is learned behavior. To others, it is not behavior at all, but an abstraction from behavior—whatever that is. Stone axes and pottery bowls are culture to some anthropologists, but no material object can be culture to others. Culture exists only in the mind, according to some; it consists of observable things and events in the external world to others. Some anthropologists think of culture as consisting of ideas, but they are divided upon the question of their locus: some say they are in the minds of the peoples studied, others hold that they are in the minds of ethnologists. We go on to "culture is a psychic defense mechanism," "culture consists of *n* different social signals correlated with *m* different responses," "culture is a Rohrschach of a society," and so on, to confusion and bewilderment. One wonders what physics would be like if it had as many and as varied conceptions of energy!

There was a time, however, when there was a high degree of uniformity of comprehension and use of the term culture. During the closing decades of the nineteenth century and the early years of the twentieth, the great majority of cultural anthropologists, we believe, held to the conception expressed by E. B. Tylor, in 1871, in the opening lines of *Primitive Culture:* "Culture . . . is that complex whole which includes knowledge, belief, art, morals, law, custom, and any other capabilities and habits acquired by man as a member of society." Tylor does not make it explicit in this statement that culture is the peculiar possession of man; but it is therein implied, and in other places he makes this point clear and explicit (Tylor 1881:54, 123, where he deals with the "great mental gap between us and the animals"). Culture, to Tylor, was the name of all things and events peculiar to the human species. Specifically, he enumerates beliefs, customs, objects—"hatchet, adze, chisel," and so on— and techniques—"wood-chopping, fishing . . . , shooting and spearing game, fire-making," and so on (Tylor 1913:5–6).

The Tylorian conception of culture prevailed in anthropology generally for decades. In 1920, Robert H. Lowie began *Primitive Society* by quoting "Tylor's famous definition." In recent years, however, conceptions and defini-

*I am greatly obliged to Robert Anderson, Raymond L. Wilder, Robert Carneiro, Gertrude E. Dole, and Elman R. Service for a critical reading of this paper in typescript.

†From *American Anthropologist,* Vol. 61, No. 2 (1959). Reproduced by permission of the author and the American Anthropological Association.

tions of culture have multiplied and varied to a great degree. One of the most highly favored of these is that *culture is an abstraction*. This is the conclusion reached by Kroeber and Kluckhohn in their exhaustive review of the subject: *Culture: a Critical Review of Concepts and History* (1952:155, 169). It is the definition given by Beals and Hoijer in their textbook, *An Introduction to Anthropology* (1953:210, 219, 507, 535). In a more recent work, however, *Cultural Anthropology* (1958:16, 427), Felix M. Keesing defines culture as "the totality of learned, socially transmitted behavior."

Much of the discussion of the concept of culture in recent years has been concerned with a distinction between culture and human behavior. For a long time many anthropologists were quite content to define culture as behavior, peculiar to the human species, acquired by learning, and transmitted from one individual, group, or generation to another by mechanisms of social inheritance. But eventually some began to object to this and to make the point that culture is not itself behavior, but is an abstraction from behavior. Culture, say Kroeber and Kluckhohn (1952:155), "is an abstraction from concrete human behavior, but it is not itself behavior." Beals and Hoijer (1953:210, 219) and others take the same view.[1]

Those who define culture as an abstraction do not tell us what they mean by this term. They appear to take it for granted (1) that they themselves know what they mean by "abstraction," and (2) that others, also, will understand. We believe that neither of these suppositions is well founded; we shall return to a consideration of this concept later in this essay. But whatever an abstraction in general may be to these anthropologists, when culture becomes an "abstraction" it becomes imperceptible, imponderable, and not wholly real. According to Linton, "culture itself is intangible and cannot be directly apprehended even by the individuals who participate in it" (1936:288–89). Herskovits also calls culture "intangible" (1945:150). Anthropologists in the imaginary symposium reported by Kluckhohn and Kelly (1945:79, 81) argue that "one can see" such things as individuals and their actions and interactions, but "has anyone ever seen 'culture'?" Beals and Hoijer (1953:210) say that "the anthropologist cannot observe culture directly; . . ."

If culture as an abstraction is intangible, imperceptible, does it exist, is it real? Ralph Linton (1936:363) raises this question in all seriousness: "If it [culture] can be said to exist at all. . . ." Radcliffe-Brown (1940:2) declares that the word culture "denotes, not any concrete reality, but an abstraction, and as it is commonly used a vague abstraction." And Spiro (1951:24) says that according to the predominant "position of contemporary anthropology . . . culture has no ontological reality. . . ."

[1]One of the earliest instances of regarding culture as an abstraction is Murdock's statement: "realizing that culture is merely an abstraction from observed likenesses in the behavior of individuals . . ." (1937:xi).

Thus when culture becomes an abstraction it not only becomes invisible and imponderable; it virtually ceases to exist. It would be difficult to construct a less adequate conception of culture. Why, then, have prominent and influential anthropologists turned to the "abstraction" conception of culture?

A clue to the reason—if, indeed, it is not an implicit statement of the reason itself—is given by Kroeber and Kluckhohn (1952:155):

> Since behavior is the first-hand and outright material of the science of psychology, and culture is not—being of concern only secondarily, as an influence on this material—it is natural that psychologists and psychologizing sociologists should see behavior as primary in their field, and then extend this view farther to apply to the field of culture also.

The reasoning is simple and direct: if culture is behavior, then (1) culture becomes the subject matter of psychology, since behavior is the proper subject matter of psychology; culture would then become the property of psychologists and "psychologizing sociologists"; and (2) nonbiological anthropology would be left without a subject matter. The danger was real and imminent; the situation, critical. What was to be done?

The solution proposed by Kroeber and Kluckhohn was neat and simple: let the psychologists have behavior; anthropologists will keep for themselves abstractions from behavior. These abstractions become and constitute *culture.*

But in this rendering unto Caesar, anthropologists have given the psychologists the better part of the bargain, for they have surrendered unto them real things and events, locatable and observable, directly or indirectly, in the real external world, in terrestrial time and space, and have kept for themselves only intangible, imponderable abstractions that "have no ontological reality." But at least, and at last, they have a subject matter—however insubstantial and unobservable—of their own!

Whether or not this has been the principal reason for defining culture as "not behavior, but abstractions from behavior," is perhaps a question; we feel, however, that Kroeber and Kluckhohn have made themselves fairly clear. But whatever the reason, or reasons—for there may have been several —may have been for the distinction, the question whether culture is to be regarded as behavior or as abstractions from it is, we believe, the central issue in recent attempts to hammer out an adequate, usable, fruitful, and enduring conception of culture.

The present writer is no more inclined to surrender culture to the psychologists than are Kroeber and Kluckhohn; indeed, few anthropologists have taken greater pains to distinguish psychological problems from culturological problems than he has.[2] But he does not wish to exchange the hard substance

---

[2]Several of the essays in *The Science of Culture* (1949)—"Culturological vs. Psychological Interpretations of Human Behavior," "Cultural Determinants of *Mind,*" "Genuis: Its Causes and Incidence," "Ikhnaton: The Great Man vs. the Culture Process," "The Definition and Prohibition if Incest," etc.—deal with this distinction.

of culture for its wraith, either. No science can have a subject matter that consists of intangible, invisible, imponderable, ontologically unreal "abstractions"; a science must have real stars, real mammals, foxes, crystals, cells, phonemes, gamma rays, and culture traits to work with.[3] We believe that we can offer an analysis of the situation that will distinguish between psychology, the scientific study of behavior on the one hand, and culturology, the scientific study of culture, on the other, and at the same time give a real, substantial subject matter to each.

Science makes a dichotomy between the mind of the observer and the external world[4]—things and events having their locus outside the mind of this observer. The scientist makes contact with the external world with and through his senses, forming percepts. These percepts are translated into concepts which are manipulated in a process called thinking[5] in such a way as to form premises, propositions, generalizations, conclusions, and so on. The validity of these premises, propositions, and conclusions is established by testing them in terms of experience of the external world (Einstein 1936:350). This is the way science proceeds and does its work.

The first step in scientific procedure is to observe, or more generally to experience, the external world in a sensory manner. The next step—after percepts have been translated into concepts—is the classification of things and events perceived or experienced. Things and events of the external world are thus divided into classes of various kinds: acids, metals, stones, liquids, mammals, stars, atoms, corpuscles, and so on. Now it turns out that there is a class of phenomena, one of enormous importance in the study of man, for which science has as yet no name: this is the class of things and events consisting of or dependent upon symboling.[6] It is one of the most remarkable facts in the

[3]I made this point in my review of Kroeber and Kluckhohn, "Culture: a Critical Review etc." (1954:464–65). At about the same time Huxley was writing (1955:15–16): "If anthropology is a science, then for anthropologists culture must be defined, not philosophically or metaphysically, nor as an abstraction, nor in purely subjective terms, but as something which can be investigated by the methods of scientific inquiry, a phenomenal process occurring in space and time."

[4]"The belief in an external world independent of the perceiving subject is the basis of all natural science," says Einstein (1934:6).

[5]Thinking, in science, means "operations with concepts, and the creation and use of definite functional relations between them, and the co-ordination of sense experiences to these concepts," according to Einstein (1936:350). Einstein has much to say in this essay about the manner and process of scientific thinking.

[6]By "symboling" we mean bestowing meaning upon a thing or an act, or grasping and appreciating meanings thus bestowed. Holy water is a good example of such meanings. The attribute of holiness is bestowed upon the water by a human being, and it may be comprehended and appreciated by other human beings. Articulate speech is the most characteristic and important form of symboling. Symboling is trafficking in nonsensory meanings, i.e., meanings which, like the holiness of sacramental water, cannot be comprehended with the senses alone. Symboling is a kind of behavior. Only man is capable of symboling.

We have discussed this concept rather fully in "The Symbol: the Origin and Basis of Human Behavior," originally published in *The Philosophy of Science,* Vol. 7, pp. 451–63 (1940).

recent history of science that this important class has no name, but the fact remains that it does not. And the reason why it does not is because these things and events have always been considered and designated, not merely and simply as the things and events that they are, in and of themselves, but always as things and events in a particular context.

A thing is what it is; "a rose is a rose is a rose." Acts are not first of all ethical acts or economic acts or erotic acts. An act is an act. An act becomes an ethical datum or an economic datum or an erotic datum when—and only when—it is considered in an ethical, economic, or erotic context. Is a Chinese porcelain vase a scientific specimen, an object of art, an article of commerce, or an exhibit in a lawsuit? The answer is obvious. Actually, of course, to call it a "Chinese porcelain vase" is already to put it into a particular context; it would be better first of all to say "a glazed form of fired clay is a glazed form of fired clay." As a Chinese porcelain vase, it becomes an object of art, a scientific specimen, or an article of merchandise when, and only when, it is considered in an esthetic, scientific, or commercial context.

Let us return now to the class of things and events that consist of or are dependent upon symboling: a spoken word, a stone axe, a fetich, avoiding one's mother-in-law, loathing milk, saying a prayer, sprinkling holy water, a pottery bowl, casting a vote, remembering the sabbath to keep it holy—"and any other capabilities and habits [and things] acquired by man as a member of [human] society" (Tylor 1913:1). They are what they are: things and acts dependent upon symboling.

We may consider these things-and events-dependent-upon-symboling in a number of contexts: astronomical, physical, chemical, anatomical, physiological, psychological, and culturological, and, consequently, they become astronomic, physical, chemical, anatomical, physiological, psychological, and culturological phenomena in turn. All things and events dependent upon symboling are dependent also upon solar energy which sustains all life on this planet; this is the astronomic context. These things and events may be considered and interpreted in terms of the anatomical, neurological, and physiological processes of the human beings who exhibit them. They may be considered and interpreted also in terms of their relationship to human organisms, i.e., in a somatic context. And they may be considered in an extrasomatic context, i.e., in terms of their relationship to other like things and events rather than in relationship to human organisms.

When things and events dependent upon symboling are considered and

It has been reprinted in slightly revised form in *The Science of Culture*. It has also been reprinted in Etc., A Review of General Semantics, Vol. 1, pp. 229–37 (1944); S.I. Hayakawa (ed.), *Language, Meaning, and Maturity* (New York, 1954); E. Adamson Hoebel et al. (eds.), *Readings in Anthropology (New York, 1955); Readings in Introductory Anthropology,* (Ann Arbor, Mich., 1956); Lewis A. Coser and Bernard Rosenberg (eds.), *Sociological Theory,* (New York, 1957); and in Walter Goldschmidt (ed.), *Readings in the Ways of Mankind,* (1957).

interpreted in terms of their relationship to human organisms, i.e., in a somatic context, they may properly be called *human behavior,* and the science, *psychology.* When things and events dependent upon symboling are considered and interpreted in an extrasomatic context, i.e., in terms of their relationships to one another rather than to human organisms, we may call them *culture,* and the science, *culturology.* This analysis is expressed diagrammatically in Fig. 1.

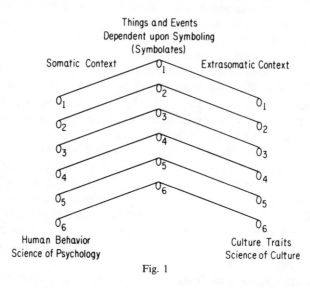

Fig. 1

In the middle of the diagram we have a vertical column of circles, O_1, O_2, O_3, etc., which stand for things (objects) and events (acts) dependent upon symboling. These things and events constitute a distinct class of phenomena in the realm of nature. Since they have had heretofore no name we have ventured to give them one: *symbolates.* We fully appreciate the hazards of coining terms, but this all-important class of phenomena needs a name to distinguish it from other classes. If we were physicists we might call them "Gamma phenomena." But we are not physicists, and we believe a simple word would be better—or at least more acceptable—than a Greek letter. In coining our term we have followed a well-established precedent: if an *isolate* is something that results from the process or action of isolating, then something that results from the action or process of symboling might well be called a symbolate. The particular word with which we designate this class of phenomena is not of paramount importance, and perhaps a better term than symbolate can be found. But it is of paramount importance that this class have a name.

A thing or event dependent upon symboling—a symbolate—is just what it is, but it may become significant in any one of a number of contexts. As we have already seen, it may be significant in an astronomic context: the performance of a ritual requires the expenditure of energy which has come from the sun. But within the sciences of man we may distinguish two significant contexts: the somatic and the extrasomatic. Symbolates may be considered and interpreted in terms of their relationship to the human organism, or they may be considered in terms of their relationships to one another, quite apart from their relationship to the human organism. Let us illustrate with some examples.

I smoke a cigarette, cast a vote, decorate a pottery bowl, avoid my mother-in-law, say a prayer, or chip an arrowhead. Each one of these acts is dependent upon the process of symboling;[7] each therefore is a symbolate. As a scientist, I may consider these acts (events) in terms of their relationships to me, to my organism; or, I may treat them in terms of their relationships to one another, to other symbolates, quite apart from their relationship to my organism.

In the first type of interpretation I consider the symbolate in terms of its relationship to my bodily structure: the structure and functions of my hand, for example; or to my stereoscopic, chromatic vision; or to my needs, desires, hopes, fears, imagination, habit formation, overt reactions, satisfactions, and so forth. How do I feel when I avoid my mother-in-law or cast a ballot? What is my attitude toward the act? What is my conception of it? Is the act accompanied by heightened emotional tone, or do I perform it in a mechanical, perfunctory manner? And so on. We may call these acts *human behavior;* our concern is *psychological.*

What we have said of acts (events) will apply to objects (things) also. What is my conception of a pottery bowl, a ground axe, a crucifix, roast pork, whisky, holy water, cement? What is my attitude and how do I react toward each of these things? In short, what is the nature of the relationship between each of these things and my own organism? We do not customarily call these things human behavior, but they are the embodiments of human behavior; the difference between a nodule of flint and a stone axe is the factor of human labor. An axe, bowl, crucifix—or a haircut—is congealed human labor. We have then a class of objects dependent upon symboling that have a significance in terms of their relationship to the human organism. The scientific consideration and interpretation of this relationship is *psychology.*

But we may treat symbolates in terms of their relationships to one

---

[7]"How is chipping an arrowhead dependent upon symboling?" it might be asked. I have answered this question in "On the Use of Tools by Primates." *Journal of Comparative Psychology,* Vol. 34, pp. 369–74 (1942); reprinted in White, *The Science of Culture;* in *Man in Contemporary Society,* prepared by the Contemporary Civilization staff of Columbia University (New York, 1955); and in E. R. Service (ed), *Readings in Introductory Anthropology* (Ann Arbor, Mich., 1956). There is a fundamental difference between the tool process in the human species and the tool process among subhuman primates. This difference is due to symboling.

another, quite apart from their relationship to the human organism. Thus, in the case of the avoidance of a mother-in-law, we would consider it in terms of its relationship to other symbolates, or symbolate clusters, such as customs of marriage—monogamy, polygyny, polyandry—place of residence of a couple after marriage, division of labor between the sexes, mode of subsistence, domestic architecture, degree of cultural development, etc. Or, if we are concerned with voting we would consider it in terms of forms of political organization (tribal, state), kind of government (democratic, monarchical, fascist); age, sex, or property qualifications; political parties and so on. In this context our symbolates become *culture*—culture traits or trait clusters, i.e., institutions, customs, codes, etc., and the scientific concern is *culturology*.

It would be the same with objects as with acts. If we were concerned with a hoe we would regard it in terms of its relationships to other symbolates in an extrasomatic context: to other instruments employed in subsistence, the digging stick and plow in particular; or to customs of division of labor between the sexes; the stage of cultural development, etc. We would be concerned with the relationship between a digital computer and the degree of development of mathematics, the stage of technological development, division of labor, the social organization within which it is used (corporation, military organization, astronomical laboratory), and so on.

Thus we see that we have two quite different kinds of sciencing[8] with regard to things and events—objects and acts—dependent upon symboling. If we treat them in terms of their relationship to the human organism, i.e., in an organismic, or somatic context, these things and events become *human behavior* and we are doing *psychology*. If, however, we treat them in terms of their relationship to one another, quite apart from their relationship to human organisms, i.e., in an extrasomatic, or extraorganismic, context, the things and events become *culture*—cultural elements of culture traits—and we are doing *culturology*. Human psychology and culturology have the same phenomena as their subject matter: things and events dependent upon symboling (symbolates). The difference between the two sciences derives from the difference between the contexts in which their common subject matter is treated.[9]

The analysis and distinction that we have made with regard to things and events dependent upon symboling in general is precisely like the one that linguists have been making for decades with regard to a particular kind of these things and events, namely, words.

A word is a thing (a sound or combination of sounds, or marks made upon some substance) or an act dependent upon symboling. Words are just what they are: words. But they are significant to scientific students of words

---

[8]"Sciencing," too, is a kind of behavior. See our essay, "Science is *Sciencing*," *Philosophy of Science*, Vol. 5, pp. 369–89 (1938); reprinted in *The Science of Culture*.

[9]Importance of context may be illustrated by contrasting attitudes toward one and the same class of women: as mothers they are revered; as mothers-in-law, reviled.

in two different contexts: somatic or organismic, and extrasomatic or extraorganismic. This distinction has been expressed customarily with the terms *la langue* and *la parole,* or language and speech.[10]

Words in a somatic context constitute a kind of human behavior: speech behavior. The scientific study of words in a somatic context is the psychology (plus physiology, perhaps, and anatomy) of speech. It is concerned with the relationship between words and the human organism: how the words are produced and uttered, the meanings of words, attitudes toward words, perception of and response to words, and so on.

In the extrasomatic context, words are considered in terms of their relationships to one another, quite apart from their relationship to the human organism. The scientific concern here is linguistics, or the science of language. Phonetics, phonemics, syntax, lexicon, grammar, dialectic variation, evolution or historical change, etc., indicate particular focuses, or emphases, within the science of linguistics.

The difference between these two sciences may be illustrated by citing two books: *The Psychology of Language* by Walter B. Pillsbury and Clarence L. Meader (New York, 1928), and *Language* by Leonard Bloomfield (New York, 1933). In the former we find chapter titles such as "The Speech Organs," "The Senses Involved in Speech," "Mental Processes in Speech," etc. In the latter the chapter headings are "The Phoneme," "Phonetic Structure," "Grammatical Forms," "Sentence-Types," etc. We illustrate the distinction between these two sciences in Fig. 2.

Figures 1 and 2 are fundamentally alike. In each case we are concerned with a class of things and events dependent upon symboling. In Fig. 1, we are concerned with a general class: symbolates; in Fig. 2 we are dealing with a particular class: words (a subclass of the class symbolates). In each case we refer the things and events to a somatic context on the one hand, and to an extrasomatic context on the other, for purposes of consideration and interpretation. And in each case we have two distinct kinds of science, or sciencing: the psychology of human behavior or of speech; and the science of culture or of language.

Culture, then, is a class of things and events, dependent upon symboling, considered in an extrasomatic context. This definition rescues cultural anthropology from intangible, imperceptible, and ontologically unreal abstractions and provides it with a real, substantial, observable subject matter. And it

---

[10] "According to [Ferdinand] de Sassure the study of human speech is not the subject matter of *one* science but of two sciences. . . . De Sassure drew a sharp line between *la langue* and *la parole.* Language (*la langue*) is universal, whereas the process of speech (*la parole*) . . . is individual" (Cassirer 1944:122). Huxley (1955:16), citing Cassirer's discussion of de Sassure's distinction between *la langue* and *la parole,* speaks of the former as "the super-individual system of grammar and syntax," and of the latter as "the actual words or way of speaking used by particular individuals." He goes on to say that "we find the *same distinction in every cultural activity*—in law, . . .; in art . . .; in social structure . . .; in science . . ." (emphasis ours).

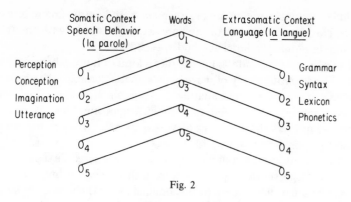

Fig. 2

distinguishes sharply between behavior—behaving organisms—and culture; between the science of psychology and the science of culture.

It might be objected that every science should have a certain class of things per se as its subject matter, not things-in-a-certain-context. Atoms are atoms and mammals are mammals, it might be argued, and as such are the subject matter of physics and mammalogy, respectively, regardless of context. Why therefore should cultural anthropology have its subject matter defined in terms of things in context rather than in terms of things in themselves? At first glance this argument might appear to be a cogent one, but actually it has but little force. What the scientist wants to do is to make intelligible the phenomena that confront him. And very frequently the significant thing about phenomena is the context in which they are found. Even in the so-called natural sciences we have a science of organisms-in-a-certain-context: parasitology, a science of organisms playing a certain role in the realm of living things. And within the realm of man-and-culture we have dozens of examples of things and events whose significance depends upon context rather than upon the inherent qualities of the phenomena themselves. An adult male of a certain animal species is called a man. But a man is a man, not a slave; a man becomes a slave only when he enters a certain context. So it is with commodities: corn and cotton are articles of use-value, but they were not commodities—articles produced for sale at a profit—in aboriginal Hopi culture; corn and cotton become commodities only when they enter a certain socioeconomic context. A cow is a cow, but she may become a medium of exchange, money (*pecus,* pecuniary) in one context, food in another, mechanical power (Cartwright used a cow as motive power for his first power loom) in another, and a sacred object of worship (India) in still another. We do not have a science of cows, but we do have scientific studies of mediums of exchange, of mechanical power, and of sacred objects in each of which cows may be significant. And so we have a science of symboled things and events in an extrasomatic context.

The locus of culture. If we define culture as consisting of real things and events observable, directly or indirectly, in the external world, where do these things and events exist and have their being? What is the locus of culture? The answer is: the things and events that comprise culture have their existence, in space and time, (1) within human organisms, i.e., concepts, beliefs, emotions, attitudes; (2) within processes of social interaction among human beings; and (3) within material objects (axes, factories, railroads, pottery bowls) lying outside human organisms but within the patterns of social interaction among them.[11] The locus of culture is thus intraorganismal, interorganismal, and extraorganismal (see Fig. 3).

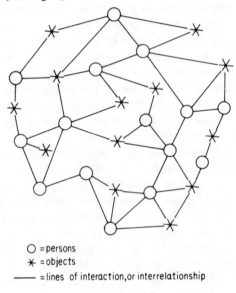

O = persons
✳ = objects
—— = lines of interaction, or interrelationship

Fig. 3. The locus of culture.

But, someone might object, you have said that culture consists of extrasomatic phenomena and now you tell me that culture exists, in part, within human organisms. Is this not a contradiction? The answer is, No, it is not a contradiction; it is a misunderstanding. We did not say that culture consists of extrasomatic things and events, i.e., phenomena whose locus is outside human organisms. What we said is that culture consists of things and events considered within an extrasomatic context. This is quite a different thing.

Every cultural element has two aspects: subjective and objective. It might appear that stone axes are "objective," and ideas and attitudes are "subjective." But this is a superficial and inadequate view. An axe has a subjec-

[11]"The true locus of culture," says Sapir (1932:236), "is in the interactions of . . . individuals and, on the subjective side, in the world of meanings which each one of these individuals may unconsciously abstract for himself from his participation in these interactions." This statement is like ours except that it omits objects: material culture.

tive component; it would be meaningless without a concept and an attitude. on the other hand, a concept or an attitude would be meaningless without overt expression, in behavior or speech (which is a form of behavior). Every cultural element, every culture trait, therefore, has a subjective and an objective aspect. But conceptions, attitudes, and sentiments—phenomena that have their locus within the human organism—may be considered for purposes of scientific interpretation in an extrasomatic context, i.e., in terms of their relation to other symboled things and events rather than in terms of their relationship to the human organism. Thus, we may consider the subjective aspect of the mother-in-law taboo, i.e., the conceptions and attitudes involved, in terms of their relationship, not to the human organism, but to other symbolates such as forms of marriage and the family, place of residence after marriage, and so on. On the other hand, we may consider the axe in terms of its relationship to the human organism—its meaning; the person's conception of it; his attitude toward it—rather than to other symboled things and events such as arrows, hoes, and customs regulating the division of labor in society.

We shall now pass in review a number of conceptions of culture, or conceptions with regard to culture, widely current in ethnological literature, and comment critically upon each one from the standpoint of the conception of culture set forth in this paper.

"Culture consists of ideas." Some anthropologists like to define culture in terms of ideas only. The reason for this, apparently, is the notion that ideas are both basic and primary, that they are prime movers and as such originate behavior which in turn may produce objects such as pottery bowls. "Culture consists of ideas," says Taylor (1948:98–110, passim), it "is a mental phenomenon . . . not . . . material objects or observable behavior. . . . For example, there is present in an Indian's mind the idea of a dance. This is the trait of culture. This idea influences his body so that he behaves in a certain way," i.e., he dances.

This conception of sociocultural reality is a naive one. It is based upon a primitive, prescientific, and now obsolete metaphysics and psychology. It was Thought-Woman among the Keresan Pueblo Indians who brought about events by thinking and willing them to happen. Ptah created Egyptian culture by objectifying his thoughts. And God said "Let there be light," and there was light. But we no longer explain the origin and development of culture by simply saying that it has resulted from man's ideas. To be sure, an idea was involved in the invention of firearms, but we have explained nothing when we say that firearms are the fruit of thought, because the ideas themselves have not been accounted for. Why did the idea occur when and where it did rather than at some other time and place? And, actually, ideas—matter of fact, realistic ideas —enter the mind from the outside world. It was working with soils that gave man, or woman, the idea of pottery; the calendar is a by-product of intensive agriculture. Culture does indeed consist in part of ideas; but attitudes, overt acts, and objects are culture, also.

"*Culture consists of abstractions.*" We return now to the presently popular definition: "culture is an abstraction, or consists of abstractions." As we observed earlier, those who define culture in these terms do not tell us what they mean by "abstraction," and there is reason to believe that they are not very clear as to what they do mean by it. They make it emphatically clear, however, that an abstraction is not an observable thing or event. The fact that doubts have been raised as to the "reality" of an abstraction indicates that those who use this term are not sure what "it means," i.e., what they mean by it. We do have some clues, however.

Culture is "basically a form or pattern or way," say Kroeber and Kluckhohn (1952:155, 169), "even a culture trait is an abstraction. A trait is an 'ideal type' because no two pots are identical nor are two marriage ceremonies ever held in precisely the same way." The culture trait "pot" therefore appears to be the ideal form of which each particular pot is an exemplification—a sort of Platonic idea, or ideal. Each and every pot, they reason, is real; but the "ideal" is never realized in any particular pot. It is like the "typical American man": 5'8½" high, weighs 164.378 pounds, is married, has 2.3 children, and so on. This is, we suppose, what they mean by an abstraction. If so, we know it well: it is a conception in the mind of the observer, the scientist.

There is a slightly different way of looking at an "abstraction." No two marriage ceremonies are ever held in precisely the same way. Well, let us tabulate a large sample of marriage ceremonies. We find that 100 percent contain element *a* (mutual acceptance of spouses). Ninety-nine percent contain element *b*. Elements *c, d,* and *e* appear in only 96, 94, and 89 percent, respectively, of the cases. We construct a distribution curve and determine an average or norm about which all particular instances are distributed. This is the typical marriage ceremony. But, like the typical American who has 2.3 children, this ideal is never fully and perfectly realized in any actual instance. It is an "abstraction," that is, a conception, worked out by the scientific observer and which exists in his own mind.

The failure to recognize the fact that abstractions are conceptions has led to confusion both as to their locus and their reality. Recognition of the fact that the so-called abstractions of science (such as a "rigid body" in physical theory; rigid bodies do not exist in actuality) are conceptions in the mind of the scientist clears up both these points: cultural "abstractions" are conceptions ("ideas") in the mind of the anthropologist. And as for their "ontological reality," conceptions are none the less real for being in the minds of men—nothing is more real, for example, than an hallucination.

This point was well made by Bidney (1954:488–89) in his review of *Culture, a Critical Review etc.:*

The real crux of the problem centers about what is meant by abstraction and what is its ontological import. Some anthropologists maintain that they are dealing only with logical abstractions and that culture has no reality other than that of an abstraction, but they can hardly expect other social scientists to agree with them, conceding that the objects of their sciences have no ontological, objective reality. *Thus Kroeber and Kluckhohn have confused the concept culture, which is a logical construct, with the actual existential culture* . . . [emphasis ours].

It is interesting to note in this connection that one anthropological theorist, Cornelius Osgood (1951:208; 1940), has defined culture explicitly as consisting of ideas in the minds of anthropologists: "Culture consists of all ideas of the manufactures, behavior, and ideas of the aggregate of human beings which have been directly observed or communicated to one's mind and of which one is conscious." Spiro (1951:24), also, holds that "culture is a logical construct, abstracted from human behavior, and as such, it exists only in the mind of *the investigator*" (Spiro's emphasis).

"There is no such thing as 'material' culture." Those who define culture in terms of ideas, or as an abstraction, or as behavior, find themselves obliged logically to declare that material objects are not, and cannot be, culture. "Strictly speaking," says Hoebel (1956:176), "material culture is really not culture at all." Taylor (1948:102, 98) goes farther: " . . . the concept of 'material culture' is fallacious" because "culture is a mental phenomenon." Beals and Hoijer (1953:210): " . . . culture is an abstraction from behavior and not to be confused with acts of behavior or with material artifacts, such as tools. . . ." This denial of material culture is rather awkward in view of the long established tradition among ethnographers, archeologists, and museum curators of calling tools, masks, fetiches, and so on, "material culture."[12]

Our definition extricates us from this dilemma. As we have already seen, it would not be absurd to speak of sandals or pottery bowls as behavior; their significant attribute is not mere deer hide or clay, but human labor; they are congelations of human labor. But in our defintion, symboling is the common factor in ideas, attitudes, acts, and objects. There are three kinds of symbolates: (1) ideas and attitudes, (2) overt acts, and (3) material objects. All may be considered in an extrasomatic context; all are to be reckoned as culture. This conception brings us back to long established usage in cultural anthropology: "Culture is that which is described in an ethnographic monograph."

"Reification of culture." There is a kind of conception of culture held by

---

[12]It is interesting to note that Durkheim (1951:313–14), who uses the term "society" when many an American anthropologist would say culture, or socio-cultural system, remarks that "it is not true that society is made up only of individuals; it also includes material things, which play an essential role in the common life." He cites as examples such things as houses, instruments and machines used in indudstry, etc. "Social life . . . is thus crystallized . . . and fixed on material supports . . . externalized. . . ."

some anthropologists that is much deplored by others who call it "reification." As one who has been especially singled out as a "reifier" of culture,[13] I may say that the term is singularly inappropriate. To reify is to make a thing of that which is not a thing, such as hope, honesty, or freedom. But it is not I who have made culture things. I have merely found real things and events in the external world which are distinguishable as a class by being dependent upon symboling, and which may be treated in an extrasomatic context, and I have called these things and events culture. This is precisely what E. B. Tylor did. It is what Lowie, Wissler, and most early American anthropologists have done. To Durkheim (1938:xliii) "the proposition which states that social facts [i.e., culture traits] are to be treated as things" lay "at the very basis of our method." It is not we who have reified culture; the elements comprising culture, according to our definition, were things to start with.

To be sure, if culture is defined as consisting of intangible, imponderable, ontologically unreal "abstractions," then to transform these wraiths into real, substantial bodies would indeed be to reify them. But we do not subscribe to such a definition.

"Culture: a process sui generis." "Culture is a thing *sui generis . . .*" said Lowie many years ago (1917:66, 17). This view has been held also by Kroeber. Durkheim, and others (for citation of examples see White 1949:89–94). It has been misunderstood and opposed by many. But what Lowie meant by this statement is made clear in the rest of the passage cited above (1917:66): "Culture is a thing *sui generis* which can be explained only in terms of itself . . . the ethnologist . . . will account for a given cultural fact by merging it in a group of cultural facts or by demonstrating some other cultural fact out of which it has been developed." For example, the custom of reckoning descent patrilineally may be explained in terms of customs of division of labor between the sexes, customs of residence—patrilocal, matrilocal, or neolocal—of a married couple; mode of subsistence; rules of inheritance, and so on. Or, to express it in terms of our definition of culture: "a symbolate in an extrasomatic context (i.e., a culture trait) is to be explained in terms of its relationship to other symbolates in the same context."

This conception of culture, like "reification" with which it is closely related, has been much misunderstood and opposed. In general, it has been regarded as "mystical." How can culture grow and develop by itself? ("Culture . . . seems to grow of itself"; Redfield 1941:134.) "It seems hardly necessary," says Boas (1928:235), "to consider culture a mystic entity that exists outside the society of its individual carriers, and that moves by its own force." Bidney (1946:535) brands this view of culture as a "mystical metaphysics of

---

[13]Max Gluckman "reifies structure in precisely the way that White reifies culture . . ." says Murdock (1951:470). Strong (1953:392) feels that "White reifies, and at times almost deifies, culture. . . ." See, also, Herrick 1956:196.

fate." And it has been opposed by Benedict (1934:231), Hooton (1939:370), Spiro (1951:23), and others.

But no one has ever said that culture is an entity that exists and moves by, and of, itself, quite apart from people. Nor has anyone ever said, as far as we know, that the origin, nature, and functions of culture can be understood without taking the human species into consideration. Obviously, if one is to understand culture in these aspects he must consider the biological nature of man. What has been asserted is that, given culture, its variations in time and place, and its processes of change are to be explained in terms of culture itself. This is precisely what Lowie meant when he said that "culture is a thing [process would have been a better term] *sui generis,*" as the above quotation from him (1917:66) makes clear. A consideration of the human organism, individually or collectively, is irrelevant to an explanation of processes of culture change. "This is not mysticism," says Lowie (1917:66), "but sound scientific method." And, as everyone knows, scholars have been working in accordance with this principle of interpretation for decades. One does not need to take human organisms into account in a scientific explanation of the evolution of currency, writing, or of Gothic art. The steam engine and textile machinery were introduced into Japan during the closing decades of the nineteenth century and certain changes in social structure followed; we add nothing to our explanation of these events by remarking that human beings were involved. Of course they were. And they were not irrelevant to the events which took place, but they are irrelevant to an explanation of these events.

"It is people, not culture, that do things." "Culture does not 'work,' 'move,' 'change,' but is worked, is moved, is changed. It is people who do things," says Lynd (1939:39). He supports this argument with the bold assertion that "culture does not enamel its fingernails . . . but people do . . ." (ibid.). He might have clinched it by demonstrating that culture has no fingernails.

The view that "it is people, not cultures, that do things" is widely held among anthropologists. Boas (1928:236) tells us that "the forces that bring about the changes are active in the individuals composing the social group, not in the abstract culture." Hallowell (1945:175) remarks that "in a literal sense cultures never have met nor will ever meet. What is meant is that peoples meet and that, as a result of the processes of social interaction, acculturation— modifications in the mode of life of one or both peoples—may take place. Individuals are the dynamic centers of this process of interaction." And Radcliffe-Brown (1940:10–11) pours fine scorn on the notion that cultures, rather than peoples, interact:

A few years ago, as a result perhaps of re-defining social anthropology as the study, not of society, but of culture, we were asked to abandon this kind of investigation in favor of what is now called the study of "culture contact." In place of the study of the formation of new composite societies, we are supposed to regard what is happening in Africa as a process in which an entity called African culture comes into contact with an entity called European or Western culture, and a third new entity is produced . . . which is to be described as Westernized African culture. To me this seems a fantastic reification of abstractions. European culture is an abstraction and so is the culture of an African tribe. I find it fantastic to imagine these two abstractions coming into contact and by an act of generation producing a third abstraction.

We call this view, that people rather than culture do things, the fallacy of pseudo-realism. Of course culture does not and could not exist independently of people.[14] But, as we have pointed out earlier, cultural processes can be explained without taking human organisms into account; a consideration of human organisms is irrelevant to the solution of certain problems of culture. Whether the practice of mummification in pre-Columbian Peru was indigenous or the result of Egyptian influence is an example of a kind of problem that does not require a consideration of human organisms. To be sure the practice of mummification, its invention in Peru, or its diffusion from Egypt to the Andean highlands, could not have taken place without the action of real, flesh-and-blood human beings. Neither could Einstein have worked out the theory of relativity without breathing, but we do not need to take his respiration into account when we trace the history, or explain the development, of this theory.

Those who argue that it is people, not culture, that do this or that mistake a description of what they see for an explanation of these events. Seated in the Senate gallery they see men making laws; in the shipyards men are building freighters; in the laboratory human beings are isolating enzymes; in the fields they are planting corn, and so on. And, for them, a description of these events, as they observe them, is a simple explanation of them: it is people who pass laws, build freighters, plant corn, and isolate enzymes. This is a simple and naive form of anthropocentrism.

A scientific explanation is more sophisticated. If a person speaks Chinese, or avoids his mother-in-law, loathes milk, observes matrilocal residence, places the bodies of the dead on scaffolds, writes symphonies, or isolates enzymes, it is because he has been born into, or at least reared within, an extrasomatic tradition that we call culture which contains these elements. A people's behavior is a response to, a function of, their culture. The culture is the independent, the behavior the dependent, variable; as the culture varies so will the behavior. This is, of course, a commonplace that is usually expounded and demonstrated during the first two weeks of an introductory course in

[14]"To be sure, these cultural events could not have taken place had it not been for human organisms . . . the culturologist knows full well that culture traits do not go walking about like disembodied souls interacting with each other . . ." (White, *The Science of Culture,* pp. 99–100).

anthropology. It is indeed people who treat disease with prayers and charms or with vaccines and antibiotics. But the question, "Why does one people use charms while another uses vaccines?" is not explained by saying that "this people does this, that people does that." It is precisely this proposition that needs to be explained: why do they do what they do? The scientific explanation does not take the people into account at all. And as for the question, Why does one extrasomatic tradition use charms while another uses vaccines, this also is one to which a consideration of people, of human organisms, is irrelevant; it is answered culturologically: culture, as Lowie has observed, is to be explained in terms of culture.

Culture "cannot be realistically disconnected from those organizations of ideas and feelings which constitute the individual," i.e., culture cannot be realistically disconnected from individuals, says Sapir (1932:233). He is quite right, of course; in actuality culture is inseparable from human beings. But if culture cannot be realistically (in actuality) disconnected from individuals it most certainly can be disconnected in logical (scientific) analysis, and no one has done a better job of "disconnecting" than Edward Sapir: there is not a single Indian—or even a nerve, muscle, or sense organ—in his monograph, *Southern Paiute, a Shoshonean Language* (1930). Nor are there any people roaming about in his *Time Perspective in Aboriginal American Culture* (1916). "Science must abstract some elements and neglect others," says Morris Cohen (1931:226) "because *not all things that exist together are relevant to each other*" (emphasis ours). Comprehension and appreciation of this fact would be an enormous asset to ethnological theory. "Citizenship cannot be realistically disconnected from eye color," i.e., every citizen has eyes and every eye has a color. But, in the United States at least, color of eyes is not relevant to citizenship: "things that exist together are not always relevant to each other."

And so it is perfectly true, as Hallowell, Radcliffe-Brown, and others say, that "it is *peoples* who meet and interact." But this should not keep us from confining our attention, in the solution of certain problems, to symbolates in an extrasomatic context: to tools, utensils, customs, beliefs, and attitudes; in short, to culture. The meeting and mixing of European culture with African culture and the production thereby of a mixture, Euro-African culture, may seem "a fantastic reification of abstractions" to Radcliffe-Brown and others. But anthropologists have been concerned with problems of this sort for decades and will continue to deal with them. The intermingling of customs, technologies, and ideologies is just as valid a scientific problem as the intermingling of human organisms or genes.

We have not asserted, nor do we imply, that anthropologists in general have failed to treat culture as a process sui generis, i.e., without taking human organisms into account; many, if not most, cultural anthropologists have in fact done this. But some of them, when they turn to theory, deny the validity of this kind of interpretation. Radcliffe-Brown himself provides us with exam-

ples of purely culturological problems and culturological solutions thereof—
in "The Social Organization of Australian Tribes" (1930–31), "The Mother's
Brother in South Africa" (1924), etc. But when he dons the philosopher's cap
he denies that this procedure is scientifically valid.[15]

However, some anthropologists have recognized, on the theoretical level,
that culture can be scientifically studied without taking human organisms into
account, that a consideration of human organisms is irrelevant to the solution
of problems dealing with extrasomatic traditions. We have cited a number—
Tylor, Durkheim, Kroeber, Lowie, et al.—who have done this.[16] But we may
add one or two new references here. "The best hope . . . for parismonious
description and 'explanation' of cultural pheonmena," say Kroeber and
Kluckhohn (1952:167) "seems to rest in the study of cultural forms and
processes as such, largely . . . abstracted from individuals and personalities."
And Steward (1955:46) remarks that "certain aspects of a modern culture can
best be studied quite apart from individual behavior. The structure and function of a system of money, banking, and credit, for example, represents supra-
individual aspects of culture." Also, he says: "form of government, legal
system, economic institutions, religious organizations, educational systems,"
and so on, "have aspects which are national . . . in scope and which must be
understood apart from the behavior of the individuals connected with them"
(ibid.:47).

There is nothing new about this; anthropologists and other social scientists have been doing this for decades. But it seems to be difficult for some of
them to accept this as a matter of theory and principle as well as of actual
practice.

"It takes two or more to make a culture." There is a conception, not
uncommon in ethnological theory, that whether a phenomenon is an element
of culture or not depends upon whether it is expressed by one, two, or "several" individuals. Thus Linton (1945:35) says that "any item of behavior
. . . which is peculiar to a single individual in a society is not to be considered
as a part of the society's culture. . . . Thus a new technique for weaving baskets
would not be classed as a part of culture as long as it was known only to one
person." Wissler (1929:358), Osgood (1951:207–08), Malinowski (1941:73),
Durkheim (1938:lvi), et al., have subscribed to this view.

Two objections may be raised against this conception of culture: (1) if
plurality of expression of learned behavior be the significant distinction between culture and not-culture, then the chimpanzees described by Wolfgang
Köhler in *The Mentality of Apes* (New York, 1925) had culture, for innovations made by a single individual were often quickly adopted by the whole

[15]Cf. White, *The Science of Culture,* pp. 96–98, for further discussion of this point.
[16]In our essays "The Expansion of the Scope of Science" and "The Science of Culture,"
in *The Science of Culture.*

group. Other subhuman species also would have culture according to this criterion. (2) The second objection is: if expression by one person is not enough to qualify an act as a cultural element, how many persons will be required? Linton (1936:274) says that "as soon as this new thing has been transmitted to and is shared by even one other individual in the society, it must be reckoned as a part of culture." Osgood (1951:208) requires "two or more." Durkheim (1938:lvi) needs "several individuals, at the very least." Wissler (1929:358) says that an item does not rise to the level of a culture trait until a standardized procedure is established in the group. And Malinowski (1941:73) states that a "cultural fact starts when an individual interest becomes transformed into public, common, and transferable systems of organized endeavor."

Obviously such a conception does not meet the requirements of science. What agreement could one find on the point at which an "individual interest becomes transformed into public, common, and transferable systems of organized endeavor"? Or, suppose an ornithologist said that if there were but one specimen of a kind of bird it could not be a carrier pigeon or a whooping crane, but that if there were an indefinite number then they could be pigeons or cranes. Or, suppose a physicist said that if there were but one atom of a certain element that it could not be copper, but if there were "a lot of such atoms" then it might properly be called copper. One wants a definition that says that item x belongs to class y or it does not, regardless of how many items of x there may be (and a class, in logic, may have only one member, or even none).

Our defintion meets the requirements of a scientific definition: an item —a conception or belief, an act, or an object—is to be reckoned an element of culture (1) if it is dependent upon symboling, and (2) when it is considered in an extrasomatic context. To be sure, all cultural elements exist in a social context; but so do such nonhuman (not dependent upon symboling) traits as grooming, suckling, and mating exist in a social matrix. But it is not sociality, duality, or plurality that distinguishes a human, or cultural, phenomenon from a nonhuman or noncultural phenomenon. The distinguishing characteristic is symboling. Secondly, whether a thing or an event can be considered in an extrasomatic context does not depend upon whether there is only one such thing or event, or two, or "several." A thing or event may be properly considered an element of culture even if it is the only member of its class, just as an atom of copper would still be an atom of copper even if it were the only one of its kind in the cosmos.

And, of course, we might have pointed out in the first place that the notion that an act or an idea in human society might be wholly the work of a single individual is an illusion, another one of the sorry pitfalls of anthropocentrism. Every member of human society is of course always subjected to sociocultural stimulation from the members of his group. Whatever a man does as a human being, and much of what he does as a mere animal, is a function of his group as well as of his organism. Any human act, even in its first expression in the person of a single individual, is a group product to begin with.[17]

Culture as "characteristic" traits. "Culture may be defined," says Boas (1938:159), "as the totality of the mental and physical reactions and activities that *characterize* the behavior of the individuals composing a social group . . ." (emphasis ours). Herskovits (1948:28) tells us that "when culture is closely analyzed, we find but a series of patterned reactions that characterize the behavior of the individuals who constitute a given group." (Just what "close analysis" has to do with this conception is not clear.) Sapir (1917:442): "The mass of typical reactions called culture. . . ." This view has, of course, been held by others.

Two objections may be raised against this conception of culture: (1) how does one determine which traits characterize a group and which traits do not —how does one draw the line between the two classes, culture and not-culture? And, (2) if we call the traits that characterize a group *culture,* what are we to call those traits that do not characterize it?

It seems probable that anthropologists who hold this view are really thinking of *a* culture, or cultures, plural, rather than of culture in general, culture as a particular kind of phenomena. Thus, "French culture" might be distinguished from "English culture" by those traits which characterize each. But if, on the one hand, the French and the English may be distinguished from each other by differences of traits, they will on the other hand be found to be very similar to each other in their possession of like traits. And the traits that resemble each other are just as much a part of the "way of life" of each people as the traits that differ. Why should only one class be called culture?

These difficulties and uncertainties are done away with by our conception of culture: culture consists of all of the ways of life of each people which are dependent upon symboling and which are considered in an extrasomatic context. If one wished to distinguish the English from the French on the basis of their respective culture traits he could easily specify "those traits which characterize" the people in question. But he would not assert that nontypical traits were not culture.

In this connection we may note a very interesting distinction drawn by Sapir (1917:442) between the behavior of individuals and "culture."

> It is always the individual that really thinks and acts and dreams and revolts. Those of his thoughts, acts, dreams, and rebellions that somehow contribute in sensible degree to the modification or retention of the mass of typical

[17]More than one hundred years ago Karl Marx wrote: "Man is in the most literal sense of the word a *zoon politikon,* not only a social animal, but an animal which can develop into an individual only in society. Production by isolated individuals outside of society . . . is as great an absurdity as the idea of the development of language without individuals living together and talking to one another," *A Contribution to the Critique of Political Economy* (Chicago: Charles H. Kerr & Co., 1904), p. 268.

reactions called culture we term social data; *the rest, thought they do not, psychologically considered, in the least differ from these, we term individual and pass by as of no historical or social moment* [i.e., they are not culture]. It is highly important to note that the differentiation of these two types of reaction is essentially arbitrary, resting, as it does, entirely on a principle of selection. The selection depends on the adoption of a scale of values. Needless to say, the threshold of the social (or historical) [i.e., cultural] *versus* the individual shifts according to the philosophy of the evaluator or interpreter. I find it utterly inconceivable to draw a sharp and eternally valid dividing line between them [emphases ours].

Sapir finds himself confronted by a plurality, or aggregation, of individuals. (He would have preferred this wording rather than "society," we believe, for he speaks of "a theoretical [fictitious?] community of human beings," adding that "the term 'society' itself is a cultural construct"; Sapir, 1932:236.) These individuals do things: dream, think, act, and revolt. And "it is always the individual," not society or culture, who does these things. What Sapir finds then is: individuals and their behavior; nothing more.

Some of the behavior of individuals is culture, says Sapir. But other elements of their behavior are not-culture, although, as he says, psychologically considered they do not differ in the slightest from those elements which he calls culture. The line thus drawn between "culture" and "not-culture" is purely arbitrary, and depends upon the subjective evaluation of the one who is drawing the line.

A conception of culture could hardly be less satisfactory than this one. It says, in effect: "culture is the name that we give to some of the behavior of some individuals, the selection being arbitrary and made in accordance with subjective criteria."

In the essay from which we have been quoting, "Do We Need a Superorganic?" (1917), Sapir is opposing the culturological point of view presented by Kroeber in "The Superorganic" (1917). He (Sapir) virtually makes culture disappear; it is dissolved into the totality of the reactions of individuals. Culture becomes, as he has elsewhere called it, a "satistical fiction" (Sapir 1932:-237). If there is no significant reality that one can call culture, then there can be no science of culture. Sapir's argument was skillful and persuasive. But it was also unsound, or at least misleading.

Sapir's argument was persuasive because he bolstered it with authentic, demonstrable fact. It was unsound or misleading because he makes it appear that the only significant distinction between the behavior of individuals and culture is the one that he had made.

It is perfectly true that the elements which comprise the human behavior of individuals and the elements which comprise culture are identical classes of things and events. All are symbolates—dependent upon man's unique ability to symbol. It is true, also, that "psychologically considered," they are all alike.

But Sapir overlooks, and by his argument effectively obscures, the fact that there are two fundamentally different kinds of contexts in which these "thinkings, actings, dreamings, and revolts" can be considered for purposes of scientific interpretation and explanation: the somatic and the extrasomatic. Considered in a somatic context, i.e., in terms of their relationship to the human organism, these acts dependent upon symboling constitute *human behavior*. Considered in an extrasomatic context, i.e., in terms of their relationships to one another, these acts constitute *culture*. Instead, therefore, of arbitrarily putting some in the category of culture and the rest in the category human behavior, we put all acts, thoughts, and things dependent upon symboling in either one context or the other, somatic or extrasomatic, depending upon the nature of our problem.

Summary. Among the many significant classes of things and events distinguishable by science there is one for which science has had no name. This is the class of phenomena dependent upon symboling, a faculty peculiar to the human species. We have proposed that things and events dependent upon symboling be called symbolates. The particular designation of this class is not as important, however, as that it be given a name of some kind in order that its distinction from other classes be made explicit.

Things and events dependent upon symboling comprise ideas, beliefs, attitudes, sentiments, acts, patterns of behavior, customs, codes, institutions, works and forms of art, languages, tools, implements, machines, utensils, ornaments, fetiches, charms, and so on.

Things and events dependent upon symboling may be, and traditionally have been, referred to two fundamentally different contexts for purposes of observation, analysis, and explanation. These two contexts may properly and appropriately be called somatic and extrasomatic. When an act, object, idea or attitude is considered in the somatic context it is the relationship between that thing or event and the human organism that is significant. Things and events dependent upon symboling considered in the somatic context may properly he called human behavior—at least, ideas, attitudes, and acts may; stone axes and pottery bowls are not customarily called behavior, but their significance is derived from the fact that they have been produced by human labor; they are, in fact, congelations of human behavior. When things and events are considered in the extrasomatic context they are regarded in terms of the interrelationships among themselves rather than in terms of their relationship to the human organism, individually or collectively. Culture is the name of things and events dependent upon symboling considered in an extrasomatic context.

Our analysis and distinctions have these advantages. The distinctions made are clear cut and fundamental. Culture is clearly distinguished from human behavior. Culture has been defined as all sciences must define their subject matter, namely, in terms of real things and events, observable directly or indirectly in the actual world that we live in. Our conception rescues anthropology from the incubus of intangible, imperceptible, imponderable "abstractions" that have no ontological reality.

Our defintion extricates us, also, from the dilemmas in which many other conceptions place us, such as whether culture consists of ideas and whether these ideas have their locus in the minds of peoples studied or in the minds of anthropologists; whether material objects can or cannot be culture; whether a trait must be shared by two, three, or several people in order to count as culture; whether traits have to characterize a people or not in order to be culture; whether culture is a reification or not, and whether a culture can enamel its fingernails.

Our distinction between human behavior and culture, between psychology and culturology, is precisely like the one that has been in use for decades between speech and language, between the psychology of speech and the science of linguistics. If it is valid for the one it is valid for the other.

Finally, our distinction and definition is in very close accord with anthropological tradition. This is what Tylor meant by culture as a reading of *Primitive Culture* will make clear. It is the one that has actually been used by almost all nonbiological anthropologists. What is it that scientific field workers among primitive peoples have studied and described in their monographs? Answer: real observable things and events dependent upon symboling. It can hardly be said that they were studying and describing imperceptible, intangible, imponderable, ontologically unreal abstractions. To be sure, the field worker may be interested in things and events in their somatic context, in which case he would be doing psychology (as he would be if he considered words in their somatic context). And anthropology, as this term is actually used, embraces a number of different kinds of studies: anatomical, physiological, genetic, psychological, psychoanalytic, and culturological. But this does not mean that the distinction between psychology and culturology is not fundamental. It is.

The thesis presented in this paper is no novelty. It is not a radical departure from anthropological tradition. On the contrary, it is in a very real sense and to a great extent, a return to tradition, the tradition established by Tylor and followed in practice by countless anthropologists since his day. We have merely given it concise and overt verbal expression.

REFERENCES

Beals, Ralph L., and Harry Hoijer. 1953. *An Introduction to Anthropology.* New York: The Macmillan Co.

Benedict, Ruth. 1934. *Patterns of Culture.* Boston and New York: Houghton, Mifflin Co.

Bidney, David. 1946. "The Concept of Cultural Crisis," *American Anthropologist,* 48:534–552.

———.1954. "Review of Culture, A Critical Review, etc., by Kroeber and Kluckhohn," *American Journal of Sociology,* 59:488–489.

Boas, Franz. 1928. *Anthropology and Modern Life.* New York: W. W. Norton and Co., Inc.

———. 1938. *The Mind of Primitive Man.* Revised edition; New York: The Macmillan Co.

Cassirer, Ernst. 1944. *An Essay on Man.* New Haven: Yale University Press.

Cohen, Morris R. 1931. *"Fiction,"* Encyclopedia of the Social Sciences, 7:225–228. New York: The Macmillan Co.

Durkheim, Emile. 1938. In George E. G. Catlin (ed.), *The Rules of Sociological Method.* Chicago: The University of Chicago Press.

———.1951. In George Simpson (ed.), *Suicide, A Study in Sociology.* Glencoe, Ill.: The Free Press.

Einstein, Albert. 1934. *The World as I See It.* New York: Covici, Friede.

———. 1936. "Physics and Reality," *Journal of the Franklin Institute,* 221:313–347, in German; 349–382 in English.

Hallowell, A. Irving. 1945. "Sociopsychological Aspects of Acculturation," in Ralph Linton (ed.), *The Science of Man in the World Crisis.* New York: Columbia University Press.

Herrick, C. Judson. 1956. *The Evolution of Human Nature.* Austin: University of Texas Press.

Herskovits, Melville J. 1945. "The Processes of Cultural Change," in Ralph Linton (ed.)., *The Science of Man in the World Crisis.* New York: Columbia University Press.

———. 1948. *Man and His Works.* New York: Alfred A. Knopf.

Hoebel, E. Adamson. 1956. "The Nature of Culture," in Harry L. Shapiro (ed.), *Man, Culture and Society.* New York: Oxford University Press.

Hooton, Earnest A. 1939. *Crime and the Man.* Cambridge, Mass: Harvard University Press.

Huxley, Julian S. 1955. In Wm. L. Thomas, Jr. (ed.), *Evolution, Cultural and Biological.* Yearbook of Anthropology

Keesing, Felix M. 1958. *Cultural Anthropology.* New York: Rinehart and Co., Inc.

Kluckhohn, Clyde, and Wm. H. Kelly. 1945. "The Concept of Culture," in Ralph Linton (ed.), *The Science of Man in the World Crisis.* New York: Columbia University Press.

Kroeber, A. L. 1917. "The Superorganic," *American Anthropologist,* 19:163–213; reprinted in *The Nature of Culture.* Chicago: University of Chicago Press.

Kroeber, A. L., and Clyde Kluckhohn. 1952. *Culture, A Critical Review of Concepts and Definitions.* Papers of the Peabody Museum of American Archaeology and Ethnology, Harvard University, 47(1):1–223. Cambridge, Mass.

Linton, Ralph. 1936. *The Study of Man.* New York: D. Appleton-Century Co.

———. 1945. *The Cultural Background of Personality.* New York: D. Appleton-Century Co.

Lowie, Robert H. 1917. *Culture and Ethnology.* New York: Boni and Liveright.

Lynd, Robert S. 1939. *Knowledge for What?* Princeton, N. J.: Princeton University Press.

Malinowski, Bronislaw. 1941. "Man's Culture and Man's Behavior," *Sigma Xi Quarterly,* 29:170–196.

Murdock, George P. 1937. Editorial preface to *Studies in the Science of Society,* presented to Albert Galloway Keller. New Haven, Conn.: Yale University Press.

———. 1951. "British Social Anthropology," *American Anthropologist,* 53:465–473.

Osgood, Cornelius. 1940. *Ingalik Material Culture.* Yale University Publications in Anthropology No. 22.

———. 1951. "Culture: Its Empirical and Non-Empirical Character, "*Southwestern Journal of Anthropology,* 7:202–214.

Radcliffe-Brown, A. R. 1924. "The Mother's Brother in South Africa," *South African Journal of Science,* 21:542–555. Reprinted in *Structure and Function in Primitive Society.*

———. 1930–31. "The Social Organization of Australian Tribes," *Oceania.* 1:34–63; 206–246; 322–341; 426–456.

———. 1940. "On Social Structure," *Journal of the Royal Anthropological Institute,* 70:1–12. Reprinted in *Structure and Function in Primitive Society.* Glencoe, Ill.: The Free Press.

———. 1952. *Structure and Function in Primitive Society.* Glencoe, Ill.: The Free Press.

Redfield, Robert. 1941. *The Folk Culture of Yucatan.* Chicago: The University of Chicago Press.

Sapir, Edward. 1916. *Time Perspective in Aboriginal American Culture.* Canada Department of Mines, Geological Survey Memoir 90. Ottawa.

———. 1917. "Do We Need a Superorganic?" *American Anthropologist,* 19:441–447.

———. 1930. *Southern Paiute, a Shoshonean Language.* Proceedings of the American Academy of Arts and Sciences 65:1–296.

———. 1932. "Cultural Anthropology and Psychiatry," *Journal of Abnormal and Social Psychology,* 27:229–242.

Spiro, Melford E. 1951. "Culture and Personality," *Psychiatry,* 14:19–46.

Steward, Julian H. 1955. *Theory of Culture Change.* Urbana, Ill.: University of Illinois Press.

Strong, Wm. Duncan. 1953. "Historical Approach in Anthropology," in A. L. Kroeber (ed.), *Anthropology Today.* Chicago: The University of Chicago Press, pp. 386–397.

Taylor, Walter W. 1948. *A Study of Archeology.* American Anthropological Association Memoir No. 69.

Tylor, Edward B. 1881. *Anthropology.* London.

———. 1913. *Primitive Culture.* 5th ed., London.

White, Leslie A. 1949. *The Science of Culture.* New York: Farrar, Straus and Cudahy; paperbound, 1958, New York: The Grove Press.

———. 1954. "Review of Culture, a critical review, by Kroeber and Kluckhohn," *American Anthropologist.* 56:461–468.

Wissler, Clark. 1929. *Introduction to Social Anthropology.* New York: Henry Holt and Co.

2 / Man and Culture *

It makes little difference whether the penguins of Antarctica know anything about the squirrels of Rock Creek Park. But it makes all the difference in the world whether the American people understand the crowded millions who inhabit Asia. Your destiny, Asia's destiny, the world's very survival, may depend on such an understanding on your part.—Carlos P. Romulo†

1. TO EACH HIS OWN

A few years ago a Walt Disney movie pictured a Through-the-Looking-Glass land in which trains stood still while the stations moved up and down the tracks, horses rode the jockeys in the races, houses caught on water and were put out by fire, and the stork brought parents to babies. It was a delightful bit of nonsense.

Westerners who go into other countries sometimes feel as if they were in some such topsy-turvy situation. Aside from any difference in physical type there is a sense of strangeness about everything. The speech seems rapid and unintelligible; gestures and facial expressions are strange; dress and ornamentation are peculiar; houses, furniture, and utensils appear odd. The food may seem tasteless or be too highly seasoned. Various behavior patterns may seem not only queer but wrong or unnatural. Any effort to find out why people behave in these seemingly queer ways rarely brings a satisfactory answer. People usually do not know why they act as they do except that they have always done it that way.

There is nothing unusual about such inability to give reasons for accepted forms of behavior. After all, an American asked why he calls the brothers of his parents and the husbands of his parents' sisters by the same kinship term, is likely to reply, "Because they are all uncles," or he may ask, "What else could you call them?" Were he asked why he doesn't eat fruit salad or ice cream and cake for breakfast, his reply would likely be, that they wouldn't be good, or that nobody does it, or that they aren't suitable breakfast foods. It is doubtful if he could make a Greenland Eskimo or a South Sea Islander understand how cold fruit juice, fresh fruits, boiled eggs, cereals with cream and sugar, or waffles with honey are particularly different from fruit salad, ice cream, and cake. If it isn't the cold or the sweet, the fruit or the eggs,

*From *Understanding Other Cultures* (Englewood Cliffs, N.J.: Prentice-Hall, Inc., 1963). Reprinted by permission of the publisher.
†*The Asian Student,* January 27, 1957.

the cream or the flour—all of which we find acceptable for breakfast in other forms—then what is it? The simple fact is that people usually think, feel, and act as they do because they were brought up in a culture in which these ways were accepted, not only as good and right, but as natural.

Many social patterns, customs, or folkways—whatever we choose to call them—are not inherently right or wrong, but they are important because their observance by everybody makes large areas of life predictable. Without them we would not know what to expect of other people or what they might be expecting of us. Furthermore, little would ever get done if we had to decide each time on procedure for these now patterned ways. Such patterns are like traffic laws: it doesn't really matter whether people drive to the left as in Britain or to the right as in the United States, but it becomes a matter of life and death that all drivers in any given place follow the same rules. When patterns involve basic values important to the society's well-being, they get into the category of what people think of as right and wrong.

Westerners are sometimes surprised to discover that many other peoples not only regard their own ways as right but may consider themselves superior to the rest of the world. The notion that "We are the people" is an old one. Back in the fifth century B.C. Herodotus said he was sure the Persian king must be mad because no one in his right mind would go about mocking other people's long established customs as Cambyses had done. "For," said Herodotus, "if one were to offer men the choice of all the customs in the world, they would examine the whole number and end up by preferring their own."

Many of the more isolated peoples of the world refer to themselves by terms that mean men or human beings. When Europeans first met Carib Indians, the Caribs announced that "we alone are people." The Hottentots' name for themselves meant men of men. Numerous other groups in Africa, aboriginal America, and elsewhere called themselves by terms that translate the wealthy ones, the intelligible ones, or, as the Navaho, simply people. The Greenland Eskimos thought the Europeans who arrived on their shores had come to learn virtue and good manners from their hosts. Numerous tribal peoples living in places that struck Europeans as particularly desolate were not only content with themselves but felt they lived in the best of all possible worlds.

The view that one's own country is the center of everything and that all others may be scaled or rated with reference to it is generally recognized as being associated with the integration and solidarity of the group. When not carried too far this ethnocentric attitude serves a useful purpose in that the very existence of a society depends on a fairly high degree of consensus. An orderly society is possible only so long as a considerable number of its members believe that their own particular habits and customs are right and proper and therefore, presumably, superior. So long as most peoples lived in relatively small and isolated groups such attitudes were not a serious threat to other societies. Today, however, the peoples of the world are so bound together that survival on our planet depends on knowledge and understanding of one another and respect for peoples whose ways are different from one's own.

Understanding the ways of other people is important also because such understanding increases our own self-knowledge and objectivity. We grow up with the assumption that our own way of doing things is the right way, if not the only way. Yet we are aware of many problems for which we do not know the solutions. A knowledge of the variety of ways in which other peoples have met similar problems gives us new perspectives and new clues to human behavior. "He knows not England who only England knows" applies equally to any society.

2. CULTURE AND SOCIETY

In its popular use the word culture usually refers to refinement or cultivation. The cultured person is thought to be one who is well educated, well mannered, and refined in behavior; who appreciates a certain type of art and prefers Beethoven to the latest hit tunes. As used in ths book culture has a different and more specialized meaning. It refers to all the accepted and patterned ways of behavior of a given people. It is a body of common understandings. It is the sum total and the organization or arrangement of all the group's ways of thinking, feeling, and acting. It also includes the physical manifestations of the group as exhibited in the objects they make—the clothing, shelter, tools weapons, implements, utensils, and so on. In this sense, of course, every people—however primitive—has a culture, and no individual can live without culture.

It is our culture that enables us to get through the day because both we and the other people we encounter attach somewhat the same meanings to the same things. Our culture is our routine of sleeping, bathing, dressing, eating, and getting to work. It is our household chores and the actions we perform on the job; the way we buy goods and services, write and mail a letter, take a taxi or board a bus, make a telephone call, go to a movie, or attend church. It is the way we greet friends or address a stranger, the admonitions we give our children and the way they respond, what we consider good and bad manners, and even to a large extent what we consider right and wrong. All these and thousands of other ways of thinking, feeling, and acting seem so natural and right that we may even wonder how else one could do it. But to millions of other people in the world every one of these acts would seem strange, awkward, incomprehensible, unnatural, or wrong. These people would perform many, if not all, of the same acts, but they would be done in different ways that to them would seem logical, natural, and right.

There are various approaches we can make to culture. We can look at it descriptively, that is, simply describe what it looks like, the form it takes. We can, for example, talk about the differences in material culture by describing the different tools used in getting food. We can compare the digging stick —a sharp pointed stick used for digging up roots and plants for food—with the short-handled hoe, the plow, or the complicated tractors, threshers, reapers, and binders, used in modern mechanized agriculture. Or we can talk about forks versus chopsticks (or fingers), or mats or hammocks versus beds, or moccasins, straw sandals and leather shoes, or bows and arrows, swords, spears, guns, cannon, or atomic bombs and guided missiles. All of these things represent different ways in which people have developed certain material objects which are used as means to certain ends. But in each case the material object represents an idea, not only an accepted way of making an object but an accepted conception of its use.

We can look at other aspects of culture in the same way. We can look at certain institutions that are found everywhere, such as marriage, and say that one society is monogamous while another allows polygamy, though the specialist will use different terms if he means plural wives or plural husbands. We can also talk about different patterns of classifying relatives, performing the marriage ceremony, handling a corpse, or approaching the gods of spirits.

But these descriptions do not in themselves help us to understand other peoples. We could compile a whole book of such descriptions and come out with the idea merely that other people are a queer lot who have never learned the right way to do things. A culture consists not only of elements or traits but also of their interrelationships and organization. Two buildings may consist of the same number of bricks of the same shape and size, put together by the same amount of mortar, and yet bear little resemblance to one another either in structure of function. Different cultures may have many specific patterns that are similar, but within each culture there is an organization or configuration that makes of it an integrated whole. This fact suggests at once that a change in one part of the culture affects all other parts.

The most profitable way to look at culture is to see it as an adaptive mechanism, that is, to see what it does. In this sense a culture is a body of ready-made solutions to the problems encountered by the group. It is, as someone has put it, a cushion between man and his environment. In order to meet their needs, people must devise ways of dealing with their environment so as to get food, clothing, and shelter. They must establish and maintain certain patterns of relationships, for in each society there will be males and females, infants, growing children, youths, adults, and the aged. They must care for the children and train them in the ways of the society so they may take their places as responsible members of the group. They must find ways to maintain the cohesion of the group and preserve consensus. In all societies the members must come to have strong sentiments about various ideas, purposes, and goals—the things we call values. And if men are to be willing to live by the society's rules, they must have some outlet for the expression of self and some way of relating to the forces outside themselves. No society limits itself to the strictly utilitarian. In all of them there is some form of art, music, dance, song, or story, and there are rites and ceremonies which, in the broadest sense of the word, we may call religious.

The resulting culture has form and pattern. There is a degree of order and system that gives to the people who participate in it a certain style of life that is peculiarly their own. It is not that the people sit down together and consciously plan these things. Most people accept their culture as "given" and usually they are not aware of why they do things in a particular way.

It is easy to see why there are fundamental likenesses in all cultures when we remember that all human organisms are essentiatly alike and that, by virtue of this fact, man's basic needs are the same. Moreover, man has essentially the same resources and the same cues offered by nature though, of course, these vary in specific ways. Everywhere man is dependent on land, water, minerals, plants, and animals. Everywhere he deals with climate and weather. Everywhere he has before him the forms, colors, and textures offered by nature. There is almost everywhere some sort of seasonal cycle of warm and cold, or wet and dry, and there is the day and the night. There is the life cycle of plants and animals. There is the human organism itself, male and female, and the developmental sequence from infancy to old age. And, finally, there is over him and around him the mystery of birth and death, of sleeping and waking, of dreams, of sickness and health, of the changing seasons, the sun and the moon and the stars. All of these and more offer to peoples the clues and the cues they need and use to build their cultures. No people uses them all and no two groups use them in exactly the same way. And so our cultures are alike in many ways, different in others.

The terms culture and society are frequently used interchangeably, and there is usually no great harm in doing so as long as we know what the difference is. In simplest form, we can say that a society is always made up of people; their culture is the way they behave. In other words, a society is not a culture; it has a culture. In one sense a society is any kind of associational group that has some degree of permanence. In this sense churches and clubs are societies and we speak of a debating society or a medical society. In the anthropological sense a society is a more or less permanent, relatively large, relatively stable, aggregate of people who live and work together, and who share a common body of meanings and a common system of values. It is this type of aggregate that we mean when we speak of *our society, Japanese society* or *Crow Indian society.*

Although we can say that each society has a culture, it does not follow that there are no cultural differences within a given society or that several different societies may not share, at least to a large extent, a common culture. As a geopolitical unity, the United States constitutes one society yet, even if we exclude groups like the American Indians or the foreign born, there is considerable variation in culture patterns within the continental United States. On the other hand, we share to a large extent a common culture with Canada, a separate, well-defined society that forms an independent political unit.

Some writers have used the term The Great Society to refer to civilization as a whole. Others have used civilization in contrast with the term culture. In this book, culture will be used as an inclusive term referring to the patterned ways of all peoples, however simple or complex their life may be. Civilization will be used only when we need to distinguish a certain kind of culture, usually a fairly sophisticated one that uses writing, has an urban life, and a complex economic and political organization. Civilization, then, is not "better than" but only more complex in certain ways than other types of culture.

We are, however, still confronted with the problem of distinguishing various cultures and societies by their degrees of complexity. The term *savages,* once used to refer to the peoples who were not considered "civilized," now sounds strange to our ears. The word *primitive* is still commonly used even by anthropologists, who refer to primitive society, primitive culture, primitive art and primitive religion, and various peoples are still referred to as primitives. But anthropologists are not happy with the word primitive used in this way, and "the primitives" probably won't be happy with it either when they find out about it. The term came into use at a time when it was commonly assumed that the way the so-called primitives live today represented the way "early man" was supposed to have lived. Now we know that the way of life of people in even the simplest culture today does not represent a form of arrested development. Moreover, the term has another disadvantage in that it carries the implication that such societies, or cultures, are all alike and this, of course, is not true.

Various other terms have been suggested, such as *simple, preliterate, nonliterate,* and *small scale,* but none of these designations is wholly satisfactory. In this book the word *primitive* has been avoided except in a few instances when nothing else seemed to fit. Most of the other common terms are used interchangeably, but always with an unspoken apology to the peoples who deserve a more suitable designation.

3. OTHER ASPECTS OF CULTURE

Religion, nationality, and language are aspects of culture that often set peoples apart from one another. In simple societies religion is usually coextensive with the political or tribal unit; in more complex societies many different religions may be represented in the same culture. Religion will be treated more fully in a later section; mention is made of it here to exphasize the fact that religion is always a part of one's learned behavior and is therefore a part of culture, not an aspect of race.

Nationality is an elusive term that is used in a variety of ways. It is often used as if it implied either religious or linguistic unity, sometimes both, though neither is necessarily involved. Many people believe that both language and religion are natural expressions of the people of a given race and that racial identity is inherent in nationality. There are, however, people of the same race who are clearly of different nationalities and other people may feel a sense of national unity though they are of different races. Brazil is a multiracial nation whose citizens feel a strong sense of national identity. India is a nation of different religions, and there is no single Indian language that is understood by everybody, yet most of the people of India feel strongly that they share a common nationality.

Language is an aspect of culture, yet people speaking different languages may share a common culture. On the other hand, a language may extend beyond national and cultural boundaries, though usually not without some modification. In the sense of being able fully to communicate with one another, most of the people of England, Australia, Canada and the United States speak the same language; in reality there are a considerable number of variations as any American visitor to England or Australia has discovered.

When they first encountered peoples with entirely different languages Europeans assumed that the forms of Latin grammer were universal categories inherent in the nature of reality. As a consequence all kinds of languages were forced into what someone has described as the procrustean bed of parts of speech, gender, case, number, tense, voice, and mode. When a given language did not lend itself to these particular categories it was thought to be rude, uncultivated and "primitive." As anthropologists made studies of other cultures and other languages it became apparent that the categories of classical grammer were neither absolute nor universal. It was seen that language is not merely a means of communication but also a special way of looking at the world and or organizing experience and that the pie of experience can be sliced in many different ways. Today the knowledgeable student of languages avoids imposing patterns from the outside and tries instead to discover the categories inherent in each particular language.

Many people have the notion that "primitive" peoples speak "primitive" languages that are simple in structure and limited in vocabulary. The facts are otherwise. Many of the unwritten languages of the world are extremely complex with vocabularies that are full and precise with reference to aspects of the culture that are important to the people. The Navaho, for example, are reported to have more than a thousand recorded names for plants and hundreds of terms used in referring to ceremonies or to specialized occupations. Eskimos have many different words for different kinds of snow.

Languages vary in the things to which they give emphasis as well as in specialized terms. In English one plural is used whether we mean two things or two thousand, whether they are all together or separate, present or absent. "We" may mean you and me, all of a group to which I belong, or me and one or more persons who are not present. "You" may mean anything from one person to thousands. There are other languages that have one plural for things bunched together and another meaning things scattered about. There are languages that have a "we" meaning you and me only and another "we" that includes other people. There are languages in which there are separate terms used for things present and for things absent.

In English one can say "I went to town" without indicating the means used to get there. The Navaho would have no equivalent of the general "went" but would need to specify whether he walked, rode a horse, rode in a wagon, a car, a train or a plane. On the other hand there are things you cannot be general about in English unless you use extra words in which to do it. In some pronouns we have to indicate sex just as the Navaho had to indicate the means by which he went. When we cannot or do not wish to identify the sex of the person referred to, we either have to use "he" as being inclusive of "she" or we use the awkward "he or she," or, in many cases, we fall back on an incorrect plural and say "they" although one person is meant.

Every language involves a particular system of sounds to which meanings are attached, and speakers of the language learn to produce these sounds and to recognize them when they are used by other people. It is difficult for an adult to learn to speak or even to hear the significant differences in another speech system. Many Chinese and Japanese who learn English as adults simply do not hear our *l* and *r* as distinct sounds. On the other hand, most Indo-European speakers find the tone languages spoken in China, in Africa and elsewhere in the world extremely difficult. Since such tones are not significant sounds in Indo-European languages we find it difficult either to hear or to repeat them even when they are called to our attention.

Among many African languages the use of a high, middle, or low tone may not only modify but may completely change the meaning of a word. When the words of an African tone language are set to Western music, as is frequently done with hymns and songs used in Western-directed churches and schools, the meaning of the words may be so distorted by the accent and tons imposed by the music that the songs become either unintelligible to the African or completely changed in meaning. Yet many Westerners have lived for years among African peoples without "hearing" these tones as significant sounds.

While it is difficult for most adults to learn to speak a foreign language perfectly, that is, without an accent, a child readily learns as its "native" language the one it hears spoken by the people around it as it first learns to speak. Any normal human being can easily learn to speak "like a native" any language he hears from infancy.

4. RACE AND CULTURE

Religion, nationality, and language are a part of our social, not our biological, heritage. We "inherit" these social and cultural patterns in the sense that we inherit lands or property and not as we inherit the genes that account for our brown or blue eyes, our straight or curly hair, or our fair or dark skins. The basic physical characteristics that are used in setting up racial categories come to us through the mechanism of biological inheritance and they are determined by the genetic make-up of our parents and the family lines they represent. Race thus stands apart from culture in that racial characteristics are physical and inborn, not learned or acquired by the individual after birth. A person's race thus tells us nothing at all about his religion, his nationality, his language or his manners and morals. There is no French race, no Irish, Latin, Anglo-Saxon, Aryan, or Jewish races. These terms properly refer to nationalities, languages, socioreligious groups or what are sometimes called ethnic groups. Nobody knows what the original Aryan speakers looked like and the Jews of the world include almost every known physical type. Jews are thus a socioreligious group, not a race in the proper meaning of the term.

There is no definition of race that is wholly satisfactory even when we attach a long string of conditions to it. For our purposes here we can say that a race is a population having in common a combination of inherited physical characteristics that set it apart from other populations having other combinations of such physical characteristics.

But whatever definition we use there is no way by which the peoples of the world can be divided into neat, precise, and orderly racial categories. Most anthropologists agree on the broad divisions of Caucasoid, Mongoloid, and Negroid with Australoids sometimes making a fourth division. But there are wide variations within these groupings and there are many peoples of the world who do not fit into any of these categories. Moreover, peoples of different physical types have mixed with one another since the beginning of recorded history and doubtless before that time. There is therefore no clear-cut and simple way by which peoples everywhere can be placed into specific racial categories with specific characteristics.

Most of the criteria used by anthropologists in determining racial categories have to do with physical characteristics that are of little or no consequence in human behavior except as they are made so by the way people feel about them. Skin color and certain other physical characteristics may be advantageous or disadvantageous in given environments but there is no evidence that skin color, hair, or other such features are in any way correlated with a particular kind of brain or with special qualities of mind and character. Moreover, recent studies by physical anthropologists indicate that the genes responsible for different characteristics not only may be inherited independently of one another but that the physical characteristics of a population may change over a period of time even when there has been no admixture with other races.

There is no evidence that the people of any one race are innately superior or inferior in general mental ability to the peoples of other races. Unquestionably individuals come into the world with different potentialities but the evidence suggests that within any of the major racial groups the whole range of individual potentialities will be found. This does not necessarily mean that there are no statistically significant differences in specific innate abilities occurring in widely separated populations. It does mean that we do not now have any reliable way of determining whether such differences exist. Furthermore a given people might conceivably be superior in one way but inferior in another. Even if it were possible to determine that in some population there was a greater than average incidence of one kind of ability or another we would still have to reckon with the various cultural factors involved. We would also be confronted with the fact that there are no objective criteria for deciding the relative superiority of mechanical aptitude, literary or artistic gifts, philosophical bent, and so on.

There are not now and probably never were any "pure races and there is no evidence that serious biological evils result from race mixture as such. Most of the problems that arise from such mixture grow out of the way in which people think and feel about it, that is, the problems are social not biological.

It is important to note that however we define race or whatever classifications we make, human beings are more alike than they are different. It is generally accepted by most scientists that present day human beings all belong to the same species and people of the most diverse types have interbred freely when brought into contact. In fact, if people of different races had the natural antipathy sometimes attributed to them there would be no need either of laws or the threat of social penalties to keep them apart.

Although there is no evidence that the biological fact of race in any way determines culture, what people think about race and the way they feel about their own and other races are a part of their learned behavior and in this sense are aspects of culture. People in different cultures may define race in quite different ways and they may feel very strongly about their definitions.

It should be noted also that different people use different criteria in classifying the peoples of mixed racial ancestry. In the United States we classify as a Negro any person who looks like a Negro, who is known to have had a Negro ancestor, or who admits to having had such an ancestor. Actually, a number of these persons are biologically more white than Negro so that our definition is in part at least a legal and social rather than a biological one.

In other parts of the world people may define race quite differently. In most Latin American countries having considerable Negro and Indian populations persons are classified on the basis of culture rather than of race. There is a Brazilian saying that a rich Negro is a white man and a poor white man is a Negro. This does not mean that the biological facts of race are completely ignored, but economic and cultural factors enter into their interpretations. In most of Latin America an Indian is a person with Indian culture. Two brothers may be regarded one as white and the other as Indian, or a person may "become white" if he learns to talk, dress, and act according to European rather than Indian custom. These patterns vary somewhat from one Latin American country to another, but nowhere in Latin America is there the kind of segregation widely practiced in the United States, and nowhere is one's race defined on the basis of a single ancestor.

Just as most peoples seem to prefer their own culture so do most of them seem to prefer their own physical type. The people in one New Guinea tribe still refer to white people by a term that can only be translated as "monstrous" or "unnatural." Another tribe assumed that Europeans wore clothes because they were ashamed of their white skins. Among some African peoples the original idea of beauty was a jet black skin, and in one tribe it was believed that white skins were a curse that God placed on Europeans because one of their ancestors had committed incest with his mother.

The common preference for one's own physical type is illustrated in a creation myth reported from the Malay people. The Creator made the first man of clay and baked him in the oven but took him out too soon. He had a very unattractive pasty white skin and lanky hair. He became the ancestor of the white people. The Creator tried again but this time he left the man in too long. His skin was burned black and his hair frizzled by the heat. This one became the ancestor of the Negroes. Profiting by his earlier mistakes, the Creator got the third one just right, a beautiful golden brown. This one, needless to say, became the ancestor of the Malays who look just as men should.

Although preference for one's own physical type seems to have been usual, race prejudice such as we know it seems not to have existed in the civilized world until after the rise of the African slave trade to the West. There was group antipathy which those who "read history backwards" sometimes take to be race prejudice but the physical differences of race or color appear not to have been the major factors. The extreme color consciousness in the world today seems to be a special development related to such factors as slavery and European colonial expansion which resulted in the political and economic subordination of many of the world's darker peoples.

These facts are relevant to our world situation today for we are prone to assume that it is race itself that underlies our differences. The evidence, however, all points to the fact that it is not race itself, but the way in which we think, feel, and act about real or assumed biological differences that is important in our relationships with other peoples. If we are to understand other peoples we must interpret culture in cultural terms. All sorts of cultures have been produced by peoples of the same race and of different races, and the normal members of any race seem perfectly capable of normal participation in any culture into which they are born or into which they are taken as infants. Race as such then has nothing to do with nationality, language, religion, or with cultural creativity.

5. IN SEARCH OF UNDERSTANDING

It is difficult, perhaps impossible, for any person ever fully to "get inside" a culture that is not his own. There are, however, certain approaches, points of view, techniques, and procedures by which one can gain insight and a measure of understanding. The later chapters of this book are in large measure given to a discussion of the variety of ways in which human groups have met their problems. These accounts will have more meaning if we first look at some of the more fruitful ways in which one may approach the study of other cultures.

Any people's social heritage is to them what "The American Way," in its best sense, is to us. It is the Pilgrim Fathers and Thanksgiving Day, the Boston Tea Party and the Fourth of July; George Washington and a cherry tree, Abraham Lincoln and a log cabin. It is Santa Claus and a manger, Easter lilies and Easter rabbits, the flag, Coney Island, camp meetings, Sunday dinner, fried chicken, ice cream and apple pie. It is Yankee Doodle, Tipperary, and My Old Kentucky Home. It is a thousand and one things, sublime and ridiculous, good and bad, mythical and real, that make us a people and not merely an aggregate of individuals whose ancestors came from just about everywhere. Many of these patterns have come to us from other peoples but we have made them peculiarly our own.

It is a common social heritage that makes for cohesion and solidarity and that thus helps insure the continuity of group life. It is in this heritage that each new generation finds its value system and a faith to live by. People can and do modify and change their social patterns but when whole peoples are ruthlessly separated from their past the result is almost always disorganization and deterioration. We have seen this cultural breakdown in peoples who somehow seemed to lose the will to live and who literally died out under the impact of a conquest that took all the meaning out of life. We have seen it in the pathetic deterioration of many once proud Indian tribes whose cup of life was broken under the impact of the white man. We have seen it, too, in American Negroes, robbed of their African heritage and prevented from accepting in full the new heritage that was being forged as a part of the American dream. We are seeing it today take a new form as totalitarian governments consciously and ruthlessly go about making other peoples over in their own image.

In insisting that cultures must be studied as wholes we are really saying that no custom, belief, or behavior can be understood out of its social or cultural context. That is, any item of behavior, any tradition or pattern, can be evaluated correctly only in the light of its meaning to the people who practice it, its relation to other elements of the culture, and the part it plays in the adaptation of the people to their environment or to one another. No custom is "odd" to the people who practice it.

The specialist who goes into another culture sees the unusual things but he looks for the regularities and the way basic problems are met. He observes not merely the overt behavior but seeks to get at the underlying premises on which such behavior rests. Many administrators and missionaries have struggled in vain to change some custom because they did not understand that they and the people they were trying to help were operating from different sets of presuppositions. Moreover, any given act of behavior may seem familiar but may have an entirely different meaning from that of a similar pattern in one's own culture.

Persons going into other cultures as government employees or missionaries are often given what has come to be called "area orientation," a program in which they are briefed on the customs of the country. This procedure has its value but far more valuable is a point of view, an understanding of what culture is and what it does, and some knowledge of the variety of ways in which human behavior has been institutionalized. This theoretical knowledge of culture gives clues and cues to the behavior of human groups wherever they are found.

One of the problems encountered in writing such a book as this is the use of the present and the past tense. Anthropologists writing about the simple societies they study usually use what is known as the ethnological present. That is, they write in the present tense as if the situation were now as it was at the time they saw it or even as some old man remembered it. In the past the peoples described were usually nonliterate and were not likely to be self-conscious about their "progress." Today in many of these societies there is an educated and self-conscious elite who want the world to know that times have changed with them as with other peoples. For the purposes of this book it is not important whether a particular pattern still exists in the form in which it was first reported. It *is* important that the reader recognize that times are changing in even the more isolated parts of the world. Therefore in most cases when referring to specific peoples I have used what may be called the ethnological past. In any case, the world is changing so rapidly that the old and new often exist side by side and a custom that is practiced as I write may have been superseded before this book is in print.

Jerome S. Bruner
Center for Cognitive Studies
Harvard University

3 / Culture, Politics, and Pedagogy *

Despite the books and articles that are beginning to appear on the subject, the process of education goes forward today without any clearly defined or widely accepted theory of instruction. We have had to make do and are still making do on clever maxims and moralistic resolutions about what instruction is and should be. The controversy that swirls around this tortured subject is a mirror of larger discontent with our culture and our morality. And so it should be —but not to the exclusion of dispassionate appraisal of the means whereby the sought-after ends might be achieved. And perhaps that, too, is overly much to expect, for if the past decade has taught us anything, it is that educational reform confined only to the schools and not to the society at large is doomed to eventual triviality.

There are a number of reasons why a theory of instruction may have little effect on educational practice. First, it could be that the theory is wrong—yet it is difficult to find a theory that is flat wrong and won't have some reasonable proposals to make. A second reason might be that it is inappropriate to the central problems of practice. For instance, a theory that is clearly excellent in respect to the instruction of children who are already motivated to learn may prove ineffective in dealing with the alienated Negro students of the inner-city school. A third reason might be its unmanageability—one aspect of which is obscurity in the path from the abstract to the concrete. No matter how deeply one is moved by the spirit of Froebel's theory, for example, it is difficult to know what one does to assure, in his metaphor, that a child be nurtured like a plant lest he be choked by the weeds of circumstance.

But even if a pedagogical theory is correct, relevant, and manageable, it may be practically ineffective when it fails to relate to the urgencies of a society.

While American society in the first decades of the twentieth century was deeply concerned with the problem of acculturating new waves of immigrants, the favored theory was once concerned with the teaching of content per se, with minimum emphasis upon formal discipline or the training of mental faculties. Those theories were perhaps too closely related to the education of special elites. Today they are popular again.

A theory fares well when it accords with a culture's conception of its function. Each culture has conceptions of the nature of a child, some conceptions of what constitutes good adults. It also has, at some implicit level, some

*From *Saturday Review*, May 18, 1968. Reprinted by permission of the author and Saturday Review, Inc.

conceptions of what it regards as the appropriate means of getting from the nature of a child to the nature of an adult. If a pedagogical theorist is to move that culture, he must forge a theory that relates to that range of acceptable means. The failure of a theory may be that it fails to accord with or overcome or relate to the "range of acceptable means" of a culture.

The net outcome of our probing is, I think, the realization that a pedagogical theory is perforce quite different from, and hardly as neutral as, the usual type of scientific theory. Indeed, it is even questionable whether it is principally a scientific theory in the explanatory sense. Nor is it a purely normative theory such as a grammatical theory, prescribing rules for reaching specified goals (such as "well formed sentences"). A theory of instruction is a political theory in the proper sense that it derives from consensus concerning the distribution of power within the society—who shall be educated and to fulfill what roles? In the very same sense, pedagogical theory must surely derive from a conception of economics, for where there is division of labor within the society and an exchange of goods and services for wealth and prestige, then *how* people are educated and in what number and with what constraints on the use of resources are all relevant issues. The psychologist or educator who formulates pedagogical theory without regard to the political, economic, and social setting of the educational process courts triviality and merits being ignored in the community and in the classroom.

It is neither surprising nor inappropriate, then, that critiques of pedagogical theories are as often as not in the form of social and political criticism and ideological debate. It has been instructive to me to see the manner in which some of these debates take shape. A book of mine, *The Process of Education* (1960), has been translated into several languages. In Italy, the book touched off a debate on the problem of revising Italian education to cope with the changing industrial society, and it has been used for clubbing Marxists and classicists alike. In the Soviet Union, one group of social critics has used the book's emphasis on discovery and intuition to castigate the dogmatism of remaining Stalinists who wish to set the dogma of socialism on the line in the classroom. That view has been seconded in Poland, Hungary, and Czechoslovakia.

In Japan, the social critics praise the book for indicating that school subjects that are technical and mathematical need not be without a proper intellectual structure and cultural grace. In Israel, a land surrounded by a ring of hostile nations, the book has been greeted as an invitation to avoid mediocrity in the preparation of new immigrants—a mediocrity that social critics fear will bring Israel to a state of dangerous vulnerability in her present isolated position. In the United States—and perhaps this is the only country affluent enough to harbor such thoughts—the principal social criticism has been a concern for the maintenance of spontaneity of the child. It has been a sobering experience to realize in what degree a book of this sort must perforce serve social and political ends and can never remain a technical book alone.

This brings me to a second conclusion, this time about the role of manageability in the impact of pedagogical theories. Manageability encompasses not only the so-called educational technology of films, books, computers, and the like, but also the scale of the enterprise in terms of people and funds. We have now entered an era in which the federal government, through the Office of Education, has established regional research and development centers to concern themselves with the betterment of our educational effort. They provide a fresh opportunity to explore deeply the feasibility of particular theories, comprehensive or segmental, concerning effective instruction.

I have had the intimate experience over the last five or six years of participating in and observing the attempt to translate a more general theory into one single course in the social sciences, "Man: A Course of Study" (1965), designed for the fifth grade. (It is being developed by what was originally Educational Services, Inc., and has now become the regional center, Educational Development Corporation.) The experience has taught us all not to be casual about means. For it soon turns out that what seems like a simple pedagogical premise would, if implemented, produce a minor revolution in teacher training or in film-making or in school budgeting. This is the engineering part of what is properly called the theory of instruction. It is something that we are only now beginning to understand. Innovation, by whatever theoretical derivation, involves vast development and engineering. By past standards of performance, we could not absorb many new innovative ideas. If we learn how to implement these matters in our generation, we shall lay the groundwork for a truly great impact of adequate theories of instruction in the next generation.

These observations on why theories of instruction are ineffective lead to a second question: What is it that is special or different about education in the sense of schooling in contrast to other ways in which we instruct? Consider the evolution of education as a cultural means of passing on skill, knowledge, and values. It is impossible, of course, to reconstruct the evolution in techniques of instruction in the shadow zone between hominids and man. I have tried to compensate for this lack by observing contemporary analogues of earlier forms, knowing full well that the pursuit of analogy can be dangerously misleading. I have spent many hours observing uncut films of the behavior of free-ranging baboons, films shot in East Africa by my colleague Irven DeVore with a very generous footage devoted to infants and juveniles. I have also had access to the unedited film archives of a hunting-gathering people living under roughly analogous ecological conditions, the !Kung Bushmen of the Kalahari, recorded by Laurance and Lorna Marshall. I have also worked directly but informally with the Wolof of Senegal, observing children in the bush and in French-style schools.

Let me describe very briefly some salient differences in the free learning patterns of immature baboons and among !Kung children. Baboons have a highly developed social life in their troops, with well organized and stable dominance patterns. They live within a territory, protecting themselves from predators by joint action of the strongly built adult males. It is striking that the behavior of baboon juveniles is shaped principally by play with their peer group, play that provides opportunity for the spontaneous expression and practice of the component acts that, in maturity, will be orchestrated into either the behavior of the dominant male or of the infant-protective female. All this seems to be accomplished with little participation by any mature animals in the play of the juveniles. We know from the important experiments of H. F. Harlow and his colleagues how devastating a disruption in development can be produced in subhuman primates by interfering with their opportunity for peer-group play and social interaction.

Among hunting-gathering humans, on the other hand, there is constant interaction between adult and child, or adult and adolescent, or adolescent and child. !Kung adults and children play and dance together, sit together, participate in minor hunting together, join in song and storytelling together. At very frequent intervals, moreover, children are party to rituals presided over by adults—minor, as in the first hair-cutting, or major, as when a boy kills his first kudu buck and goes through the proud but painful process of scarification. Children besides, are constanting playing imitatively with the rituals, implements, tools, and weapons of the adult world. Young juvenile baboons, on the other hand, virturally never play with things or imitate, directly, large and significant sequences of adult behavior.

Note, though, that in tens of thousands of feet of !Kung film, one virtually never sees an instance of "teaching" taking place outside the situation where the behavior to be learned is relevant. Nobody "teaches" in our prepared sense of the word. There is nothing like school, nothing like lessons. Indeed, among the !Kung children there is very little "telling." Most of what we would call instruction is through showing. And there is no "practice" or "drill" as such, save in the form of play modeled directly on adult models—play hunting, play bossing, play exchanging, play baby-tending, play house-making. In the end, every man in the culture knows nearly all there is to know about how to get on with life as a man, and every woman as a woman—the skills, the rituals and myths, the obligations and rights, the attitudes.

The change in the instruction of children in more complex societies is twofold. First of all, there is knowledge and skill in the culture far in excess of what any one individual knows. And so, increasingly, there develops an economical technique of instructing the young based heavily on *telling* out of context rather than *showing* in context. In literate societies, the practice becomes institutionalized in the school or the "teacher." Both promote this necessarily abstract way of instructing the young.

The result of "teaching the culture" can, at its worst, lead to the ritual, rote nonsense that has led a generation of critics to despair. For in the detached school, what is imparted often has little to do with life as lived in the society except insofar as the demands of school are of a kind that reflect *indirectly* the demands of life in a technical society. But those indirectly imposed demands may be the most important feature of the detached school. For school is a sharp departure from indigenous practice.

It takes learning, as we have noted, out of the context of immediate action just by dint of putting it into a school. This very extirpation makes learning become an act in itself, freed from the immediate ends of action, preparing the learner for the chain of reckoning, remote from payoff that is needed for the formulation of complex ideas. At the same time, the school (if successful) frees the child from the pace-setting of the round of concrete daily activity. If the school succeeds in avoiding a pace-setting round of its own, it may be one of the great agents for promoting reflectiveness. Moreover, in school, one must "follow the lesson" which means one must learn to follow either the abstraction of written speech—abstract in the sense that it is divorced from the concrete situation to which the speech might originally have been related—or the abstraction of language delivered orally but out of the context of an ongoing action. Both of these are highly abstract uses of language. It is no wonder, then, that many recent studies report large differences between "primitive" children who are in schools and their brothers who are not: differences in perception, abstraction, time perspective, and so on.

As a society becomes yet more technical, there is a longer separation from actual doing, and education begins to take up a larger and larger portion of the life span; indeed, education becomes part of the way of life. More and more time is given over to telling (usually in print), to demonstrating out of the context of action.

We can already foresee a next step in technical progress that will impose further changes on our methods of educating. For one thing, the rate of change in the surface properties of knowledge will likely increase. That is, the theory of circuits will blossom, although likely as not it will do so on the basis of understanding more deeply some principles that are now known but not fully understood. In teaching, then, we shall be more likely to search out the deeper, underlying ideas to teach, rather than presenting the technical surface that is so likely to change. A metaphoric way of putting this is to say that technical things are more likely to appear changed to an engineer than to a physicist.

There will also be many more aids and prosthetic devices for processing information than ever before. Some of these seem certain already. For one thing, we are organizing our knowledge in a data bank accessible to a user by retrieval techniques inherent in modern computing. This makes knowledge more accessible and less subject to the ancient filing and recall gymnastics of the classical scholar. For another, there will be increasing pressure to reformulate problems in a well-formed fashion in order to make them accessible to the powerful devices of computing. Ill-formed problems do not lend themselves to computing. There are dangers and opportunities in such formalism. Whichever, the trend is already discernible. In general, I think it can be said that we shall in the next hundred years be using many more intelligent and automatic devices that we shall program in behalf of our problem-solving. We need not be Luddites about it, either.

I suspect that there are three forms of activity that no device is ever going to be able to do as well as our brain with its 5 x 10^9 cortical connections, and I would suggest that these three represent what will be special about education for the future.

The first is that we shall probably want to train individuals not for the performance of routine activities that can be done with great skill and precision by the devices, but rather to train their individual talents for research and development, which is one of the kinds of activities for which you cannot easily program computers. Here I mean research and development in the sense of problem-finding rather than problem-solving. If we want to look ahead to what is special about a school, we should ask how to train generations of children to *find* problems, to look for them. I recall that wonderful prescription of the English Platonist, Weldon, to the effect that there are three kinds of things in the world: There are troubles which we do not know quite how to handle; then there are puzzles with their clear conditions and unique solutions, marvelously elegant; and then there are problems—and these we invent by finding an appropriate puzzle form to impose upon a trouble.

What this entails for education is necessarily somewhat obscure although its outlines may be plain. For one thing, it places a certain emphasis on the teaching of interesting puzzle forms: ways of thinking that are particularly useful for converting troubles into problems. These are familiar enough in any given field of knowledge: they are the useful abstractions. What is needed is a sense of how to teach their use in converting chaotic messes into manageable problems. Much of the attraction of the use of discovery in teaching comes, I suspect, from the realization of the need to equip students in this way.

A second special requirement for education in the future is that it provide training in the performance of "unpredictable services." By unpredictable services, I mean performing acts that are contingent on a response made by somebody or something to your prior act. Again, this falls in the category of tasks that we shall do better than automata for many years to come. I include here the role of the teacher, the parent, the assistant, the stimulator, the rehabilitator, the physician in the great sense of that term, the friend, the range of things that increase the richness of individual response to other individuals. I propose this is a critical task, for as the society becomes more interdependent, more geared to technological requirements, it is crucial that it not become alienated internally, flat emotionally, and gray. Those who fret and argue that we are *bound* to go dead personally as we become proficient technically have no more basis for their assertion than traditional romanticism. Recall that the nineteenth century that witnessed the birth of the Industrial Revolution also produced that most intimate form, the modern novel.

Third, what human beings can produce and no device can is art—in every form: visual art, the art of cooking, the art of love, the art of walking, the art of address, going beyond adaptive necessity to find expression for human flair.

These three—research end development, unpredictable services, and the arts—represent what surely will be the challenge to a society which has our capacity to provide technical routine. I assume we shall teach the technical routines, for that is built into our evolving system. Will we be daring enough to go beyond to the cultivation of the uniquely human?

Another question we must ask, then, is: How can the power and substance of a culture be translated into an instructional form?

First we must look briefly at what we might mean by the nature of knowledge as such, because this will prove crucial to our concern. Perhaps the most pervasive feature of human intellect is its limited capacity at any moment for dealing with information. We have about seven slots, plus or minus two, through which the external world can find translation into experience. We easily become overwhelmed by complexity or clutter. Cognitive mastery in a world that generates stimuli far faster than we can sort them depends upon strategies for reducing the complexity and the clutter. But reduction must be selective, attuned to the things that "matter." Some of the modes of reduction require, seemingly, no learning—as with our adaptation mechanisims. What does not change ceases to register: steady states in their very nature cease to stimulate. Stabilize the image on the retina by getting rid of fine tremor, and the visual world fades away.

There is another type of selectivity that reflects man's deepest intellectual trait and its heavily dependent on learning. Man constructs models of his world, templates that represent not only what he encounters and in what context, but ones that also permit him to go behond them. He learns the world in a way that enables him to make predictions of what comes next by matching a few milliseconds of what is now experienced to a stored model and reading the rest from the model. We see a contour and a snatch of movement. "Ah, yes, that's the night watchman checking the windows. . . ." It is in the nature of the selectivity governed by such models that we come increasingly to register easily on those things in the world that we expect; indeed, we assume that the expected is there on the basis of a minimum of information.

There is compelling evidence that so long as the environment conforms to the expected patterns within reasonable limits, alerting mechanisms in the brain are quieted. But once expectancy is violated—once the world ceases strikingly to correspond to our models of it (and it must be rather striking, for we ride roughshod over minor deviations)—then all the alarms go off and we are at full alertness. So man can deal not only with information that is before him, but go far beyond the information given, with all that this implies both for swiftness of intellect and for fallibility. Almost by definition, the exercise of intellect, involving as it must the use of short cuts and leaps from partial evidence, always courts the possibility of error. It is the good fortune of our species that we are also highly adept not only at correction (given sufficient freedom from time pressure), but we have learned to institutionalize ways of keeping error within tolerable limits, science being the prime example.

The models or stored theories of the world that are so useful in inference are strikingly generic and reflect man's ubiquitous tendency to categorize. William James remarked that the life of the mind begins when the child is first able to proclaim, "Aha, thingumbob again." We organize experience to represent not only the particulars that have been experienced, but the classes of events of which the particulars are exemplars. We go not only from part to whole, but irresistibly from the particular to the general.

At least one distinguished linguist has argued in recent times that this generic tendency of human intellect must be innately human, for, without it, one could not master the complex web of categorical or substitution rules that constitutes the syntax of language—any language. Both in achieving the economy with which human thought represents the world and in effecting swift correction for error, the categorizing tendency of intelligence is central. For it yields a structure of thought that becomes hierarchically organized with growth, forming branching structures in which it is relatively easy to search for alternatives. The blunders occur, of course, where things that must be together for action or for understanding happen to be organized in different hierarchies. It is a form of error that is as familiar in science as in everyday life.

I do not mean to imply, of course, that man structures his knowledge of the world only by the categorial rules of inclusion, exclusion, and overlap, for clearly he traffics in far greater complexity, too. Witness the almost irresistible urge to see cause and effect. Rather, the categorial nature of thought underlines its rule-bound nature. The eighteenth-century assumption, that knowledge grows by a gradual accretion of associations built up by the contact with events that are contiguous in time, space, or quality does not fit the facts of mental life. There are spheres where such associative laws operate within limits—as, for example, with material that is strange and meaningless (the psychologist's nonsense syllables, for instance)—but in the main, organization is a far more active process of imposing order, as when we form a hypothesis and then check it not so much to be sure but to be clued in.

We do the greater part of our work by manipulating our representations or models of reality rather than by acting directly on the world itself. Thought is then vicarious action, in which the high cost of error is strikingly reduced. It is characteristic of human beings, and no other species, that we can carry

out this vicarious action with the aid of a large number of intellectual prosthetic devices that are, so to speak, tools provided by the culture. Natural
language is the prime example, but there are pictorial and diagrammatic
conventions as well: theories, myths, modes of reckoning and ordering. We are
even able to employ devices to fulfill functions not given man through evolution—devices that bring phenomena into the human range of registering and
computing. Today, indeed, we develop devices to determine whether the events
we watch conform to or deviate from expectancy in comprehensible ways.

A colleague, George A. Miller, put it well in speaking about computers:
"Mechanical intelligence will not ultimately replace human intelligence, but
rather, by complementing our human intelligence, will supplement and am-
plify it. We will learn to supply by mechanical organs those functions that
natural evolution has failed to provide."

The range of man's intellect, given its power to be increased from the
outside in, can never be estimated without considering the means a culture
provides for empowering mind. Man's intellect, then, is not simply his own, but
is communal in the sense that its unlocking or empowering depends upon the
success of the culture in developing means to that end. The use of such
amplifiers of mind requires, admittedly, a commonly shared human capacity,
and each society fashions and perfects this capacity to its needs. But there is,
I believe, a respect in which a lack of means for understanding one matter
places out of reach other matters that are crucial to man's condition whatever
his culture.

Consider now the nature of codified knowledge. The past half century
has surely been one of the richest, as well as the most baffling, in the history
of our effort to understand the nature of knowledge. Advances in the foundation of mathematics and logic, in the philosophy of science, in the theory of
information processing, in linguistics and in psychology—all of these have led
to new formulations and new conjectures.

Perhaps the greatest change, stemming principally from the revolutions
in physics, is in our conception of what a theory is. For Newton, inquiry was
a voyage on the seas of ignorance to find the islands of truth. We know now
that theory is more than a general description of what happens or a statement
of probabilities of what might or might not happen—even when it claims to
be nothing more than that, as in some of the newer behavioral sciences. It
entails, explicitly or implicitly, a model of what it is that one is theorizing
about, a set of propositions that, taken in ensemble, yield occasional predictions about things. Armed with a theory, one is guided toward what one will
treat as data and is predisposed to treat some data as more relevant than others.

A theory is also a way of stating tersely what one already knows without
the burden of detail. In this sense it is a canny and economical way of keeping
in mind a vast amount while thinking about a very little. What is perhaps most
important about this way of viewing theory is the attitude it creates toward
the use of mind. We now see that the construction of theory is a way of using

the mind, the imagination—of standing off from the activities of observation and inference and creating a shape of nature.

There are several conclusions to be drawn from this long excursion into the nature of intellect, into the nature of how one organizes knowledge to fit it. First of all, it becomes necessary to translate bodies of theory into a form that permits the child to get closer and closer approximations to the most powerful form of a theory, beginning with a highly intuitive and active form of a theory and moving on as the child grasps that to a more precise and powerful statement of it. I find no other way of bringing the child through the maze of particulars to the kind of power that would produce the combination of research and development, unpredictable services, and the arts. Second, this means that on a a practical level the entire university community—indeed, the entire intellectual community—must have a role in education, that the separate education faculty is a misconception and probably one that requires rearrangement in the future. (Since this was written, Cornell has disbanded its faculty of education and reassigned its responsibilities to the entire faculty of arts and sciences.)

As my colleague, Philip Morrison, put it in respect to this field, there are degrees granted by departments of physics in theoretical physics, in experimental physics, and in applied physics. Why not one in pedagogical physics? Teaching is surely an extension of the general exercise whereby one clarifies ideas to oneself. All of us who have worked on curriculum have learned tremendous amounts about our subject matter simply by trying to convert it into a form that would be courteous and comprehensible to a young learner.

Now if this is the case, if we require that there be pedagogical physics and its counterparts, there is surely some need for a *special* coalition to devise means of teaching the symbolic activity involved in the kind of theory-making we have been discussing. I do not know what to call this coalition of fields; the symbol sciences might be appropriate, but it is an absurd name. Linguists, philosophers of science, philosophers of history, logicians, psychologists, teachers, substantive specialists who most understand the simple structures of their fields, mathematicians—such a coalition might show how a university might express its concern for the symbolic powers inherent in the use of a culture. We obviously do not understand what could be done by a group of this sort. They range all the way from teaching children to be brief and compact when that is needed to hold things in the range of attention, to devising the kind of mathematical program embodied in the report of the Cambridge Conference on School Mathematics *(Goals for School Mathematics,* Houghton Mifflin, 1963).

Finally, we may ask: How is intellectual development assisted by instruction?

Let me focus on the teacher in this process. One immediately invokes the phrase "teacher training." But before we do, consider a few points to be taken into account. We know that children do not readily or easily think in school.

By school age, children expect arbitrary and meaningless (to them) demands to be made on them by adults—the result probably of the fact that adults often fail to recognize the task of conversation necessary to make their questions have some intrinsic significance for the child. Children, of course, will try to solve problems if they recognize them as such. But they are not often either predisposed to or skillful in problem-finding, in recognizing the hidden conjectural feature in tasks set them. We know now that children in school can quite quickly be led to such problem-finding by encouragement and instruction.

The need for this encouragement and instruction and its relatively swift success relates, I suspect, to what psychoanalysts refer to as the guilt-ridden over-suppression of primary process and its public replacement by secondary process. Children, like adults, need reassurance that it is all right to entertain and *express* highly subjective ideas, to treat a task as a problem where you *invent* an answer rather than *finding* out there in the book or on the blackboard. With children in elementary school, there is often a need to devise emotionally vivid special games, story-making episodes, or construction projects to re-establish in the child's mind his right not only to have his own private ideas but to express them in the public setting of a classroom.

But there is another, perhaps more serious difficulty: the interference of intrinsic problem-solving by extrinsic. Young children in school expend extraordinary time and effort figuring out what it is that the teacher wants—and usually coming to the conclusion that she or he wants tidiness or remembering or doing things at a certain time in a certain way. This I refer to as extrinsic problem-solving. There is a great deal of it in school.

There are several quite straightforward ways of stimulating problem-finding. One is to train teachers to want it, and that will come in time. But teachers can be encouraged to like it, interestingly enough, by providing them and their children with materials and lessons that *permit* legitimate problem-finding and permit the teacher to recognize it. For exercises with such materials create an atmosphere by treating things as instances of what *might* have occurred rather than simply as what did occur.

Let me illustrate by a concrete instance. A fifth-grade class was working on the organization of a baboon troop—specifically, on how they might protect against predators. They saw a brief sequence of film in which six or seven adult males go forward to intimidate and hold off three cheetahs. The teacher asked what the baboons had done to keep the cheetahs off, and there ensued a lively discussion of how the dominant adult males, by showing their formidable mouthful of teeth and making threatening gestures, had turned the trick. A boy raised a tentative hand and asked whether cheetahs always attacked together. Yes, though a single cheetah sometimes followed behind a moving troop and picked off an older, weakened straggler or an unwary, straying juvenile. "Well, what if there were four cheetahs, and two of them attacked from behind and two from in front? What would the baboons do then?"

The question could have been answered empirically—and the inquiry ended. Cheetahs *do not* attack that way, and so we do not know what baboons *might* do. Fortunately, it was not. For the question opens up the deep issues of what might be and why it is not. Is there a necessary relation between predators and prey thet share a common ecological niche? Must their encounters have a "sporting chance" outcome? It is such conjecture, in this case quite unanswerable, that produces rational, self-consciously problem-finding behavior so crucial to the growth of intellectual power. Given the materials, given some background and encouragement, teachers like it as much as the students. This is simply an example, and provided in that spirit only.

Let me now turn to dialogue. My colleague, Roman Jakobson, assures me that there is a Russian proverb to the effect that one understands only after one has discussed. There are doubtless many ways in which a human being can serve as a vicar of the culture, helping a child to understand its points of view and the nature of its knowledge. But I dare say that few are so potentially powerful as participating in dialogue. Professor Jan Smedslund, at Oslo, has recently remarked on our failure to recognize that even in the domains of formal reasoning, logic, and mathematics, the social context of discussion can be shown to be crucial.

It is a simple suggestion I am making. Entering the culture is perhaps most readily done by entering a dialogue with a more experienced member of it. Perhaps one way in which we might reconsider the issue of teacher training is to give the teacher training in the skills of dialogue—how to discuss a subject with a beginner.

Pedagogical theory, then, is not only technical, but cultural, ideological, and political. If it is to have its impact, it must be self-consciously all of these. The technical task, indeed, is more formidable than ever we suspected, and we may now be operating close to the scale where we can begin to do the appropriate engineering to realize the implications of even utopian theories.

Knowledge, to be useful, must be compact, accessible, and manipulable. Theory is the form that has these properties. It should be the aim of our teaching. But in the evolution of education, it is also the case that as we move to an ever more technical organization of our culture, and now to a period involving the use of information-processing automata, the pattern of education changes. Three uniquely human traits want especial cultivation to increase the human quatity of human societies—problem-finding, the provision of unpredictable services, and art in its myriad forms from music to cuisine.

Finally, one of the most crucial ways in which a culture provides aid in intellectual growth is through a dialogue between the more experienced and the less experienced, providing a means for the internalization of dialogue in thought. The courtesy of conversation may be the major ingredient in the courtesy of teaching.

II / ATTITUDES, VALUES, AND LANGUAGE: SOME IMPLICATIONS FOR LEARNING OUTCOMES

4 / Cultural Influences Shaping the Role of the Child *

It seems somewhat incredible that anything new or different could or should be said or written about children so soon after the close of the 1960 White House Conference on Children and Youth. The thoroughness with which the experts and the interested were solicited to participate reflects credit upon the abilities of the Conference organizers. From these efforts came an outpouring of articles from dozens of contributors covering nearly every conceivable aspect affecting youth. Their authors ranged the gamut of professional, religious, organizational, social, and intellectual segments of American life. Only one group seems to have remained unsolicited in this search for wisdom, namely, youth itself.

This type of oversight is not uncommon in the traditional American procedure of examining institutions and social problems. Those who are most directly affected by the preparation of a program are the ones most likely to be overlooked in the formulation of policy or of its instrumentation through organization. Patients, prisoners, or students are seldom consulted in the operation of hospitals, prisons, or schools. Perhaps this is as it must be, but then, again, perhaps those who suffer or benefit from the effects of the exercise of responsibility by others might also make a contribution, if it could be remembered to ask their participation.

That this remark is not completely gratuitous will become apparent as the analysis of the role of children in our society is developed in the next several pages. Possibly, an understanding of its relevance may well be the most important contribution which can be made to those who are charged with the responsibility of formal education in the early childhood years. But first, it is necessary to establish at least some minimum justification to add one more statement to this recent flood of analyses and opinions by those judged most competent to speak to the subject.

An attempt to rationalize or clarify disagreements and confusion among the experts might serve as a legitimate excuse for further treatment. Actually, differences in interpretation are surprisingly minor. The confusion is more a matter of indigestion, due to the quantity of data, than of methodological deficiencies. For this reason, such justification as is offered must be upon conceptual grounds, that it is possible through reorganization and re-examina-

---

*From Conrad M. Arensberg and Solon T. Kimball, *Culture and Community* (New York: Harcourt, Brace and World, Inc., 1965). Reprinted by permission of the publisher.

tion from a different set of assumptions and with different objectives in mind to extract more meaning from the available data than has yet been achieved.

The initial step in this process is to shift our focus away from the subject, in this case children, to the environment—physical, psychical, social, and cultural—which surrounds and influences the child in his development. This emphasis does not exclude examination of the subject; it simply recognizes the interdependency between the individual and the systems of which he is a part or representative. Precedence for this procedure has been well developed in the natural sciences. Within anthropology, for example, although culture constitutes the central focus of study, it can be objectified only as individuals are examined. Contrariwise, when we come to study personality, we assume that it reflects a mirror image of the cultural experiences of the individual.

Following these introductory comments, we can now turn to an examination of the role or roles assigned to children in our society.

FORCED ABANDONMENT OF CHILDHOOD

Although it is seldom stated in this way, the major role of the child *qua* child is to submit to and assist in the activities and processes which prepare him for adult status. The extreme dependency of early infancy permits no choice in the selection of the external environment in which the initial learning occurs. Later when, presumably, the child has developed some rational discrimination in his response to demands placed upon him, it is too late for him to make effective protest. He has already internalized the emotional set of a system which requires that he eventually abandon the thought and habit ways of children and substitute those of the adult world.

However rewarding the culture of childhood, that of the grown-up world is continuously and persistently presented as more rewarding and desirable, and childhood is defined as a transitory and to-be-abandoned stage of life. No matter how entrancing, the never-never world of Peter Pan turns out to be just that, a fantasy in which childhood is forever threatened by pirates symbolizing demanding adults who must eventually win in the age-old struggle between old and young. Although James Barrie allows the illusion of a different solution, both child and adult know that his ending is founded in the realm of dreams.

This forced abandonment of childhood in which, if it is successful, the child is a willing participant, represents the first of a sequential series of tragedies which each individual encounters on the road of life. No matter how sentimental or protective adults may be, the gradual and sometimes forcible destruction of the innocence of childhood is a necessary function of the relationship between adult and the child. The latter is not the only one who suffers in this nearly abrupt destruction of childhood certainties. The transition also demands its costs of the adult. The mother's mixed emotion of anguish and pride when her "baby" first enters school is repeated later when her child, turned young adult, leaves home for marriage, college, or the world of work. She may also carry a sense of guilt because of the contradictory desire to both hold and eject, and guilt because there can never be assurance that one has done enough or that what one has done has been right. There is solace in believing that one has done the best he could, but doubt may also nag the conscience.

The male response to these crises is different only in degree, and both parents share the knowledge that they have been parties to concealment, or perhaps even deception, in their failure to communicate to the growing child what the world is really like. This conspiracy of silence is in part a function of the inability to articulate the realities; in part, it is an attempt to continue the protective role assumed during infancy; and, in part, it is a result of the parents' own unwillingness or incapacity to face the realities of their own lives. The delusion they have perpetuated, the illusion they have lived under and passed on to their children, should not be assessed as deliberate. Not that adults and parents are blameless, for they are not. The offence with which they may be charged is the same one as that which they first permitted and then prohibited, that of innocence.

The adult world is no more free of fantasy and illusion than is that of the child. The Walter Mittys are everywhere among us. Shaw's *Pygmalion* expresses a contemporary version of the Cinderella story. Our devoted adherence to romantic love as a necessary prerequisite to marriage and adult responsibilities of family and parenthood is real enough, but do we not deceive ourselves when we act as if erotic love is the panacea for the tough job of cementing relations between men and women in domestic functions?

These beliefs, and similar ones in other spheres of life, sustain us through bitterness, tragedy, and boredom. They are undoubtedly a necessary aspect in our kind of cultural world, and as such should not, even were it possible, be either dispelled or destroyed. Our sin is that we let them delude us, that we insist upon maintaining an innocence of realities. Perhaps there is no simple way to explain why this is so, but probably these tendencies are linked with the generalized guilt which our culture so successfully inculcates during that period of defenseless infancy. If so, then it is all the more apparent why we can understand the child's role only by examining the nature of the world surrounding him. In that quest, we turn to a brief look at the distinctive aspects of the American family in its metropolitan middle-class manifestations.

THE AMERICAN FAMILY SYSTEM

We can begin by examining how labels are used to describe and perhaps also obscure. There is some advantage but also danger in using apt phrases or slogans such as "the whole child." There is the tendency to treat such slogans as statements of objectives and to assign to the words themselves some magical quality which through their repeated utterance may produce the condition desired. There is also a failure to understand that, in most instances at least, the slogan—and the movements which it represents—is an after-the-fact situation. That is, that the conditions which permit some approximate realization of stated goals called for in the slogan are, in fact, already existent. An example will illustrate the point.

The now shopworn label, "the family of togetherness," generated a profusion of slogans which served the special interests of varied groups. Some were self-seekers in their commercialization of this theme. Others were genuinely altruistic in their desire to promote the better life through encouraging praying together, playing together, learning together, and similar activities which, if performed as a family, might somehow enrich and fulfill life. The image of this family type is that of parents and their dependent children. The representation does not include grandparents, other relatives, or neighbors. In technical language, this is the "family of procreation," the biological and nuclear family typical of American culture. Neither slogans nor exhortations created it and the definition of the roles of its members has been set by conditions which do not include the effects of conscious propaganda. Its natural history and functions differ from and may be contrasted with other types of family systems such as the stem, joint, or extended.

The analysis in Chapter 11 of the small family type—its historical antecedents, gradual modifications and evolution within the specific conditions of American society, and internal structure—permits one to establish a relation between scientific analysis and popular movements and their accompanying slogans. When the family is viewed from this functional perspective, then it can be seen that what many think of as new approaches or discoveries is, in fact, only an emergent awareness by professional practitioners in education, health, and welfare of already prevalent characteristics of family life. Those who advocate democratic family life, togetherness, permissiveness, child-centered education, and individuation are less the creators of new progressive movements in family life and education than they are publicizers of an existing state of affairs.

In Chapter 11, it will be remembered, the imperatives of the American family were described as based upon the isolated conjugal pair which, in its isolation, was able to shape its destinies and satisfactions with a freedom that extended to full authority over minor children. Neither this freedom, in truth a heavy responsibility, nor achieving the ideal of the educational task can be counted as easy where each adult man and woman is expected to be spouse, parent, householder, and family head all at once. Within these imperatives each person ideally finds his own mate, and in an atmosphere of mutual love rears children, maintains a household, and in the close identity with the small family finds his chief emotional identification.

Anthropologists know of no other family system which places such heavy responsibilities upon so few. In other times and places, the burden of obligations to succor and protect, to share and alleviate the tensions which arise from internal difficulties or external threat are diffused through kin and the institutions of community. In contrast, the American family in both its ideal and actual state stands nearly alone. And if this imperative, rooted in historical continuity and contemporary conditions, applies to the family as a unity, it also applies to the individuals who comprise the unity. They, too, have been taught the necessity of standing alone. Nor does the child in his period of dependency escape the requirement. If, by circumstance, he no longer contributes economically to the whole, as in an earlier agrarian period, his total burden is not thereby lightened in some degree. The responsibility he now shoulders is, if anything, heavier and more difficult than before.

STANDARDS OF ADULTHOOD

The course which beings in infancy inevitably leads through childhood and adolescence into adulthood. This progression can be viewed in part as the result of natural processes, in part as the consequence of training received from parents, peers, and teachers, but in even larger measure as directed, purposeful, and at times aggressive activity of the child himself. If the question were asked, "Is not this the universal process of acquiring adulthood in all cultures?" the answer given could not be an unqualified affirmative. The major difference is found in the early inculcation in the American child of certain standards of self-performance, the full realization of which will be achieved simultaneously with maturity. Later on we shall show that this expectancy proves to be an illusion which is, nonetheless, also transmitted to each succeeding generation.

First, however, the problem of what these standards are and how they become internalized and are maintained should be examined. Simple observation establishes that a parent comforting a hurt child often urges that he behave like a little man and stop his crying. In hundreds of other instances in the life relationship of parent and child, each time the former holds up adult behavior as superior there is implicit in the action a denigration of child behavior and an affirmation of superior adult standards. When boys are told, "Done like a man!" the implications of the praise for the action performed are quite explicit. Has anyone ever intended praise when he exclaimed, "You act like a child!"? And when older people do childish things, we call them senile or foolish.

Just when and where do we, in our multi-faceted relations with children, ever really judge their behavior except against the measure of progress they exhibit in the acquisition of adult standards? Irrespective of the steps by which the process is initiated, it is not difficult to observe the relentless insistence upon acquiring adult standards. If, by chance or intention, parents and teachers should abandon this aspect of their role, they would then have, to this extent, abandoned their function as adults.

The other part of the problem posed earlier, the question of what should be included under any listing of adult standards, was answered in large measure in Chapter 11 in the enumeration of the imperatives of our family system. Within this framework, however, there are certain specificities that need to be mentioned and their relevance elaborated if we are to grasp the role of the child.

It is generally accepted that family, school, and church transmit a greater portion of the cultural heritage to the child than do other agencies. What, then, among the many things which adults expect the child to learn, may we count as significant? The broad categories include skills for handling, knowledge for understanding, and feelings for evaluating the things, persons, and ideas which are encountered in the business of living. These requirements are so universal, however, that their generality does not help us much. If we look at some of the requirements imposed upon the individual in the American cultural system and then examine these in their relation to the family and respective roles within it, we shall encounter those specific traits which have been idealized for all members of the society.

Commitment to Change

The central and perhaps most crucial commitment of American civilization is to the inevitability and, in most instances, the desirability of change. The activities and events of everyday life are interpreted through such terms as "progress," "advancement," and "development" within the context of the never-constant environment in which we live. If the individual is to be successful in this type of society, and the promise of success is one of the imperatives which moves him, he must at least keep up with the times. Even those not motivated by promises of success know that stagnation is penalized. For the individual, this imperative means that he must be continuously poised to take advantage of opportunities for advancement. In fact, he must actively seek and, if possible, modify the environment to insure that situations favorable to him present themselves. Favorable chances and maneuvering avail nothing if there is resistance to working in new surroundings with new people and possibly learning new skills for new activities.

The successful meeting of new demands requires, first of all, readiness to abandon the present whether it be locality, associations, or activity. Under such circumstances, it is unwise to invest too deeply either emotionally, professionally, or financially, for the wrench which change demands may require a sacrifice too great to make. The easy fashion in which Americans establish and abandon new realtionships disconcerts Europeans who accuse us of emotional superficiality. Their projection of values hardly explains the situation, nor are they likely to understand the necessity of such behavior as a function of our commitment. And the more deeply imbedded guilt with its corollary of tragedy they utterly fail to comprehend.

Self-Fulfillment

These imperatives of mobility, independence, adaptability, and the capacity for continued growth represent, in one sense, subsidiary aspects of a more central requirement, that of self-fulfillment. Implied in the objective of adulthood achieved is the acquisition of competence, wisdom, and maturity. But fulfillment in the context of perpetual change contains a contradiction incapable of resolution. Final achievement is impossible because the objectives themselves are not fixed. They expand, recede, or are modified as the conditions within the system are changed, changes to which the individual in his progression also contributes. There can be no ultimate in the world view of those who adhere to the concept of an ever-expanding system. One might suppose that these circumstances would breed frustration and defeat, but apparently this occurs rarely since one is taught to accept striving as a lifelong necessity.

Perpetual Optimism

Finally, the role must be performed in a mood of perpetual hopefulness, a trait which has also been set by the culture. The extent to which this mood has been integrated into the events of daily life may be met in many contexts. The language of salutation reveals the extraordinary extent to which we have carried our insistence upon a positive and optimistic approach to the world. No matter how we really feel, we are obligated to meet the world with a sunny disposition. Our conventional "Good day" has no relation to the actual state of the weather nor do our replies to inquiries about our well-being have relation to the actual situation. The response of "Fine," or one of its many variations, expresses how we ought to be. Any other admission is incorrect. The child learns this ritual language and the accompanying values in his earliest years. He is taught to condemn whining, complaining, crybabies, and pessimists. We should also like to deny that pain, evil, and death exist, and although we are forced to recognize them we assign them only marginal status. We would like to believe that all begins are basically good and should be trusted, a character quality which sometimes causes others to accuse us of being naïve. These optimistic and positive traits found expression in the 1920's in the ringing slogan of Coué, "Day by day in every way I am getting better and better!"

Our culture demands that we maintain this euphoric façade in our own perception of the world and our place in it. Furthermore, we demand that our children acquire and exhibit the same psychological posture. Obviously, at times, this optimistic perceptual screen through which we interpret the events of the world must lead to some distortions in our apperception of reality. The truth is that, on occasions, the situation we find ourselves in, individually or collectively, is damned bad. But our "natural" optimism carries us through with the belief that tomorrow or next year will be better, that all things work out for the best, it's always darkest before the dawn, and so on through the dozens of aphorisms which give expression to the same point of view. The fact that events usually do turn toward the better lends credence to the belief.

It is my contention that the configuration of beliefs that we have been examining is a necessary corollary to the central value of self-fulfillment. To deny, in any degree, that societal conditions are not improving (through change) or that individual incapacitation prevents further growth is to admit that this keystone (self-fulfillment) upon which the structural unity of purpose in life has been erected is faulty—denies, then, the very basis of the American's conception of himself in his life role.

It should be apparent now why it has been necessary to examine these interconnections before we could turn to the direct study of the role of the child. The American small family, relatively isolated in its activities from other communal institutions, with the insistence upon the capacity for independence and mobility of its members, building and maintaining in each person the psychological posture of perpetual optimism with its corollary of self-fulfillment, taken as a whole and as functionally interdependent with other cultural systems, provides the conditions within which the role of the individual is defined.

Under such circumstances, the role of the child is as much central to the continued functioning of the whole as is the role of any other family member. A mutual dependence exists between children and their parents since the latter seek some portion of their own fulfillment through their children. In part, they fulfill themselves by providing a sheltering environment which expresses and enforces a temporary dependence. The dependency relationship, however, contains both contradiction and conflict for eventually, as both child and parent know, the independent and mobile condition must be claimed by or forced upon the child, since adulthood is a necessary step for continued growth. This brings us to the point where we can more adequately conceptualize the child's role.

PROGRESSION INTO ADULTHOOD

Those who propose two alternative ways of viewing the child, namely, either as a miniature adult or as an undeveloped person but possessing the capacities for achieving maturity, may come to conclusions that distort reality. There is no intention to pose a conundrum by saying that the child is neither and both. For example, most children by the time they have reached the age of three or four have already learned a number of important adult skills. They walk, talk, control the elimination of bodily wastes in socially acceptable ways, and have developed habits, points of view, and skills around sleeping, eating, and their relations to a limited number of other persons. Childish ways may still adhere to some of their activities, but any realistic appraisal of the contrast between behavior in the first year of life with that of the fourth must grant that in some directions adult standards have been successfully transmitted. By six or seven, some children are judged precociously mature. For most children, however, the period of development coincides with physical growth, except that in our society the dependence is maintained for a much longer period because of the requirement for formal training through post-adolescent years.

Thus, at a very early age the child acquires some of the requisite skills of an independent individual. To this extent, he has cleared some hurdles which test for adult competency. In other areas, he remains dependent, undeveloped, and not yet capable of unguided mobility. We again restate the point made earlier that the fundamental role of the child is to become an adult. All his activities are either contributory or incidental to this end. The progression is partly a function of physical and neural growth, partly a function of the social and cultural environment within which the child learns, but it is continuous although uneven.

PRESSURES ON CHILDREN TO BE ADULT

The responsibility parents feel for converting their children into adults is so great that they impose a rigorous regime upon them during their dependent years. The intensity of parental concern reaches into every aspect of child behavior. It is expressed by an overconcern and overdirection of the child's activities. All types of special "opportunities" for developing skills are sought out. One manifestation has been the downward extension of formal schooling to pre-kindergarten classes.

The reality eventually became sloganized in the phrase "child-centered." Whatever excesses have been committed in home or school by adults who abdicated responsibility because of this doctrine, their behavior never violated the fundamental principle that children must be turned into adults. The freedoms given the child in activity or temperament were never justified on the grounds that these would permit him to remain a child; it was because this freedom ensured a healthier, better-adjusted adult. In effect, child-centered dogma was an unwitting device for putting ever-greater pressures upon the child. In its rationale, the adults deluded both themselves and the children they tended because it was never explained that this was a long-term transaction with an expected profitable pay-off at the end.

Perhaps we should be more explicit about the pressures to which the child is subject. The cultural context within which these appear is, of course, that children cannot just be allowed to grow up; they must be wisely directed. The justification is based upon the great latent "potential" in the unformed young which is waiting to be realized. Only as the potential is realized can the child fulfill himself, and fulfillment is a function of adulthood, not childhood. What is not made explicit ot the child and is probably perceived by only a few parents and teachers is that their own role is dependent upon child accomplishments. Under these conditions, the child carries a heavier burden of responsibility in the proper performance of his role than that placed upon the young in any other society.

The child is expected to grow not only into an adult but into a successful one. The definition of the latter is, of course, adult-determined. Success must be found in career, in marriage, in family, in community, and in one's personal life. The adult believes and the child comes to accept early that the route to these objectives can be reached through training. The apparatus through which much of this training is transmitted is the formal educational system. It is here that performance is judged by agreed-upon standards and a preliminary preview of the future seen. Hence, the parental pressures on the child for academic striving.

BARRIERS TO ADULTHOOD

Unfortunately, there are several conditions which inhibit and limit the child's efforts in acquiring that experience necessary for adulthood. The culturally isolating centripetence of metropolitan life reduces enormously the opportunities for significant cross-group experience. The capacity to make social adaptations cannot be learned in the severaly limited urban enclave or homogeneous suburb. Emphasis upon personal adjustment is probably related to the narrow range of interpersonal experiences and the ultimate necessity to rely upon oneself. The poverty of cultural variation must have a seriously distorting effect on capacities for comparative perception. Vicarious experiences provided by fantasy or documentary in television, cinema, drama, or literature are no substitute and cannot be truly comprehended unless there is a substantial comparative understanding from which these can be interpreted. Situations portraying romantic love, the vicissitudes of family life, or the struggle for power may be dramatized in African, Asian, or American settings but the meaning is reduced to horizons found in Scarsdale, Plainville, or Little Rock.

In spite of our insistence upon cultural pluralism and the tolerance of deviancy, the danger of cultural diversity remains a powerful threat. Is it possible that the social isolation of the American small family intensifies the internalization of its values, manners, and behavior to the exclusion of differing standards? Forced to depend largely upon its own resources, as it is, this may be an expected consequence. In any event, family restrictions present another hazard in the child's struggle to grow up. These are found in the nature of the relationships between old and young, and between the sexes; and all such relationships carry their emotional correlates. Informed observers agree that not all is well in our family system, and yet what degree of credence should we give to those who see our children as guilt-ridden and hostile (Line and King 1956)? Does the American mother exhibit the black widow spider tendencies as described by Philip Wylie? To what extent have males abdicted their role in the squeeze of demands between wife and job, and to what extent are they delinquent in claiming their sons for manhood?

Perhaps these questions really have no answers. Yet they have been repeatedly asked and answered by those with ready replies. The concern should be evidence enough that the child finds himself in a confused and hence difficult position. There seems little doubt, however, that there has been both an increase in pressure upon the child from home and school and at the same time a diminution in his opportunities and hence his ability to act independently. This combination is bound to produce serious trouble.

POSTSCRIPT

Parents and teachers are particularly susceptible to exhortations by "experts" on child rearing and child life. Their position requires that the specialist appear authoritative. And we should be tolerant of their necessity to change emphasis and direction from time to time. But parents and teachers cannot forgive themselves nor can they be forgiven by their children for the consequences of following ill-advised fads of the moment. Our attitude toward the expert should be one of hesitant caution—once bitten, twice shy. The doctrine of the 1950's which extolled the virtues of the democratic family with its security through love, its togetherness, its permissiveness, and its equalitarianism is now being modified. Although the new doctrine of the 1960's has not yet been fully formulated, we may anticipate some of the line. The avant-garde has already abandoned the term "democratic" in its application to family life. Only those who lack sensitivity to the outmoded continue to champion what is dying, not family life but a style of exhortation about it.

Perhaps Bronfenbrenner (1960) is right when he suggests that he detects a cyclical trend toward "explicit discipline techniques of an earlier era," but we question his explanation when he adds that the most important forces redirecting "both the aims and methods of child training in America emanate from behind the Iron Curtain." He believes achievement has begun "to replace adjustment as the highest goal of the American way of life." He foresees that guidance counselors, parents, and even youth itself will do their part to prepare "youngsters for survival in the new competitive world of applications and achievement tests."

Sputnik may have provided the dramatic incident which focused our attention upon competitive achievement in education, but the seeds had been sown long before. Parental pressure upon their children in high school to compete through college entrance examinations for the scarce commodity of quality higher education is no new phenomenon. The band wagon for this new party line of achievement is gaining momentum. Those who disputed adjustment as the central goal of child training were labeled "anti-democratic." Those who question achievement may be considered "anti-American." Such are the caprices of the spin of the wheels of fortune.

The serious question which should concern us all is that of the consequences of the compulsive pressures which are now force-feeding the process of turning children into adults but at the same time extending the period of dependency.

Panos D. Bardis
University of Toledo

5 / Attitudes Toward the Family Among College Students and Their Parents * †

According to Ernest W. Burgess and Harvey J. Locke, familism refers to strong in-group feelings, emphasis on family goals, common property, mutual support, and the desire to pursue the perpetuation of the family.[1] As several recent developments indicate, this type of organization is no longer so dominant among typical American families as it was a few decades ago.[2] Furthermore, it seems that the influence of modern means of transportation and communication, as well as of recent socioeconomic changes, is so extensive and pervasive that the attitudes of various groupings—parents and children, college graduates and noncollege graduates, upper and lower occupational classes, and the like—are about equally nonfamilistic.

THE PROBLEM

The purpose of the present study, which deals primarily with attitudes toward familism among college students and their parents, was to examine this theory by testing the following hypotheses: (1) College students and their parents do not differ significantly in their attitudes toward familism. (2) There is no significant relationship between familism and such variables as education, age, size of home town, occupation, and number of siblings.

METHODOLOGY

To measure attitudes toward familism, a scale[3] was constructed by means of the Likert scaling technique.[4] The validity and reliability of this device were tested repeatedly and proved satisfactory. A split-half test, for instance, ap-

*This project was financed by a grant from the Faculty Fellowship Fund of Albion College.
†From *Sociology and Social Research.* Reprinted by permission of the author and publisher.

[1] *The Family,* second ed. (New York: American Book Company, 1953), p. 60.
[2] *Ibid.,* pp. 53–95.
[3] For a detailed description of this scale, see Panos D. Bardis, "A Familism Scale," *Marriage and Social Living,* in press. Valuable suggestions concerning the scale items were given by Drs. R. Blood, E. Burgess, R. Cavan, H. Christensen, E. and S. Duvall, R. Hill, J. and P. Landis, and M. Nimkoff. Copies are available upon request from the author.
[4] Rensis Likert, *A Technique for the Measurement of Attitudes* (New York: Archives of Psychology, 1932), No. 140, especially pp. 11–33 and 44–53.

plied to the responses of 30 males and females selected at random from the sample of the present study, gave a raw reliability coefficient of .79, which, after it was corrected by means of the Spearman-Brown formula,[5] resulted in a value of .88. The 16 items[6] of this scale were preceded by a statement specifying that the subjects were not expected to describe their own families but to indicate the extent to which they approved of the practices expressed by these items with reference to the family institution in general. The theoretical range of a person's reaction to each item was 0.4, while that of his familism score resulting from all 16 items was 0–64—a high score always indicated a familistically minded individual.

Part of the group studied by means of this familism scale consisted of students enrolled in the writer's Introductory Sociology course in 1958. Only white native Americans whose parents were also white native Americans, living, and still married were included. In this way, the entire group studied consisted of 68 students and their 136 parents. Of the former, 18 were males and 50 females, their ages ranging between 18 and 24 years—the mean was 19.37. Moreover, 1 was Catholic, 66 were Protestants—of these, 31 were Methodist—and 1 was nonaffiliated. One was married, 2 engaged, and 65 single. Forty-two were sophomores, 23 juniors, and 3 seniors. Eight had spent most of their first 18 years in communities of less than 5,000 population, and 59 in cities of at least 5,000—1 failed to supply information concerning this matter. Eight were only children, 34 had one sibling each, 14 had two, 11 had three, and 1 had six. The ages of the fathers ranged between 41 and 69 years, the mean being 51.26. Four of them were Catholic, 61 were Protestant— of these 27 were Methodist—and 3 were nonaffiliated. Five had only a grade school education, 22 were high school graduates, 26 had some college training, and 15 had done graduate work. Twenty-eight had spent most of their first 18 years in communities of less than 5,000 population, and 40 in cities of at least 5,000. Twelve were skilled workers or foreman, 15 were clerks or kindred workers, 24 were proprietors, managers, or officials, and 17 were professional persons. The ages of the mothers ranged between 38 and 59 years, the mean being 48.99. Two of them were Catholic and 66 were Protestant—of these, 29 were Methodist. Six had only a grade school education, 23 were high school graduates, 34 had some college training, and 5 had done graduate work. Twenty-five had spent most of their first 18 years in communities of less than 5,000 population, and 43 in cities of at least 5,000. Finally, only 9 were gainfully employed—4 were clerks or kindred workers and 5 were professional persons—while the remaining 59 were housewives.

[5]Henry E. Garrett, *Statistics in Psychology and Education,* fourth ed. (New York: Longmans, Green and Company, 1953), p. 341.
[6]See Findings and Interpretation, *infra.*

All of the data secured from these three groups were collected through personal interviews and analyzed by means of several statistical tests.

FINDINGS AND INTERPRETATION

The means of the subjects' responses to each of the 16 scale items were as follows—the first value always represents the fathers, the second the mothers, and the third the students: a person should always support his uncles or aunts if they are in need, 1.66, 1.50, 1.91; children below 18 should give almost all their earnings to their parents, .94, .91, .59; the family should consult close relatives (uncles, aunts, first cousins) concerning its important decisions, 1.51, 1.13, 1.13; children below 18 should almost always obey their older brothers and sisters, 1.75, 1.38, 1.57; a person should always consider the needs of his family as a whole more important than his own, 3.01, 2.79, 2.76; at least one married child should be expected to live in the parental home, .41, .47, .40; a person should always be expected to defend his family against outsiders even at the expense of his own personal safety, 3.01, 2.44, 2.85; the family should have the right to control the behavior of each of its members completely, 1.00, 1.28, .96; a person should always support his parents-in-law if they are in need, 2.32, 2.59, 2.38; a person should always avoid every action of which his family disapproves, 1.50, 1.50, 1.46; a person should always share his home with his uncles, aunts, or first cousins if they are in need, 1.22, 1.28, 1.44; a person should always be completely loyal to his family, 2.90, 2.68, 2.71; the members of a family should be expected to hold the same political, ethical, and religious beliefs, 1.18, 1.00, .90; children below 18 should always obey their parents, 2.81, 2.68, 2.50; a person should always help his parents with the support of his younger brothers and sisters if necessary, 2.93, 2.66, 3.00; a person should always share his home with his parents-in-law if they are in need, 2.01, 1.93, 1.94.

The above values lead to the following conclusions: (1) The relative uniformity of the means representing each item indicates some proximity between the students' attitudes toward familism and those of their parents. (2) The item represented by the highest means referred to helping one's parents with the support of one's younger siblings, while that with the lowest means pertained to the married child's living in the parental home. (3) In general, if we divide the items into three categories represented by means found primarily between 0 and 1, 1 and 2, and 2 and 3, we observe that (a) the subjects disapproved most of policies depriving the individual of his independence with reference to finances, residence, conduct, and ideologies; (b) they approved most of practices conducive to the general security of the immediate family as a whole; and (c) the intermediate responses referred primarily to helping close relatives other than parents and siblings.

72 / **Attitudes, Values, and Language**

The means of the subjects' familism scores were 30.16 for the fathers, 28.22 for the mothers, and 28.50 for the students. (A similar study involving young people residing in a rural community in southern Greece gave a mean of 46.95.) The difference between fathers and mothers was insignificant above the .05 level (t 1.81, df 134), that between fathers and students above the .10 level (t 1.63, df 134), and that between mothers and students above the .70 level (t .27, df 134), thus tending to confirm the hypothesis that "college students and their parents do not differ significantly in their attitudes toward familism." An additional test of the difference between the mean of the male students (29.89) and that of the female students (28.00) revealed that this difference was also insignificant above the .20 level (F 1.03, df 49 and 17, insignificant much above .10;[7] (t 1.21, df 66). In other words, as far as familism is concerned, the female students were about as liberal as the males, although certain studies dealing with dating have revealed a significantly lower degree of liberalism among females.[8] It is interesting to note, however, that among both parents and students the males made consistently higher familism means, the order from the highest to the lowest being: fathers, sons, mothers, daughters.

A different pattern of attitudes was revealed when the responses to the question, "At what age do you think boys should start dating individually, that is, not in groups?————, Girls?————," were analyzed. Indeed, the fathers' means for boys and girls were 16.40 and 15.85 years, respectively, the difference between them being significant slightly above the .05 level (t 1.90, df 134), while the mothers' corresponding values were 16.22 and 15.56, the difference being significant much below the .001 level (t 3.65, df 134), and those of the students 15.29 and 14.82, the difference being also significant much below the .001 level (t 4.27, df 134). In other words, as various similar studies[9] have also shown, the tendency of females to mature and marry earlier than males as well as to be younger than their husbands seems to lead to the belief that girls should start dating earlier than boys. In addition, the fathers once again proved to be the most conservative group and the students the least conservative, while the mothers were found between the two extremes, perhaps indicating that parents still tend to consider certain modern dating practices too liberal. Indeed, when the mean ages referring to boys were compared, the difference between fathers and mothers was insignificant almost at the .50 level (t .69, df 134), that between fathers and students significant much below the .001 level (t 4.83, df 134), and that between mothers and students also significant much below the .001 level (t7.15,df 134). Again, the corresponding differences pertaining to girls were all significant much below the .001 level (t 5.37, 4.70, 4.48;

[7]See Allen L. Edwards, *Experimental Design in Psychological Research* (New York: Rinehart and Company, Inc., 1950), pp. 162–70.
[8]See, for instance, Panos D. Bardis, "Attitudes Toward Dating Among the Students of a Michigan High School," *Sociology and Social Research,* 42: 276.
[9]*Ibid.*, p. 277.

df 134). In brief, although the hypothesis concerning familism was confirmed, the two generations differed significantly with reference to attitudes toward dating.

The second hypothesis, dealing with the relationship between familism and certain variables, was also confirmed. The familism-age correlation coefficients for fathers, mothers, and students, for instance, were .20, .19, and -.04, respectively, while the corresponding figures for familism and years of education were .13, -.06, and .05. Moreover, after assigning a value of 5 to professional persons, 4 to proprietors, managers, and officials, 3 to clerks and kindred workers, 2 to skilled workers and foremen, 1 to semiskilled workers, and 0 to unskilled workers,[10] the fathers' coefficient of correlation for familism and occupation proved to be as low as -.06, while that of the students—for paternal occupations—was .15. On the other hand, of the mothers, the housewives made a mean familism score of 28.46 and the nonhousewives 26.67, the difference between these means being insignificant above the .40 level (F 1.27, df 58 and 8, insignificant much above .10; t .80, df 66). Insignificant differences were also obtained when those coming from small communities (see methodology) were compared with those coming from large cities.[11] For the fathers, for example, the mean familism score of the former was 29.96 and of the latter, 30.28, the difference being insignificant above the .80 level (F 1.23, df 39 and 27, insignificant above .10; t .21, df 66). The corresponding means for the mothers were 28.00 and 28.35, their difference being insignificant above the .80 level (F 1.20, df 42 and 24, insignificant much above .10; t .22, df 66), while those representing the students were 26.62 and 28.78, their difference being also insignificant above the .30 level (F 1.42, df 7 and 58, insignificant much above .10; t 1.00, df 65). Finally, the students' coefficient of correlation for familism and number of siblings was only -.04. It seems then that, perhaps for the reasons mentioned previously, as far as the subjects of the present study are concerned, there is no significant relationship between familism and such variables as age, education, occupation, size of home town, and number of siblings.

When, however, familism scores and the ages considered desirable for the beginning of dating were correlated, the coefficients were as follows: for boys, the fathers' coefficient was .27 (significant between .01 and .05, df 66), the mothers' .07, and the students' .47 (significant much below .01, df 66), while the corresponding values for girls were .27 (significant as above), .18, and .12. In other words, there seems to be a slight positive correlation between liberalism concerning familism and liberalism concerning dating.

Finally, an effort to determine the extent of the parents' influence on their

[10]For this classification of occupations, see Alba M. Edwards, *Comparative Occupational Statistics for the United States, 1870–1940* (Washington, D.C.: United States Government Printing Office, 1943), pp. 181–86.
[11]Cf. Burgess and Locke, *loc. cit.*

children led to what appears to be the most interesting finding of the present study.[12] Indeed, the father-son coefficients of correlation for familism, age at which boys should begin dating, and age at which girls should begin dating were .16, .08, and .01, respectively, while the corresponding father-daughter figures were .41, .47 (both significant below .01, df 48), and .04. On the other hand, the corresponding mother-son coefficients were .16, .29, and .24 (last two, insignificant much above .05, df 16), while those representing the mother-daughter data were .37, .66 (both significant below .01, df 48), and .05. In other words, because the family is ordinarily the first institution to receive the child, because the latter interacts with this group when he or she is most impressionable, because family contacts are intimate, emotional, and continual, and because parents usually satisfy many of their children's physical, psychological, and social needs, thus encouraging identification with, and imitation of, the sources of such satisfaction, it seems that, despite the atomism which is dominant in our society, thiy institution is still influential. As the above data indicate, however, such influence appears to be more extensive among daughters, since, although all twelve coefficients were positive, the average of those representing the female students was .33, whereas that of the male students was only .16. Furthermore, mothers seem more influential than fathers, since their average was .30, that of the fathers being .20. Finally, the averages representing the four parent-child relationships were as follows: mother-daughter .36, father-daughter .31, mother-son .23, and father-son .08.

SUMMARY AND CONCLUSION

In brief, a study of attitudes toward the family among 68 Michigan college students and their 136 parents has revealed that (1) the two generations do not differ significantly with reference to attitudes toward familism; (2) males tend to be more familistic than females; (3) both males and females believe that girls should begin to date earlier than boys; (4) fathers tend to be more conservative than their wives and children concerning familism and dating; (5) parents believe that dating should begin much later than the average age given by their children; (6) familism does not seem to be affected significantly and consistently by age, education, occupation, size of home town, and number of siblings; and (7) children's attitudes toward the family are definitely influenced by their parents, the order from the strongest relationship to the weakest being mother-daughter, father-daughter, mother-son, father-son.

Further research by means of the familism scale employed in the present study may be conducted in various ways. Rural samples, for instance, may be compared with others obtained from cities. Moreover, it is possible for addi-

[12]Cf. Hugh Hartshorne et al., "Testing the Knowledge of Right and Wrong," *Religious Education*, 21: 539–54, especially p. 545.

tional projects to include three generations as well as various racial ethnic or religious groups. Again, the scale may be administered before and after the completion of courses in Family Life Education to measure the influence of such work on familism. Finally, some of the effects of changing social conditions on the family could be ascertained by administering the scale in one and the same school or other institution every five or ten years.

Cora Du Bois
Harvard University

6/ The Dominant Value Profile of American Culture *

This paper is an attempt to synthesize and systematize the revelant insights
on American values advanced by a diverse group of writers from De Tocqueville through Myrdal to the authors of the polemic or conversational pieces
that have been so numerous in the last decade. It will be addressed to the
dominant value system of middle-class Americans. This system is rooted in the
Protestant ethic and eighteenth-century rationalism. Many of its specific values are shared with other societies, but its configuration has come to be
considered peculiarly American.

Since the allotted space is limited, what is said here must be condensed,
schematic, and highly selective. There is no attempt to give a new definition
of value or to adhere rigidly to existing ones. Distinctions between value and
related concepts like themes, configurations, etc., will not be argued. Furthermore, the comments made here do not stem from scientific investigations.
Readers interested in the attempt of anthropologists to grapple with such
subtle and difficult questions are referred to more competent and exhaustive
materials (e.g., Kluckhohn and others 1951; Kluckhohn 1950). Dr. Ethel
Albert's still unpublished material furnishes whatever logical coherence this
paper may have, but for the content and interpretations the writer must assume
fall responsibility.[1]

THE OPPOSITIONAL MODE

Oppositional propositions are a consistent aspect of Western European
culture. They represent recurrent dilemmas in logic and ethics. They are
reflected in, and fostered by, the structure of Indo-European languages. They
have permeated sociological and psychological conceptualization. A wide
range of oppositional propositions can be offered as illustrations: thesis-
antithesis; good-evil; subject-predicate; folk-urban; aggression-submission; su-
perordinate-subordinate; mind-body. Of these oppositional propositions some

*From *American Anthropologist*, Vol. 57, No. 6 (1955). Reprinted by permission of the
author and American Anthropological Association.

[1]The materials that are emerging from the Harvard Values Study Project, particularly
Vogt's manuscript on the Texans now in press and O'Dea's on the Mormons, should be of special
interest. Unfortunately these were not consulted by the writer. Florence Kluckhohn's still unpublished material on "Dominant and Variant Value Orientations" has been read with great benefit.

may be genuine in the sense that they are, logically speaking, contraries. But it seems probable that most oppositional propositions current in Western culture are preponderantly spurious in the sense that they are poorly conceived contradictories.

The assumption is made here that no system of values can encompass genuine contraries and therefore that the oppositional propositions in any value system are spurious. The further assumption is made that in any value system where such spurious oppositions exist there will be a strain for consistency.

The implication of these assumptions for the processes of value change are clear. Analytically, any attempt to present a value system should avoid the formulation of new and spurious oppositions. The avoidance of analytic oppositions may help to reveal those already extant in the existing value system, and the associated strains for consistency may emerge more clearly.

The strain for consistency in the American value system may be one of the forces accounting for changes in its configuration over the last three hundred years. Whether that strain is more intense in the American value system than in others it is impossible to estimate here. However, that the strain exists has been manifest in two major directions: (1) the prizing of change itself, usually expressed as effort, struggle, and progress, which will be discussed again in connection with the focal value called "effort-optimism"; and (2) compromise, which is not exclusively American but has received characteristic expression in the phrase "splitting the difference." This phrase reveals particularly an appreciation of the spurious quality of the oppositions, since it implies that neither oppositional term represents "truth" and that by retreating from false dichotomies a valid equilibrium may be achieved.

FOUR BASIC PREMISES

For our purposes the value premises of any culture can be considered to rest upon the assumptions made concerning man's cognitive view of the universe, man's relation to it, and man's relation to other men. For the American middle class it is postulated that: (1) the universe is mechanistically conceived, (2) man is its master, (3) men are equal, and (4) men are perfectible. From these four basic premises alone many of the focal and specific values, as well as the directives, of the American value system can be derived. In the context of the last three hundred years of American history these assumptions have proved valid both experientially and integratively (i.e., in a self-reinforcing sense) for the United States as a whole and, more specifically, for the American middle class. Despite changed situations and therefore the potential loss of experiential and integrative validation, we may nevertheless expect these assumptions to persist for a considerable period of time. There may be lags in a value system as there are in other aspects of culture.

FOCAL VALUES AND THEIR DIRECTIVES

Albert uses the term "focal" to designate a value about which numerous specific values cluster. Directives are used to designate the do's and dont's inherent in specific as well as in focal values (Albert 1954:22, 23).

The four premises given above yield at least three major focal values: material well-being that derives from the premise that man is master of a mechanistic universe; conformity that derives from the premise of man's equality; effort-optimism that derives from the premise of man's perfectibility. (The fortunate term "effort-optimism" was coined by the Kluckhohns [1947].)

The nexus of specific values and directives clustering around each of these focal values can now be considered. Simultaneously the mutual reinforcement that occurs between the basic premises and their focal values, as well as the constant effort to resolve spurious oppositions through change, can be underlined. The inner consistency of the value system here presented accounts for much of the traditional vigor of "the American way of life" in the past. However, such vigor could not have existed without the reinforcement provided by the geographic setting of the American nation and the historic forces operative in the broader setting of Western European commercial, industrial, technical, and scientific growth in which the American nation shared.

1. Effort-Optimism

Work is a specific value in American society. It is not so much a necessary condition of existence as a positive good. It is a specific instrumental value through which man strives to reach not only the goal of his own prefectibility but also the goal of mastering a mechanistically conceived universe. But in values Vaihinger's "law of the preponderance of the means over the ends" is frequently operative. Thus work becomes a goal in itself and in the process may acquire the quality of activity for its own sake. Thus recreation, although theoretically the antithesis of work, nevertheless in its activism shows many of the aspects of work. "Fun" is something that most Americans work hard for and at, so that they must be warned at forty to give up tennis for golf, or hunting trips for painting. Touring, whether at home or abroad, acquires the quality of a marathon. And this in turn is closely associated with another specific value linked with the effort-optimism syndrome, the importance placed on education. However, as we shall see later, the educational effort acquires a particularly American cast when taken in conjunction with the other two focal values, material well-being and conformity. In sum, as many foreigners have observed, American life gives the impression of activism. The directives, as well as the virtues and vices, associated with this optimistic activism are numerous: "If at first you don't succeed, try, try again"; or, in the more contemporary idiom, "Let's get this show on the road." The optimistic quality that pervades the American mood is clearly conveyed by the "bigger ergo better" mentality; the "never say die"; the "up and at 'em."

Vigor, at least as motility, connotes biologic youth. The cult of youthfulness in this society is again a specific value frequently commented upon by foreign observers. This observation is borne out by the popularity of the heroes manufactured in Hollywood and in the world of sports, by the advertisements of styles and cosmetics. As the average age of the population increases, this value is already showing signs of being given new interpretations in terms of geriatrics, etc. This will be alluded to again in following paragraphs.

2. Material Well-Being

If indeed effort is optimistically viewed in a material universe that man can master, then material well-being is a consistent concomitant value. Not only is it consistent within the value system, but it has been amply demonstrated in our national experience. It has been manifest in the American standard of living. The nation's geographic frontier and its natural resources, combined with an era of invention, have convinced most Americans of the validity of such a proposition. In the American scene progress and prosperity have come to have almost identical meaning. So deeply convinced are most Americans of what is generally called "prosperity" that material well-being is close to being considered a "right" due to those who have conscientiously practiced the specific value of work. The congruence of this view with the new science of geriatrics, social insurance, and the growth of investment trusts is obvious. It represents a consistent adjustment of specific values to a changing situation. However, as the situational context changes it may weaken the present linkage between effort and optimism with the resulting devaluation of both and thereby set up a new strain for consistency that may alter the present configuration of the American value system.

One of the most common stereotypes about the United States is its materialism. Viewed in the context of the value system presented here, materialism is less a value *per se* than an optimistic assertion of two value premises (mastery over material nature and the perfectibility of man) that have operated in a favorable environment. What foreign observers may call materialism, with derogatory or envious innuendos, is to the American a success that carries the moral connotation of "rightness"—of a system that proves itself or, as Americans would say with complete consistency, that "works." Within the frame of American value premises, success phrased as material well-being resolves the material-spiritual opposition and becomes a proof of right-mindedness. "Hard work pays off." The old and widely known proverb that, "Virtue is its own reward" has a particularly American slant, meaning not that virtue is in itself a reward but rather that virtue is rewarded.

If hard work is a "good thing" in a material universe and since it has been rewarded by material well-being, consistency requires that manual labor should be accorded dignity or, at least, should not be considered undignified. Furthermore, manual labor is an unambiguous manifestation of that activism alluded to earlier.

The salience of material well-being as a focal value in American life leads into many by-ways, some of which confuse and confound members of societies founded on a different value configuration. In military terms, for example, Americans are so profoundly convinced of the correctness of the material well-being formula that logistics forms our basic strategy. Personal heroism, though it may amply exist, is not assumed to be the fundamental requisite for victory, as it is in France. In American terms, victory is won by the sheet of matériel laid down in front of advancing infantry and by the lines of supply that must be built up to provide such a barrier between hand-to-hand combat.

In the same vein, there is little room in the American middle-class value system for the realities of physical pain, brutality, and death. Since they are nonetheless natural and undeniable, they are given a highly stylized treatment in detective fiction, newspapers, and movies that provide an acceptable discharge of tension created by the discrepancy between values and reality. Many Americans are alienated and morally repelled when they encounter the poverty and misery prevalent in certain lands. They manage to go through life untouched experientially even by those in our own population who have not succeeded—those who exist hopelessly in rural or urban slums or those who are victims of physical or psychic disasters. We have provided for the latter so effectively that they are whisked away into institutions that our national surpluses permit us to provide comparatively lavishly. Death itself has been surrounded with appurtenances of asepsis. Evelyn Waugh's *The Loved Ones* could never have been written with India as a setting. The compelling quality of this value emerges when we consider world statistics on human welfare facilities. In this respect, the United States is consistently in the lead. Yet, if we compare these statistics with the outbursts of compassion that a newspaper account of a "blue baby" will elicit, we become aware not only of the power of this focal value but also the resultant constellation that might be summarized as compulsive compassionate activism.

3. Conformity

Viewed historically it seems probable that conformity is a more recent focal value in American culture than effort-optimism and material well-being. It may represent one of the valuational changes induced by the strain for consistency assumed earlier in the paper to be one of the forces that alter value systems. Over a century ago De Tocqueville saw with singular clarity the potential threat to national solidarity inherent in the values of individual liberty, on the one hand, and of the sovereignty of enfranchised masses, on the other hand. In the contemporary American value system, conformity represents an attempt to resolve this dilemma. The France of today, with a comparable dilemma, has still to find a resolution.

If the premises of perfectibility and equality are linked with the focal value labeled effort-optimism, then each middle-class American may legitimately aspire to maximal self-realization. But, if man is to master through his efforts a mechanistic universe, he must co-operate with his fellow-men, since no single man can master the universal machine. In other words, people are individuated and prized, but if they are to co-operate with their fellow-men for mastery of the universe or, in more modest terms, of the immediate physical and socio-political environment, too great a degree of individualization would be an impediment. Also since the American value premises—in contradistinction to much of the rest of the world—include equality, the realization of the self in such a context would not necessarily imply the development of highly personalized and idiosyncratic but rather of egalitarian traits. Self-cultivation in America has as its goal less the achievement of uniqueness and more the achievement of similarity. This is a proposition many Frenchmen, for example, find difficult to grasp. The Japanese, with their stress upon self-cultivation in order more perfectly to discharge the obligations they owe their family and society, might come closer to understanding this American formulation. (For a formulation of Japanese values, see Caudill 1952. On p. 93, the author points out the compatibility of Japanese and American middle-class values.)

The assimilation of diverse immigrant groups to middle-class American values has been one of the remarkable sociopolitical achievements of the nation and testifies to the compelling vigor of its value system. As resources and space were more fully manned, the very lack of tolerance for differences that facilitated assimilation was finally to curtail the admission to this country of those who presented such differences.

Earlier in our history self-reliance and initiative were specific values attached to the focal value of liberty. Today these specific values have a new focus. Individual self-reliance and initiative are attached to the promotion of the commonweal and to the progress of society. Conformity has replaced liberty as a focal value to which these specific traits are attached. Co-operation has been added as a specific value that has facilitated the shift-over. The present American value system manifests a highly effective integration of the individual to society.

The ramification of this nexus into the sphere of education has been alluded to already. Education is envisaged as a means by which all men through effort can realize themselves. But since co-operativeness is a specific value also inserted into this equation, education comes to be envisaged as a means to make more men more effective workers and better citizens. The land-grant colleges, the vast network of public schools, and the system of free and compulsory education with its stress on education for citizenship and on technical skills have set the American educational system apart from that of many other countries. In the American context the linkage between conformity, effort-optimism, and material well-being leads inevitably to mass education with the emphasis on the common man rather than the uncommon man, to its technical and practical cast, to what seems to many observers its low standards. Simultaneously, to many Americans schooling has acquired the weight of a goal rather than a means. A college degree is a "good thing" in itself, whether or not the education entailed is prized. This concatenation does not lead one to expect perfection as a directive for performance in American life.

In a society where co-operation and good citizenship are valued and where the commonweal is served by having each man develop himself through his own efforts, a generous friendliness, openness, and relaxation of interpersonal relations are not only possible but desirable so long as the associated expanding economy furnishes the situational possibilities. Rigid class structures and protective privacies are inconsistent with the values here enumerated. Doors need not be closed to rooms; fences need not be built around properties. The tall hedges of England and the enclosing walls of France are not appropriate to the American scene, where life faces outward rather than inward. If every individual is as "good as" the next and all are good citizens —what is there to hide? The open front yards, the porches, or more recently the picture windows that leave the home open to everyone's view, the figurative and literal klieg lights under which our public figures live are all evidence of the value placed in American life on likeness and the pressure exerted for conformity. This is very different from saying that American middle-class individuals are in fact all alike. It means merely that likeness is valued.

The American hostility to figures in authority has been frequently noted, and in this connection the almost placatory informality and familiarity of American manners that serve to play down status differences have been pointed out. The apparent contradiction between the striving for upward mobility and the distrust of those who achieve pre-eminent positions can now be seen in more balanced terms. If the argument advanced here is correct, upward mobility is valued as successful activity, but when it reaches a point where it outstrips the premise of equality and the focal value of conformity it borders on *hubris.*

In this connection then the relaxed, friendly manner of American life so frequently commented upon by foreign observers can be gauged in the broader context of an adjustment to incompatible values. The search for popularity, the desire to be like, the wish to be considered a "good fellow," are searches for reassurance that, in striving to achieve all the ends implied by the focal value of effort-optimism, one has not exceeded the bounds set by the other focal value of conformity. That this process can operate at any level of actual achievement, from the presidency of the United States to chairmanship of an Elks Club committee, need not be stressed. It is the boss, the politician, the teacher, the "big shots" who are disvalued figures to the extent that their superordinate position implies authority. It is the movie star and the baseball hero who are valued figures since their pre-eminence connotes no authority but at the same time dramatizes the meteoric rise to fame and popularity through hard work and youthful striving.

Another aspect of American social life is thrown into relief in the effort to balance effort-optimism, material well-being, and conformity and their linked specific values. In the business and financial world, despite conservative tendencies, there has been a steady trend toward consolidation and standardization. Although the familiar and now perhaps inappropriate hue and cry is still raised about monopoly and big business, the latter, at least, serves the greater material well-being of the American mass consumer, whose values are geared to conformity. "Big business' is consonant with the American value system here portrayed so long as the owners of such enterprises are pictured as the American middle class, so long as savings are invested in the stocks and bonds of these enterprises so that the middle class shares "equally" in its successes, and so long as the authorities in such enterprises are presented as servants of the people. In these terms the American value system is served. The dangers of a too extreme individualistic power-centered authority are thus allayed, and competitive rivalry is brought under control.

SUMMARY AND CONCLUSIONS

Two basic assumptions were made: (1) that no viable value system *qua* system can entertain logical contraries, and (2) that there is a strain for consistency among the spurious contradictions that may be inherent in any value system. Four major premises were assumed to underlie the American middle-class value system: (1) a mechanistically conceived universe (2) man's mastery over that universe, (3) the equality of men, and (4) man's perfectibility. From these four premises three focal values were suggested: (1) effort-optimism, (2) material well-being, and (3) conformity. Each of these focal values is envisaged as being more or less directly derived from each of the premises. Each in turn constitutes a series (here not fully explored) of specific values and directives. Each of the three focal and their constituent specific values are more or less consistently interlocked. But the viability of a value system does not rest exclusively on its internal coherence. It must also manifest a considerable degree of congruence with the situational context within which it exists. Changes in value systems will result, therefore, from a strain for consistency not only within the value system but also between values and situational factors.

REFERENCES

Albert, Ethel M. 1954. "Theory Construction for the Comparative Study of Values in Five Cultures: A Report on the Value Study," Harvard University, Laboratory of Social Relations: Value Study. (Dittoed.)

Caudill, William. 1952. "Japanese-American Personality and Acculturation," *Genetic Psychology Monographs*, 45:3–102.

Kluckhohn, Clyde, and others. 1951. "Value and Value Orientation in the Theory of Action," in Talcott Parsons and Edward A. Shils (eds.), *Toward a General Theory of Action*. Cambridge, Mass.: Harvard University Press, pp. 388–433.

Kluckhohn, Clyde, and Florence Kluckhohn. 1947. "American Culture: Generalized Orientations and Class Patterns," in Lyman Bryson (ed.), *Conflicts of Power in Modern Culture: Seventh Symposium*, pp. 106–28. New York: Conference on Science, Philosophy and Religion in Their Relation to the Democratic Way of Life, Inc. (distributed by Harper and Bros.).

Kluckhohn, Florence. 1950. "Dominant and Substitute Profiles of Cultural Orientations: Their Significance for the Analysis of Social Stratification," *Social Forces*, 28:376–93.

Seymour L. Halleck*

7 / Why They'd Rather Do Their Own Thing†

On either side of today's generation gap, the young and the old often see each other as guided by opposite values. Each group insists that his own value system is the right one. Students insist that their parents' values are misguided and out of date. Their parents fear that youth either lack values or are adopting new ones that are unwholesome.

How much do student values differ from their parents'?

The most striking change in student value systems is in the direction of values which lead to immediate gratification. Students today have little reverence for the past and little hope for the future. They are trying to live in the present.

The most important reason for this is the ever-increasing rate of change which characterizes our society. When no one can predict what the world will be like in 20, 10 or even 5 years, man must alter his psychological perspectives. The lessons of the past become less relevant; planning for the future appears futile. One is driven to gear his value systems toward enjoyment of the present.

Financial success and competitive striving for success have a revered place in the American value system—the person who devotes himself to the long-term struggle for acquisition of status and goods will be rewarded in the future. Where the future is unpredictable, however, such values lose meaning. Youth who are in the process of preparing themselves for adult roles are more likely to appreciate the uncertainty of the future than their parents. Consider, for example, the different perspectives of a mother and son in discussing the boy's prospects as a physician. The mother sees a doctor as a scientist and helper, one who does good works within the community and is rewarded with prestige and money. The son, however, is aware that by the time he spends 12 years training to become a medical specialist the nature of medical practice will hardly resemble what it is today. If he has hopes of using medicine as a vehicle for satisfying his needs for personal interaction with people, he may become uncomfortable at the thought that medicine of the future may be

---

*The author, professor of psychiatry at the University of Wisconsin, sees the widening generation gap as a problem of values. Parents live by one set of values, students by their own, and each contradicts the other. The author explains how the value crisis came about, and what might be done about it.

†From *Think,* September-October 1968. Copyright 1968 by International Business Machines Corporation. Reprinted by permission of the publisher IBM.

highly scientific and impersonal. Medicine may not, of course, go in such directions, but no one can really tell him in which direction it will go. One can consider almost any profession in a similar manner.

"YOU GOT ME, DAD"

The differences in perspectives of the generations is beautifully illustrated in *The Graduate,* a film in which the main character is "a little worried about his future." When he is angrily asked by his father, "What did I send you to college for?" the graduate replies, "You got me, Dad." I am told when this scene is viewed by student audiences they break out into wild cheers. When I saw the movie with a much older audience, the reaction was one of dismay. The graduate's remarks poignantly reflect the differing perspectives of the generations. Youth are no lazier, no more hedonistic or passive than their parents. Rather, conditions do not favor future-oriented values, and youth are being forced into the role of the "now" generation.

This, perhaps, is one reason why college students tend to downgrade the acquisition of property, why they are unimpressed and sometimes even contemptuous of it. Recruiters for industrial firms on our campuses are learning that some of the best students are not interested in business careers. Few young people can view a life that is dedicated to trade and the acquisition of wealth as meaningful. Some conservative adults fear that this new devaluation of capitalistic enterprise represents a shift to communistic or socialistic philosophies. This fear seems exaggerated. Acquisition of capital is a rational enterprise only when there is some reason to believe that it will have the same usefulness in the future as it does in the present. When this is not true the amount of self-expenditure involved in obtaining capital seems wasted.

The rejection of material values may account for certain kinds of selective stealing on the part of college students. It is probably true that more students than ever engage in shoplifting. This behavior is usually rationalized by the argument that big companies are too impersonal to be affected by minor pilfering and that since property is not very important anyway, there is no harm done in taking some of it away from those who have too much. Surprisingly, no large organization, even those created by students themselves, is immune: at the Univeristy of Wisconsin a new student cooperative is in danger of going out of business because of shoplifting.

As reverence for property has diminished, youth have come to value the intrinsic worth of human relationships. There is an emphasis on being rather than doing. Youth are preoccupied with the need for being good people who can form good relationships. Whether they are more capable than their parents of finding such relationships is debatable, but their commitment to the search for intimacy is indisputable. A "beautiful" person, in the vernacular of today's youth, is not one who is physically attractive or one who has the personal qualities that guarantee success. He is an individual who has the capacity to relate openly and warmly with others.

In focusing upon one another's personal worth, youth have emphasized the development of their innate potentialities. Unwilling to evaluate themselves by the measure of what they can produce or sustain, they focus on the process of creativity and its appreciation. The attractiveness of psychedelic drugs may be related to this new emphasis. By altering the state of their own consciousness many students hope to find new truth and power—creativity—by looking inward. But in using such drugs they also demonstrate their lack of conviction that they can shape the world and are searching for a strength and constancy within an unreal inner world.

INCREASING SKEPTICISM

Not only creative activities but also intellectual pursuits are increasingly valued as ends rather than means. This change has important ramifications for our educational system. Adults are accustomed to thinking of education as a means to success and progress. Since these values do not have the same meaning to youth, they are skeptical of the practical benefits of learning. They tend to see education as an end in itself, something to be enjoyed, even worshiped as a noble activity of man. There is much emphasis on doing away with the competitive aspects of education, with the regimentation and emphasis on grading that has served to produce citizens who would easily fit into an industrial society. Nothing enrages students more than the feeling that they are being processed to take their place in a competitive society rather than being educated to become better people.

It can be argued that youth's rejection of some of the values of the Protestant ethic or of capitalism is a result of newfound affluence and leisure. It is probably true that those who have been raised in an affluent world do not find it easy to appreciate the value of sacrifice and hard work. Yet, while affluence seems to play some role in reinforcing an emphasis on "nowness" it is also true that all classes of youth, even those who have been raised in poverty, show similar characteristics. Poor and oppressed youth may still be committed to finding a place in this capitalistic system, but even among them the rumblings of discontent with our society seem to be related to more than their inability to share in our affluence. They, too, seem to be showing an increasing skepticism toward hope and planning.

The rate of change in our society also seems to make youth more aware of the problems of commitment and fidelity. Earlier generations resolved this ambivalence by institutionalizing their commitments. Only 20 years ago the young college man's obligations to his family, his career and his community were clearly defined. Today, young people talk about the need for fidelity and at the same time emphasize the philosophy of "doing your own thing and being responsible to no one but oneself." The problem here is that while an orientation toward life in the present is more likely to increase concern with human values, it also puts a premium on flexibility. It is not easy to be flexible and committed at the same time. When the future is uncertain, one must travel lightly, must be wary of how he invests his emotional energy and must be ready to move on when there is change. Where "coolness" and intimacy are valued concurrently there exists a situation of conflict which produces a variety of unpleasant emotional reactions.

Social change influences other values, including society's attitude toward change itself. Throughout history youth have always been more open to change than their elders. There are natural reasons for this. As one grows older, his commitments to others encourage him to hold onto his position in life by supporting the status quo.

Youth today, as in the past, seem to revere change but they are also peculiarly wary of it. They are highly indignant of injustices perpetrated by the status quo. Nevertheless, in their uncertainties as to the future they have difficulty in coming up with the long-term plans for change. The New Left can propose few alternatives to our present society and can only speak of tearing it down.

A second major shift in the value systems of today's youth is also related to changes in society, particularly to the impact of new communications media. The rearing of children requires a certain degree of protectiveness and even deception; if children were prematurely exposed to information about the harsh realities of life they simply could not tolerate it. But the new media deluge today's youth with information. Children learn the cynical truths of life at a very young age. They can sense when parents and other authority figures are mildly deceptive and know when those in authority are outright deceitful or hypocritical. No institution—family, church, the university or even the law —can any longer hide behind dogma or tradition.

One of the things that is happening in every society exposed to new technology and new media, is that young people are vigorously questioning whatever arbitrary structure is imposed upon them. When students begin to perceive what is so often a weak intellectual base for behavioral demands made upon them, they become angry and rebellious. Simple answers such as, "We should do it this way because it is right," or "because we have always done it this way," will no longer satisfy them. It is futile to demand that young people bring more order into their lives unless the merits of such order can be persuasively described.

EXCESSIVE FREEDOM, EMOTIONAL CHAOS

At the moment, youth's capacity to decipher the inconsistencies and hypocrisies of the older generation has led them to adopt some rather extreme value positions with regard to the issue of freedom. Young people place increasing emphasis on the virtues of a structureless world and many seem convinced that total freedom from the dictates of authority would be an ideal existence.

This new emphasis on freedom is not without emotional consequences. Even the most rebellious student is still dominated by certain dependency needs which create an almost automatic drive toward obedience. Furthermore, as I shall attempt to elaborate later, structure and the need to rely on the wisdom or strength of others seems to be an innate human need. There comes a point when too much freedom, particularly freedom to choose from an almost unlimited set of alternatives, becomes incapacitating and paralyzing. In the struggle for autonomy some youths seem to achieve a premature or pseudomature autonomy which does not satisfy their needs, and tends to breed emotional chaos.

Another aspect of value change related to the impact of media has to do with the issue of self-revelation. In a world where deception can be easily exposed and where youth have seen so many of their faithful beliefs ruthlessly destroyed, there is a tendency to value openness in interpersonal relationships. Many of today's youth are quite willing to reveal themselves. They will talk openly of things that would have shamed their elders.

TOLERANCE AND MORALITY

A final aspect of value change related to the impact of media has to do with the issue of power. Youth are keenly aware of the capacity of the establishment to oppress others. They are also senseitive to what is often an irrational basis by which established power justifies its tenure. Students are learning they can diminish certain oppressions in their own life by attacking what often turns out to be a highly vulnerable and surprisinlgly defenseless authority.

Sometimes value differences between generations cannot be phrased in terms of direct conflict. Both adults and students, for example, advocate racial and ethnic tolerance. Yet, youth are probably more capable of adhering to this value than their parents. An adult would be more likely to limit his advocacy of tolerance when that value began to interfere with other values such as stability, status or wealth. In other situations, what appears to be a value conflict between generations is in reality an argument over which generation is more honest in its pursuit of values.

In emphasizing personal values and good relationships youth tend to maintain that they are more concerned with the needs of mankind and more compassionate than their parents. It is probably true that young people raised in a world which has been perceptually shrunk by the new media do have a great awareness of the plight of their oppressed fellows. Yet, it is rare to see this awareness translated into calls for action. The percentage of young people who are prepared to sacrifice comforts in order to help their fellowman is not overwhelming. I doubt that compassion either as a value or as an actuality is an exclusive possession of any generation. In this regard we must be aware of the existence of contradictory value systems among youth. While some are talking about the brotherhood of man, others are talking about the need for individual values and the importance of putting individual needs ahead of society's.

If we consider the values of adhering to principle versus willingness to compromise, we again find little change but much criticism between generations. Both parents and students at times accuse one another of being unwilling to adhere to principle. Both accuse one another of being unable to compromise. Students accuse parents of "selling out" for personal gain. Adults accuse students of being unwilling to compromise their idealism in the face of the realities of existence. Students accuse adults of blind adherence to irrational causes, an accusation particularly relevant to the war in Vietnam; most students see it as a conflict perpetuated by an adult generation unwilling to compromise ill-founded and destructive principles.

Is there a value crisis in American life today? In my opinion we are moving toward a crisis related to the manner in which values are generated and maintained in a changing world. As old values are attached we are not creating new ones to replace them. There is a real danger that values of any kind may be losing their power, that young people in particular may find themselves existing in a valueless world. There may be an inherent rightness in doing away with traditional values that seem irrational and cannot be justified. Yet, if such values are indiscriminately destroyed before they are replaced by more rational values, our society will experience an unprecedented degree of chaos.

Those who are entrusted with the teaching of values in our society— educators, theologians, law enforcement officers and parents—seem totally unprepared to move from dogmatic to rational presentation of value systems. As their authority is threatened, some resort to preaching and exhortation rather than to reflection. Our youth respond by despair and violence.

Our society has an obvious need for a value system based on rational efforts to enhance the well-being of man. Such a system must recognize man's biological needs. It must be practical enough to provide answers as to how men can live together in peace and stability. Finally, it must recognize that certain values at times have to be institutionalized if for no other reason than to provide stability during periods of intensive change.

SOME VALUES TO LIVE BY

It is presumptuous for anyone, including a psychiatrist, to attempt to tell other people how they should live. Yet I am convinced if one is concerned with other people's health and happiness he can find only so many guidelines by emphasizing adjustment or adaptation to what is. I do not believe that man can go on adjusting to changing conditions of our world and still be man. If there is to be a healthy society of the future we must search for positive values which transcend the nature of the immediate environment. No one can present a value system that is relevant to all men in all ages. I believe, however, that we know enough to at least try to describe certain basic guidelines.

• There is ample scientific evidence that without some capacity to share strong feelings of affection with another person it is not possible to lead a happy or useful life. Most varieties of mental illness and many physical ailments may be traced directly to feelings that one is not receiving enough affection. This condition arises when man lacks the capacity to relate himself intimately to others. Any society then must come to value intimacy or love. Closely related to this is the value of compassion. Man is a unique animal insofar as he is able to identify with the feelings of others. He needs to feel a sense of community, to identify himself as a member of a society in which he is not a bystander.

• A second value is openness to experience. I use this expression in a broad sense to include the ability to seek and evaluate without prejudice the wide variety of experience possible within the limits of one's commitment to others. Openness to experience means openness to change and personal growth. This includes the capacity to be aware of oneself. A person cannot be fully aware of the world unless he has some capacity to understand the manner in which he perceives that world. Self-understanding also implies being at ease with one's past. The healthy man cannot live wholly in the present nor can he base his existence on future rewards.

• A third value is the ability to find an optimum amount of freedom. Although man needs to love others and rely on others if he is to survive, he must also be able to experience his destinctiveness. When man sacrifices autonomy or freedom he finds a certain amount of comfort, but this is always at the expense of adopting the role of the lesser being, someone not quite as good as others.

• Because man is the only animal who is physically and psychologically helpless for a large part of his young life, he learns to rely on structure and authority as a prerequisite to comfort. Whatever tendency he might have to outgrow this need is thwarted by his appreciation of the imminence of his own death. Man is the only animal who comprehends his own mortality and he cannot live with this knowledge without belief in some power that transcends his own. For some individuals belief in a supreme being suffices. Others sustain themselves through belief in the perfectibility of man. In either case, man must have an ideology that he can value.

• Man also has an innate need to interact with his environment and alter it in a manner which provides him with a sense of mastery. It is not crucial how he gains mastery. He may find it in daily work, in organized play or in efforts to create new art, music or literature. What is important is that man must to some extent be active and must experience his activity as either having an impact on other people or as having the capacity to alter his physical surroundings.

• On a pragmatic basis it would seem obvious that we must come to value order. Man can tolerate only so much change without experiencing his existence as chaotic. I am not speaking of change which relieves oppression and injustice. Such change is obviously useful. Changes brought about by scientific and technological progress, however, need to be rigorously scrutinized and controlled. A reverence for progress (except for that progress which directly contributes toward making man a better human being as opposed to making him a more confortable human being) must be replaced by a valuation of stability.

• Another value which is probably more correctly based on pragmatism than biology is the capacity to assume responsibility for one's own behavior. Adherence to this value provides dignity for the individual and stability for the group. It is the belief in this capacity to lead a responsible life which allows a man to experience himself as a unique animal who has some choice in his own destiny. He who denies responsibility for his actions or thought cannot be free since he must live as though he were governed by uncontrollable forces.

• Another pragmatic value is honesty, the willingness to avoid deceiving oneself or others and the willingness to search for truth. Men could lead dishonest lives and survive with comfort. Yet almost any philosophy concerned with the betterment of man advocates the honest life. While there is much disagreement as to the content of the truth, few individuals—young or old—would argue with the contention that he who deceives himself or others is leading an inadequate life.

• The events of the past months have convincingly demonstrated our society's urgent need to find a way of inculcating the value of nonviolence in our people. Because man is an aggressive animal it will no doubt be necessary to resort to institutionalized, even programmed methods of forcing real acceptance of this value. It seems to me we have no other choice.

• Finally, every society must find the means of revering their elderly members. When aging means being less respected, less powerful and less relevant to this society, there can never be any joyous anticipation of the future. The question of how we can find some means of evaluating older members of our community may ultimately be the most illuminating issue in our quest to understand student values in a changing world.

THE PRICE OF WISDOM

The calamity of modern existence is that the world changes so fast that there is little likelihood that the old will continue to remain very much wiser than the young. In this regard it is distressing to note how few young Americans can identify one older American whom they deeply admire.

As the old become relatively less wise, their influence is maintained primarily by the acquisition of political and economic power. The values which they pass onto the young are then more likely to be shaped by institution and custom than by their understanding of actual human needs. I have previously described how youth are increasingly capable of recognizing the arbitrary nature of power and values which are imposed upon them by their elders. It is likely that they will continue to use their new knowledge militantly to search for more rational values and for more pragmatic divisions of power. But even as they attack the adult world they become trapped in destroying themselves. For if they make their parents irrelevant they will surely make themselves irrelevant.

In drifting into a youth-oriented culture we have ignored the teachings of philosophers who have since the time of Plato emphasized the need to revere maturity. We are often told that our youth are our future. Yet, unless we can create a world which offers the possibility of aging with grace, honor and meaningfulness, no one can look forward to the future.

Edythe Margolin
University of California, Los Angeles

8 / What Do Group Values Mean to Young Children? *

Children four to five years old do not seem to be aware of the idea of *consensus,* the concept of *popularity,* or criteria for achievement.[1] A study was recently made of kindergarten children in thirty classrooms that represented a low, a middle, and a high degree of structure of activities and control. The findings showed that few children were aware of, or were able to express, criteria for academic achievement or for effective interpersonal relationships in a group. The children were not sure what kind of behavior their group preferred. A follow-up study was made of conditions that might be partly responsible for inhibiting the development of group norms among five-six-, or seven-year-olds.[2]

The notion of *popularity,* which is so important in later years, is anchored in the concept of *group* and in an understanding of what is valued by a specific group. A child needs to know what the majority of his group approves if he is to judge who is the most popular among them. The sharing of ideas is one essential for a group. Autonomously acting individuals who do not communicate with one another cannot know what consensus is.

Consensual standards, implicit or explicit, are part of what draws people together as a group. In classrooms where children behave autonomously and do not know what the rules or norms are, the teacher is not likely to have a group in the full sense of the concept. The suggestion that children who do not know the rules cannot become a group does not imply that the author is advocating regimentation in order to develop group awareness. Children can learn what is expected of them as norms become obvious in classroom procedures.

In the study reported here three hundred children—one hundred in kindergarten, one hundred in first grade, and one hundred in second grade—from varying socioeconomic backgrounds responded to individual interviews. The subjects were asked questions to elicit information on their impressions of classroom behavior expected of the group; their awareness of a single

*From *The Elementary School Journal,* February 1969. Reprinted by permission of the author and the *Elementary School Journal.* Copyright by The University of Chicago Press, the publisher.

[1] E. Margolin, "Group Context and Concepts of Social Status," *Sociology and Social Research,* 48 (April 1964), 324–29.

[2] This study was supported in part by the University of California, Los Angeles, Grant #2109.

popular child, of popular children, or of popularity as a concept; their knowledge of criteria for assessing achievement; and how strongly they felt impelled to submit to their peers or to be obliging.

To make up the sample of three hundred children, a random sample was taken of kindergartners, first-graders, and second-graders. Ten children were taken from each of ten kindergartens, ten children from each of ten first grades, and ten children from each of ten second grades. The children ranged in age from four years and nine months to six years and eleven months. Every third child on the teacher's class list was to be interviewed. Substitutions were made if a child on the list was absent, if he did not speak English (which was the interviewer's language), or if he seemed uncomfortable in the interview. The interviewer was familiar with children in kindergarten and primary grades, having taught at those levels, but the interviewer had not taught the children in this particular study.

THE QUESTIONS

All the children who took part in the study were asked the same questions. The children were first asked: What are the names of the children in the class? Which children do you like?

To get information about criteria that pupils used to assess achievement, they were asked: Who does the best painting? Who does the best block-building? Who is the best reader? (This question was asked only in second grade, where all children had an opportunity to be chosen, since by second grade each one had had formal instruction in reading.)

To get information about the children's awareness of rules or norms in the classroom, they were asked: What are some of the things you have to remember to do at school every day? What are some of the things your friends make you remember to do at school every day? What are some of the things you wish you did not have to remember to do at school every day?

To get information about children's awareness of a popular child or of the concept of *popularity,* they were asked: Can you name someone or some children that everybody likes? Which child or children do you think the whole class likes?

To determine whether the children felt they had to submit to the group, they were asked: If you were using something and a few children came to you and asked whether they could use it, what would you do? If you were on the swing and some children came and asked you for it, what would you do or say?

It was hoped that the answers would help provide data on the nature of "groupness" in the classroom.

Early in the interview each child was asked to express his choice of classmates; the information was sought not for sociometric purposes, but to assess the child's judgments of products. The interviewer wanted to learn whether the children chose a product not because they felt it was the best, but mainly because they knew and liked the classmate whose work it was. Children are honest enough to say they do not like something, regardless of the effect on the producer's feelings. Forthrightness comes naturally to children. Consideration for the feelings of others has to be learned: it is not a natural and spontaneous reaction.

STRUCTURE

The children's responses were related to the structure of activities in the classroom, because structure affects the process by which a classroom of pupils becomes a group or remains merely an aggregate of children who are near one another. The structure of classroom activities was classified as low, medium, or high depending on the number of, and the frequency of, teacher-planned activities in which the total classroom group was expected to take part. The teachers, who did not know that structure was going to be classified, were asked to give a written estimate of the total number of activities, planned for each day, that involved participation by the entire class, as opposed to participation by small groups. Each teacher gave the information on activities to the researcher after the interviews with the children.

The number of activities in each classroom ranged from twenty to sixty-five a week. Classrooms that had twenty to thirty-four activities for participation by the entire class were considered low in structure; classrooms that had thirty-five to forty-nine activities for participation by the entire class were classified as medium in structure. Classrooms that had fifty to sixty-five or more activities for the entire class were classified as high in structure. Differences in structure among the thirty classrooms were statistically significant at the .0005 level of confidence.

The method of coding the children's answers was tested for reliability and validity. Agreement between the judges was .90.

AN AWARENESS OF THE GROUP

Children's ability to talk about their awareness of standards, or norms, seems to vary from classroom to classroom. A child's awareness that he is a member of a group seems to be influenced by chronological age, mental age, patterns of work and play, quality and degree of interaction, and teacher-planned structure of activities.

An earlier study indicated that kindergarten children did not have a sense of being part of a group, of achieving consensus. One might think that children in first grade would begin to grasp the concept of *groupness*. However, children's maturity is not the major element in understanding the concept of *group*. The structure of the teacher's plans does seem to influence the children's understanding of what a group is.

FIRST-GRADERS

In the study reported here, it was found that children in the first grade knew less than kindergartners about school routines. As the children progressed from kindergarten to first grade, their responses to questions about rules and norms showed less consensus. One might expect first-graders to show more knowledge of classroom routines than kindergarten children. The study does not support this expectation.

Perhaps the pressures of a schedule that includes many new tasks—reading, writing, mathematics—plus the routines that usually accompany children's production of materials in those tasks are confusing to pupils in first grade. In the sense of building on routines and knowledge of what happens in school, first grade is not a continuation of the schooling process of kindergarten.

From the time children enter school at the age of five and begin to become familiar with the institution, with the teacher, and with the pupils, they learn about norms, or rules, for achieving, academically and socially, not gradually and evenly, but at different rates of progress. By second grade, most of the children were more aware of norms, rules, and expectations of their peers and of the teacher. While first grade may introduce children to many new tasks and rules, the experience may also provide the groundwork for easier acquisition of routines in second grade. There may be an accumulative effect in children's learning of social and academic norms, from grade to grade.

From kindergarten to second grade the per cent of children who showed an awareness of norms increased. In kindergarten there was an increase of 10 per cent; in first grade, an increase of 15 per cent; and in second grade, an increase of 20 per cent. The increases are based on the children's responses to the question: Are there some things your friends remind you to do at school every day?

THE EFFECT OF STRUCTURE

There was a positive relationship between the degree of classroom structure and the per cent of children's responses that indicated an awareness of classroom rules. The more highly structured the classroom, the greater the number of children who were aware of rules related to the classroom. The children in classrooms that were more highly structured were supporting rules that were based on teachers' expectations (not peers'), because the children reminded their classmates of those expectations.

The per cent of responses indicated that awareness of criteria for achievement increased from kindergarten to second grade. One hypothesis to be tested was that children's awareness of criteria for achievement would increase as they advanced from kindergarten, to first grade, and to second grade. To test this hypothesis, the children's responses to questions on painting were used as important data for comparisons. Painting is the only activity that children in all three grades—kindergarten, first grade, and second grade—engaged in. Comparisons of responses about painting could be made that were not possible for other activities, which varied from grade to grade.

Activities other than painting—such as clay-modeling and reading—also provided sources of subject matter the children could use to answer questions about the work of their peers. By using these responses the children's awareness of criteria for achievement generally could be tested within each grade. Children's criteria on painting made it possible to make comparisons across the grades in one activity.

Children do no play with blocks in all grades, but there is a great deal of block play in kindergarten to give children an opportunity to show what they understand about social studies concepts. There is less play with blocks in first grade, and still less in second grade.

Thus, in this study various activities offered to children at each grade level provided the foundation for children's judgment of criteria for achievement in a specific activity.

REASONS FOR RATINGS

From first grade to second, there was an increase in the per cent of responses that showed an awareness of criteria for achievement. The highly structured classrooms at each grade level showed a lower per cent of statements that were classified as non-discriminatory. For example, when the children were asked, "Who does the best painting?" and then "Why do you think so?" or "Why do you like them?" a smaller per cent of the children replied, "I don't know," or "Just because—," or "Because I do." A larger per cent said, "He used good colors," or "She has good ideas for her paintings," or "He makes nice designs."

UNDERSTANDING—NOT DOCILITY

In second grade, the per cent of children's responses that indicated an awareness of criteria for the best reader in the class was highest for the highly structured classroom. It does not necessarily follow that if teachers want children to know criteria for achievement they should strive to create a highly structured classroom. The nature of the material, the difficulty of the material, its appeal for children, and the teacher's skill in helping children focus on specific problems all contribute to the pupils' understanding of criteria for achievement.

All too often, in the earlier grades at least, teachers are led to believe that their class is a group if the children appear docile. Submissiveness to the teacher and to peers is not sound evidence that children know what a group is. More important is children's understanding of norms, criteria for achievement, and classroom routines of various kinds.

PREMIUM QUALITIES

The qualities that help children realize that they are members of a total classroom group are the same qualities that contribute to the structural or more stable aspects of group behavior. Certain criteria for assessing popularity, academic achievement in skills, or the ability to express classroom norms or rules emerge in the context of a specific group. What is important to children when they are part of a classroom group is not always important to the same children when they are part of another group. Certain values arise in particular groups as people interact daily with one another in those groups.

Specific accomplishments are expected at school that may not be expected elsewhere. What is more important, a child knows that at school he is constantly being evaluated and must try to do his best at all times. In the school group, he tries to find out what the criteria for the "best performance" are. A pupil's knowledge of group rules may be evidence that he knows he is a member of the classroom group and is held accountable, just as his peers are, for certain standards of behavior.

GROUP PRESSURES ON CHILDREN?

How much does the group affect the behavior of children five to seven years of age? Perhaps children in this age range are not pressured by a group in the same way that adults can be. Children may not "see" the existence of a group among themselves. They may see a number of individuals and may have no interest in guessing what they are thinking. When we assume that we have some notion of the ideas of others, we have a basis for social interchange, which can, in turn, contribute to "groupness."

Young children are somewhat unpredictable; they often try out different styles of behavior. Sometimes they copy others, children as well as adults; sometimes young children create their own style. Yet, some consistency of behavior in individuals who see one another day to day lends a measure of predictability to expectations. Expectations lead to the development of norms in certain groups. Children who are rarely exposed to the thinking of their classmates as a group have little awareness of group structure.

WHAT INFLUENCES GROUP AWARENESS?

Some view the problem of group structure as one that is due mainly to children's lack of maturity. Children are too young, some believe, to understand certain abstractions. Others see children's mental development as an important consideration. Maturity and development need to be placed in a perspective of cultural concepts. Our culture and the emphasis it places on individuality at certain times and on adjustment to the group at other times affect the direction that may be taken in the development of groups in the classroom. Pupils' ideas about rules and criteria for achievement are also influenced by the teacher's style of controlling pupils and the activities planned for a curriculum.

More information is needed on how rules enforced in the home relate to, or deviate from, peer values, especially peer values that develop at school in the formal and informal networks of relationships. Also, the fact must be considered that some values are more important to children at one time in their lives than at another.

In encouraging a class to function as a democratic group, the teacher is often deceived by appearances. Group behavior seems to be a subtle blend of peer relationships and the teacher's structuring of activities.

To many, the idea of structuring conjures up an image of restrictions and rigidity. But structure can take many forms. A structure that permits children to participate in small groups of their own choosing may be appropriate for certain activities—the expressive forms of the arts or various science projects that are carried on simultaneously, for example.

WHAT IS STRUCTURE?

Structure, whatever its form, is a description of how a classroom works. Even if the teacher permits the children to do what they prefer, she must still prepare choices to offer the pupils. Pre-planning and spontaneous planning with the children are both part of a structural design; this does not mean that the design must be rigid or without choices for children.

A broad and flexible framework for examining structure in a classroom can result if structure is viewed as a concept that merely describes the geographical location of children, the number of times they meet in a total classroom group, and the specificity of the teacher's directions. If it is decided that group awareness is important for young children's development, and if it is found that certain types of structure encourage group awareness, then the teacher's problem is to find out which of the effective types of structure he prefers. If it is decided that group awareness is not important for young children, then the teacher has another problem, a different problem.

MISGIVINGS

In any case, the teacher will not be deluded into thinking that a group is forming when nothing of the sort if happening. It can be frustrating to the teacher who is trying to encourage children to become "group-minded" to feel that he is not succeeding. It can be just as frustrating to a teacher who thinks that group spirit is necessary to find that the means for achieving it are autocratic. The method defeats the goal. It is true that certain kinds of structure can get in the way of groupness. It is also true that other kinds of structure can facilitate groupness. Means and goals need to be separated so that the teacher does not feel frustrated and guilty for using one way or another to achieve what may not really be valued by educators—in this case group behavior defined as unified action, which presumably lies at the basis of democratic behavior. Can the end justify the means? These issues need to be faced. Many young teachers are confused about what constitutes democratic behavior on the teacher's part and are feeling guilty about their methods of dealing with children in the classroom.

Educational ideals conflict at many points. The ideal of developing cooperation and consideration for others in children may seem to conflict with the ideal of developing qualities such as individualism, self-protection, or self-enhancement. We want children to retain their individualism, but at certain times we also want them to listen to the ideas of others. It is not easy to teach these qualities simultaneously.

Co-operation develops from within and requires time to take on meaning for children. When teachers introduce the concept of *co-operation,* they realize that at first children will be compliant, not co-operative. Co-operation comes much later, after children learn the satisfactions that come from being thoughtful of others.

SUMMING UP

There seem to be greater differences than one might suspect in the quality of choices that children make as they move from kindergarten, to first grade and to second. In the interviews, the children's answers varied greatly in style and vocabulary. The school process had a variety of meaning for them. While it must be acknowledged that home backgrounds affect pupils' views, classroom structure seems to be important in influencing children's perceptions of classroom values. Some children seemed to know exactly what the school routines were; other children seemed to be visitors in the school. The half-hearted and unwilling pupils are somewhat like people who are not sure that they want to stay where a particular event is occurring. These children are evidence of weakness, sometimes in themselves, sometimes in the situation.

The results of the study, some of which are reported in this paper, seem to suggest that children are not affected by pressures of their own group as much as one might think. Group constraints appear to begin operating about the second grade. Group spirit is part of the socialization process at school; it does not come as part of the child's psychological equipment. For this reason, the teacher who wants to understand group behavior may well look to sociological explanations as much as to the psychological.

Mary W. Wakefield
N. J. Silvaroli*

9/A Study of Oral Language Pattern of Low Socioeconomic Groups †

Oral Language Patterns of the low socioeconomic Negro, Spanish surname, and Anglo children are thought to be sufficiently different from the middle class American children to cause difficulty in the learning process. There is evidence that children of these low socioeconomic sub-culture groups are at a distinct disadvantage in schools where the linguistic skill of the middle-class English speaking American prevails.

Inattention of lower socioeconomic class children may be due to inability to anticipate speech patterns. Bernstein (1961) found that these children used limited syntax which may hamper comprehension. Strickland (1963) found certain levels of skill in listening and talking seemed necessary to success in beginning reading. The academic and reading failure of children from low socioeconomic sub-culture groups is a major educational problem.

A study was conducted to determine whether there is a significant difference in speech patterns as measured by the Indiana Conference Scheme of 1959 among low socioeconomic Negro, Spanish surname, and Anglo children entering first grade. The study attempted to gain insight into whether a difference, if it exists, is influenced more by *ethnic* or *economic* backgrounds of the children in these subgroups. A significant similarity in their oral language pattern might indicate that low economic status rather than ethnic background has considerable influence on the oral language development of these children.

A random sample of twenty beginning first grade pupils who qualified as low socioeconomic on Warner's Index of Status Characteristics or for aid under Public Law 89–10 was chosen for each of the subgroups involved in the study. The Anglo sample was drawn from Flora Thew School in Tempe, Arizona; the Negro and Spanish surname samples were drawn from schools in the Phoenix Arizona area.

The oral language of each subject was recorded on magnetic tape in the following manner: the subject was brought into a room that was a familiar part of his school environment and was seated at a low table with the investigator. The interview, following a standard procedure, began with the investigator's

*Mary Wakefield is Director of the Reading Center at Sam Houston State College, Hunstville, Texas. N. J. Silvaroli is Director of Reading Education at Arizona State University, Tempe, Arizona.

†Reprinted by permission of the major author Mary W. Wakefield and the International Reading Association.

talking to the child about pictures and stories. The interviewer said, "I'm going to show you some pictures and I want you to tell me stories about them." The child held each of the five stimulus pictures as he talked. When he indicated that he had finished talking about a particular picture, the examiner handed him the next one. After the child began to look at the picture, he seemed to pay no attention to the recording equipment.

The recorded language samples were transcribed to typewritten form. Each transcript was analyzed, first, for the kinds and frequency of basic sentence patterns and, second, for the kinds and frequency of mazes. Mazes, as defined by Loban (1963), are sounds in speech which are not pertinent to the structure or meaning of what is being said. They consist of hesitations, false starts, and meaningless repetitions.

The Indiana Conference Scheme (sponsored by United States Office of Education, Department of Health, Education, and Welfare, 1959), a method

Pattern	Symbols	Examples
A	1 2 or 1 (2)	1 2 1 (2) The little boy sings. (or) She is in school.
B	1 2 4	1 2 4 The boy has a truck.
C	1 (2) 5	1 (2) 5 Puzzles are fun.
D	1 2 3 4	1 2 3 4 He gives the man the tomatoes.
E	1 2 4 6	1 2 4 6 He made the pumpkin pretty.
F	(2) 1	(2) 1 Here is South Mountain. There are two girls.
G	Questions	What is that? Is this a ball?
H	Passive forms	The tomatoes were picked by the men.
I	Requests, commands	Let me see it.
J	Partials	This is not a pattern; it is any incomplete unit.
	Mazes	Nonstructural elements such as:
K	Noises	"uhm," "uh"
L	Holders	"well," "see"
M	Repeats	"here is, here is"
N	Edits	Words indicating a change or correction.

of analysis used in language research, was adapted for this study in a simplified form. Numbers and symbols were used in analyzing syntactical units such as subject, verb (transitive, intransitive, and copulative), direct object, complements, etc. Mazes were also analyzed in four classes: noises, holders, repeats, and edits.

After the transcriptions had been analyzed by use of the above symbols, judges listened to the magnetic tape recordings while reading the typescripts.

The judges indicated whether or not, according to their judgment, there were any syntactic descrepancies or errors in the original judging of the speech samples.

Table 1
Analysis of Variance of Specific Speech Patterns

Sentence, Patterns Sources of Variation	Degrees of Freedom	F Ratio
A Subj. verb	2 57	1.42
B Subj. verb obj.	2 57	1.99
C Subj. verb predicate nom. or adj.	2 57	0.39
D Subj. verb ind. obj. object	2 57	1.44
F Expletive verb subj. object compliment	2 57	1.75
G Question	2 57	1.70
H Passive Forms	2 57	1.00
I Request, commands	2 57	3.91*

*p < 0.05.

RESULTS AND CONCLUSIONS

An analysis of variance for total sentence patterns revealed that mean scores for the three ethnic groups—Negro, Spanish surnames, and Anglo—were not significantly different.

The analysis of variance for specific sentence patterns summarized in Table 1 revealed that the ethnic groups were not significantly different for each of the discrete patterns except for pattern I, requests or commands. The Spanish surname children used this pattern more frequently than the Anglo or Negro children. The structure of the interview seemed to have elicited this response.

The similarity found would seem to indicate that the economic background seems a stronger influence on language than the ethnic background. This might suggest that the economically disadvantaged child comes to school and is overwhelmed with the overall language system; consequently, there is little language production. The results of this study suggest that rather than concentrate on unique materials for these ethnic groups, the school could focus on their general adjustment to the school environment.

REFERENCES

Bernstein, B. 1961. "Social Class and Linguistic Development: A Theory of Social Learning," in A. H. Halsey, *et al.* (eds.), *Education, Economy, and Society.* New York: The Free Press of Glencoe, Inc.

Loban, W. D. 1963. *The Language of Elementary School Children.* Champaign, Illinois: National Council of Teachers of English.

Strickland, Ruth G. "The Language of Elementary School Children: Its Relationship to the Language of Reading Textbooks and the Quality of Reading of Selected Children," *Bulletin of the School of Education.* Indiana University (1962) 38.

10 / Language Development in Socially Disadvantaged Children *

Conspicuous deficits in language and speech are a handicap which socially disadvantaged children often have. Because adverse environmental circumstances have not equipped many of these children to conceptualize clearly or to verbalize adequately, their ability to profit from compensatory opportunities provided them, especially those of the school, seems to be limited. Two main questions then become relevant for an understanding of their difficulties: (a) How is the language acquisition of these children different from that of middle class children? (b) How do language and speech characteristics vary according to social class? Since studies pertaining to middle class children have been summarized elsewhere (McCarthy, 1954), this review will be limited to a presentation of investigations concerned specifically with language development and characteristics in children of low socioeconomic status.

BACKGROUND STUDIES

In the 25-year period between 1930 and 1955, research on children has focused to a limited degree on the effects lower social class, institutionalization of infants, and minority membership have on language development. The classic studies of McCarthy (1930), Day (1932), and Davis (1937), which utilized paternal occupation as a criterion of selection in efforts to secure representative samplings, concur in indicating that group differences favor children from the upper socioeconomic levels on practically all aspects of language studied. Irwin (1948a, b) also showed the superiority of the speech sounds of infants whose fathers were in a business or profession over those of infants whose fathers were skilled, semiskilled, or unskilled. That the absence of verbally oriented interactions between a significant adult and a very young child can have lasting and detrimental effects on his language has been documented by research done on infants cared for in hospitals or orphanages (Brodbeck and Irwin, 1946; Dawe, 1942; Fleming, 1942; Goldfarb, 1943, 1945; Williams and McFarland, 1937.)

Membership in minority groups and its adverse influence on language facility was first pointed out by Klineberg (1935) in regard to interpretation of mental tests administered to Negro children. Brown (1944) and Anastasi

*From *Review of Educational Research,* Vol. 35, No. 5 (December 1965). Reprinted by permission of the publisher, American Educational Research Association.

and D'Angelo (1952) compared young Negro and white children on the relationship of language development to IQ measures. In a longitudinal study of a low socioeconomic Negro group in New Haven, Pasamanick (1946), Pasamanick and Knobloch (1955), and Knobloch and Pasamanick (1953) pointed out that at the end of two years the infants' language behavior, though not retarded, was significantly lower than were other fields of behavior. Anastasi and Cordova (1953) and Anastasi and de Jesús (1953) dealt with the effects of bilingualism on intelligence in two groups of Puerto Rican children. The older group of sixth graders showed a lower level of intellectual functioning than normal, an effect ascribed in part to a very low socioeconomic level and to severe language handicaps during initial school experiences. The younger group, however, did not differ in IQ measures or in language from a white and Negro group studied previously (Anastasi and D'Angelo, 1952).

The outcomes of the work done in the two and a half decades summarized above were to foreshadow much contemporary work. The finding that children from the middle class with adequate mothering revealed marked and persistent superiority in language facility over those who for reasons of low socioeconomic level or institutionalization had received less than adequate mothering was to contribute to a revival of interest in the whole area of educability of pre school age children (Fowler, 1962; Hunt, 1961). In addition, the frequently reported finding that socioeconomic status and racial or ethnic membership appeared to be important correlates of performance on measures of ability—measures known to be highly dependent on verbal factors—served to stimulate research designed to identify the particular environmental factors which enhance or inhibit language development.

ANTECEDENTS OF LANGUAGE DEFICIENCY

The following factors will be considered in the review of current studies on the process of language acquisition under socially disadvantaged circumstances: infant vocalization, development of comprehension, development of cognition, and family interactive patterns.

Infant Vocalization

Knowledge regarding some determinants of vocal output in infants and the relationship of vocalization to the development of language has been extended by several experimental studies. Rheingold, Gewirtz, and Ross (1959) demonstrated the responsiveness of vocalizations to conditioning in the three-month-old infant. Irwin (1960a) showed that in homes of lower occupational status the phonetic production of infants between 13 and 30 months could be increased beginning around 18 months by systematic reading to and talking with the infant for a short period each day, an increase greater than would occur without the sound enrichment. Rheingold and Bayley (1959), in a follow-up at 18 months of 16 institutionalized infants who had received attentive care by one person from the sixth to the eighth month of life, found that more of their experimental subjects vocalized during the social test procedure than of the control subjects, who had been cared for under the usual institutional routine. Other differences in social responsiveness and developmental status were not found, suggesting that verbal behavior of infants appears to be more sensitive to interactive influences in the environment than are other classes of behavior, a conclusion confirmed by Pringle and Tanner (1958) and Pringle (1959). To the extent that the lack of attentive mothering in an institution resembles the minimal care a child receives in a lower class home —where marginal income, crowding, and noise often make it difficult for the caretaker to give the infant much beyond bare sustenance—the likelihood of language and speech impairment in the lower class child is evident.

Development of Comprehension

Comprehension and verbal responsiveness through language represent two different functions and as such need to be considered separately with regard to facility in lower class children. Pasamanick and Knobloch (1955) divided language behavior items on the *Gesell Developmental Schedules* into three spheres: language comprehension, verbal responsiveness, and reported language behavior. They found that their two-year-old Negro subjects excelled to a statistically significant degree in the sphere of comprehension in comparison with verbal responsiveness. Reported verbal behavior did not differ significantly from the other two spheres of language behavior. Such findings have to be interpreted in the light of developmental expectations, however, where comprehension tends to precede verbalization in the normal course of events. Carson and Rabin (1960), in a comparison of school age Negro and white children equated for comprehension and from different geographical locations, showed marked difference favoring Northern white children with respect to communication on the Vocabulary subtest of the *Wechsler Intelligence Scale for Children* and on a qualitative scale applied to the oral definitions in the *Ammons Full-Range Vocabulary Test.* Here results appear to be a bona fide function of socioeconomic factors.

John and Goldstein (1964) noted the disproportionate reliance the lower class child has on what he hears for his learning in contrast to the middle class child, who has the benefit of numerous conversational dialogues with adults to assist him in his verbal responses. While it might appear likely that the lower class child begins to grasp meanings in advance of any opportunity he has for verbalizing them, even here a lack of differentiation among mental abilities based on lower verbal meaning and lower fluency scores was found to be characteristic of low status children compared with high status children studied by Mitchell (1956). Pavenstedt (1965) described children from low class families as frequently not attending to instructions and needing to rely on concrete demonstrations to translate instructions into action, a conclusion which could, however, reflect short attention span rather than comprehension difficulties. The language models to which impoverished children are exposed are often not only meager, restricted, and incorrect grammatically but also punitive, according to Gray and Klaus (1963) and Bernstein (1961), limiting divergence and elaboration in children's thinking, and thereby inhibiting the development of their ability to comprehend.

Development of Cognitive Behavior

The Verbal Survey project being conducted by Deutsch and associates at the Institute of Developmental Studies of the New York Medical College is generating a number of investigations regarding the relationship of language development and cognition. John's (1963) and John and Goldstein's (1964) extensive work on certain patterns of linguistic and cognitive behavior in children from various social classes showed some of the specific limitations in the disadvantaged group's acquisition of the ability to label, discriminate, categorize, and generalize. Brown and Deutsch (1965), drawing from the same sample, demonstrated that within a socioeconomic status group particular levels of cognitive performance reflected certain specific environmental characteristics such as race and relative deprivation. Deutsch and Brown (1964) noted additional elements of pre-school educational experience and family stability as sources of variance in IQ scores; IQ scores were higher among those children who had attended a day care center or a nursery school and among those whose fathers had been present in the home.

From the above series of studies employing a first and a fifth grade core sample of 292 children and an extended population of about 2,500 children of various racial and social class groupings, Deutsch (1965) concluded that the cumulative deficit effect advanced by Klineberg (1963) does indeed exist. On the basis of a large number of measured variables studied, with language functioning at the core, Deutsch (1965) inferred that children from low socioeconomic backgrounds and minority status became less able to handle intellectual and linguistic tasks as they moved through school.

Effects of Family Interactions

Studies on the effect of the family on language development have centered around three main variables: the frequency, quality, and continuity of interactions. McCarthy (1961) emphasized the relationship between verbal skills and parental availability, particularly the amount and kind of contact the child experiences with his mother. The small amount of contact between parent and child with many siblings seemed to explain in part Nibet's (1961) finding that a large family is a handicap to verbal development. Walters, Connor, and Zunich (1964) supported the same hypothesis of significantly fewer interactions between lower class mothers and children than between mothers and children in other social groups, on the basis of an experimental study of the observed facilitating-inhibiting behaviors used by lower class mothers in the guidance of their preschool children. Although the authors' categories did not differentiate between verbal and nonverbal interactions, the lack of communication between mother and child was clear.

Two studies penetrate beyond the fact of relative frequency of verbal exchange to the quality of the contact maintained. Milner (1951) offered promising retrospective information on the specific value of early language experience. She compared the social backgrounds of two groups of first grade Negro children who scored contrastingly high and low on language development tests. The high language scorers were found to have participated more widely in adult family conversation and to have received more overt demonstrations of affection. Bernstein (1961), a British sociologist, compared the language of working class and middle class groups of adolescents. From his work he deduced a series of highly provocative postulates pertinent to origins of language deficiencies in culturally impoverished groups. He noted the tendency of the lower class parents to exercise arbitrary authority and categorical demands in disciplining their children, without giving any explanation or allowing the child to deviate or question. In this way, children were thought to be deprived of the opportunity to explore alternatives verbally and to lack experience in conceptualizing and reasoning.

One study of lower class children was concerned with the duration of the adult-child relationship. Pringle and Bossio (1958) in their study of 8-, 11-, and 14-year-old orphans examined the effects of regular contacts with adults living outside the orphanage. Backwardness in language development was least marked among those children who, since their removal from home, had maintained a continuing relationship with a member of their family or family substitute.

CHARACTERISTICS OF LANGUAGE DEFICIENCY

The general picture of language inadequacy in lower class children is currently being subject to scrutiny not only in an effort to determine why language and speech vary according to social class but also to ascertain what the distinctive qualities of the various groups may be. Studies which relate to these efforts will be reported below according to sensory modalities, quantitative language usage, qualitative language usage, and articulatory characteristics.

Sensory Modalities

It has been hypothesized that sensory modalities contribute differentially to learning. The work of Sievers (1955) on the *Illinois Test of Psycholinguistic Abilities* (*ITPA*) based on the formulations of Osgood (1954) has made it possible to test how children of varying intellectual endowments utilize their abilities differently. Weaver (n.d.) studied the psycholinguistic abilities of three groups of culturally deprived children. Their performance on the *ITPA* showed a similarity of language patterning with relative strength in the visual-motor channels and relative weakness in auditory-vocal channels. Moreover, children in the study who had been exposed to an early training project (Gray and Klaus, 1963) did significantly better than did those in the control group. C. P. Deutsch (1964) investigated auditory discrimination as a factor in verbal behavior and in reading achievement of a lower class group. She postulated that children raised in a very noisy environment with little directed and sustained speech stimulation might will be deficient in their discrimination and recognition of speech sounds, and that they would also be relatively inattentive to auditory stimuli and would have difficulty with any other skill which is primarily or largely dependent on good auditory discrimination. Her well designed study employing poor readers and good readers at grades one, three, and five indicated the poor readers had poorer auditory discrimination and greater difficulty shifting from one modality to another than did the good readers. Her results again confirm the apparent importance of auditory discrimination and general auditory responsiveness for verbal performance and reading ability. Inferences to be drawn from these studies point to the advantages of employing visual and motor avenues in dealing with socially deprived children.

Quantitative Characteristics of Language Usage

Thomas (1962) studied sentence development and vocabulary usage in the spoken language of white and Negro kindergarten children from low socioeconomic circumstances in a Midwestern urban setting. Verbal utterances were obtained in a structured oral interview conducted by the investigator. The traditional measures of length of verbal responses, complexity of sentence structure, proportion of parts of speech, and types and frequency of grammatical errors yielded a large number of comparisons. Notable among these was the finding that his subjects used significantly fewer words per remark than did Templin's (1957) subjects drawn from a middle class socioeconomic group. Of importance to the process of beginning reading was Thomas' finding that his subjects failed to use 20 to 50 percent of the words contained in five of the standard word lists recommended for primary grades.

Deutsch and others (1964) evaluated selected aspects of expressive and receptive speech in 167 pupils from 12 New York City public schools chosen to represent various combinations of two school grades, three socioeconomic levels, sex, and Negro and white race. Continuous speech samples were obtained by use of two reinforcement techniques and were recorded on tapes. Twenty measures were applied to the transcribed language protocols including such variables as total verbal output, mean sentence length, number of different word uses, and so forth. On the basis of numerous correlations applied to these variables and the use of a factor analysis, they found that differences in language performance which correlate with social class or race also correlate with significant differences in IQ performance. This relationship is even more clear in the fifth grade than in the first grade. Such a finding suggests the importance of improving language skills if IQ scores are to be raised, a task which would need to be undertaken during the crucial preschool years.

Qualitative Characteristics of Language Usage

Qualitative characteristics of language have not been considered to any extent in relation to the culturally impoverished but are useful for tapping certain features of the way they talk, particularly to their peers. Bernstein's (1961) theoretical formulations refer to a number of dimensions of linguistic behavior in British working class children which he sees as responsible for the large proportion of educational failures in that group. Their inability to plan verbally, to develop and maintain a sequence of thought, and to deal cognitively and conversationally with specificity and relativity were proposed as barriers to academic achievement. Riessman (1962) observed that such children have considerable facility with informal language expressed best in unstructured spontaneous situations and give unusual and original responses in word-association tests. Such distinctive properties of communication as presented by these two authorities, however, are not yet substantiated through systematic research.

Articulatory Characteristics of Language Usage

There are few current studies on the pronuniciation and articulation aspects of the speech of the lower class child. Davis (1937) showed that the percentage of children with good articulation was higher among upper occupational groups than among lower. Beckey (1942) found that significantly more children with retarded speech belonged to lower socioeconomic groups. Templin (1953) demonstrated a significant difference between children of upper and lower socioeconomic groups on both screening and diagnostic tests of articulation, the difference being in favor of the upper group. She stated that according to her extensive data children of the lower socioeconomic group take about a year longer to reach essentially mature articulation than do those of the upper group. Pavenstedt (1965) said children from very low class families form their words so poorly as to make it almost impossible to understand them at three and four years of age.

The sparseness of information in this area is due probably to several factors. (a) The presence of subcultural variation in pronunication, while known generally to act as a crucial deterrent to learning and to later vocational adjustment, has only very recently received any major or focused consideration as it occurs in underprivileged groups. (b) Problems of unclear or unintelligible pronunciation have not usually been brought to the attention of the speech therapist or psychologist prior to the lower class child's entrance to school; a body of knowledge emanating from study of such problems, therefore, does not yet exist. Once these culturally disadvantaged children are in school their problems have been so great and severe as to render largely ineffective the usual services the school might have available for dealing with their needs, especially in the congested urban schools and the substandard schools in the economically poorer sections of the country. (c) The speech problems posed by groups of children from different low socioeconomic circumstances vary with geographic location, race, and ethnic origin. It has not been clear where responsibility for remediation should be assigned. The regular classroom teacher, through no fault of his own, has been largely ineffective. The time of the speech therapist has, of necessity and by training, been devoted to remediation of organic and functional speech pathologies not primarily cultural in origin.

CONCLUSIONS AND NEEDED RESEARCH

Research to date indicates that the process of language acquisition for socially disadvantaged children, in contrast to that of middle class children, is more subject (a) to a lack of vocal stimulation during infancy, (b) to a paucity of experiences in conversation with more verbally mature adults in the first three or four years of life, (c) to severe limitations in the opportunities to develop mature cognitive behavior, and (d) to the types of emotional encounters which result in the restricting of the children's conceptual and verbal skills. Distinctive qualities of their language and speech include (a) a deficit in the auditory-vocal modality greater than in the visual-motor areas; (b) a meagerness of quantity and quality of verbal expression, which serves to depress intellectual functioning as they grow older; and (c) a slower rate and lower level of articulatory maturation.

In view of the recognized communication difficulties of lower class children, there is a pressing demand for both developmental and cross-cultural studies on the multiple factors related to their language and speech. Methodology needs to be developed which will make possible age and sub-group comparisons through carefully controlled standard-stimulus situations. These situations should be sufficiently simple and practical to be easily used in a variety of settings and with many types of disadvantaged children. Techniques such as those described by Irwin (1960b) for obtaining and transcribing accurately taped recordings of language samples need to be further refined to tap spontaneous language behavior among children rather than to elicit only the more sterotyped responses obtained through adult questions. Procedures need to be developed which will enable researchers to investigate the various modes of verbal functioning and adaptation employed by the child, including attention to his language in the context of his activities with peers. The gesture accompaniments of his talking should be studied. This suggests the possibility of combining narrative and descriptive methods of describing total behavior with use of mechanical recording devices. Lastly, investigation is needed into the influence of adult models on child language and the extent to which the patterns and expressions of the parents are imitated and modified by the child.

BIBLIOGRAPHY

Anastasi, Anne, and Fernando A. Cordova. 1953. "Some Effects of Bilingualism upon the Intelligence Test Performance of Puerto Rican Children in New York City," *Journal of Educational Psychology,* 44: 1–19, January.

Anastasi, Anne, and Rita Y. D'Angelo. 1952. "A Comparison of Negro and White Preschool Children in Language Development and Goodenough Draw-a-Man IQ," *Journal of Genetic Psychology,* 81: 147–65, December.

Anastasi, Anne, and Cruz De Jesús. 1953. "Language Development and Nonverbal IQ of Puerto Rican Preschool Children in New York City," *Journal of Abnormal and Social Psychology,* 48: 357–66, July.

Beckey, Ruth Elizabeth. 1942. "A Study of Certain Factors Related to Retardation of Speech," *Journal of Speech Disorders,* 7: 223–49, September.

Bernstein, Basil. 1961. "Social Class and Linguistic Development: A Theory of Social Learning," *Education, Economy and Society.* (Edited by A. H. Halsey, Jean Floud, and C. Arnold Anderson.) New York: Free Press of Glencoe. Chapter 24, pp. 288–314.

Brodbeck, Arthur J., and Orvis C. Irwin. 1946. "The Speech Behavior of Infants Without Families," *Child Development,* 17: 145–56, September.

Brown, Bert R., and Martin Deutsch. 1965. "Some Effects of Social Class and Race on Children's Language and Intellectual Abilities: A New Look at an Old Problem." Paper read at the Biennial Meeting of the Society for Research in Child Development, March. New York: Institute for Developmental Studies, Department of Psychiatry, New York Medical College, 1965. 9 pp. (Mimeo.)

Brown, Fred. 1944. "An Experimental and Critical Study of the Intelligence of Negro and White Kindergarten Children," *Journal of Genetic Psychology*, 65: 161–75, September.

Carson, Arnold S., and A. I. Rabin. 1960. "Verbal Comprehension and Communication in Negro and White Children," *Journal of Educational Psychology*, 51: 47–51, April.

Davis, Edith A. 1937. *The Development of Linguistic Skill in Twins, Singletons with Siblings and Only Children from Age Five to Ten Years.* Institute of Child Welfare Monograph Series No. 14. Minneapolis: University of Minnesota Press. 165 pp.

Dawe, Helen C. 1942. "A Study of the Effect of an Educational Program upon Language Development and Related Mental Functions in Young Children," *Journal of Experimental Education,* 11: 200–209, December.

Day, Ella J. 1932. "The Development of Language in Twins: I. A Comparison of Twins and Single Children," *Child Development,* 3: 179–99, September.

Deutsch, Cynthia P. 1964. "Auditory Discrimination and Learning: Social Factors," *Merrill-Palmer Quarterly,* 10: 277–96, July.

Deutsch, Martin. 1965. "The Role of Social Class in Language Development and Cognition," *American Journal of Orthopsychiatry,* 35: 78–88, January.

Deutsch, Martin, and Bert Brown. 1964. "Social Influences in Negro-White Intelligence Differences," *Journal of Social Issues,* 20: 24–35, April.

Deutsch, Martin, and others. 1964. *Communication of Information in the Elementary School Classroom.* Cooperative Research Project No. 908. New York: Institute for Developmental Studies, Department of Psychiatry, New York Medical College. 133 pp. (Mimeo.)

Fleming, Virginia Van Dyne. 1942. "A Study of Stanford-Binet Vocabulary Attainment and Growth in Children in the City of Childhood, Mooseheart, Illinois, as Compared with Children Living in Their Own Homes," *Journal of Genetic Psychology,* 60: 359–73, June.

Fowler, William. 1962. "Cognitive Learning in Infancy and Early Childhood," *Psychological Bulletin,* 59: 116–52, March.

Goldfarb, William. 1943. "Infant Rearing and Problem Behavior," *American Journal of Orthopsychiatry,* 13: 249–65, April.

Goldfarb, William. 1945. "Effects of Psychological Deprivation in Infancy and Subsequent Stimulation," *American Journal of Psychiatry,* 102: 18–33, July.

Gray, Susan W., and Rupert Klaus. 1963. *Early Training Project: Interim Report.* Murfreesboro, Tenn.: The City Schools and George Peabody College for Teachers, November. 25 pp. (Mimeo.)

Hunt, J. McV. 1961. *Intelligence and Experience.* New York: Ronald Press Co. 416 pp.

Irwin, Orvis C. 1948. "Infant Speech: The Effect of Family Occupational Status and of Age on Use of Sound Types," *Journal of Speech and Hearing Disorders,* 13: 224–26, September. (a)

Irwin, Orvis C. 1948. Infant Speech: The Effect of Family Occupational Status and of Age on Sound Frequency," *Journal of Speech and Hearing Disorders,* 13: 320–23, December. (b)

Irwin, Orvis C. 1960. "Infant Speech: The Effect of Systematic Reading of Stories,"

Journal of Speech and Hearing Research, 3: 187–90, June. (a)

Irwin, Orvis C. 1960. "Language and Communication," *Handbook of Research Methods in Child Development.* (Edited by Paul H. Mussen.) New York: John Wiley & Sons. Chapter 12, pp. 487–516. (b)

John, Vera P. 1963. "The Intellectual Development of Slum Children: Some Preliminary Findings," *American Journal of Orthopsychiatry,* 33: 813–22, October.

John, Vera P., and Leo S. Goldstein. 1964. "The Social Context of Language Acquisition," *Merrill-Palmer Quarterly,* 10: 265–76, July.

Klineberg, Otto A. 1935. *Negro Intelligence and Selective Migration.* New York: Columbia University Press. 66 pp.

Klineberg, Otto. 1963. "Negro-White Differences in Intelligence Test Performance: A New Look at an Old Problem," *American Psychologist,* 18: 198–203, April.

Knobloch, Hilda, and Benjamin, Pasamanick. 1953. "Further Observations on the Behavioral Development of Negro Children," *Journal of Genetic Psychology,* 83: 137–57, September.

McCarthy, Dorothea A. 1930. *The Language Development of the Preschool Child.* Institute of Child Welfare, Monograph Series No. 4. Minneapolis: University of Minnesota Press. 174 pp.

McCarthy, Dorothea A. 1954. "Language Development in Children," *Manual of Child Psychology.* (Edited by Leonard Carmichael.) Second edition. New York: John Wiley & Sons. Chapter 9, pp. 492–630.

McCarthy, Dorothea A. 1961. "Affective Aspects of Language Learning." Presidential address, Division of Developmental Psychology, American Psychological Association. September. *Newsletter,* APA Division of Developmental Psychology, Fall, pp. 1–11.

Milner, Esther. 1951. "A Study of the Relationship Between Reading Readiness in Grade One School Children and Patterns of Parent-Child Interaction," *Child Development,* 22: 95–112, June.

Mitchell, James V., Jr. 1956. "A Comparison of the Factorial Structure of Cognitive Functions for a High and Low Status Group," *Journal of Educational Psychology,* 47: 397–414, November.

Nisbet, John D. 1961. "Family Environment and Intelligence," *Education, Economy and Society.* (Edited by A. H. Halsey, Jean Floud, and C. Arnold Anderson.) New York: Free Press of Glencoe. Chapter 23, pp. 273–87.

Osgood, Charles E., issue editor. 1954. "Psycholinguistics: A Survey of Theory and Research Problems," *Journal of Abnormal and Social Psychology,* Vol. 49, Supplement 1954, No. 4. October. 203 pp.

Pasamanick, Benjamin. 1946. "A Comparative Study of the Behavioral Development of Negro Infants," *Journal of Genetic Psychology,* 69: 3–44, September.

Pasamanick, Benjamin, and Hilda Knobloch. 1955. "Early Language Behavior in Negro Children and the Testing of Intelligence," *Journal of Abnormal and Social Psychology,* 50: 401–402, May.

Pavenstedt, Eleanor. 1965. "A Comparison of the Child-Rearing Environment of Upper-Lower and Very Low Lower Class Families," *American Journal of Orthopsychiatry,* 35: 89–98, January.

Pringle, M. L. Kellmer. 1959. "Comparative Study of the Effects of Early Deprivation

118 / Attitudes, Values, and Language

on Speech Development," *Perceptual and Motor Skills,* 9: 345, December.
Pringle, M. L. Kellmer, and Victoria Bossio. 1958. "A Study of Deprived Children: Part II. Language Development and Reading Attainment," *Vita Humana,* 1: 142–70.
Pringle, M. L. Kellmer, and Margaret Tanner. 1958. "The Effects of Early Deprivation on Speech Development: A Comparative Study of Four Year Olds in a Nursery School and in Residential Nurseries," *Language and Speech,* 1: 269–87, October-December.
Rheingold, Harriet L., and Nancy Bayley. 1959. "The Later Effects of an Experimental Modification of Mothering," *Child Development,* 30: 363–72, September.
Rheingold, Harriet L., Jacob L. Gerwirtz, and Helen W. Ross. 1959. "Social Conditioning of Vocalizations in the Infant." *Journal of Comparative and Physiological Psychology* 52: 68–73, February.
Riessman, Frank. 1962. *The Culturally Deprived Child.* New York: Harper & Row. 140 pp.
Sievers, Dorothy Jean. 1955. *Development and Standardization of a Test of Psycholinguistic Growth in Preschool Children.* Doctor's thesis. Chicago: University of Illinois. 148 pp. (Abstract: *Dissertation Abstracts* 16: 286–87; No. 1, 1956)
Templin, Mildred C. 1953. "Norms on Screening Test of Articulation for Ages Three Through Eight," *Journal of Speech and Hearing Disorders,* 18: 323–31, December.
Templin, Mildred C. 1957. *Certain Language Skills in Children.* Institute of Child Welfare Monograph Series No. 26. Minneapolis: University of Minnesota Press. 183 pp.
Thomas, Dominic Richard. 1962. *Oral Language, Sentence Structure and Vocabulary of Kindergarten Children Living in Low Socio-Economic Urban Areas.* Doctor's thesis. Detroit, Mich.: Wayne State University, 1962. 393 pp. (Abstract: *Dissertation Abstracts,* 23: 1014. No. 3.)
Walters, James, Ruth Connor, and Michael Zunich. 1964. "Interaction of Mothers and Children from Lower-Class Families," *Child Development,* 35: 433–40, June.
Weaver, S. Joseph. 0000. *Interim Report: Psycholinguistic Abilities of Culturally Deprived Children,* Nashville, Tenn.: George Peabody College for Teachers, n.d. 3 pp. (Mimeo.)
Williams, Harold M., and Mary L. McFarland. 1937. "A Revision of the Smith Vocabulary Test for Preschool Children, Part III." *Development of Language and Vocabulary in Young Children.* (Edited by Harold M. Williams, Mary L. McFarland, and Marguerite F. Little.) University of Iowa Studies in Child Welfare No. 13. Iowa City: University of Iowa, June. pp. 35–46.

III / THE CULTURALLY DIFFERENT PUPIL

Cleo O. Hearnton Cook*

11/Self Concept and the Culturally Different Learner†

Self concept theory is increasingly useful as greater effort is made to educate all of the children. At the center of this theory is the learner's perception of himself. These include such phenomena as the defense of self; regard for self; aspiration; involvement of self with other objects, other people, groups and organizations.

The teacher as he considers the manner in which the learner sees himself must relate the self concept of another person, to his own self perception and to his function in the teaching act. All of this must be placed in the context of the teacher's societal goals and the societal goals of the learner. The teacher must address himself to five major elements: (1) another's self concept, (2) his own self concept, (3) his perception of the teaching act, (4) his perception of his own society, and (5) his perception of the learner's society.

Because of the uniqueness of SELF, and its attending phenomena, the related research has certain limitations:

— the several measuring instruments are inadequate
— research designs are often questionable
— many difficulties are encountered when certain variables are isolated or made independent
— control is highly difficult
— the use of independent demographic or sociological variables which may have unknown relevance to psychological variables may preclude or obscure clear psychological interpretations of obtained associations

Accepting the limitations just stated Wylie,[1] after reviewing more than 300 published studies and 120 unpublished doctoral disertations concluded that research evidence about self concept supports the following generalizations:

*Dr. Cleo Cook, of California State College at Los Angeles, served as resource consultant at the 1964 CASCD conference which had as its theme *The Learner—In His Society and as He Sees Himself.* Several members who heard her presentation requested an article elaborating the views she expressed in one of the action assemblies.

†Reprinted from the *California Journal for Instructional Improvement,* a quaterly publication of the California Association for Supervision and Curriculum Development.

[1]Ruth Wylie, *The Self Concept. A Critical Survey of Pertinent Research Literature* (Lincoln: University of Nebraska Press, 1961).

82592

1. A child's self concept is similar to the view of himself which he attributes to his parents.
2. A child's level of self regard is associated with his parent's reported level of regard for him.
3. One's body characteristics which are highly valued enhance his self regard; his body characteristics which are lowly valued undermine his self regard.
4. Failure on a capacity which one sees as being most instrumental to his goal achievement will affect negatively his evaluation of other areas related to self.
5. The extent to which failure or success changes one's self evaluation is tied up inextricably with (a) certain personality characteristics, (b) the extent to which one values the source of his failure or success, (c) the extent to which he feels that the source of information is viewed as adequate.
6. Social desirability in our culture is seen as having much in common with health over sickness—personal well-being over maladjustment. Therefore, the influence of social desirability is so great that one must be confronted with the "Ideal Self," the "Actual Self," and the "Social Self."
7. One's self concept is shaped through his interaction with others.
8. One's self concept influences his interaction with others.

These eight tendencies suggest situational frames, frames in which the teacher may operate as a facilitator or blocker. They further suggest that a learner *may* see himself in many ways according to the structure of the situations in which he finds himself. As a corollary, no learner can be categorically labeled with specific self concept brands.

A learner usually sees himself as a *someone*. This *someone* has a *role*—a real role, which may be present-oriented only, present-past-oriented, or present-past-future-oriented. The *role* is *acted* out for *himself* and for *others*. This *himself* or *someone* may or may not be acceptable to the learner himself or to his *others*. The *others* (teachers and other people) may or may not be acceptable to the learner or, alas, to the *others* themselves. This *role* may or may not result in fulfillment, depending upon the learner's need to achieve, the relevance of the *role* to his purposes, and the extent to which interaction between *himself* and *others* has supported his feeling of being worthwhile.

Appropriate here is the exciting construct of motivation presented by Cattell, Radcliff and Sweeney.[2] They define the construct as a learning attitude:

[2]R. B. Cattell, J. A. Radcliff, and A. B. Sweeney, "The Nature and Measurement of Components of Motivation," *Genetic Psychology Monographs,* 68: 49–211 (1963).

1. Stimulus Situation	2. Organism	3. Interest-need of a certain intensity	4. Specific Goal, course of action	5. Object conceived in action
In these circumstances	I, the learner,	want so much	to do this	with that.

The interest and intrigue inherent in applying the Cattell, Radcliff, Sweeney construct to each learner is apparent. Let us conduct one *SELF* through this pattern:

1. *Stimulus Situation:* In these circumstances—

A school which I am required to attend . . . where symbols are important . . . books, alphabet, numerals are applied to social esteem and acceptance . . . where verbal fluency and "thing" sophistication are important to communication and well-being . . . where activities by necessity are structured-timeness and timeliness are the order . . . where groupness obscures individual focus . . . where objectivity and record keeping obtain . . . where competitiveness in the use of symbols, words, and movement means survival . . . and where there are people who may or may not be like me—

2. *The Organism:*

I am a product of another group of cricumstances . . . I appear with a background of socializing experiences quite different from those evidenced here . . . a background that represents social failure . . . the t.v., radio, and billboards by exclusion of folk that look like me have led me to suspect that I am ugly, doomed to failure, fenced in as far as aspirations for job opportunities, housing and the ingredients of "good living" are concerned . . . denied! My clothing, speech, and manners reinforce this suspicion now that I view myself in these new surroundings . . .

You see, it was not until I ventured out—away from home that I felt the real difference . . . I know few of the objects in the classroom, and the many and varied objects that I use at home and in my neighborhood are not valued here. The responsibilities that I have accepted as being very important to the well-being of my "great family" and neighborhood have no place here . . . I have cared for the baby . . . made my own bed . . . prepared meals for my brothers and sisters . . . dressed myself, done the marketing every morning before school time, washed dishes, and even picked and chopped cotton to help support the family—

3. *Interest-Need of a Certain Intensity:*

I want so much

4. *Specific Goal:*

to do something that has relevance for me

5. *Object Conceived in Action:*

with something which will give me a pride in myself at this very moment in this very place. . . . It is significant that the most relevant thing might be a good rest, a hot nourishing meal . . . a toy to call my own . . . a tender pat on the shoulder . . . or for you, dear teacher, to tell me I am beautiful . . . (at this moment I may take my comb from my hip pocket and comb the front of my hair.)

Truly at first I will have difficulty understanding my teacher's directions . . . sustaining my listening because by necessity I have had to develop inattentiveness . . . relating symbols to action and to the expression of ideas, seeing syntax in planning and movement . . . identifying with the pictures and other visual materials that consistently exclude people like me.

But my teacher, my *Significant Other*, will see me as her *Significant Other*, because we share the same goal. Both of us are striving to become "actualizing persons." The teacher is aware of Combs'[3] findings that underachievers (1) see themselves as less adequate and less acceptable to others, (2) see their peers as less acceptable and adults as less acceptable, (3) show an inefficient and less effective approach to problems and (4) show less freedom or adequacy of emotional expression. ("The basic thread running through this study relates to a larger hypothesis that persons can only function to the degree that they feel adequate to function. Underachievement is often seen by the underachiever as less fraught with danger than actually trying to achieve.")

I keep asking myself, "Shall I lose my masculinity and really do this kid stuff ? Shall I be prissy and talk nice the way my teacher wants me to? If no adult like her has ever related to me, what makes me so sure that I can trust her?"

My teacher will help me succeed and think well of myself. She is aware that the Lamy study[4] supported the theory that a child's self concept and the perceptions he holds of himself in relationship to various aspects of his world are related to his reading achievement and may be causal factors in his subsequent reading achievement.

And finally my teacher's words and actions shall be enhancing and supportive. The Staines'[5] report shows that in classrooms taught by teachers whose words and actions are enhancing to students, more learning occurs.

The above is a simplification of a highly complex phenomenon related to the culturally different learner. For some children the teacher's task is facilitating the "self actualizing process." For others it is the *undoing* of the *Nobody Image* that has emerged from different circumstances, being socially disadvantaged or being confronted with a new value system.

It is not easy for the teacher or the learner for that matter, to slip into

[3]Charles Franklin Combs, *A Study of the Relationship Between Certain Perceptions of Self and Scholastic Underachievement in Academically Capable High School Boys,* Doctoral Dissertation, Syracuse University. *Dissertation Abstracts,* 63–5034 (1963), pp. 620–21.

[4]Mary W. Lamy, *Relationship of Self-Perceptions of Early Primary Children to Achievement in Reading.* Doctoral Dissertation, University of Florida. *Dissertation Abstracts,* 63–5796 (1962), p. 628.

[5]J. W. Staines, "The Self Picture as a Factor in the Classroom," *British Journal of Educational Psychology,* 28:97–111 (June 1958).

another's value system (as he must often do) and relate to the other person in this most sensitive area of self-image development. Relating to the learner in a self image development process may require:

(1) Seeing beauty in bodily or physical traits that are different from one's own
(2) Developing an awareness of another's models and another's available choices of behavior that have become a part of him
(3) Breaking through accumulated hostility
(4) Leading the learner to a point of identification with foreign models, models outside of his own past experiences, which should enhance his development for living in democracy's mainstream
(5) Broadening one's context of expectancy—an expectancy that a person different from the teacher himself might find reason for achieving —and that reason is this: there is a possibility that the learner can and will operate efficiently, effectively and affectively now and later in the broader democratic community
(6) Reconstructing values as to what is worthy of reward
(7) Pushing beyond what the learner finds relevant, once the relevance point or meaning point has been reached, to an enlargement of skills and function. It simply is not enough to reach a learner through athletics, for example, and permit him to remain at this point of relevance. The basic limitations that would ensue would render him helpless in a "mathematicking," communicating, expressing society and return him subsequently to his Nobody Image.

In this respect another aspect related to motivation is crucial: if the learner has a deep problem, that problem appears to be orbital; that is, he may interpret every blocking, every failure, or every facilitating act as being related to that problem. A fifth grade underachieving pupil instigated a fight with a classmate. This prevented his completing his assignment and detained his group from going out for recess. A visitor asked him what was the trouble. He answered (referring to the teacher), "She doesn't like me. Look at the way she does her hands."

The Self is subject to change. The task confronting school people is not only that of increasing the possibility of the learner's achievement in order that he may see himself as an adequate achiever, but of associating successful achievement with a positive affective-orientation-reinforcement. The learner must increase his vividness of a goal wide enough to embrace the real fulfillment of being an adequate democratic citizen. If he and his teacher can see him as such, he has a good chance of so becoming.

REFERENCES

ASCD. 1962. Perceiving, Behaving, Becoming. Yearbook. Washington, D.C. ASCD.

Bledsoe, J. C. and Garrison. 1962. *The Self Concepts of Elementary School Children in Relation to Academic Achievement, Intelligence, Interests and Manifest Anxiety.* Athens: University of Georgia.

Cattell, R. R., J. Radcliff, and A. B. Sweeney, "The Nature and Measurement of the Components of Motivation," *Genetic Psychology Monographs,* 68:49–211.

Combs, Charles Franklin. 1963. *A Study of the Relationship Between Certain Perceptions of Self and Scholastic Underachievement in Academically Capable High School Boys.* Doctoral Dissertation, Syracuse University. *Dissertation Abstracts,* 63–5034, pp. 620–21.

Lamy, Mary W. 1962. *Relationship of Self-Perceptions of Early Primary Children to Achievement in Reading.* Doctoral Dissertation, University of Florida. *Dissertation Abstracts,* 63–5796, p. 628.

Staines, J. W. 1958. "The Self Picture as a Factor in the Classroom," *British Journal of Educational Psychology,* 28:97–111, June.

Wylie, Ruth. 1961. *The Self Concept. A Control Survey of Pertinent Literature* (Lincoln: University of Nebraska Press).

Patricia C. Hishiki*

12 / The Self Concepts of Sixth Grade Girls of Mexican-American Descent†

Since the development of an individual's self concept is one of the most vital areas of human growth, educators concerned with child growth and development have become increasingly cognizant of its importance. The home, the school, and the community offer varied and important experiences for the acquisition of values and for the development of self.

For a minority population within the larger society the opportunities for the full range of experiences open to members of the majority are limited. In addition, certain handicaps among individual members of a minority group may be present which significantly affect the development of self. In the case of the Mexican-American, the problems include disadvantages in the areas of educational attainment, occupational structure, income, housing, effective community organization, and political strength. Lack of facility in the language of the majority contributes to language problems.

Thus, the background of experiences for the Mexican-American is shaped and colored by the cultural milieu. The child brings to school a historical framework of culture which cannot be described as "culturally deprived." Rather, he enters school with a "culture" of his own, with many positive characteristics that have developed out of coping with a "different" environment.

There is some belief that membership either in a low socio-economic group or in a minority culture tends to depress self concept because of discrimination by the larger society against these groups. Studies by Dreger and Miller, and Keller found that depressed self concepts as well as tendencies toward self-depreciation were noted in disadvantaged children (7). No systematic studies, however, dealing with the self concepts of Mexican-Americans have been found to date.

In the Southwest, which includes the states of California, Texas, New Mexico, Arizona, and Colorado, the Mexican-Americans number approximately four million. In the state of California no single concentration of Mexican-Americans within a metropolitan area is more important than the

*Patricia C. Hishiki is an Elementary Teacher at the Palo Alto Unified School District. She received her B.A. degree from Trinity College, her M.A. degree from the California State College, Los Angeles.

†From *California Journal of Educational Research*, Vol. 20, No. 2 (March 1969). Permission to reprint granted by California Journal of Educational Research, California Teachers Association.

community in East Los Angeles. It was to this area that the focus of this study was directed.

Literature pertaining to the Mexican-American indicates that this group has been found to score low on tests of intelligence (8), and to be characteristically low on tests of academic achievement (3, 6) as well. There are, however, within this population many students who are academically successful. The role of self concept and the sense of adequacy in relation to intelligence and academic achievement may contribute to further understanding of differences among individuals that arise.

THE PROBLEM

Bledsoe and Garrison studied groups of Caucasian fourth and sixth grade children in Clarke County, Georgia, in order to determine relationships between self concept and academic achievement, intelligence, interests, and manifest anxiety (1). The major purpose of this pilot study was to investigate in similar fashion the self concepts of sixth grade girls of Mexican-American descent. Further concerns focused upon relationships between self concept and intelligence and academic achievement.

HYPOTHESES OF CONCERN

Two groups of sixth grade girls, one, a group of Mexican-American girls in California schools examined for this study, and the other, a group of Caucasian girls attending school in Clark County, Georgia would not differ (1) in self concept, (2) in the relationships between measures of self concept and measures of intelligence and academic achievement, and (3) patterns of self description.

PROCEDURES

For the study of Bledscoe and Garrison in Georgia a *Self Concept Scale* was developed and a *Child Self-Description Scale* adapted from a previous study by Carlson. Permission to use these scales for this study was obtained. The *Self Concept Scale* consisted of thirty adjectives, twenty-five which signified positive qualities and five of which signified negative qualities. The subjects indicated on a three-point scale (Nearly Always, About One-Half the Time, or Just Now and Then) how each adjective was descriptive of himself. The *Self Concept Scale* was scored obtaining a numerical indication of self concept and ideal self by assigning values to the choices.

The ninety-five items of the *Child Self-Description Scale* were selected to describe feelings and preferences toward important and meaningful activities and situations in a child's life. The items were organized into nineteen pentads or sets of five. A pretest administered to a group of students of similar background determined the appropriateness of the choices.

The two instruments were administered to all the sixth grade girls attending two schools located in the area of East Los Angeles in the Montebello School District. Over 80 per cent of the students attending the two schools were identified as pupils with Spanish surnames. The final sample selected consisted of sixty-five girls of Mexican-American descent, over three-fourths of whom spoke Spanish in addition to English.

Scholastic characteristics were defined by the *Lorge-Thorndike Intelligence Test* scores and by the *Stanford Achievement Test* scores obtained as part of a long-range program of educational measurement in the district.

In the Georgia study the subjects were selected to represent a cross section of the white student population in Clarke County School District. The data reported in this study were based on 70 sixth grade girls with the *Self Concept Scale* and 158 sixth grade girls with the *Child Self-Description Scale*. For the Georgia sample scores were reported for the *California Short Form Test of Mental Maturity* and the *California Achievement Test*.

The hypotheses were tested statistically by comparison of means, "t" tests, and Pearson Product Moment Correlation Coefficients. When statistical tests were applied, the .05 confidence level was required to reject the null hypothesis.

FINDINGS

There was a significant difference between the self concepts of sixth grade girls of Mexican-American descent and white sixth grade girls in Georgia. The comparison between groups as shown in Table I revealed that the mean concept scores for both self and ideal self were higher for the Georgia group than the Mexican-American group.

Although it was not within the scope of this study to specifically investigate intelligence and academic achievement of the two groups, certain differences were apparent. The scores of both groups could not be equated because different measures were used in each case. In the areas of intelligence, mean scores for the white sixth grade girls as measured by the instrument used in the Georgia study were higher than the scores of Mexican-American girls in both Language and Non-Language. The Georgia sample deviated by half a standard deviation above the mean from a hypothetical national norm, and the Mexican–American group deviated by the same half a standard deviation but below the norm.

There were significant relationships between self concept and factors of

TABLE I

Means, Standard Deviations, and Tests of Significance
of the Self Concept Scale of Groups of Sixth Grade Girls

Group	Self Concept	Ideal Self
Georgia (N = 70)		
mean	78.41	88.02
standard deviation	6.51	3.31
Mexican-American (N = 65)		
mean	71.82	81.25
standard deviation	8.66	8.69
Tests of Significance	4.99*	5.94*

*significant at .001 level

intelligence and academic achievement for the Mexican-American group, according to the results presented in Table II. The correlations were low (.32–.58) and moderately positive, but were more positive and significant than the correlations of the group in Georgia.

TABLE II

Correlations Between Self Concept Scale and Intelligence
and Academic Achievement for Groups of Sixth Grade Girls

	Self Concept		Ideal Self	
Intelligence	Georgia	Mexican-American	Georgia	Mexican-American
Verbal	.004	.584°°	.243	.620°°
Nonverbal	−.038	.388°°	.093	.359°°
Achievement				
Word Meaning	.091	.321°	.528°°	.382°°
Paragraph Meaning	.111	.392°°	.478°°	.453°°
Arithmetic Concepts	−.019	.368°°	.259°°	.534°°
Arithmetic Computation	.035	.332°	−.030	.284°
Arithmetic Application	—	.330°	—	.429°°

°significant at .05 level
°°significant at .01 level

In describing characteristics most and least like themselves, the patterns of self descriptions of the two groups did not differ: eleven of the first choices and nine of the last choices were similar for both groups.

The group of girls in Georgia preferred reading and art most frequently and favored science least frequently, whereas the Mexican-American group was similar in its preference for art, but differed in selecting arithmetic as last choice. Other selected findings from the nineteen pentad descriptions found the Georgia group choosing actor most frequently as a vocational choice and rejecting engineer and scientist, whereas the Mexican-American group chose teacher and secretary most frequently and rejected newspaper reporter.

Over two-thirds of both groups selected "to go to college" as a first choice. Georgia girls placed greatest emphasis on "I'm not doing as well as I should in my school work," but the Mexican-American girls indicated that "I have to be very careful of my health" was of greater importance and gave the school work as their second choice. Neither group felt that their parents were too strict.

CONCLUSIONS

1. The sixth grade girls of Mexican-American descent investigated in this pilot study were found to possess significantly different self concepts from white sixth grade girls in Georgia. Likewise, their perceptions of ideal selves were different when measured on the similar instrument.

2. The finding that there were statistically significant and positive correlations between scores of the *Self Concept Scale* and the scores of the *Lorge-Thorndike Intelligence Test* was in accord with earlier research, such as the studies by Davidson and Lang (4), and Piers and Harris (9), and differed from the findings in the Georgia study. These earlier studies of self concept and intelligence were conducted using samples of white students at various age levels. An even greater correlation between the factors was found for Mexican-American girls than for the girls in the study by Bledsoe and Garrison.

3. The relationship between self concept and academic achievement was verified in the case of Mexican-American students. This finding is comparable to those of white students recently investigated by Brookover, Thomas, and Paterson (2), and Fink (5). However, the investigator, unlike Fink and Bledsoe and Garrison, found an even greater correlation between the factors in this study of Mexican-American girls.

4. Since the findings of comparison between groups illustrated more positive and significant relationships of self concept to the factors of intelligence and academic achievement among the Mexican-American group of students, the importance of these areas is underscored. In the present study the mean scores for Mexican-American sixth grade girls on the intelligence test were below an intelligence quotient norm of 100. Mean grade placements on the achievement test were two grade levels lower than actual grade.

5. The findings of the present study suggested that Mexican-American sixth grade girls and white sixth grade girls in Georgia assigned similar patterns of self-description to themselves. It can therefore be concluded that the choices describing feelings and preferences occurring in a child's life as measured by the instrument were similar for the Mexican-American group and the group of girls in Georgia.

6. The comparison of case studies of students of high and low self concepts revealed differences in achievement levels. The Mexican-American sixth grade girl with a high self concept had more success in academic achievement than did the sixth grade girl of similar background with a low self concept.

RECOMMENDATIONS

The reflections of self concept which were presented in this study pointed out the differences between groups of sixth grade girls of Mexican-American descent and white sixth grade girls in Georgia. Yet many of the goals, ideals, and aspirations for the future of the two groups of girls were similar. For example, both groups of girls indicated that they expected to "go to college."

In view of the results of intelligence and achievement testing, the group of girls from Georgia would have a better chance of entering and succeeding in college. However, other factors which contribute to achieving the desired goal of college attendance include future performance in school and individual motivation and sense of purpose. Therefore, it is the role of the school to provide every opportunity for bringing the reality and the aspiration level of the Mexican-American student closer together.

REFERENCES

1. Bledsoe, Joseph C., and Karl C. Garrison. 1962. *The Self Concepts of Elementary School Children in Relation to Their Academic Achievement, Intelligence, Interests, and Manifest Anxiety.* Cooperative Research Project No. 1003. Athens, Georgia: The University of Georgia, College of Education.
2. Brookover, Wilbur B., Shailor Thomas, and Ann Paterson. 1964. "Self-Concept of Ability and School Achievement," *Sociology of Education*, 37, 271–278.
3. Carlson, Hilding B., and Norman Henderson. 1950. "The Intelligence of American Children of Mexican Parentage," *Journal of Abnormal and Social Psychology*, 45, 544–551
4. Davidson, Helen H., and Gerhard Lang. 1960. "Children's Perceptions of Their Teachers' Feelings Toward Them Related To Self Perception, School Achievement, and Behavior," *Journal of Experimental Education*, 29, 107–118.
5. Fink, Martin B. 1962. "Self-Concept as It Relates to Academic Underachievement," *California Journal of Educational Research*, 13, 57–62.
6. Garth, Thomas R., and Harper D. Johnson. 1934. "The Intelligence and Achievement of Mexican Children in the United States," *Journal of Abnormal and Social Psychology*, 29, 222–229.
7. Gordon, Edmund W. 1965. "Characteristics of Socially Disadvantaged Children," *Review of Educational Research*, 35, 377–388.
8. Pasamanick, Benjamin. 1951. "The Intelligence of American Children of Mexican Parentage: A Discussion of Uncontrolled Variables," *Journal of Abnormal and Social Psychology*, 46, 598–602.
9. Piers, Ellen V., and Dale B. Harris. 1964. "Age and Other Correlates of Self-Concept in Children," *Journal of Educational Psychology*, 55, 91–95.

Lee Sechrest
Northwestern University
Luis Flores
University of the Philippines
Lourdes Arellano
Ateneo de Manila

13 / Language and Social Interaction in a Bilingual Culture *†[1]

A. INTRODUCTION

For individuals proposing to do research in bilingual cultures, there is always a question about the importance of the language chosen for the conduct of the study. It has been shown, for example, that among bilingual French-women there were distinct differences in Thematic Apperception Test responses obtained in English and in French, and it has been suggested that the differences are congruent with the biases of English-speaking and French cultures (1). Ervin (2) has also found that bilingual English–Italian speakers had better recall for verbal materials when both learning and recall were in their first-learned language. The first author of the present study became interested in possible attitude differences associated with the use of English and Tagalog among bilingual Filipinos. For all, or nearly all, of their lives educated Filipinos are bilingual (and many are multilingual), but there are many reasons to believe that the two languages they speak have different implications for them.

Solee (6) studied differential perceptual defense in English and Tagalog among bilingual school children. The real ingenuity of her research lay in the fact that she was able to divide her subjects into two groups: (*a*) those who first learned Tagalog at home and who were exposed to English at a later date, and (*b*) those who first learned English at home and who were exposed to Tagalog at some later time. She reasoned that the language used in the home for the child's earliest training would be of greater importance from an emotional point of view. More and earlier emotional experiences should have taken place in the context of the first-learned language. Therefore, more perceptual

*Received in the Editorial Office, Provincetown, Massachusetts, on June 10, 1968, and given special consideration in accordance with our policy for cross-cultural research. Copyright, 1968, by The Journal Press.

†From *The Journal of Social Psychology*, Vol. 76 (1968), pp. 155–161. Reprinted by permission of the major author, Lee Sechrest, and the publisher.

[1]This research was supported by Grant No. MH 07906–01 from the National Institute of Mental Health.

133

defense would be expected for taboo words printed in the child's first language. Her hypothesis was firmly supported.

Evidence of an anecdotal nature became available to the writers when a few married, bilingual Filipinos were asked in what language they made love. In spite of the fact that many of them habitually spoke English, even in their homes, all of them seemed to find the idea of making love in English quite amusing.

To study social interaction, a first, and admittedly crude, investigation was focused upon the preference for English or a Philippine vernacular in different social situations: viz, when speaking with someone of the same sex or when speaking with a person of the opposite sex. On the basis of observations reported above, it was supposed that the vernacular would be the preferred language for emotional discourse and, therefore, that mixed-sex couples would more often be speaking in the vernacular than same-sex couples. While it is not necessarily the case that conversations between mixed-sex couples would be more emotionally charged, it seemed probable to all three writers that such would be the case among Filipino college students.

TABLE 1

Language Spoken by Pairs of Bilingual Persons Observed in
Casual Interaction on a University Campus

Sexes of Pair	English		Philippine Dialect	
	N	%	N	%
Male-Male	14	18	64	82
Female-Female	12	14	79	86
Male-Female	18	28	47	72

The University of the Philippines is a large, state supported, coeducational school located in Quezon City. Although it draws students from all over the Philippines, the greatest proportion of them are Tagalog speaking. The school is coeducational, but Filipino students are, on the average, a year or two younger than comparable American students; and the current social mores do not promote obviously close relationships between students of the opposite sex.

Several Filipino student observers were hired to go around campus and simply note the occasions on which two persons were talking to each other, the sexes of the pair, and whether they were speaking in English or one of the many Filipino dialects. No special efforts were made to obtain a genuinely *random* sample of two-person conversations on campus, but the observations obtained were quite diverse with respect to physical location and time of day. The results are given in Table 1 in the form of a cross-classification for language and sex of the pair involved.

Contrary to expectations, the mixed-sex couples were *more* likely to be speaking English than same-sex pairs, the mixed-sex couples differing significantly from the same-sex couples ($X^2 = 4.65$, $df = 1$, $p < .05$). Perforce the authors must invent an explanation for their findings, and they believe that it lies in the nature of boy-girl relations in the Phillippines, relations still colored strongly by the Spanish tradition: in public, boys and girls are expected to keep their feelings toward each other under strick control, and public physical contact between them is all but prohibited. It is our tentative hypothesis that English tends to be used somewhat more frequently in boy-girl conversations because it is the "language of the intellect" and permits greater control of the social interaction.

The above observations and considerations suggested the possibility that in this bilingual culture social interactions might be influenced by the language chosen for the interaction: e.g., use of English might tend to produce a more formal and "distant" interaction. Previous work by Sommer (7, 8, 9) and Leipold (4), as well as the general theorizing of Hall (3), indicated that spatial distance between interacting persons might be taken as an index of social distance. In our experiment it was expected that the language used between two Filipinos might affect the social distance and hence the physical distance between them.

B. METHOD

The experiment was conducted in a room about 25 feet long, opening off a corridor. The right side of the room as the subject entered was screened off by movable screens, but the subject could not see anything behind them. At the end of the room away from the door was a chair where the experimenter was seated. Subjects were recruited from the corridor by being handed a card by a second experimenter, on which was typed a brief request to participate in a "perception" experiment that would take only a very few minutes. Then, depending on the condition, the instructions, which were written in English, requested the subject either to go ahead and enter the room or wait until he was called. These were the "No invitation" and "Invitation" conditions. If the subject was in the Invitation condition, he very shortly was requested to "Come in, please," either in English or in Tagalog.

When the subject entered the room, he saw either a male or a female experimenter, all seniors or graduate students, seated at the far end of the room. It was up to the subject to determine how closely he would approach. As soon as he stopped his forward progress, an observer hidden behind the screen noted the distance in terms of six-inch units from the desk, small marks having been placed on the wall to facilitate the measurement. And at that time the experimenter seated at the table asked the first of four innocuous, standard questions. These questions were asked either in English or Tagalog according to the condition. After pretesting on 30 subjects, the last 166 were asked: (a) What do you think of Tagalog movies? (b) What is your favorite kind of music? (c) Where would you like to spend a vacation? (d) What can you say about the administration? Questions were asked in random order for each subject. The subject's answers were recorded verbatim, and later a score amounting to the total number of words emitted was assigned to each subject.

When the subject had finished speaking, the distance from the desk was noted again, and the subject was given a simple visual perception task as a "cover" for the experiment; then was asked about his age, course of study, and familiarity with the experimenter. Afterwards he was thanked for his participation and dismissed.

1. Design

The social distance experiment involved four variables with two values of each. The language used by the experimenter was either English or Tagalog; the subject either received a verbal invitation to enter the room or did not; the experimenter was either male or female; and the subject was either male or female. In addition, the amount of speech was analyzed as a second measure of the social interaction. Thus, the design produced a $2 \times 2 \times 2 \times 2$ analysis of variance for both distance and amount of speech, but in the case of distance there were two measures so that a repeated measures analysis was required.

2. Experimenters

Six male and six female experimenters were employed in the experiment and each tested from three to 32 subjects. An effort was made to have each experimenter test subjects in every condition and in equal numbers, but that desideratum was impossible to achieve, in part, because availability of subjects depended on the number of persons passing in the corridor at any one time. Nonetheless, there were no strong biases associated with experimenters.

3. Subjects

Subjects were all college students and were from all year levels except graduate. An effort was made to get equal numbers of subjects in every condition, but that proved difficult; and the ultimate number per cell ranged from nine to 14. Some few subjects were lost because of errors or erratic behavior or previous familiarity with the experimenter. A total of 196 subjects provided usable data for the experiment.

C. RESULTS

The data for social distance as reflected in linear distance were analyzed by an analysis of variance for repeated measures, with the use of an unweighted means solution in view of the unequal cell frequencies (10). There were only two significant findings for the between-subjects part of the analysis and one within subjects. Sex of subject was significant as a main effect, and sex of subject interacted with sex of experimenter to produce another significant finding. As can be seen from the means given in Table 2, males made a closer approach than females. Males also approached more closely when the experimenter was a male, while females maintained a particularly great distance with a male experimenter. No other main effect even approached significance, *including language spoken*, for which the *F* was less than 1.00. Nor were any

TABLE 2
Means of Distance and Verbal Productivity Measures for Experimental
Variables Involved in Significant Findings

Variable	Mean Distance, in ft.	Mean Number Words
English spoken	5.27	22.96
Tagalog spoken	4.78	17.77
Male subjects	4.03	24.44
Female subjects	6.02	16.29
Male *S*-Male *E*	3.29	
Male *S*-Female *E*	4.95	
Female *S*-Male *E*	7.06	
Female *S*-Female *E*	4.80	

other interactions close to significance, the largest *F* being 1.08 for the quadruple interaction. The only significant finding within subjects was for measures, the *F* being significant at well beyond the .01 level. There was a strong tendency for subjects to decrease distance during the time of the interaction, perhaps a reflection of decreasing discomfort. No variables interacted in any way with measures, most *F*s being less than 1.00.

For amount of speech, the analysis of variance, again for unweighted means owing to unequal cell frequencies, only two main effects were significant, the means of which are reported in Table 2. Both language and sex of subject produced significant *F*s. Use of English by the Experimenter produced longer replies to the questions than did Tagalog ($F = 5.80$; df $= 1,150$; $p < .05$), and males emitted longer replies than females ($F = 14.21$; $df = 1,150$; $p < .01$). No other findings were significant, the largest *F* being 2.50 for the quadruple interaction.

D. DISCUSSION

On the basis of the investigations reported above, the authors are led to conclude that among Filipino bilinguals in a university setting choice of language is of little significance for social interaction. To be sure, the results of the first investigation suggest some bias in the language *preferred* in different kinds of interactions, but the results of the experiment in which language employed was manipulated indicate no effect on social distance produced by employing either English or Tagalog. Apparently the use of English or Tagalog was optional, Lynch, *et al.* (5) have found that language skill—i.e., in the dialect—plays but a small part in the impression made by Peace Corps volunteers in the Philippines. Even the findings of the first investigation are attenuated by noting that English was relatively little used for informal conversation and hence can only have limited effects. That the use of Tagalog in questioning produced briefer replies is of definite interest, but the import of that finding will be ambiguous until it is known whether Tagalog is inherently more efficient in communicating ideas of the kind expressed in response to the questions used here. However, an analysis of 25 Tagalog and 25 English replies to Tagalog questions showed no difference in length of reply, suggesting that it may be the language of the question rather than the response that is important.

Of considerable interest is the fact that, except for the use of occasional words having a special meaning not easily rendered in English, all subjects questioned in English answered completely in English. But many questioned in Tagalog answered in English or shifted to English during their answer (about 50 per cent). Several stated that they were accustomed to answering in English questions of the type asked and felt more comfortable in doing so. Yet, as can be seen, English is apparently not the preferred language of communication among these students in their casual interpersonal dealings. The authors are left to conclude, tentatively, that English is probably the preferable language for matters of an affectively neutral cast; but to guess that, if issues of a more intimate nature were being probed, there might be advantages to the use of common dialect.

The linear distance measure of social distance seemed to tap an important aspect of the social interaction between subject and experimenter. The fact that males showed less "distancing" than females and that females and males produced especially great distance when mixed are quite consistent with Filipino culture. These suppositions are supported by the amount of speech emitted, with males again being bolder than females. The findings reported here, therefore, seem relevant to social interaction in the Philippine culture.

E. SUMMARY

The present study grew out of a concern for the possible effects of language on experimental work done in bilingual cultures. In an initial study of casual conversations on a Philippine university campus, it was found that the great majority were being conducted in a local dialect although the university's language of instruction is English. English was more likely to be the language of conversation when the couples speaking were of mixed sex. A second study focused on the effects of language on social distance as reflected by physical distance in an experimental setting. The language used by the experimenter did not affect distance taken by his subjects, but cross-sex experimenter-subject pairs showed greater distancing. Use of English by the experimenter did produce longer replies by subjects.

REFERENCES

1. Ervin, S. M. 1961. "Learning and Recall in Bilinguals," *Amer. J. Psychol.*, 74, 446–451.
2. _____.1964. "Language and TAT Content in Bilinguals," *J. Abn. & Soc. Psychol.*, 68, 500–507.
3. Hall, E. T. 1966. *The Hidden Dimension.* New York: Doubleday.
4. Leipold, W. D. "Psychological Distance in a Dyadic Interview as a Function of Introversion-Extraversion, Anxiety, Social Desirability and Stress." Unpublished Doctoral dissertation, University of North Dakota, Grand Forks.
5. Lynch, F., T. Martezki, A. Bennett, Jr., S. M. Bennett, & L. D. Nelson. The Philippines Peace Corps Survey. Univ. Hawaii, Honolulu.
6. Sollee, N. 1963. "A Study of Perceptual Defense Involving Bilinguals: An Experiment." Unpublished Master's thesis, University of the Philippines, Quezon City, Philippines.
7. Sommer, R. 1959. "Studies in Personal Space," *Sociometry,* 22, 247–260.
8. _____. 1960. "Personal Space," *Can. Arch.,* pp. 76–80.
9. _____. 1962. "The Distance for Comfortable Conversations: A Further Study," *Sociometry,* 25, 111–116.
10. Winer, B. J. 1962. *Statistical Principles in Experimental Design.* New York: McGraw-Hill.

Lee Rainwater

14 / Crucible of Identity: The Negro Lower-Class Family *

But can a people . . . live and develop for over three hundred years by simply reacting? Are American Negroes simply the creation of white men, or have they at least helped create themselves out of what they found around them? Men have made a way of life in caves and upon cliffs, why can not Negroes have made a life upon the horns of the white man's dilemma? . . . American Negro life is, for the Negro who must live it, not only a burden (and not always that) but also a discipline just as any human life which has endured so long is a discipline teaching its own insights into the human conditions, its own strategies of survival. . . .

For even as his life toughens the Negro, even as it brutalizes him, sensitizes him, dulls him, goads him to anger, moves him to irony, sometimes fracturing and sometimes affirming his hopes; even as it shapes his attitude towards family, sex, love, religion; even as it modulates his humor, tempers his joy—it conditions him to deal with his life and with himself. Because it is his life and no mere abstraction in someone's head. He must live it and try consciously to grasp its complexity until he can change it; must live it as he changes it. He is no mere product of his socio-political predicament. He is a product of interaction between his racial predicament, his individual will and the broader American cultural freedom in which he finds his ambiguous existence. Thus he, too, in a limited way, is his own creation.—Ralph Ellison

As long as Negroes have been in America, their marital and family patterns have been subjects of curiosity and amusement, moral indignation and self-congratulation, puzzlement and frustration, concern and guilt, on the part of white Americans.[1] As some Negroes have moved into middle-class status, or

*From *Daedalus*, Vol. 95, No. 1. Reprinted by permission of the American Academy of Arts and Sciences, Boston, Mass.

[1]This paper is based in part on research supported by a grant from the National Institutes of Mental Health, Grant No. MH–09189, "Social and Community Problems in Public Housing Areas." Many of the ideas presented stem from discussion with the senior members of the Pruitt-Igoe research staff—Alvin W. Gouldner, David J. Pittman, and Jules Henry—and with the research associates and assistants on the project. I have made particular use of ideas developed in discussions with Boone Hammond, Joyce Ladner, Robert Simpson, David Schulz, and William Yancey. I also wish to acknowledge helpful suggestions and criticisms by Catherine Chilman, Gerald Handel, and Marc J. Swartz. Although this paper is not a formal report of the Pruitt-Igoe research, all of the illustrations of family behavior given in the text are drawn from interviews and observations that are part of that study. The study deals with the residents of the Pruitt-Igoe housing projects in St. Louis. Some 10,000 people live in these projects which comprise forty-three eleven-story buildings near the downtown area of St. Louis. Over half of the households have female heads, and for over half of the households the principal income comes from public

acquired standards of American common-man respectability, they too have shared these attitudes toward the private behavior of their fellows, sometimes with a moral punitiveness to rival that of whites, but at other times with a hard-headed interest in causes and remedies rather than moral evaluation. Moralism permeated the subject of Negro sexual, marital, and family behavior in the polemics of slavery apologists and abolitionists as much as in the Northern and Southern civil rights controversies of today. Yet, as long as the dialectic of good or bad, guilty or innocent, overshadows a concern with who, why, and what can be, it is unlikely that realistic and effective social planning to correct the clearly desperate situation of poor Negro families can begin.

This paper is concerned with a description and analysis of slum Negro family patterns as these reflect and sustain Negroes' adaptations to the economic, social, and personal situation into which they are born and in which they must live. As such it deals with facts of lower-class life that are usually forgotten or ignored in polite discussion. We have chosen not to ignore these facts in the belief that to do so can lead only to assumptions which would frustrate efforts at social reconstruction, to strategies that are unrealistic in the light of the actual day-to-day reality of slum Negro life. Further, this analysis will deal with family patterns which interfere with the efforts slum Negroes make to attain a stable way of life as working-or middle-class individuals and with the effects such failure in turn has on family life. To be sure, many Negro families live *in* the slum ghetto, but are not *of* its culture (though even they, and particularly their children, can be deeply affected by what happens there). However, it is the individuals who succumb to the distinctive family life style of the slum who experience the greatest weight of deprivation and who have the greatest difficulty responding to the few self-improvement resources that make their way into the ghetto. In short, we propose to explore in depth the family's role in the "tangle of pathology" which characterizes the ghetto.

The social reality in which Negroes have had to make their lives during the 450 years of their existence in the western hemisphere has been one of victimization "in the sense that a system of social relations operates in such a way as to deprive them of a chance to share in the more desirable material and non-material products of a society which is dependent, in part, upon their

assistance of one kind or another. The research has been in the field for a little over two years. It is a broad community study which thus far has relied principally on methods of participant observation and open-ended interviewing. Data on families come from repeated interviews and observations with a small group of families. The field workers are identified as graduate students at Washington University who have no connection with the housing authority or other officials, but are simply interested in learning about how families in the project live. This very intensive study of families yields a wealth of information (over 10,000 pages of interview and observation reports) which obviously cannot be analyzed within the limits of one article. In this article I have limited myself to outlining a typical family stage sequence and discussing some of the psychosocial implications of growing up in families characterized by this sequence. In addition, I have tried to limit myself to findings which other literature on Negro family life suggests are not limited to the residents of the housing projects we are studying.

labor and loyalty." In making this observation, St. Clair Drake goes on to note that Negroes are victimized also because "they do not have the same degree of access which others have to the attributes needed for rising in the general class system—money, education, 'contacts,' and 'know-how.' "[2] The victimization process started with slavery; for 350 years thereafter Negroes worked out as best they could adaptations to the slave status. After emancipation, the cultural mechanisms which Negroes had developed for living the life of victim continued to be serviceable as the victimization process was maintained first under the myths of white supremacy and black inferiority, later by the doctrines of gradualism which covered the fact of no improvement in position, and finally by the modern Northern system of ghettoization and indifference.

When lower-class Negroes use the expression, "Tell it like it is," they signal their intention to strip away pretense, to describe a situation or its participants as they really are, rather than in a polite or euphemistic way. "Telling it like it is" can be used as a harsh, aggressive device, or it can be a healthy attempt to face reality rather than retreat into fantasy. In any case, as he goes about his field work, the participant observer studying a ghetto community learns to listen carefully to any exchange preceded by such an announcement because he knows the speaker is about to express his understanding of how his world operates, of what motivates its members, of how they actually behave.

The first responsibility of the social scientist can be phrased in much the same way: "Tell it like it is." His second responsibility is to try to understand why "it" is that way, and to explore the implications of what and why for more constructive solutions to human problems. Social research on the situation of the Negro American has been informed by four main goals: (1) to describe the disadvantaged position of Negroes, (2) to disprove the racist ideology which sustains the caste system, (3) to demonstrate that responsibility for the disadvantages Negroes suffer lies squarely upon the white caste which derives economic, prestige, and psychic benefits from the operation of the system, and (4) to suggest that in reality whites would be better rather than worse off if the whole jerry-built caste structure were to be dismantled. The successful accomplishment of these *intellectual* goals has been a towering achievement, in which the social scientists of the 1920's, '30's, and '40's can take great pride; that white society has proved so recalcitrant to utilizing this intellectual accomplishment is one of the great tragedies of our time, and provides the stimulus for further social research on "the white problem."

Yet the implicit paradigm of much of the research on Negro Americans has been an overly simplistic one concentrating on two terms of an argument:

White cupidity————Negro suffering.

[2]St. Clair Drake, "The Social and Economic Status of the Negro in the United States," *Daedalus* (Fall 1965), p. 772.

As an intellectual shorthand, and even more as a civil rights slogan, this simple model is both justified and essential. But, as a guide to greater understanding of the Negro situation as human adaptation to human situations, the paradigm is totally inadequate because it fails to specify fully enough the *process* by which Negroes adapt to their situations as they do, and the limitations one kind of adaptation places on possibilities for subsequent adaptations. A reassessment of previous social research, combined with examination of current social research on Negro ghetto communities, suggests a more complex, but hopefully more vertical, model:

> White cupidity creates Structural Conditions Highly Inimical to Basic Social Adaptation (low-income availability, poor education, poor services, stigmatization) to which Negroes adapt by Social and Personal Responses which serve to sustain the individual in his punishing world but also generate aggressiveness toward the self and others which results in Suffering directly inflicted by Negroes on themselves and on others.

In short, whites, by their greater power, create situations in which Negroes do the dirty work of caste victimization for them.

The white caste maintains a cadre of whites whose special responsibility is to enforce the system in brutal or refined ways (the Klan, the rural sheriff, the metropolitan police, the businessman who specializes in a Negro clientele, the Board of Education). Increasingly, whites recruit to this cadre middle-class Negroes who can soften awareness of victimization by their protective coloration. These special cadres, white and/or Negro, serve the very important function of enforcing caste standards by whatever means seems required, while at the same time concealing from an increasingly "unprejudiced" public the unpleasant facts they would prefer to ignore. The system is quite homologous to the Gestapo and concentration camps of Nazi Germany, though less fatal to its victims.

For their part, Negroes creatively adapt to the system in ways that keep them alive and extract what gratification they can find, but in the process of adaptation they are constrained to behave in ways that inflict a great deal of suffering on those with whom they make their lives, and on themselves. The ghetto Negro is constantly confronted by the immediate necessity to suffer in order to get what he wants of those few things he can have, or to make others suffer, or both—for example, he suffers as exploited student and employee, as drug user, as loser in the competitive game of his peer-group society; he inflicts suffering as disloyal spouse, petty thief, knife- or gun-wielder, petty con man.

It is the central thesis of this paper that the caste-facilitated infliction of suffering by Negroes on other Negroes and on themselves appears most poignantly within the confines of the family, and that the victimization process as it operates in families prepares and toughens its members to function in the ghetto world, at the same time that it seriously interferes with their ability to operate in any other world. This, however, is very different from arguing that "the family is to blame" for the deprived situation ghetto Negroes suffer; rather we are looking at the logical outcome of the operation of the widely ramified and interconnecting caste system. In the end we will argue that only palliative results can be expected from attempts to treat directly the disordered family patterns to be described. Only a change in the original "inputs" of the caste system, the structural conditions inimical to basic social adaptation, can change family forms.

Almost thrity years ago, E. Franklin Frazier foresaw that the fate of the Negro family in the city would be a highly destructive one. His readers would have little reason to be surprised at observations of slum ghetto life today:

> . . . As long as the bankrupt system of southern agriculture exists, Negro families will continue to seek a living in the towns and cities. . . . They will crowd the slum areas of southern cities or make their way to northern cities where their families will become disrupted and their poverty will force them to depend upon charity.[3]

THE AUTONOMY OF THE SLUM GHETTO

Just as the deprivations and depredations practiced by white society have had their effect on the personalities and social life of Negroes, so also has the separation from the ongoing social life of the white community had its effect. In a curious way, Negroes have had considerable freedom to fashion their own adaptations within their separate world. The large society provides them with few resources but also with minimal interference in the Negro community on matters which did not seem to affect white interests. Because Negroes learned early that there were a great many things they could not depend upon whites to provide they developed their own solutions to recurrent human issues. These solutions can often be seen to combine, along with the predominance of elements from white culture, elements that are distinctive to the Negro group. Even more distinctive is the *configuration* which emerges from those elements Negroes share with whites and those which are different.

It is in this sense that we may speak of a Negro subculture, a distinctive *patterning* of existential perspectives, techniques for coping with the problems of social life, views about what is desirable and undesirable in particular situations. This subculture, and particularly that of the lower-class, the slum, Negro, can be seen as his own creation out of the elements available to him

[3]E. Franklin Frazier, *The Negro Family in the United States* (Chicago, 1939), p. 487.

in response to (1) the conditions of life set by white society and (2) the selective freedom which that society allows (or must put up with given the pattern of separateness on which it insists).

Out of this kind of "freedom" slum Negroes have built a culture which has some elements of intrinsic value and many more elements that are highly destructive to the people who must live in it. The elements that whites can value they constantly borrow. Negro arts and language have proved so popular that such commentators on American culture as Norman Mailer and Leslie Fiedler have noted processes of Negro-ization of white Americans as a minor theme of the past thirty years.[4] A fairly large proportion of Negroes with national reputations are engaged in the occupation of diffusing to the larger culture these elements of intrinsic value.

On the negative side, this freedom has meant, as social scientists who have studied Negro communities have long commented, that many of the protections offered by white institutions stop at the edge of the Negro ghetto: there are poor police protection and enforcement of evil equities, inadequate schooling and medical service, and more informal indulgences which whites allow Negroes as a small price for feeling superior.

For our purposes, however, the most important thing about the freedom which whites have allowed Negroes within their own world is that it has required them to work out their own ways of making it from day to day, from birth to death. The subculture that Negroes have created may be imperfect but it has been viable for centuries; it behooves both white and Negro leaders and intellectuals to seek to understand it even as they hope to change it.[5]

Negroes have created, again particularly within the lower-class slum group, a range of institutions to structure the tasks of living a victimized life and to minimize the pain it inevitably produces. In the slum ghetto these institutions include prominently those of the social network—the extended kinship system and the "street system" of buddies and broads which tie (although tenuously and upredictably) the "members" to each other—and the institutions of entertainment (music, dance, folk tales) by which they instruct, explain, and accept themselves. Other institutions function to provide escape from the society of the victimized: the church (Hereafter!) and the civil rights movement (Now!).

[4]Norman Mailer, "The White Negro" (City Light Books, San Francisco, Calif., 1957); and Leslie Fiedler, *Waiting For The End* (New York, 1964), pp. 118–137.

[5]See Alvin W. Gouldner, "Reciprocity and Autonomy in Functional Theory," in Llewellyn Gross (ed.), *Symposium of Sociological Theory* (Evanston, Ill., 1958), for a discussion of functional autonomy and dependence of structural elements in social systems. We are suggesting here that lower-class groups have a relatively high degree of functional autonomy *vis à vis* the total social system because that system does little to meet their needs. In general the fewer the rewards a society offers members of a particular group in the society, the more autonomous will that group prove to be with reference to the norms of the society. Only by constructing an elaborate repressive machinery, as in concentration camps, can the effect be otherwise.

THE FUNCTIONAL AUTONOMY OF THE NEGRO FAMILY

At the center of the matrix of Negro institutional life lies the family. It is in the family that individuals are trained for participation in the culture and find personal and group identity and continuity. The "freedom" allowed by white society is greatest here, and this freedom has been used to create an institutional variant more distinctive perhaps to the Negro subculture than any other. (Much of the content of Negro art and entertainment derives exactly from the distinctive characteristics of Negro family life.) At each stage in the Negro's experience of American life—slavery, segregation, de facto ghettoization—whites have found it less necessary to interfere in the relations between the sexes and between parents and children than in other areas of the Negro's existence. His adaptations in this area, therefore, have been less constrained by whites than in many other areas.

Now that the larger society is becoming increasingly committed to integrating Negroes into the main stream of American life, however, we can expect increasing constraint (benevolent as it may be) to be placed on the autonomy of the Negro family system.[6] These constraints will be designed to pull Negroes into meaningful integration with the larger society, to give up ways which are inimical to successful performance in the larger society, and to adopt new ways that are functional in that society. The strategic questions of the civil rights movement and of the war on poverty are ones that have to do with how one provides functional equivalents for the existing subculture before the capacity to make a life within its confines is destroyed.

The history of the Negro family has been ably documented by historians and sociologists.[7] In slavery, conjugal and family ties were reluctantly and ambivalently recognized by the slave holders, were often violated by them, but proved necessary to the slave system. This necessity stemmed both from the profitable offspring of slave sexual unions and the necessity for their nurture, and from the fact that the slaves' efforts to sustain patterns of sexual and parental relations mollified the men and women whose labor could not simply be commanded. From nature's promptings, the thinning memories of African heritage, and the example and guilt-ridden permission of the slave holders, slaves constructed a partial family system and sets of relations that generated conjugal and familial sentiments. The slave holder's recognition in advertise-

[6]For example, the lead sentence in a St. Louis Post Dispatch article of July 20, 1965, begins "A White House study group is laying the ground work for an attempt to better the structure of the Negro family."

[7]See Kenneth Stampp, The Peculiar Institution (New York, 1956); John Hope Franklin, From Slavery to Freedom (New York, 1956); Frank Tannenbaum, Slave and Citizen (New York, 1946); E. Franklin Frazier, op. cit.; and Melville J. Herskovits, The Myth of the Negro Past (New York, 1941).

ments for run-away slaves of marital and family sentiments as motivations for absconding provides one indication that strong family ties were possible, though perhaps not common, in the slave quarter. The mother-centered family with its emphasis on the primacy of the mother-child relation and only tenuous ties to a man, then, is the legacy of adaptations worked out by Negroes during slavery.

After emancipation this family design often also served well to cope with the social disorganization of Negro life in the late nineteenth century. Matrifocal families, ambivalence about the desirability of marriage, ready acceptance of illegitimacy, all sustained some kind of family life in situations which often made it difficult to maintain a full nuclear family. Yet in the hundred years since emancipation, Negroes in rural areas have been able to maintain full nuclear families almost as well as similarly situated whites. As we will see, it is the move to the city that results in the very high proportion of mother-headed households. In the rural system the man continues to have important functions; it is difficult for a woman to make a crop by herself, or even with the help of other women. In the city, however, the woman can earn wages just as a man can, and she can receive welfare payments more easily than he can. In rural areas, although there may be high illegitimacy rates and high rates of marital disruption, men and women have an interest in getting together; families are headed by a husband-wife pair much more often than in the city. That pair may be much less stable than in the more prosperous segments of Negro and white communities but it is more likely to exist among rural Negroes than among urban ones.

The matrifocal character of the Negro lower-class family in the United States has much in common with Caribbean Negro family patterns; research in both areas has done a great deal to increase our understanding of the Negro situation. However, there are important differences in the family forms of the two areas.[8] The impact of white European family models has been much greater in the United States than in the Caribbean both because of the relative population proportions of white and colored peoples and because equalitarian values in the United States have had a great impact on Negroes even when they have not on whites. The typical Caribbean mating pattern is that women go

[8]See Raymond T. Smith, *The Negro Family in British Guiana* (New York, 1956); J. Mayone Stycos and Kurt W. Back, *The Control of Human Fertility in Jamaica* (Ithaca, N. Y., 1964); F. M. Henriques, *Family and Colour in Jamaica* (London, 1953); Judith Blake, *Family Structure in Jamaica* (Glencoe, Ill., 1961); and Raymond T. Smith, "Culture and Social Structure in The Caribbean," *Comparative Studies in Society and History*, Vol. VI (The Hague, The Netherlands, October 1963), pp. 24–16. For a broader comparative discussion of the matrifocal family see Peter Kunstadter, "A Survey of the Consanguine or Matrifocal Family," *American Anthropologist*, Vol. 65, No. 1 (February 1963), pp. 56–66; and Ruth M. Boyer, "The Matrifocal Family Among the Mescalero: Additional Data," *American Anthropologist*, Vol. 66, No. 3 (June 1964), pp. 593–602.

through several visiting and common-law unions but eventually marry; that is, they marry legally only relatively late in their sexual lives. The Caribbean marriage is the crowning of a sexual and procreative career; it is considered a serious and difficult step.

In the United States, in contrast, Negroes marry at only a slightly lower rate and slightly higher age than whites.[9] Most Negro women marry relatively early in their careers; marriage is not regarded as the same kind of crowning choice and achievement that it is in the Caribbean. For lower-class Negroes in the United States marriage ceremonies are rather informal affairs. In the Caribbean, marriage is regarded as quite costly because of the feasting which goes along with it; ideally it is performed in church.

In the United States, unlike the Caribbean, early marriage confers a kind of permanent respectable status upon a woman which she can use to deny any subsequent accusations of immorality or promiscuity once the marriage is broken and she becomes sexually involved in visiting or common-law relations. The relevant effective status for many Negro women is that of "having been married" rather than "being married"; having the right to be called "Mrs." rather than currently being Mrs. Someone-in-Particular.

For Negro lower-class women, then, first marriage has the same kind of importance as having a first child. Both indicate that the girl has become a woman but neither one that this is the last such activity in which she will engage. It seems very likely that only a minority of Negro women in the urban slum go through their childrearing years with only one man around the house.

Among the Negro urban poor, then, a great many women have the experience of heading a family for part of their mature lives, and a great many children spend some part of their formative years in a household without a father-mother pair. From Table 1 we see that in 1960, forty-seven per cent of

TABLE 1

Proportion of *Female Heads* for Families with Children by Race, Income, and Urban-Rural Categories

Negroes	Rural	Urban	Total
under $3000	18%	47%	36%
$3000 and over	5%	8%	7%
Total	14%	23%	21%
Whites			
under $3000	12%	38%	22%
$3000 and over	2%	4%	3%
Total	4%	7%	6%

Source: U. S. Census: 1960, PC (1) D. U. S. Volume, Table 225; State Volume, Table 140.

[9]Paul C. Glick, *American Families* (New York, 1957), pp. 133 ff.

the Negro poor urban families with children had a female head. Unfortunately cumulative statistics are hard to come by; but, given this very high level for a cross-sectional sample (and taking into account the fact that the median age of the children in these families is about six years), it seems very likely that as many as two-thirds of Negro urban poor children will not live in families headed by a man and a woman throughout the first eighteen years of their lives.

One of the other distinctive characteristics of Negro families, both poor and not so poor, is the fact that Negro households have a much higher proportion of relatives outside the mother-father-children triangle than is the case with whites. For example, in St. Louis Negro families average 0.8 other relatives per household compared to only 0.4 for white faimilies. In the case of the more prosperous Negro families this is likely to mean that an older relative lives in the home providing baby-sitting services while both the husband and wife work and thus further their climb toward stable working- or middle-class status. In the poor Negro families it is much more likely that the household is headed by an older relative who brings under her wings a daughter and that daughter's children. It is important to note that the three-generation household with the grandmother at the head exists only when there is no husband present. Thus, despite the high proportion of female-headed households in this group and despite the high proportion of households that contain other relatives, we find that almost all married couples in the St. Louis Negro slum community have their own household. In other words, when a couple marries it establishes its own household; when that couple breaks up the mother either maintains that household or moves back to her parents or grandparents.

Finally we should note that Negro slum families have more children than do either white slum families or stable working- and middle-class Negro families. Mobile Negro families limit their fertility sharply in the interest of bringing the advantages of mobility more fully to the few children that they do have. Since the Negro slum family is both more likely to have the father absent and more likely to have more children in the family, the mother has a more demanding task with fewer resources at her disposal. When we examine the patterns of life of the stem family we shall see that even the presence of several mothers does not necessarily lighten the work load for the principal mother in charge.

THE FORMATION AND MAINTENANCE OF FAMILIES

We will outline below the several stages and forms of Negro lower-class family life. At many points these family forms and the interpersonal relations that exist within them will be seen to have characteristics in common with the life styles of white lower-class families.[10] At other points there are differences, or the Negro pattern will be seen to be more sharply divergent from the family life of stable working- and middle-class couples.

It is important to recognize that lower-class Negroes know that their particular family forms are different from those of the rest of the society and that, though they often see these forms as representing the only ways of behaving given their circumstances, they also think of the more stable family forms of the working class as more desirable. That is, lower-class Negroes know what the "normal American family" is supposed to be like, and they consider a stable family-centered way of life superior to the conjugal and familial situations in which they often find themselves. Their conceptions of the good American life include the notion of a father-husband who functions as an adequate provider and interested member of the family, a hard working home-bound mother who is concerned about her children's welfare and her husband's needs, and children who look up to their parents and perform well in school and other outside places to reflect credit on their families. This image of what famly life can be like is very real from time to time as lower-class men and women grow up and move through adulthood. Many of them make efforts to establish such families but find it impossible to do so either because of the direct impact of economic disabilities or because they are not able to sustain in their day-to-day lives the ideals which they hold.[11] While these ideals do serve as a meaningful guide to lower-class couples who are mobile out of the group, for a great many others the existence of such ideas about normal family life represents a recurrent source of stress within families as individuals become aware that they are failing to measure up to the ideals, or as others within the family and outside it use the ideals as an aggressive weapon for criticizing each other's performance. It is not at all uncommon for husbands or wives or children to try to hold others in the family to the norms of stable family life while they themselves engage in behaviors which vilate these norms. The effect of such criticism in the end is to deepen commitment to the deviant sexual and parental norms of a slum subculture. Unless they are careful, social workers

[10]For discussions of white lower-class families, see Lee Rainwater, Richard P. Coleman, and Gerald Handel, *Workingman's Wife* (New York, 1959); Lee Rainwater, *Family Design* (Chicago, 1964); Herbert Gans, *The Urban Villagers* (New York, 1962); Albert K. Cohen and Harold M. Hodges, "Characteristics of the Lower-Blue-Collar-Class," *Social Problems, Vol. 10, No. 4 (Spring 1963), pp. 303–334;* S. M. Miller, "The American Lower Classes: A Typological Approach," in *Arthur B. Shostak and William Gomberg, Blue Collar World* (Englewood Cliffs, N. J., 1964); and Mirra Komarovsky, *Blue Collar Marriage* (New York, 1964). Discussions of Negro slum life can be found in St. Clair Drake and Horace R. Cayton, *Black Metropolis* (New York, 1962), and Kenneth B. Clark, *Dark Ghetto* (New York, 1965); and of Negro community life in small-town and rural settings in Allison Davis, Burleigh B. Gardner, and Mary Gardner, *Deep South* (Chicago, 1944), and Hylan Lewis, *Blackways of Kent* (Chapel Hill, N. C., 1955).

[11]For general discussions of the extent to which lower-class people hold the values of the larger society, see Albert K. Cohen, *Delinquent Boys* (New York, 1955); Hyman Rodman, "The Lower Class Value Stretch," *Social Forces,* Vol. 42, No. 2 (December 1963), pp. 205 ff; and William L. Yancey, "The Culture of Poverty: Not So Much Parsimony," unpublished manuscript, Social Science Institute, Washington University.

and other professionals exacerbate the tendency to use the norms of "American family life" as weapons by supporting these norms in situations where they are in reality unsupportable, thus aggravating the sense of failing and being failed by others which is chronic for lower-class people.

Going Together

The initial steps toward mating and family formation in the Negro slum take place in a context of highly developed boys' and girls' peer groups. Adolescents tend to become deeply involved in their peer-group societies beginning as early as the age of twelve or thirteen and continue to be involved after first pregnancies and first marriages. Boys and girls are heavily committed both to their same sex peer groups and to the activities that those groups carry out. While classical gang activity does not necessarily characterize Negro slum communities everywhere, loosely-knit peer groups do.

The world of the Negro slum is wide open to exploration by adolescent boys and girls: "Negro communities provide a flow of common experience in which young people and their elders share, and out of which delinquent behavior emerges almost imperceptibly."[12] More than is possible in white slum communities, Negro adolescents have an opportunity to interact with adults in various "high life" activities; their behavior more often represents an identification with the behavior of adults than an attempt to set up group standards and activities that differ from those of adults.

Boys and young men participating in the street system of peer group activity are much caught up in games of furthering and enhancing their status as significant persons. These games are played out in small and large gatherings through various kinds of verbal contests that go under the names of "sounding," "signifying," and "working game." Very much a part of a boy's or man's status in this group is his ability to win women. The man who has several women "up tight," who is successful in "pimping off " women for sexual favors and material benefits, is much admired. In sharp contrast to white lower-class groups, there is little tendency for males to separate girls into "good" and "bad" categories.[13] Observations of groups of Negro youths suggest that girls and women are much more readily referred to as "that bitch" or "that whore" than they are by their names, and this seems to be a universal tendency carrying no connotation that "that bitch" is morally inferior to or different from other women. Thus, all women are essentially the same, all women are

[12]James F. Short, Jr., and Fred L. Strodtbeck, *Group Process and Gang Delinquency* (Chicago, 1965), p. 114. Chapter V (pages 102–115) of this book contains a very useful discussion of differences between white and Negro lower-class communities.
[13]Discussions of white lower-class attitudes toward sex may be found in Arnold W. Green, "The Cult of Personality and Sexual Relations," *Psychiatry*, Vo. 4 (1941), pp. 343–348; William F. Whyte, "A Slum Sex Code," *American Journal of Sociology*, Vol. 49, No. 1 (July 1943), pp. 24–31; and Lee Rainwater, "Marital Sexuality in Four Cultures of Poverty," *Journal of Marriage and the Family*, Vo. 26, No. 4 (November 1964), pp. 457–466.

legitimate targets, and no girl or woman is expected to be virginal except for reason of lack of opportunity or immaturity. From their participation in the peer group and according to standards legitimated by the total Negro slum culture, Negro boys and young men are propelled in the direction of girls to test their "strength" as seducers. They are mercilessly rated by both their peers and the opposite sex in their ability to "talk" to girls; a young man will go to great lengths to avoid the reputation of having a "weak" line.[14]

The girls share these definitions of the nature of heterosexual relations; they take for granted that almost any male they deal with will try to seduce them and that given sufficient inducement (social not monetary) they may wish to go along with his line. Although girls have a great deal of ambivalence about participating in sexual relations, this ambivalence is minimally moral and has much more to do with a desire not to be taken advantage of or get in trouble. Girls develop defenses against the exploitative orientations of men by devaluing the significance of sexual relations ("he really didn't do anything bad to me"), and as time goes on by developing their own appreciation of the intrinsic rewards of sexual intercourse.

The informal social relations of slum Negroes begin in adolescence to be highly sexualized. Although parents have many qualms about boys and, particularly, girls entering into this system, they seldom feel there is much they can do to prevent their children's sexual involvement. They usually confine themselves to counseling somewhat hopelessly against girls becoming pregnant or boys being forced into situations where they might have to marry a girl they do not want to marry.

Girls are propelled toward boys and men in order to demostrate their maturity and attractiveness; in the process they are constantly exposed to pressures for seduction, to boys "rapping" to them. An active girl will "go with" quite a number of boys, but she will generally try to restrict the number with whom she has intercourse to the few to whom she is attracted or (as happens not infrequently) to those whose threats of physical violence she cannot avoid. For their part, the boys move rapidly from girl to girl seeking to have intercourse with as many as they can and thus build up their "reps." The activity of seduction is itself highly cathected; there is gratification in simply "talking to" a girl as long as the boy can feel that he has acquitted himself well.

> At sixteen Joan Bemias enjoys spending time with three or four very close girl friends. She tells us they follow this routine when the girls want to go out and none of the boys they have been seeing lately is available: "Every time we get ready to go someplace we look through all the telephone numbers of boys we'd have and we call them and talk so sweet to them that they'd come on around.

[14]See Boone Hammond. "The Contest System: A Survival Technique," Master's Honors papers. Washington University, 1965. See also Ira L. Reiss, "Premarital Sexual Permissiveness Among Negroes and Whites," *American Sociological Review*, Vol. 29, No. 5 (October 1964), pp. 688–698.

All of them had cars you see. (I: What do you do to keep all these fellows interested?) Well nothing. We don't have to make love with all of them. Let's see, Joe, J. B., Albert, and Paul, out of all of them I've been going out with I've only had sex with four boys, that's all." She goes on to say that she and her girl friends resist boys by being unresponsive to their lines and by breaking off relations with them on the ground that they're going out with other girls. It is also clear from her comments that the girl friends support each other in resisting the boys when they are out together in groups.

Joan has had a relationship with a boy which has lasted six months, but she has managed to hold the frequency of intercourse down to four times. Initially she managed to hold this particular boy off for a month but eventually gave in.

Becoming Pregnant

It is clear that the contest elements in relationships between men and women continue even in relationships that become quite steady. Despite the girls' ambivalence about sexual relations and their manifold efforts to reduce its frequency, the operation of chance often eventuates in their becoming pregnant.[15] This was the case with Joan. With this we reach the second stage in the formation of families, that of premarital pregnancy. (We are outlining an ideal-typical sequence and not, of course, implying that all girls in the Negro slum culture become pregnant before they marry but only that a great many of them do.)

Joan was caught despite the fact that she was considerably more sophisticated about contraception than most girls or young women in the group (her mother had both instructed her in contraceptive techniques and constantly warned her to take precautions). No one was particularly surprised at her pregnancy although she, her boy friend, her mother, and others regarded it as unfortunate. For girls in the Negro slum, pregnancy before marriage is expected in much the same way that parents expect their children to catch mumps or chicken pox; if they are lucky it will not happen but if it happens people are not too surprised and everyone knows what to do about it. It was quickly decided that Joan and the baby would stay at home. It seems clear from the preparations that Joan's mother is making that she expects to have the main responsibility for caring for the infant. Joan seems quite indifferent to the baby; she shows little interest in mothering the child although she is not particularly adverse to the idea so long as the baby does not interfere too much with her continued participation in her peer group.

Establishing who the father is under these circumstances seems to be important and confers a kind of legitimacy on the birth; not to know who one's father is, on the other hand, seems the ultimate in illegitimacy. Actually Joan had a choice in the imputation of fatherhood; she chose J.B. because he is older

---

[15]See the discussion of aleatory processes leading to premarital fatherhood in Short and Strodtbeck, *op. cit.,* pp. 44–45.

than she, and because she may marry him if he can get a divorce from his wife. She could have chosen Paul (with whom she had also had intercourse at about the time she became pregnant), but she would have done this reluctantly since Paul is a year younger than she and somehow this does not seem fitting.

In general, when a girl becomes pregnant while still living at home it seems taken for granted that she will continue to live there and that her parents will take a major responsibility for rearing the children. Since there are usually siblings who can help out and even siblings who will be playmates for the child, the addition of a third generation to the household does not seem to place a great stress on relationships within the family. It seems common for the first pregnancy to have a liberating influence on the mother once the child is born in that she becomes socially and sexually more active than she was before. She no longer has to be concerned with preserving her status as a single girl. Since her mother is usually willing to take care of the child for a few years, the unwed mother has an opportunity to go out with girl friends and with men and thus become more deeply involved in the peer-group society of her culture. As she has more children and perhaps marries she will find it necessary to settle down and spend more time around the house fulfilling the functions of a mother herself.

It would seem that for girls pregnancy is the real measure of maturity, the dividing line between adolescence and womanhood. Perhaps because of this, as well as because of the ready resources for child care, girls in the Negro slum community show much less concern about pregnancy than do girls in the white lower-class community and are less motivated to marry the fathers of their children. When a girl becomes pregnant the question of marriage certainly arises and is considered, but the girl often decides that she would rather not marry the man either because she does not want to settle down yet or because she does not think he would make a good husband.

It is in the easy attitudes toward premarital pregnancy that the matrifocal character of the Negro lower-class family appears most clearly. In order to have and raise a family it is simply not necessary, though it may be desirable, to have a man around the house. While the AFDC program may make it easier to maintain such attitudes in the urban situation, this pattern existed long before the program was initiated and continues in families where support comes from other sources.

Finally it should be noted that fathering a child similarly confers maturity on boys and young men although perhaps it is less salient for them. If the boy has any interest in the girl he will tend to feel that the fact that he has impregnated her gives him an additional claim on her. He will be stricter in seeking to enforce his exclusive rights over her (though not exclusive loyalty to her). This exclusive right does not mean that he expects to marry her but only that there is a new and special bond between them. If the girl is not willing to accept such claims she may find it necessary to break off the relationship rather than tolerate the man's jealousy. Since others in the peer group have a vested interest in not allowing a couple to be too loyal to each other they go out of their way to question and challenge each partner about the loyalty of the other, thus contributing to the deterioration of the relationship. This same kind of questioning and challenging continues if the couple marries and represents one source of the instability of the marital relationship.

Getting Married

As noted earlier, despite the high degree of premarital sexual activity and the rather hgih proportion of premarital pregnancies, most lower-class Negro men and women eventually do marry and stay together for a shorter or longer period of time. Marriage is an intimidating prospect and is approached ambivalently by both parties. For the girl it means giving up a familiar and comfortable home that, unlike some other lower-class subcultures, places few real restrictions on her behavior. (While marriage can appear to be an escape from interpersonal difficulties at home, these difficulties seldom seem to revolve around effective restrictions placed on her behavior by her parents.) The girl also has good reason to be suspicious of the likelihood that men will be able to perform stably in the role of husband and provider; she is reluctant to be tied down by a man who will not prove to be worth it.

From the man's point of view the fickleness of women makes marriage problematic. It is one thing to have a girl friend step out on you, but it is quite another to have a wife do so. Whereas premarital sexual relations and fatherhood carry almost no connotation of responsibility for the welfare of the partner, marriage is supposed to mean that a man behaves more responsibly, becoming a provider for his wife and children even though he may not be expected to give up all the gratifications of participation in the street system.

For all of these reasons both boys and girls tend to have rather negative views of marriage as well as a low expectation that marriage will prove a stable and gratifying existence. When marriage does take place it tends to represent a tentative commitment on the part of both parties with a strong tendency to seek greater commitment on the part of the partner than on one's own part. Marriage is regarded as a fragile arrangement held together primarily by affectional ties rather than instrumental concerns.

In general, as in white lower-class groups, the decision to marry seems to be taken rather impulsively.[16] Since everyone knows that sooner or later he will get married, in spite of the fact that he may not be sanguine about the prospect, Negro lower-class men and women are alert for clues that the time has arrived. The time may arrive because of a pregnancy in a steady relation-

[16]Rainwater, *And the Poor Get Children, op. cit.,* pp. 61–63. See also Carlfred B. Broderick, "Social Heterosexual Development Among Urban Negroes and Whites," *Journal of Marriage and the Family.* Vol. 27 (May 1965), pp. 200–212. Broderick finds that although white boys and girls, and Negro girls become more interested in marriage as they get older, Negro boys become *less* interested in late adolescence than they were as preadolescents.

ship that seems gratifying to both partners, or as a way of getting out of what seems to be an awkward situation, or as a self-indulgence during periods when a boy and a girl are feeling very sorry for themselves. Thus, one girl tells us that when she marries her husband will cook all of her meals for her and she will not have any housework; another girl says that when she marries it will be to a man who has plenty of money and will have to take her out often and really show her a good time.

Boys see in marriage the possibility of regualr sexual intercourse without having to fight for it, or a girl safe from venereal disease, or a relationship to a nurturant figure who will fulfill the functions of a mother. For boys, marriage can also be a way of asserting their independence from the peer group if its demands become burdensome. In this case the young man seeks to have the best of both worlds.[17]

Marriage as a way out of an unpleasant situation can be seen in the case of one of our informants, Janet Cowan:

> Janet has been going with two men, one of them married and the other single. The married man's wife took exception to their relationship and killed her husband. Within a week Janet and her single boy friend, Howard, were married. One way out of the turmoil the murder of her married boy friend stimulated (they lived in the same building) was to choose marriage as a way of "settling down." However, after marrying the new couple seemed to have little idea how to set themselves up as a family. Janet was reluctant to leave her parents' home because her parents cared for her two illegitimate children. Howard was unemployed and therefore unacceptable in his parent-in-law's home, nor were his own parents willing to have his wife move in with them. Howard was also reluctant to give up another girl friend in another part of town. Although both he and his wife maintained that it was all right for a couple to step out on each other so long as the other partner did not know about it, they were both jealous if they suspected anything of this kind. In the end they gave up on the idea of marriage and went their separate ways.

In general, then, the movement toward marriage is an uncertain and tentative one. Once the couple does settle down together in a household of their own, they have the problem of working out a mutually acceptable organization of rights and duties, expectations and performances, that will meet their needs.

Husband-Wife Relations

Characteristic of both the Negro and white lower class is a high degree of conjugal role segregation.[18] That is, husbands and wives tend to think of themselves as having very separate kinds of functioning in the instrumental

[17]Walter Miller, "The Corner Gang Boys Get Married," *Trans-action,* Vol. 1, No. 1 (November 1963), pp. 10–12.
[18]Rainwater, *Family Design, op. cit.,* pp. 28–60.

organization of family life, and also as pursuing recreational and outside interests separately. The husband is expected to be a provider; he resists assuming functions around the home so long as he feels he is doing his proper job of bringing home a pay check. He feels he has the right to indulge himself in little ways if he is successful at this task. The wife is expected to care for the home and children and make her husband feel welcome and comfortable. Much that is distinctive to Negro family life stems from the fact that husbands often are not stable providers. Even when a particular man is, his wife's conception of men in general is such that she is pessimistic about the likelihood that he will continue to do well in this area. A great many Negro wives work to supplement the family income. When this is so the separate incomes earned by husband and wife tend to be treated not as "family" income but as the individual property of the two persons involed. If their wives work, husbands are likely to feel that they are entitled to retain a larger share of the income they provide; the wives, in turn, feel that the husbands have no right to benefit from the purchases they make out of their own money. There is, then, "my money" and "your money." In this situation the husband may come to feel that the wife should support the children out of her income and that he can retain all of his income for himself.

While white lower-class wives often are very much intimidated by their husbands, Negro lower-class wives come to feel that they have a right to give as good as they get. If the husband indulges himself, they have the right to indulge themselves. If the husband steps out on his wife, she has the right to step out on him. The commitment of husbands and wives to each other seems often a highly instrumental one after the "honeymoon" period. Many wives feel they owe the husband nothing once he fails to perform his provider role. If the husband is unemployed the wife increasingly refuses to perform her usual duties for him. For example one woman, after mentioning that her husband had cooked four eggs for himself, commented, "I cook for him when he's working but right now he's unemployed; he can cook for himself." It is important, however, to understand that the man's status in the home depends not so much on whether he is working as on whether he brings money into the home. Thus, in several of the families we have studied in which the husband receives disability payments his status is as well-recognized as in families in which the husband is working.[19]

Because of the high degree of conjugal role segregation, both white and Negro lower-class families tend to be matrifocal in comparison to middle-class families. They are matrifocal in the sense that the wife makes most of the

[19]Yancey, *op. cit.* The effects of unemployment on the family have been discussed by E. Wright Bakke. *Citizens Without Work* (New Haven, Conn., 1940); Mirra Komarovsky, *The Unemployed Man and His Family* (New York, 1960); and Earl L. Kees, *Families in Trouble* (New York, 1946). What seems distinctive to the Negro slum culture is the short time lapse between the husband's loss of a job and his wife's considering him superfluous.

decisions that keep the family going and has the greatest sense of responsibility to the family. In white as well as in Negro lower-class families women tend to look to their female relatives for support and counsel, and to treat their husbands as essentially uninterested in the day-to-day problems of family living.[20] In the Negro lower-class family these tendencies are all considerably exaggerated so that the matrifocality is much clearer than in white lower-class families.

The fact that both sexes in the Negro slum culture have equal right to the various satisfactions of life (earning an income, sex, drinking, and peer-group activity which conflicts with family responsibilities) means that there is less pretense to patriarchal authority in the Negro than in the white lower class. Since men find the overt debasement of their status very threatening, the Negro family is much more vulnerable to disruption when men are temporarily unable to perform their provider roles. Also, when men are unemployed the temptations for them to engage in street adventures which repercuss on the marital relationship are much greater. This fact is well-recognized by Negro lower-class wives: they often seem as concerned about what their unemployed husbands will do instead of working as they are about the fact that the husband is no longer bringing money into the home.

It is tempting to cope with the likelihood of disloyalty by denying the usual norms of fidelity by maintaining instead that extra-marital affairs are acceptable as long as they do not interfere with family functioning. Quite a few informants tell us this, but we have yet to observe a situation in which a couple maintains a stable relationship under these circumstances without a great deal of conflict. Thus one woman in her forties who has been married for many years and has four children first outlined this deviant norm and then illustrated how it did not work out:

> My husband and I, we go out alone and sometimes stay all night. But when I get back my husband doesn't ask me a thing and I don't ask him anything. . . . A couple of years ago I suspected he was going out on me. One day I came home and my daughter was here. I told her to tell me when he left the house. I went into the bedroom and got into bed and then I heard him come in. He left in about ten minutes and my daughter came in and told me he was gone. I got out of bed and put on my clothes and started following him. Soon I saw him walking with a young girl and I began walking after them. They were just laughing and joking right out loud right on the sidewalk. He was carrying a large package of hers. I walked up behind them until I was about a yard from them. I had a large dirk which I opened and had decided to take one long slash across the both of them. Just when I decided to swing at them I lost my balance—I have a bad hip. Anyway, I didn't cut them because I lost my balance. Then I called

[20]See particularly Komarovsky's discussion of "barriers to marital communications" (Chapter 7) and "confidants outside of marriage" (Chapter 9), in *Blue Collar Marriage, op. cit.*

his name and he turned around and stared at me. He didn't move at all. He was shaking all over. That girl just ran away from us. He still had her package so the next day she called on the telephone and said she wanted to come pick it up. My husband washed his face, brushed his teeth, took out his false tooth and started scrubbing it and put on a clean shirt and everything, just for her. We went downstairs together and gave her the package and she left.

So you see my husband does run around on me and it seems like he does it a lot. The thing about it is he's just getting too old to be pulling that kind of stuff. If a young man does it then that's no so bad—but an old man, he just looks foolish. One of these days he'll catch me but I'll just tell him, "Buddy you owe me one," and that'll be all there is to it. He hasn't caught me yet though.

In this case, as in others, the wife is not able to leave well enough alone; her jealousy forces her to a confrontation. Actually seeing her husband with another woman stimulates her to violence.

With couples who have managed to stay married for a good many years, these peccadillos are tolerable although they generate a great deal of conflict in the marital relationship. At earlier ages the partners are likely to be both prouder and less innured to the hopelessness of maintaining stable relationships; outside involvements are therefore much more likely to be disruptive of the marriage.

Marital Breakup

The precipitating causes of marital disruption seem to fall mainly into economic or sexual categories. As noted, the husband has little credit with his wife to tide him over periods of unemployment. Wives seem very willing to withdraw commitment from husbands who are not bringing money into the house. They take the point of view that he has no right to take up space around the house, to use its facilities, or to demand loyalty from her. Even where the wife is not inclined to press these claims, the husband tends to be touchy because he knows that such definitions are usual in his group, and he may, therefore, prove difficult for even a well-meaning wife to deal with. As noted above, if husbands do not work they tend to play around. Since they continue to maintain some contact with their peer groups, whenever they have time on their hands they move back into the world of the street system and are likely to get involved in activities which pose a threat to their family relationships.

Drink is a great enemy of the lower-class housewife, both white and Negro. Lower-class wives fear their husband's drinking because it costs money, because the husband may become violent and take out his frustrations on his wife, and because drinking may lead to sexual involvements with other women.[21]

[21]Rainwater, *Family Design, op. cit.,* pp. 305–308.

The combination of economic problems and sexual difficulties can be seen in the case of the following couple in their early twenties:

When the field worker first came to know them, the Wilsons seemed to be working hard to establish a stable family life. The couple had been married about three years and had a two-year-old son. Their apartment was very sparsely furnished but also very clean. Within six weeks the couple had acquired several rooms of inexpensive furniture and obviously had gone to a great deal of effort to make a liveable home. Husband and wife worked on different shifts so that the husband could take care of the child while the wife worked. They looked forward to saving enough money to move out of the housing project into a more desirable neighborhood. Six weeks later, however, the husband had lost his job. He and his wife were in great conflict. She made him feel unwelcome at home and he strongly suspected her of going out with other men. A short time later they had separated. It is impossible to disentangle the various factors involved in this separation into a sequence of cause and effect, but we can see something of the impact of the total complex.

First Mr. Wilson loses his job: "I went to work one day and the man told me that I would have to work until 1:00. I asked him if there would be any extra pay for working overtime and he said no. I asked him why and he said, 'If you don't like it you can kiss my ass.' He said that to me. I said, 'Why do I have to do all that?' He said, 'Because I said so.' I wanted to jam (fight) him but I said to myself I don't want to be that ignorant, I don't want to be as ignorant as he is, so I just cut out and left. Later his father called me (it was a family firm) and asked why I left and I told him. He said, 'If you don't want to go along with my son then you're fired.' I said O.K. They had another Negro man come in to help me part time before they fired me. I think they were trying to have him work full time because he worked for them before. He has seven kids and he takes their shit."

The field worker observed that things were not as hard as they could be because his wife has a job, to which he replied, "Yeah, I know, that's just where the trouble is. My wife has become independent since she began working. If I don't get a job pretty soon I'll go crazy. We have a lot of little arguments about nothing since she got so independent." He went on to say that his wife had become a completely different person recently; she was hard to talk to because she felt that now that she was working and he was not there was nothing that he could tell her. On her last pay day his wife did not return home for three days; when she did she had only seven cents left from her pay check. He said that he loved his wife very much and had begged her to quit fooling around. He is pretty sure that she is having an affair with the man with whom she rides to work. To make matters worse his wife's sister counsels her that she does not have to stay home with him as long as he is out of work. Finally the wife moved most of their furniture out of the apartment so that he came home to find an empty apartment. He moved back to his parents' home (also in the housing project).

One interesting effect of this experience was the radical change in the husband's attitudes toward race relations. When he and his wife were doing well together and had hopes of moving up in the world he was quite critical of Negroes; "Our people are not ready for integration in many cases because they really don't know how to act. You figure if our people don't want to be bothered with whites then why in hell should the white man want to be bothered with them. There are some of us who are ready; there are others who aren't quite ready yet so I don't see why they're doing all of this hollering." A scarce eight months later he addressed white people as he spoke for two hours into a tape recorder, "If we're willing to be with you, why aren't you willing to be with us? Do our color make us look dirty and low down and cheap? Or do you know the real meaning of 'nigger'? Anyone can be a nigger, white, colored, orange or any other color. It's something that you labeled us with. You put us away like you put a can away on the shelf with a label on it. The can is marked 'Poison: stay away from it.' You want us to help build your country but you don't want us to live in it. . . . You give me respect; I'll give you respect. If you threaten to take my life, I'll take yours and believe me I know how to take a life. We do believe that man was put here to live together as human beings; not one that's superior and the one that's a dog, but as human beings. And if you don't want to live this way then you become the dog and we'll become the human beings. There's too much corruption, too much hate, too much one individual trying to step on another. If we don't get together in a hurry we will destroy each other." It was clear from what the respondent said that he had been much influenced by Black Muslim philosophy, yet again and again in his comments one can see the displacement into a public, race relations dialogue of the sense of rage, frustration and victimization that he had experienced in his ill-fated marriage.[22]

Finally, it should be noted that migration plays a part in marital disruption. Sometimes marriages do not break up in the dramatic way described above but rather simply become increasingly unsatisfactory to one or both partners. In such a situation the temptation to move to another city, from South to North, or North to West, is great. Several wives told us that their first marriages were broken when they moved with their children to the North and their husbands stayed behind.

"After we couldn't get along I left the farm and came here and stayed away three or four days. I didn't come here to stay. I came to visit but I liked it and so I said, 'I'm gonna leave!' He said, "I'll be glad if you do.' Well, maybe he didn't mean it but I thought he did. . . . I miss him sometimes, you know. I think about him I guess. But just in a small way. That's what I can't understand about life sometimes; you know—how people can go on like that and still break up and meet somebody else. Why couldn't—oh, I don't know!"

[22]For a discussion of the relationship between Black Nationalist ideology and the Negro struggle to achieve a sense of valid personal identity, see Howard Brotz, *The Black Jews of Harlem* (New York, 1963), and E. U. Essien-Udom, *Black Nationalism: A Search for Identity in America* (Chicago, 1962).

The gains and losses in marriage and in the post-marital state often seem quite comparable. Once they have had the experience of marriage, many women in the Negro slum culture see little to recommend it in the future, important as the first marriage may have been in establishing their maturity and respectability.

The House of Mothers

As we have seen, perhaps a majority of mothers in the Negro slum community spend at least part of their mature life as mothers heading a family. The Negro mother may be a working mother or she may be an AFDC mother, but in either case she has the problems of maintaining a household, socializing her children, and achieving for herself some sense of membership in relations with other women and with men. As is apparent from the earlier discussion, she often receives her training in how to run such a household by observing her own mother manage without a husband. Similarly she often learns how to run a three-generation household because she herself brought a third generation into her home with her first, premarital, pregnancy.

Because men are not expected to be much help around the house, having to be head of the household is not particularly intimidating to the Negro mother if she can feel some security about income. She knows it is a hard, hopeless, and often thankless task, but she also knows that it is possible. The maternal household in the slum is generally run with a minimum of organization. The children quickly learn to fend for themselves, to go to the store, to make small purchases, to bring change home, to watch after themselves when the mother has to be out of the home, to amuse themselves, to set their own schedules of sleeping, eating, and going to school. Housekeeping practices may be poor, furniture takes a terrific beating from the children, and emergencies constantly arise. The Negro mother in this situation copes by not setting too high standards for herself, by letting things take their course. Life is most difficult when there are babies and preschool children around because then the mother is confined to the home. If she is a grandmother and the children are her daughter's, she is often confined since it is taken as a matter of course that the mother has the right to continue her outside activities and that the grandmother has the duty to be responsible for the child.

In this culture there is little of the sense of the awesome responsibility of caring for children that is characteristic of the working and middle class. There is not the deep psychological involvement with babies which has been observed with the working-class mother.[23] The baby's needs are cared for on a catch-as-catch-can basis. If there are other children around and they happen to like babies, the baby can be over-stimulated; if this is not the case, the baby

[23]Rainwater, Coleman, and Handel, *op. cit.*, pp. 88–102.

is left alone a good deal of the time. As quickly as he can move around he learns to fend for himself.

The three-generation maternal household is a busy place. In contrast to working-and middle-class homes it tends to be open to the world, with many non-family members coming in and out at all times as the children are visited by friends, the teenagers by their boy friends and girl friends, the mother by her friends and perhaps an occasional boy friend, and the grandmother by fewer friends but still by an occasional boy friend.

The openness of the household is, among other things, a reflection of the mother's sense of impotence in the face of the street system. Negro lower-class mothers often indicate that they try very hard to keep their young children at home and away from the streets; they often seem to make the children virtual prisoners in the home. As the children grow and go to school they inevitably do become involved in peer-group activities. The mother gradually gives up, feeling that once the child is lost to this pernicious outside world there is little she can do to continue to control him and direct his development. She will try to limit the types of activities that go on in the home and to restrict the kinds of friends that her children can bring into the home, but even this she must give up as time goes on, as the children become older and less attentive to her direction.

The grandmothers in their late forties, fifties, and sixties tend increasingly to stay at home. The home becomes a kind of court at which other family members gather and to which they bring their friends for sociability, and as a by-product provide amusement and entertainment for the mother. A grandmother may provide a home for her daughters, their children, and sometimes their children's children, and yet receive very little in a material way from them; but one of the things she does receive is a sense of human involvement, a sense that although life may have passed her by she is not completely isolated from it.

The lack of control that mothers have over much that goes on in their households is most dramatically apparent in the fact that their older children seem to have the right to come home at any time once they have moved and to stay in the home without contributing to its maintenance. Though the mother may be resentful about being taken advantage of, she does not feel she can turn her children away. For example, sixty-five-year-old Mrs. Washington plays hostess for weeks or months at a time to her forty-year-old daughter and her small children, and to her twenty-three-year-old granddaughter and her children. When these daughters come home with their families the grandmother is expected to take care of the young children and must argue with her daughter and granddaughter to receive contributions to the daily household ration of food and liquor. Or, a twenty-year-old son comes home from the Air Force and feels he has the right to live at home without working and to run up an eighty-dollar long-distance telephone bill.

Even aged parents living alone in small apartments sometimes acknowledge such obligations to their children or grandchildren. Again, the only clear return they receive for their hospitality is the reduction of isolation that comes from having people around and interesting activity going on. When in the Washington home the daughter and granddaughter and their children move in with the grandmother, or when they come to visit for shorter periods of time, the occasion has a party atmosphere. The women sit around talking and reminiscing. Though boy friends may be present, they take little part; instead they sit passively, enjoying the stories and drinking along with thw women. It would seem that in this kind of party activity the women are defined as the stars. Grandmother, daughter, and granddaughter in turn take the center of the stage telling a story from the family's past, talking about a particularly interesting night out on the town or just making some general observation about life. In the course of these events a good deal of liquor is consumed. In such a household as this little attention is paid to the children since the competition by adults for attention is stiff.

Boy Friends, not Husbands

It is with an understanding of the problems of isolation which older mothers have that we can obtain the best insight into the role and function of boy friends in the maternal household. The older mothers, surrounded by their own children and grandchildren, are not able to move freely in the outside world, to participate in the high life which they enjoyed when younger and more foot-loose. They are disillusioned with marriage as providing any more secure economic base than they can achieve on their own. They see marriage as involving just another responsibility without a concomitant reward—"It's the greatest thing in the world to come home in the afternoon and not have some curly headed twot in the house yellin' at me and askin' me where supper is, where I've been, what I've been doin', and who I've been seein'." In this situation the woman is tempted to form relationships with men that are not so demanding as marriage but still provide companionship and an opportunity for occasional sexual gratification.

There seem to be two kinds of boy friends. Some boy friends "pimp" off mothers; they extract payment in food or money for their companionship. This leads to the custom sometimes called "Mother's Day," the tenth of the month when the AFDC checks come.[24] On this day one can observe an influx of men into the neighborhood, and much partying. But there is another kind of boy friend, perhaps more numerous than the first, who instead of being paid for his services pays for the right to be a pseudo family member. He may be the father of one of the woman's children and for this reason makes a steady contribution to the family's support, or he may simply be a man whose com-

[24]Cf. Michael Schwartz and George Henderson, "The Culture of Unemployment: Some Notes on Negro Children," in Schostak and Gomborg, *op. cit.*

pany the mother enjoys and who makes reasonable gifts to the family for the time he spends with them (and perhaps implicitly for the sexual favors he receives). While the boy friend does not assume fatherly authority within the family, he often is known and liked by the children. The older children appreciate the meaningfulness of their mother's relationship with him—one girl said of her mother's boy friend:

> "We don't none of us (the children) want her to marry again. It's all right if she wants to live by herself and have a boy friend. It's not because we're afraid we're going to have some more sisters and brothers, which it wouldn't make us much difference, but I think she be too old."

Even when the boy friend contributes ten or twenty dollars a month to the family he is in a certain sense getting a bargain. If he is a well-accepted boy friend he spends considerable time around the house, has a chance to relax in an atmosphere less competitive than that of his peer group, is fed and cared for by the woman, yet has no responsibilities which he cannot renounce when he wishes. When women have stable relationships of this kind with boy friends they often consider marrying them but are reluctant to take such a step. Even the well-liked boy friend has some shortcomings—one woman said of her boy friend:

> "Well he works; I know that. He seems to be a nice person, kind hearted. He believes in survival for me and my family. He don't much mind sharing with my youngsters. If I ask him for a helping hand he don't seem to mind that. The only part I dislike is his drinking."

The woman in this situation has worked out a reasonably stable adaptation to the problems of her life; she is fearful of upsetting this adaptation by marrying again. It seems easier to take the "sweet" part of the relationship with a man without the complexities that marriage might involve.

It is in the light of this pattern of women living in families and men living by themselves in rooming houses, odd rooms, here and there, that we can understand Daniel Patrick Moynihan's observation that during their mature years men simply disappear; that is, that census data show a very high sex ratio of women to men.[25] In St. Louis, starting at the age range twenty to twenty-four there are only seventy-two men for every one hundred women. This ratio does not climb to ninety until the age range fifty to fifty-four. Men often do not have real homes; they move about from one household where they have kinship or sexual ties to another; they live in flop houses and rooming houses; they spend time in institutions. They are not household members in the only "homes" that they have—the homes of their mothers and of their girl friends.

It is in this kind of world that boys and girls in the Negro slum community learn their sex roles. It is not just, or even mainly, that fathers are often

---

[25]Daniel Patrick Moynihan, "Employment, Income, and the Ordeal of the Negro Family," *Daedalus* (Fall 1965), pp. 760–61.

absent but that the male role models around boys are ones which emphasize expressive, affectional techniques for making one's way in the world. The female role models available to girls emphasize an exaggerated self-sufficiency (from the point of view of the middle class) and the danger of allowing oneself to be dependent on men for anything that is crucial. By the time she is mature, the woman learns that she is most secure when she herself manages the family affairs and when she dominates her men. The man learns that he exposes himself to the least risk of failure when he does not assume a husband's and father's responsibilities but instead counts on his ability to court women and to ingratiate himself with them.

IDENTITY PROCESSES IN THE FAMILY

Up to this point we have been examining the sequential development of family stages in the Negro slum community, paying only incidental attention to the psychological responses family members make to these social forms and not concerning ourselves with the effect the family forms have on the psychosocial development of the children who grow up in them. Now we want to examine the effect that growing up in this kind of a system has in terms of socialization and personality development.

Household groups function for cultures in carrying out the initial phases of socialization and personality formation. It is in the family that the child learns the most primitive categories of existence and experience, and that he develops his most deeply held beliefs about the world and about himself.[26] From the child's point of view, the household *is* the world; his experiences as he moves out of it into the larger world are always interpreted in terms of his particular experience within the home. The painful experiences which a child in the Negro slum culture has are, therefore, interpreted as in some sense a reflection of this family world. The impact of the system of victimization is transmitted through the family; the child cannot be expected to have the sophistication an outside observer has for seeing exactly where the villains are. From the child's point of view, if he is hungry it is his parents' fault; if he experiences frustrations in the streets or in the school it is his parents' fault; if that world seems incomprehensible to him it is his parents' fault; if people are aggressive or destructive toward each other it is his parents' fault, not that of a system of race relations. In another culture this might not be the case; if a subculture could exist which provided comfort and security within its limited

---

[26]Talcott Parsons concludes his discussion of child socialization, the development of an "internalized family system" and internalized role differentiation by observing, "The internalization of the family collectivity as an object and its values should not be lost sight of. This is crucial with respect to . . . the assumption of representative roles outside the family on behalf of it. Here it is the child's family membership which is decisive, and thus his acting in a role in terms of its values for 'such as he.' " Talcott Parsons and Robert F. Bales, *Family, Socialization and Interaction Process* (Glencoe, Ill., 1955), p. 113.

world and the individual experienced frustration only when he moved out into the larger society, the family might not be thought so much to blame. The effect of the caste system, however, is to bring home through a chain of cause and effect all of the victimization processes, and to bring them home in such a way that it is often very difficult even for adults in the system to see the connection between the pain they feel at the moment and the structured patterns of the caste system.

Let us take as a central question that of identity formation within the Negro slum family. We are concerned with the question of who the individual believes himself to be and to be becoming. For Erikson, identity means a sense of continuity and social sameness which bridges what the individual *"was* as a child and what he is *about to become* and also reconciles his *conception of himself* and his community's recognition of him." Thus identity is a "self-realization coupled with a mutual recognition."[27] In the early childhood years identity is family-bound since the child's identity is his identity *vis-à-vis* other members of the family. Later he incorporates into his sense of who he is and is becoming his experiences outside the family, but always influenced by the interpretations and evaluations of those experiences that the family gives. As the child tries on identities, *announces* them, the family sits as judge of his pretensions. Family members are both the most important judges and the most critical ones, since who he is allowed to become affects them in their own identity strivings more crucially than it affects anyone else. The child seeks a sense of valid identity, a sense of being a particular person with a satisfactory degree of congruence between who he feels he is, who he announces himself to be, and where he feels his society places him.[28] He is uncomfortable when he experiences disjunction between his own needs and the kinds of needs legitimated by those around him, or when he feels a disjunction between his sense of himself and the image of himself that others play back to him.[29]

"Tell It Like It Is"

When families become involved in important quarrels the psychosocial underpinnings of family life are laid bare. One such quarrel in a family we have been studying brings together in one place many of the themes that seem to dominate identity problems in Negro slum culture. The incident illustrates in

---

[27]Erik H. Eriksen, "Identity and the Life Cycle," *Psychological Issues,* Vol. 1, No. 1 (1959).

[28]For discussion of the dynamics of the individual's *announcements* and the society's *placements* in the formation of identity, see Gregroy Stone, "Appearance and the Self," in Arnold Rose, *Human Behavior in Social Process* (Boston, 1962), pp. 86–118.

[29]The importance of identity for social behavior is discussed in detail in Ward Goodenough, *Cooperation and Change* (New York, 1963), pp. 176–251, and in Lee Rainwater, "Work and Identity in the Lower Class," in Sam H. Warner, Jr., *Planning for the Quality of Urban Life* (Cambridge, Mass., forthcoming). The images of self and of other family members is a crucial variable in Hess and Handel's psychosocial analysis of family life; see Robert D. Hess and Gerald Handel, *Family Worlds* (Chicago, 1959), especially pp. 6–11.

a particularly forceful and dramatic way family processes which our field work, and some other contemporary studies of slum family life, suggests unfold more subtly in a great many families at the lower-class level. The family involved, the Johnsons, is certainly not the most disorganized one we have studied; in some respects their way of life represents a realistic adaptation to the hard living of a family nineteen years on AFDC with a monthly income of $202 for nine people. The two oldest daughters, Mary Jane (eighteen years old) and Esther (sixteen) are pregnant; Mary Jane has one illegitimate child. The adolescent sons, Bob and Richard, are much involved in the social and sexual activities of their peer group. The three other children, ranging in age from twelve to fourteen, are apparently also moving into this kind of peer-group society.

When the argument started Bob and Esther were alone in the apartment with Mary Jane's baby. Esther took exception to Bob's playing with the baby because she had been left in charge; the argument quickly progressed to a fight in which Bob cuffed Esther around, and she tried to cut him with a knife. The police were called and subdued Bob with their nightsticks. At this point the rest of the family and the field worker arrived. As the argument continued, these themes relevant to the analysis which follows appeared:

1) The sisters said that Bob was not their brother (he is a half-brother to Esther, and Mary Jane's full brother). Indeed, they said their mother "didn't have no husband. These kids don't even know who their daddies are." The mother defended herself by saying that she had one legal husband, and one common-law husband, no more.

2) The sisters said that their fathers had never done anything for them, nor had their mother. She retorted that she had raised them "to the age of woman-hood" and now would care for their babies.

3) Esther continued to threaten to cut Bob if she got a chance (a month later they fought again, and she did cut Bob, who required twenty-one stitches).

4) The sisters accused their mother of favoring their lazy brothers and asked her to put them out of the house. She retorted that the girls were as lazy, that they made no contribution to maintaining the household, could not get their boy friends to marry them or support their children, that all the support came from her AFDC check. Mary Jane retorted that "the baby has a check of her own."

5) The girls threatened to leave the house if their mother refused to put their brothers out. They said they could force their boy friends to support them by taking them to court, and Esther threatened to cut her boy friend's throat if he did not co-operate.

6) Mrs. Johnson said the girls could leave if they wished but that she would keep their babies; "I'll not have it, not knowing who's taking care of them."

7) When her thirteen-year-old sister laughed at all of this, Esther told her not to laugh because she, too, would be pregnant within a year.

8) When Bob laughed, Esther attacked him and his brother by saying that both were not man enough to make babies, as she and her sister had been able to do.

9) As the field worker left, Mrs. Johnson sought his sympathy. "You see, Joe, how hard it is for me to bring up a family. . . . They sit around and talk to me like I'm some kind of a dog and not their mother."
10) Finally, it is important to note for the analysis which follows that the following labels—"black-assed," "black bastard," "bitch," and other profane terms—were liberally used by Esther and Mary Jane, and rather less liberally by their mother, to refer to each other, to the girls' boy friends, to Bob, and to the thirteen-year-old daughter.

Several of the themes outlined previously appear forcefully in the course of this argument. In the last year and a half the mother has become a grandmother and expects shortly to add two more grandchildren to her household. She takes it for granted that it is her responsibility to care for the grandchildren and that she has the right to decide what will be done with the children since her own daughters are not fully responsible. She makes this very clear to them when they threaten to move out, a threat which they do not really wish to make good nor could they if they wished to.

However, only as an act of will is Mrs. Johnson able to make this a family. She must constantly cope with the tendency of her adolescent children to disrupt the family group and to deny that they are in fact a family—"He ain't no brother of mine"; "The baby has a check of her own." Though we do not know exactly what processes communicate these facts to the children it is clear that in growing up they have learned to regard themselves as not fully part of a solidary collectivity. During the quarrel this message was reinforced for the twelve-, thirteen-, and fourteen-year-old daughters by the four-way argument among their older sisters, older brother, and their mother.

The argument represents vicious unmasking of the individual members' pretenses to being competent individuals.[30] The efforts of the two girls to present themselves as masters of their own fate are unmasked by the mother. The girls in turn unmask the pretensions of the mother and of their two brothers. When the thirteen-year-old daughter expresses some amusement they turn on her, telling her that it won't be long before she too becomes pregnant. Each member of the family in turn is told that he can expect to be no more than a victim of his world, but that this is somehow inevitably his own fault.

In this argument masculinity is consistently demeaned. Bob has no right to play with his niece, the boys are not really masculine because at fifteen and sixteen years they have yet to father children, their own fathers were no goods who failed to do anything for their family. These notions probably come originally from the mother, who enjoys recounting the story of having her common-law husband imprisoned for nonsupport, but this

[30]See the discussion of "masking" and "unmasking" in relation to disorganization and re-equilibration in families by John P. Spiegel, "The Resolution of Role Conflict within the Family," in Norman W. Bell and Ezra F. Vogel, *A Modern Introduction to the Family* (Glencoe, Ill., 1960), pp. 375–377.

comes back to haunt her as her daughters accuse her of being no better than they in ability to force support and nurturance from a man. In contrast, the girls came off somewhat better than the boys, although they must accept the label of stupid girls because they have similarly failed and inconveniently become pregnant in the first place. At least they can and have had children and therefore have some meaningful connection with the ongoing substance of life. There is something important and dramatic in which they participate, while the boys, despite their sexual activity, "can't get no babies."

In most societies, as children grow and are formed by their elders into suitable members of the society they gain increasingly a sense of competence and ability to master the behavioral environment their particular world presents. But in Negro slum culture growing up involves an ever-increasing appreciation of one's shortcomings, of the impossibility of finding a self-sufficient and gratifying way of living.[31] It is in the family first and most devastatingly that one learns these lessons. As the child's sense of frustration builds he too can strike out and unmask the pretensions of others. The result is a peculiar strength and a pervasive weakness. The strength involves the ability to tolerate and defend against degrading verbal and physical aggressions from others and not to give up completely. The weakness involves the inability to embark hopefully on any course of action that might make things better, particularly action which involves cooperating and trusting attitudes toward others. Family members become potential enemies to each other, as the frequency of observing the police being called in to settle family quarrels brings home all too dramatically.

The conceptions parents have of their children are such that they are constantly alert as the child matures to evidence that he is as bad as everyone else. That is, in lower-class culture human nature is conceived of as essentially bad, destructive, immoral.[32] This is the nature of things. Therefore any one child must be inherently bad unless his parents are very lucky indeed. If the mother can keep the child insulated from the outside world, she feels she may be able to prevent his inherent badness from coming out. She feels that once he is let out into the larger world the badness will come to the fore since that is his nature. This means that in the identity development of the child he is constantly exposed to identity labeling by his parents as a bad person. Since as he grows up he does not experience his world as particularly gratifying, it is very easy for him to conclude that this lack of gratification is due to the fact

---

[31]See the discussion of self-identity and self-esteem in Thomas F. Pettigrew, *A Profile of the Negro American* (Princeton, N. J., 1964), pp. 6–11.

[32]Rainwater, Coleman, and Handel, *op. cit.,* pp. 44–51. See also the discussion of the greater level of "anomie" and mistrust among lower-class people in Ephriam Mizruchi, *Success and Opportunity* (New York, 1954). Unpublished research by the author indicates that for one urban lower-class sample (Chicago) Negroes scored about 50 per cent higher on Srole's anomie scale than did comparable whites.

that something is wrong with him. This, in turn, can readily be assimilated to the definitions of being a bad person offered him by those with whom he lives.[33] In this way the Negro slum child learns his culture's conception of being-in-the-world, a conception that emphasizes inherent evil in a chaotic, hostile, destructive world.

Blackness

To a certain extent these same processes operate in white lower-class groups, but added for the Negro is the reality of blackness. "Black-assed" is not an empty pejorative adjective. In the Negro slum culture several distinctive appellations are used to refer to oneself and others. One involves the terms, "black" or "nigger." Black is generally a negative way of naming, but nigger can be either negative or positive, depending upon the context. It is important to note that, at least in the urban North, the initial development of racial identity in these terms has very little directly to do with relations with whites. A child experiences these identity placements in the context of the family and in the neighborhood peer group; he probably very seldom hears the same terms used by whites (unlike the situation in the South). In this way, one of the effects of ghettoization is to mask the ultimate enemy so that the understanding of the fact of victimization by a caste system comes as a late acquisition laid over conceptions of self and of other Negroes derived from intimate, and to the child often traumatic, experience within the ghetto community. If, in addition, the child attends a ghetto school where his Negro teachers either overtly or by implication reinforce his community's negative conceptions of what it means to be black, then the child has little opportunity to develop a more realistic image of himself and other Negroes as being damaged by whites and not by themselves. In such a situation, an intelligent man like Mr. Wilson (quoted on pages 160-161) can say with all sincerity that he does not feel most Negroes are ready for integration—only under the experience of certain kinds of intense personal threat coupled with exposure to an ideology that places the responsibility on whites did he begin to see through the direct evidence of his daily experience.

To those living in the heart of a ghetto, black comes to mean not just "stay back," but also membership in a community of persons who think poorly of each other, who attack and manipulate each other, who give each other small comfort in a desperate world. Black comes to stand for a sense of identity as no better than these destructive others. The individual feels that he must embrace an unattractive self in order to function at all.

We can hypothesize that in those families that manage to avoid the

[33]For a discussion of the child's propensity from a very early age for speculation and developing explanations, see William V. Silverberg, *Childhood Experience and Personal Destiny* (New York, 1953), pp. 81 ff.

destructive identity imputations of "black" and that manage to maintain solidarity against such assaults from the world around, it is possible for children to grow up with a sense of both Negro and personal identity that allows them to socialize themselves in an anticipatory was for participation in the larger society.[34] This broader sense of identity, however, will remain a brittle one as long as the individual is vulnerable to attack from within the Negro community as "nothing but a nigger like everybody else" or from the white community as "just a nigger." We can hypothesize further that the vicious unmasking of essential identity as black described above is least likely to occur within families where the parents have some stable sense of security, and where they therefore have less need to protect themselves by disavowing responsibility for their children's behavior and denying the children their patrimony as products of a particular family rather than of an immoral nature and an evil community.

In sum, we are suggesting that Negro slum children as they grow up in their families and in their neighborhoods are exposed to a set of experiences —and a rhetoric which conceptualizes them—that brings home to the child an understanding of his essence as a weak and debased person who can expect only partial gratification of his needs, and who must seek even this level of gratification by less than straight-forward means.

Strategies for Living

In every society complex processes of socialization inculcate in their members strategies for gratifying the needs with which they are born and those which the society itself generates. Inextricably linked to these strategies, both cause and effect of them, are the existential propositions which members of a culture entertain about the nature of their world and of effective action within the world as it is defined for them. In most of American society two grand strategies seem to attract the allegiance of its members and guide their day-to-day actions. I have called these strategies those of *the good life and of career success.*[35] A good life strategy involves efforts to get along with others and not to rock the boat, a comfortable familism grounded on a stable work career for husbands in which they perform adequately at the modest jobs that enable them to be good providers. The strategy of career success is the choice of ambitious men and women who see life as providing opportunities to move from a lower to a higher status, to "accomplish something," to achieve greater than ordinary material well-being, prestige, and social recognition. Both of these strategies are predicated on the assumption that the world is inherently rewarding if one behaves properly and does his part. The rewards of the world may come easily or only at the cost of great effort, but at least they are there.

---

[34] See Ralph Ellison's autobiographical descriptions of growing up in Oklahoma City in his *Shadow and Act* (New York, 1964). The quotations at the beginning of this article are taken from pages 315 and 112 of this book.

[35] Rainwater, "Work and Identity in the Lower Class," *op cit.*

In the white and particularly in the Negro slum worlds little in the experience that individuals have as they grow up sustains a belief in a rewarding world. The strategies that seem appropriate are not those of a good, family-based life or of a career, but rather *strategies for survival.*

Much of what has been said above can be summarized as encouraging three kinds of survival strategies. One is the strategy of the *expressive life style* which I have described elsewhere as an effort to make yourself interesting and attractive to others so that you are better able to manipulate their behavior along lines that will provide some immediate gratification.[36] Negro slum culture provides many examples of techniques for seduction, of persuading others to give you what you want in situations where you have very little that is tangible to offer in return. In order to get what you want you learn to "work game," a strategy which requires a high development of a certain kind of verbal facility, a sophisticated manipulation of promise and interim reward. When the expressive strategy fails or when it is unavailable there is, of course, the great temptation to adopt a *violent strategy* in which you force others to give you what you need once you fail to win it by verbal and other symbolic means.[37] Finally, and increasingly as members of the Negro slum culture grow older, there is the *depressive strategy* in which goals are increasingly constricted to the bare necessities for survival (not as a social being but simply as an organism).[38] This is the strategy of "I don't bother anybody and I hope nobody's gonna bother me; I'm simply going through the motions to keep body (but not soul) together." Most lower-class people follow mixed strategies, as Walter Miller has observed, alternating among the excitement of the expressive style, the desperation of the violent style, and the deadness of the depressed style.[39] Some members of the Negro slum world experiment from time to time with mixed strategies that also incorporate the stable working-class model of the good American life, but this latter strategy is exceedingly vulnerable to the threats of unemployment or a less than adequate pay check, on the one hand, and the seduction and violence of the slum world around them, on the other.

Remedies

Finally, it is clear that we, no less than the inhabitants of the ghetto, are not masters of their fate because we are not masters of our own total society. Despite the battles with poverty on many fronts we can find little evidence to

[36] *Ibid.*

[37] Short and Strodtbeck see violent behavior in juvenile gangs as a kind of last resort strategy in situations where the actor feels he has no other choice. See Short and Strodtbeck, *op. cit.,* pp. 248-264.

[38] Wiltse speaks of a "pseudo depression syndrome" as characteristic of many AFDC mothers. Kermit T. Wiltse, "Orthopsychiatric Programs for Socially Deprived Groups," *American Journal of Orthopsychiatry,* Vol. 33, No. 5 (October 1963), pp. 806-813.

[39] Walter B. Miller, "Lower Class Culture as a Generating Milieu of Gang Delinquency," *Journal of Social Issues,* Vol. 14, No. 3 (1958), pp. 5-19.

sustain our hope of winning the war given current programs and strategies.

The question of strategy is particularly crucial when one moves from an examination of destructive cultural and interaction patterns in Negro families to the question of how these families might achieve a more stable and gratifying life. It is tempting to see the family as the main villain of the piece, and to seek to develop programs which attack directly this family pathology. Should we not have extensive programs of family therapy, family counseling, family-life education, and the like? Is this not the prerequisite to enabling slum Negro families to take advantage of other opportunities? Yet, how pale such efforts seem compared to the deepseated problems of self-image and family process described above. Can an army of social workers undo the damage of three hundred years by talking and listening without massive changes in the social and economic situations of the families with whom they are to deal? And, if such changes take place, will the social-worker army be needed?

If we are right that present Negro family patterns have been created as adaptations to a particular socioeconomic situation, it would make more sense to change that socioeconomic situation and then depend upon the people involved to make new adaptations as time goes on. If Negro providers have steady jobs and decent incomes, if Negro children have some realistic expectation of moving toward such a goal, if slum Negroes come to feel that they have the chance to affect their own futures and to receive respect from those around them, then (and only then) the destructive patterns described are likely to change. The change, though slow and uneven from individual to individual, will in a certain sense be automatic because it will represent an adaptation to changes socioeconomic circumstances which have direct and highly valued implications for the person.

It is possible to think of three kinds of extra-family change that are required if family patterns are to change; these are outlined below as pairs of current deprivations and needed remedies:

Deprivation Effect of Caste Vicitimization	Needed Remedy
I. Poverty	Employment income for men; income maintenance for mothers
II. Trained incapacity to function in a bureaucratized and industrialized world	Meaningful education of the next generation
III. Powerlessness and stigmatization	Organizational participation for aggressive pursuit of Negroes' self-interest
	Strong sanctions against callous or indifferent service to slum Negroes
	Pride in group identity, Negro *and* American

Unless the major effort is to provide these kinds of remedies, there is a very real danger that programs to "better the structure of the Negro family" by direct intervention will serve the unintended functions of distracting the country from the pressing needs for socioeconomic reform and providing an alibi for the failure to embark on the basic institutional changes that are needed to do anything about abolishing both white and Negro poverty. It would be sad, indeed, if, after the Negro revolt brought to national prominence the continuing problem of poverty, our expertise about Negro slum culture served to deflect the national impulse into symptom-treatment rather than basic reform. If that happens, social scientists will have served those they study poorly indeed.

Let us consider each of the needed remedies in terms of its probable impact on the family. First, the problem of poverty: employed men are less likely to leave their families than are unemployed men, and when they do stay they are more likely to have the respect of their wives and children. A program whose sole effect would be to employ at reasonable wages slum men for work using the skills they now have would do more than any other possible program to stabilize slum family life. But the wages must be high enough to enable the man to maintain his self-respect as a provider, and stable enough to make it worthwhile to change the nature of his adaptation to his world (no one-year emergency programs will do). Once men learn that work pays off it would be possible to recruit men for part-time retraining for more highly skilled jobs, but the initial emphasis must be on the provision of full-time, permanent unskilled jobs. Obviously it will be easier to do this in the context of full employment and a tight labor market.[40]

For at least a generation, however, there will continue to be a large number of female-headed households. Given the demands of socializing a new generation for non-slum living, it is probably uneconomical to encourage mothers to work. Rather, income maintenance programs must be increased to realistic levels, and mothers must be recognized as doing socially useful work for which they are paid rather than as "feeding at the public trough." The bureaucratic morass which currently hampers flexible strategies of combining employment income and welfare payments to make ends meet must also be modified if young workers are not to be pushed prematurely out of the home.

Education has the second priority. (It is second only because without stable family income arrangements the school system must work against the tremendous resistance of competing life-style adaptations to poverty and eco-

---

[40]This line of argument concerning the employment problems of Negroes, and poverty war strategy more generally, is developed with great congency by James Tobin, "On Improving the Economic Status of the Negro," *Daedalus* (Fall 1965), and previously by Gunnar Myrdal, in his *Challenge to Affluence* (New York, 1963), and Orville R. Gursslin and Jack L. Roach, in their "Some Issues in Training the Employed," *Social Problems,* Vol. 12, No. 1 (Summer 1964), pp. 68-77.

nomic insecurity.) As Kenneth Clark has argued so effectively, slum schools now function more to stultify and discourage slum children than to stimulate and train them. The capacity of educators to alibi their lack of commitment to their charges is protean. The making of a different kind of generation must be taken by educators as a stimulating and worthwhile challenge. Once the goal has been accepted they must be given the resources with which to achieve it and the flexibility necessary to experiment with different approaches to accomplish the goal. Education must be broadly conceived to include much more than classroom work, and probably more than a nine-months schedule.[41]

If slum children can come to see the schools as representing a really likely avenue of escape from their difficult situation (even before adolescence they know it is the only *possible* escape) then their commitment to school activities will feed back into their families in a positive way. The parents will feel proud rather than ashamed, and they will feel less need to damn the child as a way to avoid blaming themselves for his failure. The sense of positive family identity will be enriched as the child becomes an attractive object, an ego resource, to his parents. Because he himself feels more competent, he will see them as less depriving and weak. If children's greater commitment to school begins to reduce their involvement in destructive or aimless peer-group activities this too will repercuss positively on the family situation since parents will worry less about their children's involvement in an immoral outside world, and be less inclined to deal with them in harsh, rejecting, or indifferent ways.

Cross-cutting the deprivations of poverty and trained incapacity is the fact of powerlessness and stigmatization. Slum people know that they have little ability to protect themselves and to force recognition of their abstract rights. They know that they are looked down on and scape-goated. They are always vulnerable to the slights, insults, and indifference of the white and Negro functionaries with whom they deal—policemen, social workers, school teachers, landlords, employers, retailers, janitors. To come into contact with others carries the constant danger of moral attack and insult.[42] If processes of status degradation within families are to be interrupted, then they must be interrupted on the outside first.

One way out of the situation of impotence and dammed-up in-group aggression is the organization of meaningful protest against the larger society. Such protest can and will take many forms, not always so neat and rational as the outsider might hope. But, coupled with, and supporting, current programs of economic and educational change, involvement of slum Negroes in organizational activity can do a great deal to build a sense of pride and potency. While only a very small minority of slum Negroes can be expected

[41]See Chapter 6 (pages 111-153) of Kenneth Clark, *op. cit.,* for a discussion of the destructive effects of ghetto schools on their students.

[42]See the discussion of "moral danger" in Lee Rainwater, "Fear and the House-as-Haven in the Lower Class," *Journal of the American Institute of Planners,* February 1966 (in press).

to participate personally in such movements, the vicarious involvement of the majority can have important effects on their sense of self-respect and worth.

Some of the needed changes probably can be made from the top, by decision in Washington, with minimal effective organization within the slum; but others can come only in response to aggressive pressure on the part of the victims themselves. This is probably particularly true of the entrenched tendency of service personnel to enhance their own sense of self and to indulge their middle-class *ressentiment* by stigmatizing and exploiting those they serve. Only effective protest can change endemic patterns of police harassment and brutality, or teachers' indifference and insults, or butchers' heavy thumbs, or indifferent street cleaning and garbage disposal. And the goal of the protest must be to make this kind of insult to the humanity of the slum-dweller too expensive for the perpetrator to afford; it must cost him election defeats, suspensions without pay, job dismissals, license revocations, fines, and the like.

To the extent that the slum dweller avoids stigmatization in the outside world, he will feel more fully a person within the family and better able to function constructively within it since he will not be tempted to make up deficits in self-esteem in ways that are destructive of family solidarity. The "me" of personal identity and the multiple "we" of family, Negro, and American identity are all inextricably linked; a healthier experience of identity in any one sector will repercuss on all the others.

15 / Newcomers from the Southern Mountains *

Some people stoutly maintain that there is nothing which distinguishes Southern Mountain people from any one else in the United States. I think, however, that going to church on Saturday night in the summertime and families with eight and ten children are indicators of significant cultural differences.

Despite this evidence and much more which is available, people of and from this area are often very resistant to being given any specific identification. For purposes of this presentation they will be identified as Southern Mountain Newcomers. . . .

There are important variations among the approximately 7,000,000 people in the Appalachian South which complicates the task of making valid generalizations. A third difficulty is the lack of adequate research data to document some of the hypotheses.

MAGNITUDE AND CAUSES OF THE MIGRATION FROM THE SOUTHERN MOUNTAINS

The Southern Mountain States have long been an important source of population for such industrial states of the Midwest as Illinois, Michigan, Indiana, and Ohio. I have estimated that nearly 800,000 people have moved out of the counties in the Appalachian South between 1950–1956. Not all of these have come north by any means, for Southern cities are also growing. But there is much evidence that the road north has attracted a great many of them.

Many factors are involved in this population movement. Perhaps if we classify them by area or origin and area of destination, the factors can be summarized readily. Within the mountain states in which these people originate the following factors are operative. First, dissatisfaction with the possibilities of life there is increasing as a result of receiving and accepting the knowledge and values of urban living. Second, the population carrying capacity of the resources of the area are already strained to such a point that further population increases will reduce the already low levels of living. The area as a whole is characterized by high birth rates, declining agricultural resources,

*Reprinted from the report of the Institute of Cultural Patterns of Newcomers (Chicago: Welfare Council of Metropolitan Chicago, 1959), pp. 15–40, by permission of the publisher.

and only a few opportunities for industrial employment. A third cause of the outmigration is the rapid mechanization of coal-mining and the declining demand for coal. . . .

Most of the (migrants) are young and in reasonably good health. They thus offer many years of productive labor. Despite all the handicaps for urban living which their situational background imposes upon them, we can take encouragement from the evidence that, like most other people, they have a capacity to learn the ways and demands of a new environment.

They have no responsibility for the fact that they are "Old American" stock, but in the scales of group membership by which people are judged in America, the balance is tipped in favor of such groups. I have received numerous favorable reports of the work of Southern Mountain men in factories and with machinery. This particular strength comes almost as a "natural" to men who have been reared on the near-subsistence farm of the mountains or who have worked in mines and logging woods. Their ability to keep their elderly cars and trucks operating is evidence of a mechanical ability and ingenuity which few people I know possess.

Places of Residence Are Dominantly Rural and Relatively Isolated in a Mountainous Region

The social, economic, and political manifestations of a rural background have been noted frequently in recent research studies, such as those of the Detroit Area Study.

A recent Indianapolis study which showed that the limited capacity of southern migrants to make new friends constituted one of their major sources of adjustment difficulty.

For many . . . concerned with the adjustment problems of such migrants as these, the difficulties are those of involving them in programs of churches, neighborhood centers, or helping their children develop a feeling of belonging in large urban schools. The areas of our great cities in which the Southern Mountain people concentrate are generally lacking in active churches. The buildings may be there, but their congregations have moved away. In many cases the staffs of such churches have done all they knew to get the newcomers to participate.

I know of a Cincinnati case where only one family from the hills attended church after seven years of concentrated effort by the church staff. Finally, the staff gave up and turned to the task of ministering to its own membership. But I'm sure it will not be long before this church moves out to the suburbs where its membership is.

There are no easy remedies for this problem. One difficulty seems to be the tendency of rural people to define large impersonal organizations as unfriendly. Also, there is the fact that they simply are not accustomed to regular church attendance as are many urban people. For many in the mountain areas, going to church has been something you do only in the summer while the revivals are being held. . . .

Most of the Area Must Be Characterized as One of Low Economic Productivity

The meaning of a thin economic base for urban adjustment can perhaps only be understood as we gain some comprehension of the effects of poverty upon attitudes and behavior. Although most of our knowledge of these effects are derived from studies of urban poverty, there are many insights which can be appropriated and applied to the case of rural poverty.

Not all mountain families have adequate food, nor are their houses always warm in winter despite the general abundance of fuels. Allison Davis has shown how from such circumstances come anxiety patterns which may show up as excesses of eating and getting warm when resources are abundant instead of rational budgeting for future needs. I wish I had a nickel for every time I've heard a middle-class mountain person of secure income condemn the improvidence of coal mining families. Poverty seems to develop a certain defensive hardening and insensitivity which James Plant interprets as a product of insecurity and deprivation. There is no reason why we should not expect to find all of these manifestations among the Southern Mountain Newcomers. . . .

The Relatively Large Families Perform Numerous Functions Through a System of Roles Allocated by Age and Sex in Which the Father Is Generally the Authority Center and Mother the Affection Center

Both in terms of structure and function the extended families to which this proposition refers are in conflict with the need to prepare children for migration. In place of rigid systems of role allocation, there is a need for flexibility, and instead of activities mainly in concert with other members of the family, there is a need for variety of personal contacts. Rather than seeking to bind its members to it by continual involvement in activities centering in the family, a major function should be to prepare children emotionally for leaving home by a gradual process of separation and new experiences.

But the ties that pull these people towards their childhood home are not only those of family. There are also the bonds to place, to the beauty and serenity of the hills. As one who left behind the mountain grandeur of Colorado in exchange for those broad, green plains fo Urbana, Illinois, I think I can empathize with the writer of "The Hills of Home." And also with the mountain man who left a good Indiana farm to return to Kentucky because he just couldn't get along without some hills to "lean his eyes agin" when he got up in the morning. . . .

Child-Rearing Practices Are Generally Permissive in the Early Years of Life and Continue for Boys in Regard to Their Outside Activities and Choices of Age-Related Activities

Research studies on this point are few and far between, but the writings of various novelists and able observers all seem in line with my own numerous observations on the permissive character of parent-child relations. One of the most interesting documents in this field was written by a former New York City nursery school teacher, Claudia Lewis, in her book, *Children of the Cumberlands.* Perhaps such permissiveness is but a general characteristic of families with numerous children, crowded living quarters, and limited and uncertain incomes. Numerous studies of lower class urban families point to this conclusion. . . .

In the hills the children seem to be rather free to roam about the roads, woods, and streams doing much as they please. This is not necessarily a healthy pattern, but it does not exist amidst the variety of dangers of the city. Transplanted to the city such permissiveness becomes neglect. In view of the small living quarters available to most of these newcomers and their own behavioral patterns, there is an obvious need for play areas, made safe both by absence of traffic and by the presence of adult supervision.

Houses Are Generally Small and Cheaply Constructed

Both in absolute size and more importantly in terms of the number of persons per dwelling unit, the houses of the area must be classed as "small." I have run some data through my slide rule and come up with a few figures which might be thought of as an Index of Crowding. For the mountain counties of Kentucky the index ranges from 100 up to nearly 125, but for the urban counties it ranges around 70. In the midwestern states the index stands at about 60. It is no exaggeration to say that living space per occupant in Leslie County, Kentucky, is less than half that available, on the average, in Illinois.

In such crowded houses there is an obvious problem of order. How families of four, six, eight children even keep out of each other's way in such small quarters remains a mystery to me. In my own interviewing experience in the mountains, I've yet to enter a home in which the beds were not made, regardless of the time of day. And remember living room and bedroom may all be the same.

There is some evidence that such order purchased at the price of harsh authoritarianism which demands conformity from the children, and the repression of hostility among the family members. The scope of this authority among farm families extends also to the work-sets. One careful student of mountain culture who lived in many homes while gathering his data has offered the hypothesis that the displacement of repressed feelings may explain the widespread bickering, lawin', and various forms of conflict which are so obviously present in Southern Mountain neighborhoods.

Religious Beliefs and Practices Are Dominated by the Fundamentalist and Literalist Interpretations of the Bible, and Although Not Promoted by Active Church Organizations, These Beliefs Permeate the Society

It is considerably easier to provide evidence for the low level of church participation than for the idea of religious beliefs permeating the society. Membership rates in the eastern mountain area of Kentucky are probably not much above 20 per cent of the population, and when we note further the infrequency of services for rural churches and the general shortage of pastors, it is evident that participation rates will be well below those of our urban areas.

The degree to which religion permeates the society is difficult to measure. It's something you learn about as you listen to and talk with people, as you listen to school children, note the signs along the highways and in the country stores. The following summarizes the matter well: "To an outsider coming in, it is a source of wonder how universally religion is recognized in the mountains. Practically everyone acknowledges its claims, whether he does anything about them or not. Almost no one opposes or deprecates religion."

Emphasis on a hereafter, lovely in its promise of tangible goods and a reversal of the ranks of the present society, has been noted frequently by observers of religious behavior among the poor. Rural church services in the mountains among the various "holiness" groups are noted for their extremes of emotional display. To interpret this as a culturally acceptable outlet for normally restrained emotions would seem to be a logical extension of the preceding analysis.

Education Through the Schools Has Been Serving the Rather Minimal Needs for the 3 r's in a Family-Centered, Low Productivity Economy Infused with Other Worldly Values

Throughout the rural farm areas of the Southern States the proportion of adults aged 25 and over whose formal schooling stopped before the completion of the eighth grade averages close to 75 per cent. In rural nonfarm regions two-thirds is a fair approximation.

In recent years much interest has been focused on the dropout problem. In one study of the percentage of children enrolled in the fifth grade in 1943–1944 who graduated eight years later from high school, Wisconsin topped the list with 80 per cent; Illinois was 65, well above the national average of 52. The Southern States with mountain counties ranged from a low in Georgia of 22 per cent to 41 in West Virginia. The Kentucky figure of 35 per cent means that only 35 out of every 100 in the fifth grade as of 1943–1944 finished high school within eight years. We are on the upward road in this regard but the vista that I see ahead is long and steep.

Such data can only mean that the vast majority of the Southern Mountain Newcomers will have received inadequate formal education, judged by urban standards. For both the teachers of children and those who would find some way to involve the older newcomers in adult education, getting acceptance of the value of schooling is a difficult undertaking. Most of our schools are probably oriented to the values of the middle class and taught by representatives of this class. Such values are not part of the experience world of most people from the mountains, and their values are, conversely, not part of the experience world of their teachers and those who would help them.

The present concern with dropouts, and the discovery of the extent to which this is concentrated among lower status persons has intensified the concern of educators to find some way to bridge these cultural worlds. We have plenty of evidence that these people have adequate learning capacity. The problem is one of getting them to accept the values and experiences which the educational system has to offer.

The Leisure Time of Adults and Children Is Not Usually Organized Around Competitive Activities

Rural life in the mountains has a relaxed quality about it which may lead one to the erroneous conclusion that they never work hard. This is far from the truth as anyone knows who has shared in the tasks of a household of numerous children but devoid of running water, automatic heating, and the like. The largely unmechanized agriculture requires a large output of energy, and those who cut the timber from precipitous mountain slopes or mine the coal are hardly engaged in sedentary occupations. Such activities surely do not call for a game of gold or tennis, when the day's work is over. "Jus' settin' " on the porch is much more appropriate. . . .

It Is Expected that Fear, Pain, and Hardship Will Not Be Expressed, and Demonstrations of Affection and Joy Are Subject to Cultural Controls

I have no statistical measurement of the extent to which mountain people are conditioned to repress open expression of the feelings associated with hardship, pain, and fear. Pride is of course involved in these phenomena, but one psychiatric social worker has written of the way in which coal miners drive themselves back to the mines, never admitting their fears, until for some the repressions come forth as a characteristic neurosis.

And then I recall a conversation with a Red Cross worker in Hazard, Kentucky, during the great flood there one January and February. She spoke of having worked in disaster situations in many parts of the nation, but she had never encountered people so unwilling to reveal the extent to which they had been damaged by the flood. Perhaps some of the high rejection rates noted by Selective Service in this area is a result of the patterned emphasis on not admitting the need for medical care and taking steps to get it. . . .

The need the children show for openly expressed affection is an observation which has been impressed on me repeatedly and which others who visit mountain schools notice. To get close to a warmly affectionate adult, to touch the person—these seem experiences of great value to mountain children. From what I know of their family life, this search for affection is understandable.

The Rights of Individuals to Independence of Relief and Action Are to be Vigorously Defended Against Criticism and Interference by Others

The two aspects of this proposition probably find their best documentation in novels and stories of mountain life, plus the daily newspapers of the region. Both the independence and vigorous defense of this independence probably have their cultural roots in isolated rural living, historic rebellion against the landed classes of the seaboard states and the cotton economy of the South, and the permissiveness of child-rearing practices.

I find such independence manifesting itself in the "right-to-differ." One expects this right for himself, and extends it to others. But those who differ must adopt a laissez-faire attitude toward each other's differences. Among many examples of this spirit let me cite a few. On learning about a unique way of house construction proposed by a visitor whose idea had been subject to much scoffing by urban acquaintances, one mountain man remarked, "It's a free country, ain't it? A man's got a right to do what he wants. . . ."

Racial integration in schools has taken place in numerous mountain counties of eastern Kentucky and West Virginia without serious difficulties. For about 30 years following the Civil War the student body of Berea College was about equally divided between white and Negro, and our integration today, though on much smaller scale, has been without difficulty. I submit that such events as I have mentioned could not have occurred unless the culture of these people had given them the expectation of accepting the different.

To have someone out of the South make such a statement today must indeed give rise to honest doubts. I am aware that there are thousands of low-status whites coming into northern cities bearing a heavy load of prejudice towards all sorts of differences. But I do not believe my mountain neighbors have been the victims of this spiritual disease quite so intensively. Those responsible for programs calling for integration where Southern Mountain Newcomers are involved can, I believe, act with the confidence that clearly stated and well-administered programs will be accepted with tolerance.

CONCLUSION

As with other migrant groups who have come to Chicago, a considerable amount of acculturation of the newcomers is to be expected; many of their children will lose most evidences of their mountain background. But many of them will simply exchange the status of "newcomer from the Southern Mountains" for the status of lower class.

We have every reason to expect the continuation of this migration-stream if the following assumptions hold true: first, the continued growth of employment opportunities in the Chicago Metropolitan Area; second, the continuation of the high effective fertility rate now present in the mountains.

Our economic analyst has concluded that eastern Kentucky has presently twice as many people as can be adequately employed. There is good reason to believe this applies to much of the rest of the mountain South. Presently most of these people are deeply attached to the values of land ownership and farming. Industrial employment will not attract them except on terms far beyond what employers would be willing to offer. If the expectations of these people ever rise above the level which can be met by staying on their small farms, the potential stream of out-migrants will have expanded greatly.

The satisfactoriness both for the newcomers and for the oldtimers of future movements population groups such as this one would seem to depend upon the following conditions. First, if helping agents can obtain and make use of insights into not only the cultural background of the newcomers but also the meaning of the urban situation for them, then a more beneficial adjustment for all can result. Second, I believe there is no doubt that a better solution must be found for the problems of housing and residential areas than has yet been achieved. Third, the youngsters in the mountains need to be prepared for urban adjustment through improving and extending their formal education, through diversifying their social and cultural experiences with other people, and through orienting and training them for the possible kinds of employment the city has to offer.

The accomplishment of this tremendous task requires resources far beyond those which can be supplied by any of the states from which these folks come. Is it possible that those states which get the best years of the newcomers' lives might transfer resources to the states which are responsible for preparing them for adult living?

Frank Riessman
Psychologist, Mobilization for Youth, Inc.

16/ The Overlooked Positives of Disadvantaged Groups * †

I have been interested in the problems of lower socio-economic groups for about 15 years, during most of which time there has been a lack of concern for the educational problems of children from low-income families. In the last five years, however, this attitude has changed markedly. There is now an enormous interest on the part of practitioners and academic people in this problem. I think we are on the point of a major breakthrough in terms of dealing with this question.

After appraising a good deal of the recent work that has been done on the education of disadvantaged children, I feel that there is a considerable agreement regarding many of the recommendations for dealing with the problem, although there are some very different emphases. What is missing, however, is a theoretic rationale to give meaning and direction to the action suggestions. I should like to attempt to provide the beginnings of such a rationale.

I think that a basic theoretic approach here has to be based on the culture of lower socio-economic groups and more particularly the elements of strength, the positives in this culture. The terms "deprived," "handicapped," "underprivileged," "disadvantaged," unfortunately emphasize environmental limitations and ignore the positive efforts of low-income individuals to cope with their environment. Most approaches concerned with educating the disadvantaged child either overlook the positives entirely, or merely mention in passing that there are positive features in the culture of low socio-economic groups, that middle-class groups might learn from, but they do not spell out what these strengths are, and they build educational programs almost exclusively around the weaknesses or deficits.

I want to call attention to the positive features in the culture and the psychology of low income individuals. In particular, I should like to look at the cognitive style, the mental style or way of thinking characteristics of these people. One major dimension of this style is slowness.

---

*This is a revision of an opening address at the Conference on Education of Disadvantaged Children, held by the Office of Education, May 21–23, 1962, Washington, D. C.

†Permission to reprint granted by the publishers, the *Journal of Negro Education* (Washington, D.C.: Howard University).

SLOW VS. DULL

Most disadvantaged children are relatively slow in performing intellectual tasks. This slowness is an important feature of their mental style and it needs to be carefully evaluated. In considering the question of the slowness of the deprived child, we would do well to recognize that in our culture there has probably been far too much emphasis on speed. We reward speed. We think of the fast child as the smart child and the slow child as the dull child. I think this is a basically false idea. I think there are many weaknesses in speed and many strengths in slowness.

The teacher can be motivated to develop techniques for rewarding slow pupils if she has an appreciation of some of the positive attributes of a slow style of learning. The teacher should know that pupils may be slow for other reasons than because they are stupid.

A pupil may be slow because he is extremely careful, meticulous or cautious. He may be slow because he refuses to generalize easily. He may be slow because he can't understand a concept unless he does something physically, e.g., with his hands, in connection with the idea he is trying to grasp.

The disadvantaged child is typically a physical learner and the physical learner is generally a slower learner. Incidentally, the physical style of learning is another important characteristic of the deprived individual and it, too, has many positive features hitherto overlooked.

A child may be slow because he learns in what I have called a one-track way. That is, he persists in one line of thought and is not flexible or broad. He does not easily adopt other frames of reference, such as the teachers, and consequently he may appear slow and dull.

Very often this single-minded individual has considerable creative potential, much of which goes unrealized because of lack of reinforcement in the educational system.

Analysis of the many reasons for slowness leads to the conclusion that slowness should not be equated with stupidity. In fact, there is no reason to assume that there are not a great many slow, gifted children.

The school in general does not pay too much attention to the slow gifted child but rather is alert to discover fast gifted children. Excellence comes in many packages and we must begin to search for it among the slow learner's as well as among the faster individuals.

My own understanding of some of the merits of the slow style came through teaching at Bard College, where there is an enrollment of about 350 students. There I had the opportunity of getting to know quite well about 40 students over a period of four years. I could really see what happened to them during this time. Very often the students I thought were slow and dull in their freshman year achieved a great deal by the time they became seniors. These are not the overall bright people who are typically selected by colleges, but in some area, in a one-tract way, these students did some marvelous creative work. It was too outstanding to be ignored. I discovered in talking with students that most of them had spent five or six years in order to complete college. They had failed courses and made them up in summer school. Some had dropped out of college for a period of time and taken courses in night school. These students are slow learners, often one-tract learners, but very persistent about something when they develop an interest in it. They have a fear of being overpowered by teachers in situations where they don't accept the teacher's point of view, but they stick to their own particular way of seeing the problem. They don't have a fast pace, they don't catch on quickly and they very often fail subjects.

At the present time, when there is a measure of public excitement for reducing the four-year college to three years, I would submit that many potentially excellent students need a five or six year span to complete a college education.

The assumption that the slow pupil is not bright functions, I think, as a self-fulfilling prophecy. If the teachers act toward these pupils as if they were dull, the pupils will frequently come to function in this way. Of course, there are pupils who are very well developed at an early age and no teacher can stop them. But in the average development of the young person, even at the college level, there is need for reinforcement. The teacher must pick up what he says, appeal to him, and pitch examples to him. Typically this does not occur with the slow child. I find in examining my own classroom teaching that I easily fall into the habit of rewarding pupils whose faces light up when I talk, who are quick to respond to me and I respond back to them. The things they say in class become absorbed in the repertoire of what I say. I remember what they say and I use it in providing examples, etc. I don't pick up and select the slower pupil and I don't respond to him. He has to make it on his own.

In the teacher training program future teachers should be taught to guard against the almost unconscious and automatic tendency of the teacher to respond to the pupil who responds to him.

HIDDEN VERBAL ABILITY

A great deal has been said about the language or verbal deficit supposedly characteristic of disadvantaged children. Everybody in the school system, at one time or another, has heard that these children are inarticulate, non-verbal, etc. But is not this too simple a generalization? Aren't these children quite verbal in out-of-school situations? For example, that the educationally deprived child can be quite articulate in conversation with his peers is well illustrated by the whole language developed by urban Negro groups, some of which is absorbed into the main culture via the Beatnick and the musician, if you dig what I mean.

Many questions about the verbal potential of disadvantaged children must be answered by research. Under what conditions are they verbal? What kind of stimuli do they respond to verbally? With whom are they verbal? What do they talk about? What parts of speech do they use? Martin Deutsch of New York Medical College is doing some very significant research trying to specify these factors and I surveyed some of his findings in my book, *The Culturally Deprived Child*. I think Deutsch is getting at some very interesting things. One technique he uses is a clown that lights up when the children say something. "Inarticulate" children can be very verbal and expressive in this situation.

Disadvantaged children are often surprisingly articulate in role-playing situations. One day when I was with a group of these youngsters, sometimes mistaken for a "gang," I asked them, "Why are you sore at the teachers?" Even though I was on good terms with them, I could not get much of a response. Most of them answered in highly abbreviated sentences. However, after I held a role-playing session in which some of the youngsters acted out the part of the teachers while others acted out the parts of the pupils, these "inarticulate" youngsters changed sharply. Within a half-hour they were bubbling over with very verbal and very sensitive answers to the questions I had asked earlier. They were telling me about the expressions on the teachers' faces that they did not like. They reported that they knew the minute they entered the room that the teacher did not like them and that she did not think they were going to do well in school. Their analyses were specific and remarkably verbal.

However, the quality of language employed has its limitations and I think herein lies the deficit. As Basil Bernstein indicates, the difference is between formal language and public language, between a language in a written book and the informal, everyday language. There is no question in my mind that there is a deficit in formal language. Since this deficit is fairly clear, the question might be asked, why make such an issue of the positive verbal ability to these children.

The reason is that it is easy to believe, that too many people have come to believe, that this formal deficit in language means that deprived people are characteristically non-verbal.

On the other hand, if the schools have the idea that these pupils are basically very good verbally, teachers might approach them in a different manner. Teachers might look for additional techniques to bring out the verbal facility. They might abandon the prediction that deprived children will not go very far in the education system and predict instead that they can go very far indeed because, they have very good ability at the verbal level. In other words, an awareness of the positive verbal ability—not merely potential—will lead to demanding more of the disadvantaged child and expecting more of him.

EDUCATION VS. THE SCHOOL

There is a good deal of evidence that deprived children and their parents have a much more positive attitude towards education than is generally believed. One factor that obscures the recognition of this attitude is that while deprived individuals value education, they dislike the school. They are alienated from the school and they resent the teachers. For the sake of clarity, their attitude towards education and toward the school must be considered separately.

In a survey conducted a few years ago, people were asked, "What did you miss most in life that you would like your children to have?" Over 70 per cent of the lower, socio-economic groups answered, "Education." The answer was supplied by the respondents, not checked on a list. They could have answered "money," "happiness," "health," or a number of things. And I think this is quite significant. Middle-class people answer "education" less frequently because they had an education and do not miss it as much.

A nation-wide poll conducted by Roper after World War II asked, "If you had a son or daughter graduating from high school, would you prefer to have him or her go on to college, do something else, wouldn't care?" The affirmative response to the college choice was given by 68 per cent of the "poor," and 91 per cent for the more prosperous. The difference is significant, but 68 per cent of the poorer people is a large, absolute figure and indicates that a large number of these people are interested in a college education for their children.

Why then do these people who have a positive attitude towards education, hold a negative attitude towards the schools? These youngsters and their parents recognize that they are second-class citizens in the school and they are angry about it. From the classroom to the PTA they discover that the school does not like them, does not respond to them, does not appreciate their culture, and does not think they can learn.

Also, these children and their parents want education for different reasons than those presented by the school. They do not easily accept the ideas of expressing yourself, developing yourself, or knowledge for its own sake. They want education much more for vocational ends. But underneath there is a very positive attitude towards education and I think this is predominant in the lower socio-economic Negro groups. In the Higher Horizons program in New York City the parents have participated eagerly once they have seen that the school system is concerned about their children. One of the tremendously positive features about this program is the concern for disadvantaged children and the interest in them. This the deprived have not experienced before and even if the programs did nothing else, I believe that the parents and the children would be responsive and would become involved in the school, because of the demonstrated concern for them.

SOME WEAKNESSES

A basic weakness of deprived youngsters which the school can deal with is the problem of "know-how." Included here is the academic "know-how" of the school culture as well as the "know-how" of the middle class generally. Knowing how to get a job, how to appear for an interview, how to fill out a form, how to take tests, how to answer questions and how to listen.

The last is of particular importance. The whole style of learning of the deprived is not set to respond to oral or written stimuli. These children respond much more readily to visual kinesthetic signals. We should remodel the schools to suit the styles and meet the needs of these children. But no matter how much we change the school to suit their needs, we nevertheless have to change these children in certain ways; namely, reading, formal language, test taking and general "know-how."

These weaknesses represent deficienies in skills and techniques. However, there is one basic limitation at the value level, namely the anti-intellectual attitudes of deprived groups. It is the only value of lower socio-economic groups which I would fight in the school. I want to make it very clear that I am very much opposed to the school spending a lot of time teaching values to these kids. I am much more concerned—and in this I am traditional—that the schools impart skills, techniques and knowledge rather than training the disadvantaged to become good middle-class children.

However, I think there is one area indigenous to the school which has to be fought out at some point with these youngsters; that is their attitude toward intellectuals, towards knowledge for its own sake, and similar issues.

These children and their parents are pretty much anti-intellectual at all levels. They do not like "eggheads." They think talk is a lot of bull. I would consciously oppose this attitude in the school. I would make the issue explicit. There would be nothing subtle or covert about it. I would at some point state clearly that on this question the school does not agree with them and is prepared to argue about the views they hold.

OTHER POSITIVE DIMENSIONS

In my book, *The Culturally Deprived Child,* and in various speeches, I have elaborated more fully on these and other positive dimensions of the culture and style of educationally deprived people. A brief list would include the following: cooperativeness and mutual aid that mark the extended family; the avoidance of the strain accompanying competitiveness and individualism; the equalitarianism, in informality and humor; the freedom from self-blame and parental over-protection; the children's enjoyment of each other's company and lessened sibling rivalry, the security found in the extended family and a traditional outlook; the enjoyment of music, games, sports and cards; the ability to express anger; the freedom from being word-bound; an externally oriented rather than an introspective outlook; a spatial rather than temporal perspective; an expressive orientation in contrast to an instrumental one; content-centered not a form-centered mental style; a problem-centered rather than an abstract-centered approach; and finally, the use of physical and visual style in learning.

SUMMARY AND IMPLICATIONS

I have attempted to reinterpret some of the supposedly negative aspects —e.g., slowness—that characterize the cognitive style of disadvantaged individuals. I have given particular attention to the untapped verbal ability of these individuals amd have indicated the basic weaknesses of the disadvantaged child which the school must overcome, such as the lack of school know-how, anti-intellectualism, and limited experience with formal language. Others which should be noted here are poor auditory attention, poor time perspective, inefficient test-taking skills, and limited reading ability.

The school must recognize these deficiencies and work assiduously to combat them. They are by no means irreversible, but even more important, because neglected, the positive elements in the culture and style of lower socio-economic groups should become the guide lines for new school programs and new educational techniques for teaching these children.

There are a number of reasons why it is important to emphasize the positive:

1. It will encourage the school to develop approaches and techniques, including possibly special teaching machines, appropriate for the cognitive style of deprived children.

2. It will enable children of low income backgrounds to be educated without middle-classifying them.

3. It will stimulate teachers to aim high, to expect more and work for more from these youngsters. Thus, it will constrain against patronization and condescension, and determinate, double-track systems where the deprived child never arrives on the main track.

4. It will function against the current tendency of over-emphasizing both vocational, non-academic education for children of low-income background.

5. It will provide an exciting challenge for teachers if they realize that they need not simply aim to "bring these children up to grade level," but rather can actually develop new kinds of creativity.

6. It will make the school far more pluralistic and democratic because different cultures and styles will exist and interact side by side. Thus, each can learn from the other and the empty phrase that the teacher has much to learn

from deprived children will take on real meaning. General cultural interaction between equal cultures can become the hallmark of the school.

7. It will enable the teacher to see that when techniques, such as role-playing and visual aids are used with deprived children, it is because these techniques are useful for eliciting the special cognitive style and creative potential of these children. All too often these techniques have been employed with the implicit assumption that they are useful with children who have inadequate learning ability.

8. It will lead to real appreciation of slowness, one-track learning and physical learning as potential strengths which require careful nurturing. The teacher will have to receive special training in how to respond to these styles, how to listen carefully to the one-track person, how to reward the slow learner, etc. Special classes for slow learners will not culminate in the removal of these youngsters from the mainstream of the educational process on a permanent second track, and longer periods of time in school and college can be planned for these students without invidious connotations.

Dr. Irving Taylor, who has been concerned with various types of creativity in our American society, has observed that the mental style of the socially and economically disadvantaged learners resembles the mental style of one type of highly creative persons. Our schools should provide for the development of these unique, untapped national sources of creativity.

IV/ THE EDUCATION OF CHILDREN FROM DIVERSE SUBCULTURES

17 / Issues in Educating the Culturally Disadvantaged †

"The child was diseased at birth, striken with a hereditary ill that only the most vital of men are able to shake off. I mean poverty—the most deadly and prevalent of all diseases."—Eugene O'Neill, *Fog*

Culturally disadvantaged youth—and by this we usually mean poverty-stricken youth—are the subject of growing interest among the nation's educators. For the most part, the problem of educating this group is an ancient one, but it is becoming more and more visible as rural slums are transplanted to the great city, where they grow and fester. (The problem still exists in rural areas, of course, in all its depressing forms.[1]) Because urbanization and migration to the cities continue unabated, concern will mount.

Recognition of the problem and initiation of steps to solve it are manifest in many districts across the country. A recent issue of the *NEA Journal*[2] devotes fifteen pages to seven articles on programs and approaches. The progenitor of these programs began as the Guidance Demonstration Project in New York City in 1956. Eminently successful, it was later expanded and renamed Higher Horizons.

The Higher Horizons program served as a model for myriad other programs, including the Ford Foundation Great Grey Areas programs, Houston's Talent Preservation project, Phoenix's Careers for Youth, and Seattle's Disadvantaged Student program. The first state-wide program based on the Higher Horizons formula was started as Project ABLE by New York state in 1961. It provides $200,000 annually in state funds on a 50-50 matching basis to sixteen different city, village, and suburban communities. Four other states are now planning or considering similar programs: Maine, Rhode Island, Pennsylvania, and California. The California legislature recently approved a proposal for an Environment Enrichment program in which $324,000 in state funds will go to school districts.

*Mr. Kaplan (Theta 1029) is coordinator, Project ABLE, Bureau of Guidance, New York State Education Department, Albany. He was on leave during 1962–63 to serve as assistant director, NEA Project on School Dropouts.

†Reprinted by permission of the Phi Delta Kappan and author.

[1]Robert M. Isenberg, "The Rural Disadvantaged." *NEA Journal,* Vol. 52, No. 4 (April 1963).

[2]*NEA Journal,* Vol. 52, No. 4 (April 1963).

While many communities are becoming aroused to the needs and are showing interest, a number of issues connected with establishing Higher Horizons-type programs need discussion.

ISSUE I. WHO ARE THE DISADVANTAGED AND HOW ARE THEY IDENTIFIED?

Are all pupils who live in slum neighborhoods disadvantaged? Do all pupils from minority groups and urban areas qualify for such programs? Should we call them "culturally deprived," "impoverished," "disadvantaged," or something else? Can entire "culturally deprived" schools be selected for such programs, or do we work with only selected cases within these schools?

Frank Riessman, in his recent book titled *The Culturally Deprived Child,*[3] uses these terms interchangeably: culturally deprived, educationally deprived, underprivileged, disadvantaged, lower class, lower socio-economic. He points out that by 1970 one out of two public school pupils in these cities will be "culturally deprived." Indeed, this is already the case in Washington, D. C., Baltimore, Wilmington, and Philadelphia.

Whether we choose to call these pupils disadvantaged, culturally deprived, or economically impoverished, they usually exhibit two characteristics: they are from the lower socio-economic groups in the community and they are notably deficient in cultural and academic strengths. The latter characteristic is usually, but not always, a consequence of the first factor. The parents of these children have simply been unable to provide the quality of background, outlook, initial grounding, and readiness for formal learning that middle- and upper-class parents provide as a matter of course. And all too often our schools have been almost exclusively geared to the mores of the latter group.

Identifying or designating certain pupils or schools as culturally disadvantaged remains a local problem. Sometimes 90 per cent or more of the student body may unquestionably fit this designation, and consequently the entire school may require a special program. In other cases, perhaps 50 per cent of the student body can be regarded as culturally disadvantaged, while in most schools the ratio is more likely one disadvantaged pupil to three up to ten not underprivileged. These latter schools face the problem of how to provide a program for only a portion of the school's enrollment (usually scattered throughout all grade levels), how to select and exclude specific individuals (border-line cases are the toughest), and finally, how this group should be designated. One Project ABLE elementary school in a New York state village has students dispersed throughout the school, with anywhere from one to six in a class of twenty-five to thirty. Another Project ABLE program in a small city not far away has identified its sixth-grade disadvantaged young-

[3]Frank Riessman, *The Culturally Deprived Child* (New York: Harper and Brothers, 1962).

sters and brought them together in a pilot program in one classroom under one highly competent male teacher.

As to what terms to use, the impact of labeling individuals or schools as culturally deprived, no matter how accurate this term may in fact be, is best illustrated by what happened to an elementary principal in New York state. As a project director of a "culturally deprived" school, he had so termed it to teachers and board members. At a meeting of representatives from all Project ABLE schools in the state, he found that the neighborhood school he had attended as a boy was a Project ABLE school. When he heard this, his first reaction was, "That's ridiculous! My old school? That neighborhood's not culturally deprived!" The character of the neighborhood may have changed since his day, but the important point is that an intelligent, dedicated individual directing his efforts and ingenuity to improving the educational level of his culturally disadvantaged students failed to recognize the denigrating effect of the phrase until it was applied to *him*.

Most programs for culturally deprived pupils are now being given euphonious (or euphemistic) titles, frequently chosen by the pupils themselves. These titles can be indicative of the purpose and spirit of the programs without overtone of denigration: Higher Horizons, Project ABLE, Operation Bootstrap, Springboard, New Frontiers, Wings, Project Mercury, Project HELP, Talent Demonstration.

ISSUE II. ARE PROGRAMS FOR THE DISADVANTAGED "FAIR" TO OTHER SCHOOL CHILDREN?

In districts where special programs have been developed, the provision of extra teachers and counselors, special services, supplies and materials, cultural enrichment trips, and the like are eyed enviously by pupils, teachers, administrators, and parents from non-project schools. This is especially so when the special program is designed for only a segment of the school's enrollment. Some administrators have felt that this is an insuperable handicap and hesitate to develop special programs for this reason. It is also argued that these programs are unfair to non-project children because they cost most on a per-pupil basis.

Such objections are not new to education. They have been raised with regard to special education for the physically handicapped, mentally retarded, gifted and academically talented, and emotionally disturbed. Few people now feel that special educational problems do not merit special programs and additional costs. It is true that a compensatory educational experience for the disadvantaged group almost always entails additional expenditures. However, it can be argued that *equal* educational opportunity for these youngsters does not necessarily mean the same *kind* of education; in most cases, it means equal *plus* more of the same in greater depth, quality, and appropriateness.

If some school board members are reluctant to allocate additional funds to certain sub-groups, let them calm their doubts in the knowledge that, almost without fail, these programs bring sparkling dividends which benefit the rest of the school program and the wider community. For example, practices, approaches, and experiences developed by teachers in these programs are often transferrable, with little or no additional cost, to other classes and schools in the district. The impact on the school's morale is evident in this excerpt from a Project ABLE director's report:

> When the project began, a few teachers in the project schools were skeptical of its value. At the end of the first year of operation everyone associated with the project—students, parents, school and community personnel alike—is enthusiastic and hopeful it will be expanded. The most frequently expressed comments are "This is wonderful; let's have more of it!" or "At last we are able to do what we've always known should be done."
>
> At first it was a little difficult to interest teachers in giving the extra time required. Now we have lists of teachers, many from faculties other than those of the project schools, who are anxious to participate.

Finally, school board members and community leaders are beginning to see clearly, especially with regard to school dropouts, that a greater investment *now* constitutes a saving to the community in the long run, when this investment is balanced with resultant lower costs for welfare, unemployment benefits, institutional and rehabilitative services, and greater earnings and citizen productivity.

ISSUE III. ARE PROGRAMS FOR THE DISADVANTAGED JUST ANOTHER METHOD OF MAINTAINING DE FACTO SEGREGATION?

Some educators and observers have wondered whether these programs might not be an attempt to maintain *de facto* school segregation. This is because students in most of the programs are overwhelmingly from minority groups, especially in Northern cities where housing and neighborhood residential patterns have operated to produce *de facto* school segregation in supposedly integrated schools. Segregated schools serving segregated neighborhoods will be excused and even condoned, these people infer, if the programs and services offered by these schools are outstanding and attractive.

These programs, once instituted, in fact tend to produce the reverse effect. Project pupils are given the chance to participate in activities with pupils from all over the school district, often for the first time. Since the purpose of programs for the disadvantaged is to lift the sights and aspirations of these youngsters, the resultant effect, when these attempts are successful, is for greater numbers to select and qualify for academic and honors courses at the high-school level. At this point they associate with white students from middle-class and privileged backgrounds much more frequently and intimately than they otherwise would.

In addition, in view of what has happened to the "separate but equal" doctrine, it is unlikely that the Negro community will tolerate the extension of this practice in a new form, even on a "separate but better" basis.

Programs for the disadvantaged serve to accelerate pupil adjustment, growth in achievement and ability, and readiness, so that these pupils can assume full-fledged membership status in the schools. They develop the ability to benefit from and aspire to whatever opportunities the community's educational system and the future may offer. This is why such organizations as the National Scholarship Service and Fund for Negro Students (NSSFNS) and the National Urban League endorse them enthusiastically.

ISSUE IV. SHOULD PROGRAMS FOR THE DISADVANTAGED CONCENTRATE ON ONE SPECIFIC GRADE LEVEL, E.G., THE ELEMENTARY GRADES?

Some educators argue that programs for the disadvantaged can be most effectively and economically operated if they concentrate at one level, for example, grades 1–3, rather than at a higher level. It is not at all unusual to hear recommendations that "this approach is unquestionably a good one at this level but a far superior job could be done if it had been in effect for these same children one, two, or three years earlier."

Successful or promising programs have been inaugurated at *all* levels.[4] Pre-kindergarten programs for disadvantaged children have been conducted in New York City, Baltimore, and by the state of Pennsylvania's Environment Enrichment program. Kindergarten programs for this group are underway in Racine (Wisconsin), Dayton (Ohio), White Plains (New York), and in Texas for Mexican-American children. Other programs for the disadvantaged cover the full range of grades one through twelve. Project ABLE schools in New York state have programs underway at all levels, although most of them concentrate on grades four through eight. The Higher Horizons program is now operating in grades three through ten.

Indeed, a few colleges have started experimentation with programs and admissions policies and procedures for disadvantaged youth. Bronx Community College in New York City has experimented with special pre-college evening courses in literature, composition, mathematics, and basic study skills. Intensified guidance and counseling has been provided for these youngsters.

---

[4]Daniel Schreiber, "The Dropout and Delinquent: Promising Practices Gleaned from a Year of Study," *Phi Delta Kappan,* Vol. 44, No. 5 (February 1963)

Southern University (Baton Rouge), Dillard University (New Orleans), and Whitworth College (Spokane, Washington) are experimenting with pre-college orientation for these students. Harvard, Brown, and Rhode Island College have relaxed admissions requirements for, and are carefully following up, selected cases.

Since programs are serving the disadvantaged at all levels from pre-kindergarten through college, the important question is not the best grade level on which to focus these activities but rather the most appropriate to *begin.*

The level at which a school system chooses to introduce its program will depend, of course, on a number of factors, among them staff readiness and leadership, facilities, community resources, and parental support.

ISSUE V. DO PROGRAMS FOR THE DISADVANTAGED REQUIRE FOUNDATION FUNDS OR OUTSIDE FINANCIAL SUPPORT?

Admittedly, foundation grants and outside funds are a great asset in getting a program underway, not only because of the extra monies provided but for the aura of approval and support the staff and the community attach to a foundation program. The Ford Foundation's Great Cities Grey Areas program has provided sizeable amounts of money to metropolitan school districts. The College Entrance Examinations Board and the National Service and Scholarship Fund for Negro Students donated funds to get the original Guidance Demonstration project underway in New York City. The Johnson and Western Foundations have made grants to the Racine, Wisconsin, school system for its experimental program. State funds in New York state and Pennsylvania have permitted their respective state education departments to develop projects.

Nevertheless, in a number of cases school systems have begun their programs with little extra expenditures or with the additional funds provided entirely by the local community. In Norfolk, Virginia, a recent replication of the Higher Horizons program was attempted at that city's Jacox Junior High School without outside support. According to a study by Brazziel and Gordon, programs to help disadvantaged children make better use of public education can be carried out in any school at a modest cost.[5]

Some school systems have already developed special activities for the culturally disadvantaged without outside assistance. The National Urban League's Talent Search Bank approach, utilizing community volunteers and resources, has done this for some time.

Sometimes a small or token appropriation is sufficient to launch a suc-

---

[5]William F. Brazziel and Margaret Gordon, "Replications of Some Aspects of the Higher Horizons Program in a Southern Junior High School," *Bulletin of the NASSP,* Vol. 47, No. 281 (March 1963).

cessful demonstration. In New York state during the last few years, the State Education Department has sponsored Talent Search programs in thrity city, village, and suburban school districts. For the most part these are small-scale demonstration projects. NDEA Title V-A funds provided intensified guidance services for underachieving students at the junior high-school level.

In the future, it appears, school systems desiring programs for their culturally disadvantaged students will have to rely primarily on local funds and resources. As with other educational innovations, from programed learning to language laboratories, once educational merit has been established, the introduction of the new program becomes the joint responsibility of the school district and the state.

ISSUE VI. IS ADDITIONAL MONEY ALL THAT'S NEEDED TO LAUNCH A SUCCESSFUL PROGRAM?

Obviously an effective comprehensive program for disadvantaged children requires additional funds. While there may be disagreement about the amount, there is a general consensus that compensatory educational experiences and provisions demand additional expenditures. However, a school district must provide more than money if it is to develop a successful program.

For one thing, even if specialists are added, much will need to be done in the way of orientation and in-service training for the entire staff. Special curricular materials will have to be developed. Program activities, particularly those pertaining to cultural enrichment, work-study experiences, and group guidance will require planning and coordination. If, in addition, team teaching, ungraded primary programs, and other such innovations are to be simultaneously introduced, even greater care must be exercised in making plans. This planning takes time.

Hunter College, Yeshiva University, Newark State Teachers College, and Queens College have each been developing specialized educational programs for their students who will be teaching disadvantaged pupils. The Detroit Public Schools and Bank Street College (New York City), working independently, are developing special materials for teaching reading to culturally disadvantaged pupils at the primary level. One school in Chicago developed its own elementary school readers "replete with slums instead of suburbs as motifs and mixed ethnic groups as characters."[6]

Especially important is the need to work with the entire staff of the schools involved. Many teachers, often unconsciously, may be psychologically rejecting these students; all teachers in such a program should have the opportunity to participate in in-service training to examine their attitudes, expectations, and practices with regard to these youngsters.

[6] *Ibid.*

ISSUE VII. IS THERE A STANDARD TYPE OF SCHOOL PROGRAM FOR THE DISADVANTAGED THAT A COMMUNITY CAN ADOPT?

Some administrators assume that programs for the disadvantaged can be introduced in much the same way that a new educational practice such as television is added. However, the depth, breadth, and exact form that characterize successful programs vary considerably community to community. Some aspects are highlighted in some schools but assume secondary roles in others. Perhaps the best illustration of the variety that can occur is shown by the forty-two programs described in the recent (February, 1963) publication, *School Programs for the Disadvantaged,* prepared by the NEA's Educational Research Service.[7] While these programs share basic similarities, each is unique and must be viewed as reflecting local needs and local leadership. Each school must design and develop its own. Even the Higher Horizons program provides for variation among schools. No two programs in Project ABLE are just alike, though all were planned and initiated during 1961 under State Education Department auspices.

One community can learn from another engaged in a similar program. Visits by teachers and administrators to programs-in-action help to transplant program techniques and rationales from one community to another. In addition, a growing body of research and progress reports is available to interested districts.

ISSUE VIII. ARE PROGRAMS FOR THE DISADVANTAGED UNDULY INFLUENCED BY THE "HAWTHORNE EFFECT"?

These programs, it is claimed, are effective not because of the specific techniques and activities employed but because the children involved feel that they have been selected for special consideration. Given a sugar pill which he thinks is an aspirin, the child reports that his headache has disappeared (the "Hawthorne effect"). It is asserted that it's not *what* is done but merely that something "special" is done and that students know they have been selected for this something special; the end result will still produce substantial improvement in behavior, although the changes may be only temporary.

The research now underway with experimental and control groups will eventually illuminate the validity of these charges. However, it does appear from the evidence already reported that substantial gains in the performances of pupils (test scores, class marks and standings, attendance, educational and vocational goals) and of schools (holding power, discipline, scholarship awards, teacher retention) are achieved merely by the introduction of these

[7]Educational Research Service, *School Programs for the Disadvantaged,* National Education Association, 1963.

programs. Such gains as improved reading skills and increased holding power are not ephemeral in their effect on student achievement and accomplishments. Though student performance *may* no longer continue to improve with a cessation of program activities (thereby supporting the thesis that the "new" motivation is not fully integrated), it is likely that this criticism applies equally well to other facets of the school program, e.g., extracurricular activities or guidance services.

The goal of most Higher Horizons-type programs is to convey to each disadvantaged pupil the feeling that he is the focus of the school's concern and attention. This may be a distinct revelation for many of these pupils. Unless correspondent traits are manifested by the staff and effectively communicated to the pupil and his parents, these programs fall short of their objectives. Some observers feel it is this aspect of the program more than any other that produces the desired changes. Others feel that improved techniques and methods and new opportunities are the key components. Still a third group contends that it is a combination of these two approaches. Of course the two approaches are not mutually exclusive. The Hawthorne criticism, however, applies mainly to the first and third views, i.e, heightened motivation, no matter how it is produced, will bring about (similar) change in student performance. If this is true, a logical question is, What alternative (more effective, less costly, or more efficient) "sugar pill" activities might realistically be substituted?

Some experts suggest that these programs can accomplish their objectives by eliminating all but one or two features, these varying with the needs or resources of the community. Recent research evidence regarding motivation and underachievement suggests that these two phenomena are highly complex; therefore, it appears unlikely that oversimplified or "shortcut" solutions will produce similar changes in student behavior. In fact, even in full-scale Higher Horizons programs, where activities are multiple and varied, a minority of students make no gains.

The importance of motivation, attitudes, and the student's self-image in these programs must not be minimized. The frequency with which these programs report noticeable positive change, first in student demeanor (dress, attendance, interest, speech), and subsequently in academic accomplishments (grades, levels of achievement, skills) emphasizes the importance of including consideration of student attitudes in programs for the disadvantaged.

ISSUE IX. DO PROGRAMS FOR THE DISADVANTAGED OVERLOOK OR MINIMIZE THE ATTRIBUTES OF THE CULTURE OF THESE CHILDREN AND THEIR FAMILIES?

The term "culturally deprived" is now viewed with some disfavor by certain sociologists and educators; more accurate terms, they submit, are "culturally different" or "economically deprived." They maintain that children from impoverished families are *not* culturally deprived in the sense that they are culture*less*. Rather, their cultures and heritages *differ* from those cultivated by the middle-class schools they attend. Programs for the disadvantaged, they say, disregard the special strengths of this group, e.g., their folk humor, physical or manipulative propensities, pragmatism, etc., and condescendingly regard these children as having little if anything positive to offer or to build on in the classroom.

Some critics scold the schools for their rejection of the "culture of poverty" and insist that many of these youths who, in turn, reject the schools by dropping out are wiser and more realistic than their peers who choose to remain.[8]

The claim that school personnel in general and programs for disadvantaged specifically minimize potential non-middle-class contributions and meritorious qualities is probably a fair appraisal. However, there is evidence now that many programs are attempting to foster in their staff a better understanding of the community's disadvantaged and to adapt and develop materials and methods accordingly. For instance, primary readers and materials more realistically attuned to the actual experiences and backgrounds of these children are being developed. (The Board of Education of New York City has recently served notice on textbook publishers that it would no longer purchase social studies texts which do not adequately treat minority groups and deal realistically with intergroup tensions and efforts to relieve them. Other large city systems are considering similar stands.) The New York State Education Department has developed curriculum materials pertaining to the Negro in American history and American society today.[9] The Washington, D.C., public schools are developing similar materials.

Special courses for teachers in training and teachers in service help school personnel gain a better understanding of varying cultural and ethnic groups and their problems. Some programs for the disadvantaged make provision for home visits by teachers and counselors or arrange for periodic, informal discussions with small groups of parents (numbering four to six) in the school. These attempts at improved parental communication and participation also give school personnel more accurate perspective and insight regarding the backgrounds, values, and orientations of disadvantaged families.

Do programs for the disadvantaged, by their mere existence, indicate that the cultures and values of these groups are meaningless and unworthy of consideration in the schools? Are these programs set up primarily to stamp out

[8]Edgar Friedenburg, "An Ideology of School Withdrawal," a chapter in the forthcoming NEA publication, *School Dropouts.* Daniel Schreiber, editor, scheduled for late 1963.
[9]The New York State Education Department, *Intergroup Relations, Resource Handbook for Elementary School Teachers; The Negro in American History,* Division of Intercultural Relations in Education. The New York State Education Department, Albany 1, N. Y., 1963.

cultural differences and to fill the void with values, goals, and habits deemed more acceptable to "society" by school board members or administrators? If this were the case, it would do great violence to the American democratic tradition. It seems more likely that the real aim of these programs is not the blurring and subjugating of differences so much as providing underprivileged pupils with the tools of an education adequate to guarantee them the competence to make their own choices and decisions regarding how they wish to live, to work, to play. Otherwise, their choices are restricted by immediate circumstance and limited environments. As the Educational Policies Commission has pointed out,[10] "If the problem of the disadvantaged is to be solved, the society as a whole must give evidence of its undifferentiated respect for all persons." The commission further asserts:

> The problem of the disadvantaged arises because their cultures are not compatible with modern life. One of the greatest challenges facing the United States today is that of giving all Americans a basis for living constructively and independently in the modern age. *The requirement is not for conformity but for compatibility.* To make all people uniform would be as impractial as it would be inconsistent with American ideals. *To give all people a fair chance to meet the challenge of life* is both practicable and American. [Italics added]

Jacob Landers, coordinator of New York City's Higher Horizons program, in answer to the question, What makes a successful Higher Horizons school?[11] said:

> No amount of increased appropriations, and no change in procedures or organization, can be effective without a fundamental faith in the ability of the children. It is not enough to know intellectually that Negro and Puerto Rican children can learn as well as other children. It must be felt in the marrow of the bones and in the pit of the stomach.
> This belief in the children and pride in their accomplishments must run like a golden thread through the fabric of the school's daily existence. With this feeling, the school poor in services can yet be rich in achievement; without it, the richest services yield but the poorest results.
> Our great enemy is the phrase "as well as can be expected." It implies that the school merely reflects the community, but cannot affect it. It implies an acceptance of the *status quo,* rather than a struggle to change it.
> The true Higher Horizons program spreads faith in children and hope for their future.

The variety of programs which have been developed illustrates that this faith in children and hope for their future can be expressed and fostered in

[10] *Education and the Disadvantaged American,* Educational Policies Commission, NEA, 1962.
[11] *Higher Horizons Bulletin,* December, 1962. Board of Education of the City of New York.

different ways. There will naturally be questions about the most practicable, economical, and beneficial kind of program to develop in a given community. These questions are embraced by the issues discussed here. Only by confronting these squarely and unequivocally will school districts be able to develop successfully their own programs for disadvantaged pupils.

Lillian Dimitroff*

18 / Concept of Self and Teaching Culturally Different People †

A DESCRIPTION OF CULTURALLY DIFFERENT PEOPLE

Culturally different people are those who are not fully accepted in the mainstream of American life today. At the risk of labeling these people, one should remember that we are a culturally pluralistic nation which rather recently has come to recognize the concept of cultural pluralism as being as valid as the concept of the melting pot in describing our nation. Culturally different people have a distinct life style. Though separate from the American mainstream they are not without an Americanized culture of their own. The fact remains, however, that this distinct way of life seems more disadvantageous in meeting the demands of increasing urbanization and of competing in a technologically advanced economy. Generally speaking these people have crowded into the older parts of our major cities; their habitats are described as comprising a ghetto. The people are generally classified as belonging to the lowest socio-economic class whose style of living is not entirely devoid of positive aspects and is preferred by some people. In our major cities these people make up a considerable proportion of the population in comparison with those who could be considered middle class or upper class. At their present rate of increase, within a few years the proportion of these children enrolled in the public schools of our fourteen largest cities will increase to one in two pupils. The difficulties of teaching these children are well known.

*Dr. Dimitroff has taken a sound psychological focus for her research on culturally different people—the concept of self. It is obvious that environment has traumatic effects on this concept, and children from culturally different families are apt to have serious psychological repercussions in their adjustment to the schoolroom. The role of family and parents in such environment is often different from that of the conventional school-age child.

Interestingly, the self-concept is more secure in a younger child and is altered only after a few years in school and exposure to more complex experiences of competition and achievement which threaten his level of confidence.

Dr. Dimitroff also takes a very realistic look at integration and the interracial situation and the problems which were found in such programs as Head Start and the Higher Horizons projects. She has also developed an experimental technique for improving instruction of culturally deprived children and offers specific, practical, and realistic tips to teachers of such programs. These conclusions are based on actual experience, as observed in the inner city schools, and as reported and discussed in the seminars of teachers and intern teachers working in the area.

†Reprinted with permission of Scott, Foresman and Co. and the author.

THE EFFECTS OF A POOR CONCEPT OF SELF

Many reasons have been suggested to explain the learning problems of this segment of our school population. The fact that culturally different pupils have a poor self-concept is worth examining as one of the causes of learning difficulties inasmuch as there is a close relationship between negative self-concept and problems of learning.

A child's concept of self refers to his feeling of self-worth and competency. This self is the product of an individual's social experiences—a mirror of the interaction between the person and the society with which he has had contact. The self, moreover, is a continuum, rooted in the past and influencing behavior in the future. If the experiences of the past have been satisfying enough to build a foundation for a future, the motivation and drive to learn will be present because the self comprehends that his aspirations are within the realm of the possible. On the other hand, many culturally different people—especially Negroes—have developed a poor self-image both as a result of impoverished experiences in the home and deprivation in the community. Although an experience occurred in early childhood and is buried in the subconscious, it is, nevertheless, functioning. "The young child's identity arises partly from what is done to and for him and what he is told about himself . . ."[1] Extreme deprivation in the home has a numbing effect on the intellect of a child living in such an environment. In this type of home as in any other, the young child observes the techniques of dealing with others and their effectiveness in solving problems of daily living.

> As a child . . . begins to explore his small world, he may be continually blocked, scolded, and even punished for his curiosity and his impulsive activity, being told that he is bad and treated as unacceptable or rejected. From these verbalized statements about himself, often colored with strong parental feelings, the child begins to develop an image of the self . . . frequently with feelings of anxiety, shame, guilt, resentment and hostility.[2]

At present genetic aspects have yielded to environmental forces as the primary influence of our most challenging and baffling educational problem. "The more averse and demoralizing are his family life and his neighborhood, the more often his identity may be stunted or distorted."[3]

Such an experience emphasizes a child's observation of adult frustration, helplessness, dependency and even hopelessness. The small child internalizes these experiences especially as they apply to his mother; they become a part of his being; they are the preparation and background which he brings to the

---

[1] Lawrence K. Frank, "Clues to Children's Identity," *Childhood Education*, XLII (January 1966), p. 276.
[2] *Ibid.*, p. 277.
[3] *Loc. cit.*

school. Although the child cannot or will not verbalize how he feels or thinks about himself, his play, coloring, drawing and spontaneous dramatizations communicate his *story about himself.* It behooves teachers to cultivate the sensitivity to the particular "story" which each child brings to the classroom, and with this understanding, to comprehend the educational *milieu* in which they will have to function; it is perhaps quite different from their expectations and preparational background.

A relatively small percentage of children with a culturally disadvantaged outlook succeed in school. Coming from a deprived background, generally speaking, the self which this child brings to school does not prepare him for learning in the usual manner. In the period when this individual should have experienced a satisfying development of his mental and emotional powers, the stupefying and destructive environmental effects have retarded his growth. Consequently, his defeat by school experiences and his bitter emotional reactions to overt as well as covert rebuffs have hardened his negative self-image which, in turn, slows the mastery of skills and content needed for success in our culture. The emotional impact of a culture foreign to that of his school and teachers sometimes can be so devastating to his self as to close the avenues of communication. "A child's life is more greatly affected by the way his emotions develop than by either his physical or mental development. Within rather wide limits, success and happiness in school, in his life work, in his family relations, in his daily living depend much more on his emotional maturity than on his physical or mental maturity."[4] Each reaction, be it mental, physical, social, or emotional, leaves a person a slightly changed human being, and without a healthy means of communication, he is severely handicapped. His emotional maturity is largely a product of his ability to communicate.

Regardless of the race of the culturally different child, his environmental relationships have left him with a negative self-concept. This coupled with a mother-child communication system *lacking in range of* alternativies of thought, action, and cognitive meaning have crippled the child's ability to function in a school situation. Family relationships structure as well as communication and language shape the thought and cognitive styles of problem solving of the individual.[5]

The culturally different child comes to school with a restricted language background characterized by a limited vocabulary, sentence fragments, stereotyped expressions, short sentences, simple grammatical structure, lack of precision, and even substitution of gestures for words. Expectations about the nature of school and what takes place there have been unwittingly represented

[4]J. Murray Lee and Dorris May Lee, *The Child and His Development* (New York, 1967), p. 123.
[5]Robert D. Hess and Virginia C. Shipman, "Early Experience and the Socialization of Cognitive Modes in Children," *Child Development,* XXXVIII (December 1965), p. 870.

by the low-socio-economic mother in a manner which has not helped to prepare her child to profit from school. According to research conducted by Dr. Robert Hess of the University of Chicago this mother might give the following instructions: "Well John, it's time to go to school now. You must know how to behave. The first day at school you should be a good boy and should do just what the teacher tells you to do."[6]

In contrast, research by Dr. Hess revealed that the middle-class mother would instruct her child in the following manner:

> First of all, I would remind her that she was going to school to learn, that her teacher would take my place, and that she would be expected to follow instructions. Also that her time was to be spent mostly in the classroom with other children, and that any questions or any problems that she might have she could consult with her teacher for assistance.[7]

Whereas the first mother represented the role of the child at school as compliant, passive and dependent upon authority, the second parent portrayed the classroom situation as a place to learn. She implied that the child's role would be an active one and that school *would be an extension* of the home experience. For the first child in this comparison, a poor self-image, a disorganized home, poor language background, constant noise, lack of systematic visual stimulation and poor nutrition militate against success at school.

A REVIEW OF PERTINENT RESEARCH

Although the bulk of research relating to aspects of concept of self and the instruction of culturally different children will be reviewed in this section, some studies will be referred to in other portions of this chapter because of their close relationship to subjects under consideration.

CONCEPT OF SELF AND THE FAMILY

As stated above, a child's self-picture stems from early sources and can cast a shadow over the remaining years of his life. The earliest sources of a child's self-picture are his contact with his mother and others in his family. "Once a child has his self-picture, he acts it out. . . . It determines not only his behavior but his mental health, future success, and happiness."[8]

This same point of view concerning the effects of early experiences is

---

[6]*Ibid.*, p. 877.
[7]*Loc. cit.*
[8]Katherine Roe, "Your Child's Self-Picture," *Childhood Education*, XXXVIII (March 1962), p. 333.

supported by a study conducted by James V. Mitchell, who ascertained that the crux of the parent-child relationship seems to be that the child's perception of what his parents are is determined by other people's estimate of the parents. This he considers to be more important than specific characteristics of home life.[9]

For a Negro child, especially, this could be a devastating observation, because he observes that his *parents are relegated* to an inferior position. The above point of view was supported by Mitchell's study of 145 female sophomores at a midwest university; his conclusion follows:

Self-acceptance is influenced appreciably by a satisfying and congenial family life while the development of anxiety and neurotic symptoms will more likely be occasioned by the subject's perception that she is failing to meet standards rather than any dissatisfaction with family life *per se.*[10]

This study confirmed the importance of family life, but for these subjects, injury to ego as a result of unsuccessful competition seemed the crucial factor in good adjustment to the school situation.

The matriarchal family organization, characteristic of many lower-class families, has often been blamed for a child's personality disorders and ultimate failure in school. Certainly, older children are not likely to develop the same self-concept in such an organization. Dodd's study, briefly described below, did not go far enough for conclusive evidence. He attempted to ascertain whether drawings of women made by children who live in a matriarchal society will be more complete than their drawings of men signifying a difference in relationship. The sample consisted of 103 culturally deprived. Negro children between the ages of four and one-half and five and one-half in Buffalo, New York. The results were that both boys and girls drew a greater number of more complete women than men.[11]

The fact that children at this age are very much attached to their mothers is obvious although this study is inconclusive and needs to be followed to its logical conclusion to ascertain whether results are different with older subjects, and whether a matriarchal family organization is *productive* of more personality disorders and learning difficulties than a patriarchal order. Martin Deutsch and Bert Brown investigated 543 urban children to ascertain the effects of the father's absence from the home. Children in father-absent families as compared with those from intact families scored significantly lower on standardized tests; this fact was even more marked at fifth grade level than in the primary grades. This would seem to suggest a negative cumulative effect of

---

[9]James V. Mitchell, "Self-Family Perceptions Related to Self Acceptance, Manifest Anxiety, Neuroticism," *The Journal of Educational Research,* LVI (January 1963), p. 236.

[10]*Ibid.,* p. 242.

[11]John M. Dodd and Robert R. Randall, "A Comparison of Negro Children's Drawings of a Man and a Woman," *The Journal of Negro Education,* XXXV (Summer 1966), p. 287.

father absence.[12] This piece of research does not conclusively answer the question whether lower scores of children from father-absent homes are connected to poor self-image.

CONCEPT OF SELF AND CHILDREN'S ABILITY TO FUNCTION EFFECTIVELY

Beeman Phillips[13] felt there is a "progressive and age-related pattern of development of the self . . . and (it) is a factor in the accuracy of self-perception. As postulated above, older children would provide more accurate information in some types of research. The subjects were four classes of third grade pupils who were tested on a modification of Amatora's Children's Personality Scale to obtain self-ratings. Teacher ratings and peer ratings were also obtained. Findings indicated that sixth grade estimates were closer to reality and in nearer agreement with those of teachers and peers than third grade estimates.[14] This study also disclosed that older children with more accurate self-perception may also feel that high academic aspirations may be futile if they belong to a culturally *disadvantaged group*. This feeling may be reinforced by statistics which show that as culturally disadvantaged boys and girls progress through school both their I.Q. and performance deteriorate.

For the culturally disadvantaged, the self-concept has been shown to deteriorate as the child gets older. "In self-concept are bound up one's hopes, fears, defenses, and self-esteem . . . the nucleus of personality."[15] For the younger child, the school is a secure and protective place. It is at the third grade level that the self-concept seems to take a precipitous drop; this is also the time when many culturally disadvantaged children begin to have really serious learning problems in school. Morse analyzed the responses of more than six hundred pupils in alternate grades from three through eleven to a Self-Esteem Inventory. The third grade responded in a significantly different manner; they showed a high self-regard. After this grade, results showed a significant decrease in concept of self which improved again in the eleventh grade. Even in this improved period, 44 per cent of the eleventh graders wished they were somebody else.[16]

These replies certainly indicate the degree of discouragement in both the elementary and secondary school. Just as important is the implicit suggestion

---

[12]Benjamin S. Bloom, Allison Davis, and Robert Hess, *Compensatory Education for Cultural Deprivation* (New York, 1965), p. 104.

[13]Beeman N. Phillips, "Age Changes in Accuracy of Self-Perceptions," *Child Development,* XXXIV (December 1963), p. 1041.

[14]*Ibid.,* p. 1044.

[15]William C. Morse, "Self-Concept in the School Setting," *Childhood Education,* XLI (December 1964), p. 196.

[16]*Ibid.,* p. 197.

to educators that the longer boys and girls are in school the less positive is the self-concept. The problem is to make school children educationally productive instead of struggling with a sense of failure.

The law of this land is that schools shall be racially integrated. A pertinent piece of research by Webster and Kroger was concerned with ascertaining how integrated adolescent associations affected Negro concepts of self. In three integrated high schools in the San Francisco Bay area, over 300 Negro adolescents were tested with a questionnaire. The following information was sought:

1. Will Negro subjects with white friends score significantly higher on measures of personal independence than Negro subjects without white friends?

2. Will Negro subjects with white friends report significantly higher scores in respect to these points?

a. Social competence: this referred to a subject's feelings of social competency, that is, how competent and comfortable he felt about his abilities to interact socially with others.

b. Intellectual esteem: this focused on a subject's estimate and confidence in his intellectual ability.

c. Physical esteem: this dealt with a subject's level of esteem for his physical attributes.

d. Will total self-concept scores of Negro youths with white friends be higher than those without white friends?

3. Will Negro subjects with white friends report significantly higher scores in regard to levels of aspiration?

a. Will vocational aspirations be higher?

b. Will levels of expected vocational attainment be higher?

c. Will perceptions of potential for later occupational attainment be higher?

4. Will Negro subjects with white friends predict for themselves significantly higher levels of future social acceptance by the total society?

5. Will Negro subjects with white friends score significantly lower in respect to ethnic concern or anxiety?

6. Will Negro subjects with white friends score significantly lower on a measure of group esteem, that is, display ethnocentrism?

7. Will Negro subjects reporting no white friendships state a significantly greater preference for associations with Negroes?

Results supported an affirmative answer to all the questions. An important exception, however, was the physical esteem dimension which did not produce any significantly different scores for the two groups. As in some other studies, the possession of Negroid features with a high level of visibility constitutes a reality for all Negroes regardless of their outlook or Caucasian friendships. Concerning the sixth question regarding feelings or anxiety over being a Negro, the scores reported for the two groups were not significantly different. Likewise, no significant difference was indicated by the two groups as to their levels of esteem for Negroes as a group, but the subjects without Caucasian friendships expressed a preference for associating with Negroes.[17]

Although the self-concept of Negroes as a group is lower than among Caucasians, obviously it is not uniformly so. Inasmuch as accepted attitudes and behaviors of any ethnic group exert a powerful influence upon its members, it would seem that the adolescents with white friendships displayed a higher degree of independence, inner strength, and self-concept than the average. In addition, the group with the higher self-concepts and the Caucasian friendships would naturally raise the level of its experiences, human contacts, and vocational goals. No doubt, their lives were thus enriched. Inasmuch as a positive self-concept contributes to optimum educational attainment, this group probably displayed higher academic achievement, although this was not a part of the Webster-Kroger conclusions.

RELATIONSHIP BETWEEN CONCEPT OF SELF AND READING

Reading is a necessary skill for satisfactory educational progress, and research concerning the self in relation to the development of this skill is pertinent to the subject under consideration. There has been evidence for a period of years that there is a relationship between a poor self-concept and severe retardation in reading. The review of some of the research of the last decade supports this point of view. In an unpublished doctoral dissertation, L. Barber of the University of Michigan found that children accepted in remedial reading "displayed anxiety about self and relationships with people to a marked degree."[18]

In an unpublished doctoral study by D. D. Lumpkin at the University of Southern California in 1959, fifth grade overachievers and underachievers were matched in respect to chronological age, mental age, sex, and home background. The overachievers revealed significantly more positive self-concepts.[19]

R. F. Bodwin made a similar type of study of 100 pupils with reading disability, 100 with arithmetic disability and 100 with no educational disability. He found that the relationship between immature self-concepts and reading disability yielded a correlation of .72 at the third grade level and .62 at the sixth grade level.[20]

Research has also sought the relationship between self-concept and aca-

[17]Staten W. Webster and Marie N. Kroger, "A Comparative Study of Selected Perceptions and Feelings of Negro Adolescents with and Without White Friends in Integrated Urban High Schools," *The Journal of Negro Education,* XXXV (Winter 1966), pp. 55–61.
[18]See William W. Wattenberg and Clare Clifford, "Relation of Self-Concepts to Beginning Achievement in Reading," *Child Development,* XXXV (June 1964), p. 461.
[19]*Loc. cit.*
[20]*Loc. cit.*

demic achievement. In Flint, Michigan, M. A. Bruck of Michigan State University measured the self-concept of 300 pupils using samples from the third through sixth grades and from the eleventh grade. This doctoral dissertation revealed a positive and significant relationship between self-concept and grade-point averages *at all grade levels* in which students were considered.[21] In 1960, D. E. Homachek at the University of Michigan School discovered that high achievement and intellectual self-images were related to reading age. Also in that year at Northern Texas State College, L. C. Seay found changes in self-concept were positively associated with experiences in the remedial reading program.[22]

The objective of Wattenberg and Clifford was to determine which was the antecedent phenomenon, a poor self-concept or reading disability. Measures of mental ability and self-concept were obtained during the first semester of kindergarten of 185 children in two elementary schools in Detroit. Two and a half years later, measures of 128 children remaining in these schools were obtained of progress in reading and self-concept. Their hypotheses follow:

1. Measures and ratings of self-concept taken during the first semester of kindergarten will be predictive of later achievement in reading.

2. There will be low correlation between a mental test score and measures and ratings of self-concept.

3. The relationship between reading achievement and changes in measures of self-concept from kindergarten to second grade will be positive but low.

4. Evidence of ego strength will show a high positive correlation with achievement in reading.

5. Ratings of self-concept will display characteristics of defensive reactions; children verbalizing a high ratio of self-reference will show lower success in reading than those demonstrating little preoccupation with self-characteristics.[23]

Evaluation of data supported these hypotheses: the data indicated a definite link between competence and improvement of self-concept, and a decided correlation between kindergarten scores and later reading achievement. This study indicated that self-concept in kindergarten has greater influence in the development of reading skill than the reading experience has upon the self-concept.[24] The results of this study definitely indicated that measures and ratings of self-concept and ego strength in kindergarten were predictive of later reading achievement. Along with tests of mental ability, measures and ratings of self-concept seem to describe the child's potential more accurately than by tests alone. Definitely positive self-concepts were shown to be antece-

---

[21] *Loc. cit.*
[22] *Ibid.*, p. 462.
[23] *Ibid.*, pp. 463–464.
[24] *Ibid.*, p. 465.

dents to and predictive of reading accomplishment and also correlation between feelings of competence and of personal worth was indicated.[25]

SELF-CONCEPT AND THE TEACHER

Understanding the importance of self-concept can assist teachers, counselors, and parents to achieve a deeper understanding and insight into a child's behavior and a better working relationship with children. Information is offered in the studies which follow:

Hugh V. Perkins in 1954–1955 investigated the effects of social-emotional climate; teacher participation in an in-service child study program; and acceptance by teachers and others of the self. The relationship between grade levels and changes in children's self-concepts was defined as an indication of *congruency* between self-*concept* and self-*ideal*. The findings follow:

1. Girls generally registered greater self-ideal congruency than boys, although all children revealed greater congruency between self and ideal-self with passage of time.

2. Greater congruency of self and ideal-self was revealed by children whose teachers are participating in a child study course and by sixth graders.

3. A lack of relationship between changes in children's self-ideal—self-congruency and changes in their acceptance by peers was disclosed.

4. Children achieved increased self-ideal—self-congruency during a period of time that they were in attendance at school.[26]

The results of this study might be different if it were repeated now in a school attended largely by culturally different children.

Earl McCallon postulated that "self and ideal-self concepts are acquired through environmental influences . . . that variation in environment might facilitate or retard the movement toward . . . self-ideal—self-congruency."[27] The purpose of his study was to investigate the relationship between certain teacher characteristics and change in the congruency of children's perception of self and ideal-self. His sample consisted of 47 fifth and sixth grade teachers and their pupils. Results indicated a movement toward greater congruency of self-ideal—self-perception by the children in this study.[28] This researcher believed that teachers exert a strong influence on children's development and the perception of self-ideal—self-relationship.

There has been much research to find the personality characteristics

---

[25] *Ibid.*, p. 466.
[26] Hugh V. Perkins, "Factors Influencing Change in Children's Self-Concepts," *Child Development,* XXIX (June 1958), p. 226.
[27] Earl L. McCallon, "Teacher Characteristics and Their Relationship to Change in the Congruency of Children's Perceptions of Self and Ideal-Self," *Journal of Experimental Education,* XXXIV (Summer 1966), pp. 84–88.
[28] *Ibid.*, p. 87.

which distinguish the effective teacher, but so far no one set of characteristics have been selected as the key which distinguishes the effective teacher. Seeing that self-awareness (how teacher appears to her pupils) is an important factor in teaching behavior, a teacher who has this quality is aware of her impact on the pupils.

The Wright-Sherman study sample consisted of 40 teachers and their pupils. The instruments used for this evaluation were the "Semantic Differential Evaluative Adjectives" and the "Leader-Tyrant Evaluative Statements." These instruments sampled the past of the teachers as well as pupils' feelings towards and impressions of their teachers. The hypothesis was that teacher self-awareness is related to evaluation of childhood authority figures. Four authority figures were used: mother, father, best-liked teacher, and least-liked teacher. Multiple correlation coefficients between teachers' self-awareness and their evaluation of authority figures was .52 for girls and .62 for boys. The findings suggested that self-awareness among women teachers was contingent on the idealization of the mother rather than father and on a moderate rather than on an extreme evaluation of former teacher images. Lack of self-awareness increased with idealization of father.[29] Considering the importance of teacher self-awareness, in working with children in the classroom, one can only assume that the teacher's need for satisfaction and self-respect dictated a low self-awareness to protect the teacher's ego.

Dr. James C. Lafferty of the Wayne County, Michigan Schools found a way to improve the self-concepts of teachers as well as the classroom climate. Instructors showed improvement in mental health after participating in a consulting program which included improvement of skills and self-confidence and analysis of informational levels. The faculty were organized into small groups for discussion and self-study; this program lasted for a year. The results of this program showed positive changes in self-concepts in 50 per cent of the cases.[30]

Teacher training institutions, too, have shown concern with the self-concept of the teachers as well as of the pupil. The self-concepts of trainee-teachers in two cultures, namely, England and Jamaica, were compared. The method was to have the subjects write unstructured compositions on the topic. "I Myself; the Person I Am; the Person Others Think I Am; the Person I Would Like to Be." In addition, both groups were rated on tests of self-concept. These comparisons were stated:

1. Both male and female, Jamaican students, regardless of age, rated themselves significantly higher in respect to self-concept than English teacher-trainees.

[29]Benjamin Wright and Barbara Sherman, "Teachers' Self-Awareness and Their Evaluation of Childhood Authority Figures," *School Review,* LXXI (Spring 1963), pp. 80–84.
[30]Samuel A. Moore, "The Teacher's Self-Image," *Overview,* II (December 1961), pp. 23–25.

2. English male students rated themselves at approximately the same level as English female students; however, Jamaican female students rated themselves higher than Jamaican men and appeared to be less self-accepting.

3. There were no important differences between the self-concept scores of English students of regular age and of more mature years. In contrast, the mature Jamaican students rated themselves lower than those of usual college age.[31]

Another investigation of the self-concept of student teachers was the Lantz study. The major purpose of his investigation was to explore the relationship between concept of self of women elementary student teachers and classroom emotional climate. The following variables in the form of a questionnaire were used as predictors:

1. Self-concept score which was the expressed attitude of an individual about himself to his classroom emotional climate rating.

2. "Self-Other Discrepancy" score which was the disparity between an individual's expressed attitudes about himself and his expressed attitudes toward most other elementary teachers.

3. "Self-ideal Discrepancy" score which was the disparity between an individual's expressed attitudes about the ideal teacher and how it was related to her classroom emotional climate rating.[32]

None of the variables used as predictors was capable of predicting classroom emotional scores beyond chance. The only variable from which any prediction of classroom emotional climate could be made was the "Self-Other Discrepancy" score for the skeptical-distrustful scale. People who rated themselves thus received higher classroom emotional climate scores, possibly because they expressed their own personalities in their teaching.

The importance of these studies is the emphasis they place on a teacher's self-concept which determines her general behavior by what she perceives herself to be and which is the foundation of a harmonious personality. A teacher's personality is of prime importance to success in the classroom. Although important, it is very intangible.

SELF-CONCEPT AND LEARNING

A child's self-concept, his social anchorages, (an individual's ability to find his place in the social group) and his readiness are necessary components of learning. The purpose of this study was to ascertain the self-attitudes and

[31]A. S. Phillips, "The Self Concepts of Trainee-Teachers in Two Sub-Cultures," *The British Journal of Educational Psychology*, XXX (June 1963), p. 154.
[32]Donald L. Lantz, "Relationship Between Classroom Emotional Climate and Concepts of Self, Others, and Ideal Among Elem. Student Teachers," *Journal of Education Research*, LIX (October 1965), p. 80.

social anchorages of a select group of 61 junior high school math and science students in grades 7, 8, and 9 from Iowa public schools. It was felt that the findings might possibly indicate what should be included and what should be omitted in the junior high school curriculum. The "Twenty-Statement Test" was administered during the last week of the eight-week summer session. The conclusion was that one could surmise that the self-attitudes revealed by the "Twenty-Statement Test" could be valuable in curriculum planning, counselling and guidance, and teacher preparation.[33]

Joseph Caliguri, an elementary school principal in Las Vegas, Nevada, used four open-ended questions to explore the self-concept of 425 intermediate grade children in a minority group area. Children responded freely about aggressive behavior or feelings. Pupils' perceptions about things that made them feel important tended to show low expectations of disadvantaged children concerning ego strength. The topics which follow show the order of values children expressed:[34]

Topics	Response
Getting Material Things	31%
Personality Considerations	35%
Academic Concerns	26%
Physical Features	4%
Making Friends	3%
Receiving Praise	1%

Undoubtedly the order of importance of the above topics indicates need of material things and desire for independence. The responses also indicated significant implications for educators:

1. A need for broadening school and community activities as a basis for resolution of personal and interpersonal problems in socially approved ways.

2. Prestige-building activities as a conscious part of the school program should be included to increase feelings of self-identity and self-esteem.[35] From this study there was evidence that behavior of these children was really not controlled by what pupils knew but by their feelings, that is, their concept of self.

Whether self-concept and school achievement have a close relationship to each other was investigated by Brookover. He sampled 1050 seventh grade students. His findings indicated a significant positive correlation between self-concept and performance in the academic role, relationship between self-

[33]Leland Holt and Manford Sonstgard, "Relating Self-Conception to Curriculum Development," *The Journal of Educational Research,* LVIII (April 1965), p. 351.
[34]Joseph Caliguri, "The Self-Concept of the Poverty Child," *The Journal of Negro Education,* XXXV (Summer 1966), pp. 280–282.
[35]*Ibid.,* p. 282.

concept and performance in specialized areas, and a correlation between the perceived evaluations of significant others and pupil performance.[36]

IMPORTANCE OF SELF-CONCEPT TO TRAINING CULTURALLY DIFFERENT PUPILS

The Culturally Different Child, Home, and School

"The child can only operate in terms of the way he sees himself . . . [he] withdraws or strikes out before the other person has a chance to establish a friendly feeling."[37] This description fits many culturally different children. The self is developed by the pattern prevailing in the culture. It develops in relation to what it feeds on, being selective in regard to what it perceives and chooses. The family plays a crucial role in the development of the self. Brazziel and Terrell found that when the family, along with the child and the school, participates in readiness activities, children's learning and learning potential is increased.

The results of a six-week readiness program which included Negro children and their parents produced these results:

1. At the end of six weeks the children in the experimental group tested at the fiftieth percentile of the Metropolitan Readiness Test, in contrast to the control group which tested at the fifteenth percentile.

2. After seven months the mean I.Q. of the experimental group was 106.5 as compared to a general expectation of 90.[38]

Jackson hypothesized that learning effectiveness can be impaired by membership in a socially deprived or a stressful family environment, or classroom conditions that create a threatening climate for learning. He postulated, moreover, that learning effectiveness is enhanced by positive attitudes toward school, realistic achievement goals, and feelings of self-confidence.[39]

Another student of these educational problems has expressed a view which also affects learning:

> In a society in which mental inferiority, laziness, incompetency, and irresponsibility are part of the definition externally assigned to a group as in the case with the Negro, the group so defined will tend to confirm this definition.[40]

---

[36]Wilbur B. Brookover and Shailer Thomas, "Self-Concept and School Achievement," *Sociology of Education,* XXXVII (Spring 1964), p. 278.
[37]J. Murray Lee and Dorris M. Lee, *The Child and His Curriculum* (New York, 1960), p. 31.
[38]Bloom, Davis, and Hess, *op. cit.* p. 88.
[39]Philip W. Jackson and Nina Strattner, "Meaningful Learning and Retention: Noncognitive Variables," *Review of Educational Research,* XXXIV (December 1964), pp. 513–527.
[40]Ralph Hines, "Social Expectations and Cultural Deprivation," *Journal of Negro Education,* XXXIII (Spring 1964), p. 137.

Confirmation of these expectations has occurred as a result of cultural and institutional forces in operation in our society which reward behavior conforming to this stereotype. For many years culturally disadvantaged people have accepted a given status in society which became a part of their own self-image. Acceptance of this status coupled with resultant life changes have lowered the motivational level of these people until many seem to be without any goals beyond daily survival. They have very low levels of aspiration, and these attitudes have become internalized for large segments of population. The result has been an overwhelming number of serious learning problems which have not yielded to the usual classroom methods of instruction. This serious problem has been compounded by the large numbers of culturally different children in our largest urban centers which are faced with a serious shortage of well-trained teachers.

The concept of self not only affects how children learn but also how they behave. The problem of the Negro male to earn a decent living and to occupy a respected position in the home and community is reflected in the behavior and learning problems of many Negro boys at school. In their attempt to maintain their self-image they emphasize physical prowess and rebellion. Thus, many renounce artistic, abstract, and intellectual activities. In view of this evidence of a poor self-concept of Negro school boys, it is not strange that there are usually more Negro girls in honor classes than boys.[41] Another factor relative to the problem is family background; a relatively small percentage of Negroes are not even one generation removed from poverty. The home has not been equipped with books and other cultural artifacts, and the school experience is often not stressed or looked upon as really desirable.

Other problems stemming from disadvantaged homes which find their way into the classroom are as follows: the selective inattention cultivated by children in order to survive in a noisy environment is later used to tune out the teacher. Aggressiveness combined with quickness has demonstrated to many slum children that they will be more successful in competition for a limited supply of material comforts. With such a background, these individuals develop into impulsive children. These are the hyperactive youngsters who rush out of their seats to get the attention of the teacher, to examine something in the classroom, or to follow some explorations of their own. Such a child has a very short attention span, experiences difficulty in concentrating or sitting long enough to learn skills necessary for school success. The nonvigorous child has learned to survive in his environment by being passive. In school he is withdrawn, lethargic, and very difficult to reach. Poor nutrition is responsible for many listless children in classrooms. Also, the paucity of toys in the home has caused a failure to develop manipulative skills. Even if these children came

---

[41]Clemmont E. Vontress, "The Negro Personality Reconsidered," *The Journal of Negro Education,* XXXV (Summer 1966), p. 217.

to the classroom with a good self-image, maintaining it would be difficult in the face of the problems mentioned above.

RAISING CONCEPT OF SELF AND MORE EFFECTIVE TEACHING OF CULTURALLY DIFFERENT PEOPLE

Improvement of Concept of Self

Improving concept of self is a lengthier and more difficult process than tearing it down. To produce such a change requires experiences which help the individual perceive the self in a more favorable light. Each involvement with the environment may mean assimilating something and surrendering something. The special problems of culturally different people are of a social, economic, and legal nature evolving from the cultural isolation of these groups. As stated before, the self largely determined by a background of accumulated experiences is selective in its perception of intake; if it perceives a hostile environment, it becomes almost impermeable. A prolonged unfavorable environment in which the self seeks to protect itself produces isolation with a diminished self as the least consequence.

Any program which purports to alleviate the present dilemma must approach it on a more inclusive front than the educational alone. The causes of deprivation must be sought and relieved. Minimally, any effective program must provide for economic escalation and for constructive interaction of individuals of culturally different groups within the larger social sturcture. New techniques must be explored for eliminating the barriers of communication which impede social action.[42] In order for culturally different people to learn, there must be a drive and a visible reward to people of their own group.

METHODS AND TECHNIQUES FOR IMPROVING THE INSTRUCTION OF CULTURALLY DIFFERENT CHILDREN

Learning is what the self perceives, accepts, reviews, synthesizes, interprets, and uses from the perceptual inputs before it at every waking moment. For this reason it is important that the teacher should arrange situations and provide experiences which are designed to help students see themselves as adequate and effective agents. For every child, the experience of success in some activity is important, but the Negro child needs continued opportunities to see himself and his racial group in a realistically positive way from his earliest days through high school. There is a particular necessity for the Negro

[42]Paul B. Warren, "Guidelines for the Future—An Educational Approach for the Culturally Disadvantaged," *The Journal of Negro Education,* XXXV (Summer 1966), p. 283.

child to see examples of his own ethnic group who have made a success of their lives as a result of a good education. Dr. Sam Shepard of St. Louis has used young Negroes from McDonnell Aircraft Corp. to inspire higher levels of aspiration in Negro youth. To see Negro people who are successful in sports is not enough; sports do not emphasize the abstract levels of achievement. Schools attended by culturally different people have a great need for counselors who can fill in part of the gap of an inadequate home life. Giving a student the opportunity to talk about his problem and showing sympathetic interest make him feel he has a friend who is sincerely interested in him. Furthermore, if the problem is verbalized and viewed with perspective it is never as bad as it seemed originally. Nothing is more devastating than to feel one has a problem peculiar to himself; group therapy is, therefore, particularly helpful. A good counselling experience can truly give culturally different youth an anchor.

Many teachers have had rewarding experiences with these young people. Here are a few tips to teachers of culturally different pupils:

1. Less teacher domination of a lesson with more guidance of children to find satisfying solutions.

2. More open-ended questions and more exploration of a number of answers rather than questioning for the "right" answer.

3. Less criticism of mistakes and failure and more utilization of mistakes as a part of learning.

4. bilbiotherapy can fill a need for vicarious experience because youngsters can read about and discuss people with similar conflicts, problems, and hardships.

5. Trips provide a needed background of experience to which reading and discussion can be related.

6. School projects providing status can supply these children with needed experiences as well as pride in accomplishment. Here are a few examples of such activities:

a. Contests
b. Assembly programs
c. Bulletin boards
d. Attractive classrooms

7. Guiding the child in making some object representative of school work which can be taken home to the parent will satisfy the pride of both child and parent.

8. Use of mirrors and pictures in elementary classrooms can improve self appearance as well as grooming habits. The child should be made to feel that his own image is the most important in the world and encouraged to take pride in it.

9. Directed listening can combat tuning out the teacher. Films, filmstrips, records, tape-recorded speeches, and live reports can be used with

a listening guide sheet consisting of a skeleton outline to be completed as a student listens.

10. Scrambled outline related to familiar and well-structured material is a useful exercise for teaching relationships.

11. Negro children especially need to be made aware that this ethnic group has contributed to the history of this country from the very beginning. Such a project has been carried out at the Burns School in Chicago by student teacher Mrs. Helen Saunders of Chicago State College. This student teacher was very well informed on Negro history and wrote the materials presented to a seventh grade class. Pupils, parents, and teachers were pleased with these materials. Negroes and whites shared these feelings. When parents attending the culminating activities of the last unit were asked about their feelings concerning these materials, Negroes and whites expressed unanimous approval; moreover they felt that such material should be incorporated into the curriculum. At no time did the author observe any feeling other than pride when children were studying this material.

12. Role playing and dramatization provide understanding and gratification of children's desires to be admired and respected by their peers.

13. Raising the level of aspiration is important for children with a poor self-concept. Charles Reed, former student teacher at the Gregory School in Chicago, carried on such a project. Every week he asked his class, "What are you going to be?" Many of these children had poor adult models in the neighborhood and had not thought of an occupation. Each child had to describe what he wished to be. This exercise was very informative for the pupils, and it caused them to consider their aspirations, most important for their concepts of self.

14. Using concrete materials makes an educational experience meaningful to pupils who have difficulties with abstractions.

15. Linking lessons with making a living raises aspirations and supplies motivation.

16. Vicarious experience and less emphasis on abstractions can be provided by films, filmstrips, charts, cartoons, maps, globes, pictures, postcards, and stick figures.

17. The physical effort of writing a lesson helps many of these children concentrate and therefore retain more.

18. Introduce only one new difficulty at a time to prevent confusion and further deterioration of self-image.

19. Present small blocks of subject matter so that pupils find tasks within their reach and experience the satisfaction of completing a task.

20. Provide many simple practice exercises but allow plenty of time to complete them. These children are not speed oriented.

21. Hold frequent remedial drills; these pupils need repetition. Drills can be varied by making games of them. Having a little review just before lunch

and before the end of the day is good reinforcement and good public relations, because children may tell their parents what they learned.

22. Use variety with frequent changes of activities to provide for short attention span.

23. Use graphs to record progress, so pupil can have the satisfaction of seeing the progress he is making.

24. Give much individual help to slow learners; a one-to-one relationship is very satisfying to this type of child's ego. The learning response in this kind of situation is frequently very good.

25. Work out special projects. The ego of any child is flattered by being a part of some special activity.

26. Provide a situation in which this child can succeed. Success improves the concept of self; a positive self-concept makes learning easier.

27. Use material from a child's environment, because it is more easily learned and retained.

28. Structure the activities in the classroom; the organization and predictability provide some emotional security to a child with a poor self-concept.

29. A warm personality is flattering to a child with a poor self-concept and makes it easy for him to identify with the adult. This is very supportive to a child. Juan Cruz, a former student teacher from Chicago State College, did a special project of teaching English to Puerto Rican children. His success with these children was due to his kind of personality, interest, and dedication which enabled these children to identify with him.

30. Last, I should like to urge teachers not to place implicit faith in I. Q. tests. For children of this type, tests are inaccurate; moreover, many of this world's most creative individuals would be eliminated by these tests.

Among the people who will have a great impact on the child's concept of self will be his teacher. Since this is the case, teacher training institutions should re-evaluate their efforts of contributing to a positive self-concept of teacher-trainees. In a study by Staines, more learning took place in classrooms in which the words and actions of the teacher were enhancing to the students.[43]

[43]J. W. Staines, "The Self-Picture as a Factor in the Classroom," *British Journal of Educational Psychology*, XXXIII (June 1958), p. 108.

Allan C. Ornstein*

19/Why Ghetto School Teachers Fail†

We have the peculiar notion that we are doing good as long as we spend large sums of money. We believe that the problem of educating the disadvantaged can be solved by simply dispensing money to provide compensatory education, which we hope will guarantee "quality education" and "equality of opportunity" for the disadvantaged. Yet, despite our huge outlay of money we are not making significant gains; the problem is snowballing into a vicious, stubborn cycle. In effect, we have vaulted madly off in all directions and have adopted a saturation approach—with the hope that some programs will work —which blinds us with false hopes and makes it difficult to find the best way of solving the problem.

My purpose here is to come to grips with the problem and suggest why we are failing. I am governed by a major assumption as to the reason for the problem and the stage that it has now reached. None of the compensatory programs has come up with a substitute for good teaching. No amount of money is adequate if teachers are doing an inadequate job. New schools, smaller classes, integrated textbooks, etc., are meaningless if teachers are indifferent. In short, it profits us little to spend billions of dollars on compensatory education and then place the students under ineffective teachers.

The idea that teachers are failing to reach and teach the disadvantaged is not new, but I suggest that we explore the reasons, in turn, so that we become aware that everything we are attempting is superficial and merely a waste of time, energy, and money. The teachers are the victims of an intolerable system which causes them to become angry, frustrated, and finally indifferent.

Teacher-training institutions do an appalling job of preparing teachers. Those who are assigned to "good" schools usually manage to get by, since their students have the ability and intrinsic motivation to behave well and learn on their own. However, whenever teachers are assigned to work with the disadvantaged, poor teaching becomes obvious, because these students depend on good teaching. That a limited number of ghetto-school teachers do succeed and maintain their faith in themselves and in their students may be attributed to their unusual personality, that despite their poor training allows them to gain experience and effectively teach the disadvantaged.

*Biographical Data: Allan C. Ornstein is now assistant director of a National Defense Institute for teachers of disadvantaged youth at New York University and among other duties is a teacher in the Sands Junior High Special Service School. He has written a number of articles on the teaching of the disadvantaged.

The trouble with teacher training is that courses consist merely of descriptions, recommendations, anecdotes, and success stories, which are nothing more than opinion, but often taken as gospel. Readings consist of wonderful, glowing reports and advice, but fail to demonstrate how or why the advice works. Indeed, the advice is at best a "gimmick," a dead-end approach. What is suggested for or works with one teacher does not neccessarily work with another, even with the same group of students. The best advice, in fact, can sometimes do the most harm.

Eager but unprepared, the ghetto-school teacher is usually doomed to failure. The disadvantaged are astute appraisers and knowing manipulators of their environment; they easily see through "gimmicks." They know what will upset teachers, often better than the teachers know; they readily sense what they can or cannot do with a particular teacher. They realize that threats are ineffectual and that the teacher's authority is limited. In this connection, they usually assess the teacher as a person before they become interested in him as a teacher. A negative assessment—which is common, because of the conflict of values and life styles between the teacher and students—can provoke a dramatic incident, or it can be drawn out into a series of minor clashes. In either case, the students proceed to capitalize on the teacher's weaknesses, then ridicule and abuse him as a person, for example, derogating his personality and physical appearance. Once having demolished the teacher's self-respect and authority, they readily express indignation and contempt toward him, and all their hostility and their resentment of authority are directed at him.

Disadvantaged students at the junior-high-school level are generally the most difficult to deal with. By then, many are rebellious and too retarded in the basic skills to learn in a regular classroom. Many are strong enough to be a physical threat or sophisticated enough to probe a teacher's weaknesses. On the other hand, they lack self-control and are not mature enough to reason with or old enough to be legally suspended if they really cause trouble.

The outcome is that the teacher soon tends to see his students as adversaries. Each day leaves him emotionally and physically exhausted. Anxiety overwhelms him, too, as he becomes aware that almost anything can happen. He is confronted by a bored and hostile class, a group of thirty or thirty-five students he can no longer control. He sees no tangible results of hard work and feels no sense of accomplishment. For his own mental health and disposition, then, the teacher is forced to learn not to care. His apathy protects him; it is his defense; it is his way of coping with the meaninglessness of the possible danger of his situation. That the students are not learning is no longer his major concern. Weekends and holidays become more important; he needs to rest, recuperate, and regain his strength and rationality. Sometimes he cannot wait, and becomes "ill" a day or two before the weekend. Sometimes he does not finish the term; often he does not return for the next term.

The teacher turns to his supervisors for help, but quickly learns that he must solve his own problems. His supervisors rarely have the time to provide assistance on more than an emergency basis. Often the supervisors are suffering from many of the same problems as the teacher, for example, lack of training and experience. Many are unwillingly appointed to the school, and like teachers, they are anxiously awaiting their transfer to a better school. The only difference is that they can shut their office doors, which they often do, thereby divorcing themselves from the teacher's problems.

Of course, some supervisors are concerned and eager to provide assistance. Nonetheless, they often become inspectors. They work under the assumption that the teachers are not teaching and students are not learning—which is almost always true under the existing situation and therefore must be coerced and controlled. However, the unanticipated consequences of this teacher-supervisory relationship increases the teachers' indifference, and reinforces minimum acceptable teaching performance which in turn becomes maximum standards. Minimum performance convinces the supervisors that their assumptions are correct, and they proceed to check more closely on the teachers and treat them as subordinates. The relationship worsens and the teachers soon realize they must battle students and supervisors.

If the teacher is a substitute, his colleagues advise him not to return in September, to leave before he becomes regularly appointed. If he is already regularly appointed, he learns to "mark time" until he is allowed to transfer to a better school. Even if the teacher is regularly appointed, if he is young enough not to be trapped by a pension or a deferment from the Army, he may be so depressed that he leaves the system or the profession entirely.

The point is that most regularly certified ghetto-school teachers are trapped by the school system. In order to reduce the turnover of teachers, many urban schools require five or more years of service before a teacher can even first request a transfer. What happens during the interim? The longer the teacher has to wait to be transferred from a school he wants no part of, the more meaningless teaching becomes and the more cynical he becomes. Involvement, commitment, dedication, the joy of teaching, and the rest of the splendid jargon become cliches.

Who suffers more—the teacher or student—is questionable. Both are victims and victimize each other; both are the prisoners of the school system; both have dropped out in fact if not in name from the learning process; both aften drive each other out of the school. As for the teacher, one hundred eighty days a year he faces a living death—a feeling of hopelessness and despair— perhaps the bleakest existence any person can experience. Instead of teaching, he finds he must face a long-drawn-out humiliation, a state of helplessness and hopelessness, when the worst may be still to come in which the only certainty is there is no solution in sight to his predicament.

Prisoners adopt an air of dull-wittedness, of cooperative and willing incompetence. Subject peoples act much more incompetent and indifferent than they are, by declaring their minds free from their enslaved state. Ghetto-school teachers are subject people. Their schools are a kind of jail sentence, and "torture" is not too strong a word to describe some of the things that they have experienced in the classroom. Is this not a partial explanation of the incompetence and indifference that teachers often display in ghetto schools?

The hypocrisy of the system—compounded by its bureaucracy, inertia, pettiness, and total disregard for teachers—reinforces the teachers' indifference for teaching. The system operates by syphoning the teachers' energy and enthusiasm; it operates by first coercing teachers into and then prohibiting their escape from an almost impossible teaching situation, and therefore meaningless existence.

While the teachers are being assaulted, the system produces glowing reports. Pilot programs always seem to work, especially if evaluated by their directors. Instead of consulting their teachers, the system calls upon "experts" from local universities, governmental agencies, and foundations to reexamine and reorientate. (*The Bundy Report* is the latest example whereby an outside group of "experts," whose total teaching experience adds up to zero, is attempting to tell the teachers how they should teach and how their schools should be organized.) The belief is that teachers are rank-and-file workers with no legitimate right to define policy. Directions and decisions are passed on to teachers with no concern for them and no avenue of communication open to them, except by disrupting the system and striking. The entire system is organized to keep teachers in a second-class position, with no ego-involvement in curriculum development, no participation in policy, and no means of sharing credit given to the schools. Their supervisors, instruments of the system, run roughshod over them, because supposedly, that is "the way things get done in the system." Similarly, the supervisors decide almost everything and take whatever praise may come, but poor achievement is looked upon as an inadequacy of the teachers.

Having to fend against students, supervisors and the system, the teachers are confronted by a group of angry parents and condescending educators, who have taken to the task—of course, only with the best intentions—to vent their criticism of ghetto-school teachers. Although their criticisms are understandable, they are wholesale and generalized and overlook the reasons for poor teaching, and therefore, they have done grave injustices. Their harsh tone and constant criticism add to the problem of recruiting teachers, discourage competent and concerned teachers from remaining, and harden the already widespread feelings of indifference and futility, as well as reinforce poor teaching morale and performance.

The attackers are either too emotional or too remote from the actual classroom situation to understand the teachers' plight. They fail to recognize that these teachers were once working harder than any others in the profession, but because of impossible conditions and lack of adequate support were forced to retreat from teaching. They fail to appreciate that these teachers are over-whelmed by despair and need assistance, not criticism. They fail to realize that they have abandoned and further alienated the teachers.

In particular, the professors of education, who trained these teachers and now criticize them, would do well to accept the "challenge" they talk about and apply for teaching licenses and teach. There are many vacancies in ghetto schools, and there is much need for good teachers. One reason is that profes-sors have failed miserably in training their clientele.

To be sure, it would be interesting to see if the professors really know what they are talking about, or if they could do any better than the teachers. I dare them. At least, they ought to go into the classroom to "find out what it is really like" to teach the disadvantaged, and experience what the teachers experience. Again, I dare them. Instead of patronizing the teachers, criticizing them for negative attitudes and ineffectiveness, and berating them for failing to understand and appreciate what they have done for them, the professors should apologize for failing to do their jobs, that is, training teachers.

At the time of this writing, the proposal for decentralizing the New York City schools, and having a local ethnic group run the schools and choose the teachers and curriculum, is hotly contested. But what effect will this have on teaching morale and performance? Parents and educators urge teachers to maintain their dedication and behave as professionals while simultaneously undermining their independence which is an essential ingredient of profes-sional morale and status. Certainly, pride and power for the ghetto community would be beneficial, but lack of pride and power for the teachers is detrimental.

Why can't we have parents and teachers working together and sharing pride and power? Why can't parents and teachers, black, white, or purple stop distributing blame and sit on the same side of the fence? If parents alone fill the power structure of the schools or share it only with unwieldy, entrenched bureaucrats, the teachers, once again, will feel abandoned and remain indiffer-ent, reviving only when their contract expires and they can pursue their own self-interests.

On a large scale, it is impractical to talk about screening teachers for their attitudes or professional suitability to teach the disadvantaged when there are not enough teachers who are willing to work with such students. If a change is what we really want, let's stop attacking the teachers and start giving them support and a voice in running the school, for improving the education of the disadvantaged all boils down to what the teachers do.

Philip Reidford
University of California, Los Angeles
Michael Berzonsky
Ontario Institute for Studies in Education
University of Toronto

20 / Field Test of an Academically Oriented Preschool*

Since the beginning of Project Head Start in 1965, many experiments have been carried out to design a curriculum that could remedy the environmental deficiencies of disadvantaged preschool children (1-5).

The most highly structured of these curriculums is the Bereiter-Engelmann [2] program, which teaches language, reading, and arithmetic to disadvantaged four-year-olds. According to the authors, after three months of instruction fifteen disadvantaged preschoolers showed gains on three subtests of the Illinois Test of Psycholinguistic Abilities. The children showed a mean gain of four months on the Auditory Vocal Automatic, a mean gain of three months on the Auditory Vocal Association, and a mean gain of fifteen months on Vocal Encoding. Three months later Bereiter reported additional gains on the three subtests. He reported a mean gain of nine months on the Auditory Vocal Automatic, five months on the Auditory Vocal Association, and eight months on Vocal Encoding. He also reported, after six months of instruction, a mean gain of 6.7 in intelligence quotient, as measured by the Third Revision, 1960, of the Stanford-Binet Intelligence Scale, Form L-M.

The project reported here seeks to test the findings of Bereiter and Engelmann in a Head Start setting[6]. There are two important reasons for such an experiment. First, Head Start is based on the empirically unsubstantiated premise that early education can eliminate or greatly reduce environmental deprivation; this study seeks to provide some of the needed empirical evidence for this premise. Second, Bereiter and Engelmann have recently published a book, *Teaching Disadvantaged Children in the Preschool,* in which they explain in detail content and teaching strategies with such logic and force that the wary practitioner needs substantiating data from outside sources [2].

Two classes of twenty-four children were selected according to Project Head Start criteria. The forty-eight children ranged in age from three years and eight months to five years and seven months. The two groups attended preschool classes for two and a half hours a day, one group in the morning and one in the afternoon, five days a week, at the McKinley School in York,

*From *The Elementary School Journal,* February 1969. Reprinted by permission of the authors and the Journal. Copyright by The University of Chicago Press.

Pennsylvania. For about six months these Head Start children were instructed in the Bereiter and Engelmann curriculum for language, arithmetic, and reading. Each class was divided into four ability groups on the basis of informal performance ratings by the teachers. Each of these eight groups received an hour of instruction in a two-and-a-half-hour day. Twenty minutes were set aside for each content area. The four teachers, two for each class, received a half-day of training a week for three months in the Bereiter-Engelmann curriculum.

Because all teachers could not be trained in all subject-matter areas at the same time, it was necessary to train all the teachers in language first, then reading, and finally arithmetic. The content areas were also presented to the children in this order. Twenty minutes of daily classroom instruction in language began on October 1, 1965, in reading on December 1, 1965, and in arithmetic on January 3, 1966. The assumption is, therefore, that differences between pre- and post-tests on the measures used are due primarily to effects of eight months of language instruction, six months of reading instruction, and five months of arithmetic instruction. The instructional content, the teaching strategies, and the preschool management procedures—with the exception of the reading program—closely followed the Bereiter-Engelmann preschool program as outlined in their book *Teaching Disadvantaged Children in the Preschool* [2]. The reading curriculum was taken from an earlier work by Bereiter, Engelmann, Osborn, and Reidford [6].

TEACHING SCHEDULE

This preschool program could afford only two teachers for each class of twenty-four children. The teaching load was shared by the two teachers. Since each of the four groups was taught for an hour a day—twenty minutes in each subject area—an alternating schedule was devised so that a teacher taught two groups for a total teaching time of two hours a day. An aide was on hand to take care of children who were not being instructed. This strategy was used for two months, until the end of February, when it was decided that two hours a day of intensive teaching was too much of a load. All four teachers met and worked out a team teaching system that lightened the teaching load for each team member and insured the best possible instruction for the children.

Under the revised teaching schedule, all four teachers taught morning and afternoon. One teacher instructed three reading groups, another two arithmetic groups, another two language groups, and the fourth one language and one arithmetic group. This schedule varied, according to load and the subject taught, from morning to afternoon and from day to day on a rotating basis, which insured that each teacher was instructing the same number of classes each week. As in the earlier arrangement, however, groups of about six children had three instructional sessions a day—one in language, one in reading, and one in arithmetic.

THE TESTS

All the children were given Form L-M of the Stanford-Binet Intelligence Scale from two to ten weeks after the program began. This extended testing schedule was necessary because of the lack of qualified testers. One part-time examiner tested all the children. The delayed testing, as we see it, served only to diminish the possibility of gains on post-testing, for when some of the children took the pre-test they had already made ten weeks of progress in the program. If we were to obtain the same gains as Bereiter and Engelmann, the delayed testing could reduce the difference between results on the pre-test and the post-test by as many as three to five points in intelligence quotient [2].

Twenty-three to twenty-five weeks after the pre-testing sessions, Form L-M of the Stanford-Binet Intelligence Scale was administered as a post-test to all the children. In other words, it took only two weeks to administer the post-test to all forty-eight children. The post-test was given by the same examiner who gave the pre-test; however, during the post-testing period he worked fulltime, not part-time as during the pre-testing period. An attempt was made to schedule the children for the post-test in the same sequence as the pre-test.

A year after the program began, two subtests of the Illinois Test of Pyscholinguistic Abilities—the Auditory Vocal Automatic and the Auditory Vocal Association—were administered to thirty-eight of the forty-eight children. At this time, all the subjects had had the eight-month pre-school experience, a two-month summer program based on the Bereiter-Engelmann method and a one-month Kindergarten experience. The Auditory Vocal Automatic and the Auditory Vocal Association were chosen because Bereiter and Engelmann [2] found that disadvantaged children with a median age of four years and six months scored at three years on these tests. Gray and Klaus [3] and Hartman [4] have reported additional evidence of below average performance by disadvantaged children on these subtests of the Illinois Test of Psycholinguistic Abilities. Informal descriptive data in the form of observations by teachers, parents, and the writers were also collected.

GAINS

Generally the results obtained were similar to, but less dramatic than, those reported by Bereiter and Engelmann [2]. The children's mean intelligence quotient rose from 95.7 to 102.1, a mean gain of 6.4 points. The gain was significant at the .01 level. A gain of 6.4 in intelligence quotient is hardly astounding when compared with gains reported in other preschool studies by Gray and Klaus [3], Hartman [4], and Kirk and Johnson [7]. What is interesting, however, is where the gains occurred. The least squares fit indicated that there is a non-linear relationship between scores on the pre- and post-tests: the pre-test—post-test gain increases with increased pre-test scores. In other words, the higher the initial intelligence quotient, the greater the gain.

As one would expect, most studies of disadvantaged preschool children generally report that the lower the initial intelligence quotient, the greater the gain. Bereiter and Engelmann's [2] study is an exception. In the study reported here treatment had a differential effect. This result would seem to indicate that although the children were taught in groups formed on the basis of ability, the teachers were better able to gear their instruction to the brighter children. In fact, a number of teachers found it much easier to teach the higher level groups than the lower level groups.

Results on the subtests of the Illinois Test of Psycholinguistic Abilities revealed that the children were functioning at realistic levels for their ages. At a mean chronological age of five years and three months, the children obtained a mean score of five years and two months on the Auditory Vocal Automatic and five years and three months on the Auditory Vocal Association. These results compare favorably with Bereiter's [8]. He reported that after six months of treatment children with a mean chronological age of five years and one month drawn from a population similar to ours obtained scores of four years and nine months on the Auditory Vocal Automatic and four years and seven months on the Auditory Vocal Association. Since the scores are not derived but correspond directly to chronological age, the results are within acceptable limits.

ENCOURAGEMENT

Our results are heartening for two reasons. First, the Auditory Vocal Automatic is a test of grammatical usage and understanding, and the Auditory Vocal Association is a verbal analogy or reasoning test. We did not give pre-tests on these measures, but we have reviewed pre-test results of several studies that drew their sample from a population which approximated ours, and our test results indicate that we made considerable progress in developing these two important skills. Second, data from other studies indicate that even when there are increases in intelligence quotient, little gain is found in these two language subtests. In a study by Reidford and Berzonsky [9] that compared Head Start and control children after an eight-week period the control group had a mean chronological age of five years and two months and a mean score of three years and seven months on the Auditory Vocal Automatic and four years on the Auditory Vocal Association. The experimental group with a chronological age of five years and one month had a mean score of four years on the Auditory Vocal Automatic and four years and four months on the Auditory Vocal Association. Similar results are to be found in the study by Gray and Klaus [3] and in the study by Hartman [4].

We believe, therefore, that the importance of our study lies chiefly in the scores obtained on the two measures of the Illinois Test of Psycholinguistic Abilities, not in the scores obtained on the Stanford-Binet Intelligence Scale.

WHERE ARE THE GAINS MADE?

It is logical to conclude that all studies which show a gain in intelligence quotient have some effect on the children. The important issue, however, seems to be where the effect is occurring. For example, the profile of the Gray and Klaus study [3] indicates that the children advanced evenly and proportionately from pre-treatment levels to post-treatment levels on the nine subtests of the Illinois Test of Psycholinguistic Abilities. Initially they were below their chronological ages in five subtests: the Auditory Vocal Association, the Auditory Vocal Automatic, Auditory Decoding, the Visual Motor Sequencing, and the Motor Encoding. After three years they continued to be considerably below norms for their age level in the skills as measured by these subtests. Unlike the gains in our study, advances in the study by Gray and Klaus did not seem to be made where they were needed most.

In summary, our results indicate that long-term exposure to the Bereiter-Engelmann preschool curriculum not only raises intelligence quotient, but also, and more important, stimulates development in reasoning ability, and in grammatical usage and in understanding. It is evident from our results and from the results obtained by Bereiter and Engelmann [2] that an academically oriented curriculum reverses some of the intellectual deficits of the culturally disadvantaged. However, studies by Reidford and Berzonsky [9] and Wolff and Stein [10] indicate that such deficiencies are not sensitive to short-term educational remedies. Until evidence is gathered on the effectiveness of short-term programs, we recommend that short-term discontinuous programs for preschool disadvantaged children be replaced by long-term programs that extend their methodologies through the early grades of the elementary school.

NOTES

1. G. D. Alpern. 1966. "The Failure of a Nursery-School Enrichment Program for Culturally Disadvantaged Children." Paper read at Regional Meeting of American Association of Psychiatric Clinics for Children, Cincinnati, Ohio.
2. C. Bereiter and S. Engelmann. 1966. *Teaching Disadvantaged Children in the Preschool.* Englewood Cliffs. New Jersey: Prentice-Hall, Inc.

3. Susan Gray and R. A. Klaus. 1965. "An Experimental Preschool Program for Culturally Deprived Children," *Child Development,* 36: 887–898, December.
4. A. S. Hartman. 1966. *1964–1965, Annual Progress Report to the Ford Foundation.* Preschool and Primary Education Project. Harrisburg, Pennsylvania: Department of Public Instruction.
5. D. P. Weikhart. 1964. "Perry Preschool Project Progress Report." Ypsilanti, Michigan, June. (Mimeographed.)
6. C. Bereiter, S. Engelmann, Jean Osborn, and P. Reidford. 1966. "An Academically Oriented Preschool for Culturally Deprived Children," in Fred Hechinger (ed.), *Preschool Education Today.* New York: Doubleday and Company. Pp. 105–135.
7. S. Kirk and O. Johnson. 1951. *Educating the Retarded Child.* Cambridge, Massachusetts: Riverside Press.
8. C. Bereiter. 1965. "Progress Report on an Academically Oriented Preschool for Culturally Deprived Children." Urbana, Illinois. (Mimeographed.)
9. P. Reidford and M. D. Berzonsky. 1967. "An Evaluation of an Eight-Week Headstart Program." Paper presented at annual American Educational Research Association Convention, New York, February.
10. M. Wolff and Annie Stein. 1966. "Six Months Later, a Comparison of Children Who Had Headstart, Summer, 1965, with Their Classmates in Kindergarten." New York City: Yeshiva University, August. (Mimeographed.)

Robert L. Williams*

21 / What Are We Learning from Current Programs for Disadvantaged Students? †

During the past four years many universities in an attempt to make their resources available to an increasingly broad spectrum of the college age population have given major consideration to individuals from economically and educationally impoverished backgrounds. Recent data indicate that probably more than 50 per cent of the institutions of higher learning in this country now have special programs for such students,[1] who are frequently described as disadvantaged or high risk. Most of these programs, however, are currently little more than token efforts, and it is an ironic fact that, with the exception of predominanantly Negro colleges, private institutions have evidenced greater involvement in educating disadvantaged students than have public institutions.[2]

Disadvantaged or high risk students by no means form a homogeneous population. In fact, students which some schools consider high risk would be among the intellectual elite on other campuses. Most colleges define disadvantagement in the context of their own student bodies; that is, disadvantaged students are those whose educational and economic background is considered markedly inferior to that of their regular students. The term "high risk" may have a slightly different connotation. It usually refers to an economically poor student who according to traditional predictive criteria is not likely to succeed at a particular school. Nevertheless, program reports indicate that the terms "disadvantaged" and "high risk" are generally used interchangeably.

Although lack of sufficient funds to attend college is the most common characteristic of disadvantaged students, other characteristics have been noted with some degree of uniformity. For example, most high risk students obtain lower scores on standardized tests than those typically earned by regular students in the respective schools. American College Testing scores in the

*Robert L. Williams is assistant professor in the Department of Educational Psychology and Guidance at the University of Tennessee. His article, which is based on a study of compensatory assistance to disadvantaged students, is an adaptation of a report presented at the annual meeting of the National Association of State Universities and Land-Grant Colleges at Washington, D.C., in November 1968.

†From *Journal of Higher Education,* Vol. 40 (April 1969), pp. 274–285. Copyright 1969 by the Ohio State University Press and reprinted with its permission.

[1] John Egerton, *Higher Education for "High Risk" Students* (Atlanta: Southern Education Foundation, 1968), p. 49.

[2] *Ibid.,* p. 13.

vicinity of 13 or 14 and composite Scholastic Aptitude Test scores of 700–800 have been cited as norms for disadvantaged students. A substantial number of risk students have also had somewhat mediocre high school records. However, several colleges accept only the financially limited students with outstanding academic records or impressive standardized test scores. Actually, few institutions are recruiting impoverished ghetto students with serious academic deficiencies. Most students classified as high risk come from ethnic or cultural backgrounds different from the non-disadvantaged. Many are lower class blacks attending predominantly white institutions. Poor whites, Puerto Ricans, American Indians, and Mexican Americans are to a limited extent also represented. Inasmuch as disadvantaged students characteristically come from sociological settings which are devoid of educational incentives, it is not unusual to find that they are apathetic and even antagonistic toward education. Many do not see that education is of any practical significance to them. Certainly, very few of their own volition would pursue a college education.

Despite a multiplicity of crippling deficiencies, disadvantaged students have manifested other characteristics which personnel in high risk programs interpret as signs of educability. Criteria often employed in the selection of these students include: (1) some evidence of ability to handle academic work, for example, high school grades showing improvement, acceptable achievement at some point, or promising standardized test scores; (2) a willingness to accept some measure of personal responsibility for achievement or failure; (3) at least a minimal perception of self-worth; (4) emotional toughness evidenced by perseverance in the face of frustrating circumstances; (5) intense motivation to improve the circumstances of one's life; (6) some indication of leadership potential; (7) the capacity to think and plan creatively; (8) an ability to distinguish realistically between what is desired and what is possible; (9) a special talent (e.g., facility in music, art, or athletics); and (10) success in any activity which has required sustained effort. The one criterion which is mentioned by virtually all schools is achievement motivation, but not necessarily motivation directed toward the attainment of educational goals. In selecting disadvantaged students, many institutions have waived traditional admissions criteria such as standardized test scores and high school rank. Instead, colleges have relied heavily on subjective evaluations accruing from personal interviews and on the recommendations of high school counselors, clergymen, teachers, coaches, and social workers in impoverished areas.

What types of assistance are colleges providing for disadvantaged students? Nearly all programs for these students include provisions for financing their college education. The money has come from a variety of sources, including major foundations (notably Rockefeller and Ford), industrial firms, Educational Opportunity Grants, National Defense Education Act loans, federal work-study programs, cooperative work-study programs with industry, state funds, service organizations, civic clubs, and alumni groups. Several schools provide not only financial support but also extensive training in the personal management of financial resources. Helping students systematically save money to finance long-term goals has received particular emphasis.

The primary academic objective of most programs is the development of communication skills, especially reading, writing, speaking, and listening. It is reasoned that these students cannot hope to succeed vocationally without the ability to communicate effectively in the mainstream of society. Facility in the use of standard English is considered fundamental to effective communication. A concerted attempt is made to teach standard English in a fashion that does not disparage the student's cultural dialect. The student is first made to see how his dialect functions as a legitimate language system, and standard English is then presented as a second language.[3] Numerous programs include intensive compensatory study in standard English either during the summer prior to the freshman year or on weekends during the regular academic term. Since many universities have also discovered that high risk students are quite deficient in basic quantitative skills, a number of programs are now emphasizing compensatory study in mathematics almost as much as study in language arts.

Universities have developed several ambitious policies for maximizing the academic success of disadvantaged students. First of all, considerable use has been made of individualized instruction. In this vein, most programs provide extensive individual tutoring in all academic areas. The corps of tutors includes teachers, graduate students, regular undergraduate students, and more advanced disadvantaged students. Many tutors serve on a completely voluntary basis and receive no financial remuneration for their services. Programmed instruction is another type of individualized teaching which has been used as a supplement to classroom instruction. Universities have also arranged for disadvantaged students to take lighter than normal course loads and five to six years to finish degree programs. Some schools have very liberal probationary policies for high risk students, for example, permitting students to repeat courses several times and take a number of quarters to raise their grade point average to an acceptable level. To facilitate initial placement of students in appropriate courses, a few institutions administer extensive placement examinations. Scores on these examinations indicate whether a student should enroll in regular courses, remedial courses (credit and non-credit), or courses which integrate remedial and college level work. Concurrent with these courses is extensive instruction in basic study skills.

In the main, universities have given as much attention to the affective side of disadvantagement as to the purely academic. Many disadvantaged students initially view the college campus as foreign soil. Therefore, deliberate

---

[3]Leslie Berger, *College Now for Ghetto Youth!* (New York: City University of New York, 1968), p. 8.

efforts are usually made to soften the transition from the student's previous environment to the college community. Some colleges bring prospective students to the campus for several days during the students' senior year in high school. This visit affords an opportunity for colleges to collect important placement data and for students to develop a somewhat realistic conception of college life. Students not permitted a pre-enrollment visit may initially become distraught because of the sheer newness of the college experience.

After fully matriculating, high risk students typically receive regular personal counseling. Many programs encourage first-year students to have at least one session per week with their counselor. This arrangement permits problems to be dealt with before they become cumulative. Later, the frequency of the sessions can be reduced as a student demonstrates adequate personal and academic progress. The responsibilities of the counselor are to create a bridge between students and the academic establishment, to provide a personal orientation to college life, to advise students in the selection of courses, to facilitate formulation of appropriate career goals, to assist students in overcoming poor study habits, to help them with whatever personal problems might interfere with their academic progress, and to aid them in achieving a sense of ther own identity. Counselors also serve as resource people to instructors, since the counselor's insight into the attitudes of a student can be extremely helpful to a teacher groping to reach that student in the classroom. In addition to counseling, special courses such as Negro History, the Negro Family, Poverty, Urban Conditions, and Civil Liberties have been developed to help students more fully understand themselves and their role in society. Some schools have found that small-group discussions of pertinent social and economic issues may evoke more candid articulation of student feelings than personal counseling sessions. For this reason, counselors frequently participate in these group sessions.

Most programs attempt to provide appropriate role models for high risk students. A few program staffs include full-time personnel from disadvantaged backgrounds. Other schools employ the more advanced and successful disadvantaged students as tutors of new students. Another approach involves a cooperative work-study arrangement with industry, whereby students alternate quarters between school and work. The work experience enables a high risk student to see at first hand members of his particular minority group functioning in highly respectable positions. Many high risk students come to college feeling that the better jobs are inaccessible to them. Work experiences while in college provide not only a source of income but an opportunity for the student to appraise his vocational future in a more positive and realistic way.

How effective have these special programs been in altering the achievement patterns of disadvantaged students? Universities have assumed that high risk students possess intellectual qualities which have not been fully evidenced in their previous academic performance. Scholastic motivation, adequate study skills, and a supportive social environment are other factors which determine academic success, but these are the very conditions which are missing in the background of most disadvantaged students. The primary objective of university programs for the disadvantaged is to create such conditions and thereby alter achievement patterns. To what extent have universities been successful in attaining this goal?

Although most programs are too new to permit conclusive judgments relative to their long-term effectiveness, the initial results elicit optimism. In most instances, the academic mortality rate for disadvantaged students has been no higher than for regular students. But can we assume that this low mortality rate is a result of the special programs? Data from the few institutions with equivalent control groups provide an affirmative answer, namely, that the drop-out/flunk-out rate is much higher for the control subjects than for those in the high risk programs.[4] The grades of students in these programs have generally been much better than would have been predicted from their high school grades and standardized test scores. While the grade distribution of risk students is slightly more skewed toward the lower end of the continuum than that of regularly admitted students, some have made exceptionally high grades. In no instance has a college lowered grading or graduation standards to accommodate high risk students.

We should not conclude from these data that all efforts to enhance the educational skills of disadvantaged students have been highly successful. For example, standardized test scores obtained by risk students have not been appreciably altered by compensatory assistance. Furthermore, improverished ghetto students have usually performed poorly in the special programs. In 1965, New York University admitted sixty severely damaged ghetto students to an experimental program. Recently published information concerning the NYU effort indicates that only fifteen of these students are currently enrolled. In at least one instance a university has terminated its high risk program because it felt the program was detrimental to the self-esteem of risk students.

In evaluating programs for high risk students, it is extremely difficult to determine specifically what factors are responsible for the success or failure of these students. Financial aid, special housing, intensive orientation to university life, special courses, small-group instruction, programmed instruction, a personalized teaching approach, tutorial assistance, personal counseling, compensatory study in language arts, a reduced course load, and an extended time period to obtain a degree constitute the major features of programs for the disadvantaged. How many of these factors really make a difference? Most programs are not experimentally designed to permit empirical assessment of the effect of specific independent variables. Theoretically all of these factors are

[4]Berger, op. cit., p. 15.

important, but their specific empirical efficacy is difficult to demonstrate from existing data. Consequently, assessment of individual components is based more on the personal testimony of program personnel than on empirical fact.

Financial assistance appears to be the fundamental component of all high risk programs. Inasmuch as disadvantaged students have little money, some type of financial support is indispensible. But are all types of financial aid for the disadvantaged equally beneficial? Considering the testimony of various program directors, I would recommend that risk students be given extensive training in the management of their financial resources, that they be required to earn a portion of their support, and that the university provide sufficient funds to permit these students to purchase clothing and engage in social activities generally characteristic of the non-disadvantaged on campus. Unless the latter condition is met, the assimilation of risk students into the university community, their self-respect, and their academic survival may be severely threatened. I would also strongly recommend that universities use money or tokens as short-term reinforcers for appropriate academic effort. A specified quantity of these reinforcers could later be exchanged for clothing, personal items, tickets to entertainment events, and so on.

Another component that seems to have fundamental significance is housing. Without question, familial and sociological conditions in the ghetto are antithetical to academic development. Unless students are physically removed from these socially destructive circumstances they have little chance of success in college. However, certain types of on campus housing may be equally detrimental. At this point it appears that risk students should be housed with regular students. Typically, risk students tend to relate only to each other and isolate themselves from non-disadvantaged students. Separate housing for high risk students would be likely to destroy any real chance of their being assimilated into the mainstream of university life.

Some schools contend that the initial orientation of disadvantaged students to a special program is a basic determinant of their adjustment to college. A question often propounded regarding the orientation process is whether students should initially be made aware of their serious academic deficiencies. Some programs attempt to conceal disadvantagement, even from the students themselves. On the other hand, directors of the more significant programs contend that it is best to be realistic from the beginning in dealing with risk students. Unless a student is cognizant of his deficiencies, he will be apt to resist much of the special assistance provided for him. Students not initially made aware of their limitations usually resent later attempts by instructors and counselors to point out these limitations. Although personnel should be candid, they must also be optimistic in evaluating a student's academic potential. Otherwise much of the special assistance will seem futile. This optimism need not be fabricated. Colleges are discovering that risk students have some extraordinary virtues. They are quite often verbally adept in group discussion, analytical in human relationships, and more socially sophisticated than their middle class counterparts. In appraising a student's potential, qualities such as these can be emphasized. However, since risk students typically get off to a slow start academically, neither they nor program personnel should expect dramatic success initially. In fact, individual tutors must be prepared to provide much of the impetus for study during the student's first year in college.

Another crucial academic question is whether high risk students should be placed in specially designed courses or regular courses. Some directors affirm that a special curriculum for risk students would lead to a degree with dimininshed social and professional significance. Separate learning situations for risk students would also be incongruous with a principal objective of most programs, namely, for disadvantaged students and regular students to learn from each other. Diversity of students within classes can be as important educationally as the quality of the faculty, facilities, and curriculum. Furthermore, personnel report that having risk students in regular classes often motivates instructors to be more practical and realistic in their teaching. Despite having an aversion to a separate curriculum, several program designers have included remedial or compensatory courses in their programs. If remedial courses are included, they should carry college credit. Initially, credit may be much more important to a student than acquisition of academic skills and subject matter. Risk students have a tremendous proclivity toward the immediate and the tangible. Early in their college work they must experience tangible progress toward the attainment of a degree. A program beginning with a deluge of non-credit remedial courses is not likely to produce outstanding motivation or achievement. A much more effective way to provide remedial assistance would be through utilization of automated instruction. Teaching machines permit students to proceed at their own pace in an atmosphere free of the anxiety and frustration which many risk students associate with the classroom milieu.

Some program designers feel that disadvantagement is more of an affective disability than an academic one. Certainly many black students come to the university with a keen distrust of whites and a deep-seated resistance to authority. Frequently, students are so preoccupied with personal and social problems that they have little time and energy to devote to purely academic pursuits. For Negro students the concept of black power and accepting assistance from whites will probably be in painful conflict. Universities have adjudged several factors to be important in helping students to deal with personal vexations without jeopardizing their academic growth. A major finding thus far is that the teaching relationship with disadvantaged students must be highly personal, that is, the instructor must convey concern for the student as a person. A personalized teacher-student relationship requires much more small-group instruction and individual contact between teacher and students than is typical in most university settings.

It seems reasonable that intensive personal counseling would also be an extremely important affective feature of high risk programs. Many students must change their perceptions of themselves and of others before academic progress can be expected. Personal counseling is perhaps the most logical way to rectify these debilitating perceptions. My only reservation about the utility of counseling in many of the programs is the possibility of creating an emotional barrier by requiring risk students to see counselors. The long-range benefit derived from counseling might be far more pronounced if counseling assistance was made completely voluntary. Special courses dealing with the unique heritage and problems of a minority group have proven to be two-edged swords in altering the personal adjustment of students in that minority group. These courses seem to facilitate racial and ethnic pride, but they may also create an attitude of provincialism which impedes a student's social adjustment. The latter tendency can be minimized if non-disadvantaged students are encouraged to participate actively in these courses. Program reports suggest that individual tutoring can be a major source of affective support for disadvantaged students. Some of the most effective tutors appear to be advanced high risk students. Quite frequently new students have never been exposed to anyone of their age, race, background, and intelligence who is a college person. The success of these advanced risk students is tangible evidence to the new student that he has a real chance to succeed in college. Risk students also profit from serving as tutors. In so doing, they reinforce their newly acquired knowledge and have the satisfaction of transmitting it to someone else.

If high risk programs are to succeed, they must have the support of students, particularly of students actually in the programs. Resistance to administrative and faculty paternalism will probably be more intense among disadvantaged students than among the non-disadvantaged. Unless high risk students are involved in the development of a program, they may reject it and subsequently fall prey to activist movements working toward the overthrow of existing administrative authority. Ideally, administrators should actively seek feedback from risk students concerning their recommendations for developing and improving a program.

To achieve success, a program must also have the full support of top level administrators. These programs entail a tremendous expenditure of money, time, effort, and talent. In essence, a university must change the total environment of disadvantaged students. To be successful in this area a university must also modify many of its own practices, such as rigid entrance requirements, mass instruction, teaching by means of lectures, and impersonal faculty-student relationships. Not the least of the university's tasks is training a faculty entrenched in middle class values to communicate with disadvantaged students. Quite often, programs for disadvantaged students encounter strong resistance from within the university community. Many professors contend that by the time they are of college age disadvantaged youths are academically irredeemable and their presence on campus severely threatens academic standards. Consequently, without the full support of administrators who make the decisions concerning money, facilities, and staff, a high risk program may be destroyed by apathy and criticism from within the university community.

Historically, most colleges have admitted good students and graduated good students. We are now finding that institutions of higher learning can do more, that is, they can educate students with a history of mediocrity and failure. We do not yet know the full impact of high risk programs on a person's attitude toward himself, his future vocational success, or his contribution to society. Neither co we know how much waste of human resources and social discord will result from our failure to provide the disadvantaged a realistic chance to obtain a college education.

V/ TESTING THE CULTURALLY DIFFERENT

Nadine M. Lambert
Berkeley, California

22 / The Present Status of the Culture Fair Testing Movement*

The historical development of tests of mental ability has not ignored the fact that environment influences performance. What the development of the intelligence test movement has shown us, however, is that the degree to which psychologists have wished to deal with environment and the totality of cultural influences as they affect measured intellectual performance has vacillated.

The problem of culture bias in tests has not been ignored in the literature. Notable among those who have argued for a clear-headed look at how much tests handicap such children and in turn perpetuate a particular system of educational emphasis is Davis (1948). In the Midcentury White House Conference on Children and Youth (1951) he pointed out that unless America finds and trains effectively more children from the vast lower socio-economic groups with undeveloped educational potential, this country will be seriously threatened by the competive developments of European and Asian countries. He contended that the discovery of such children has been restricted by the fact that "standard" intelligence tests have have been culturally biased in favor of the higher socio-economic groups. A great amount of evidence is available to demonstrate that children from higher socio-economic families do consistently better as a group on traditional intelligence tests than those from lower economic levels (Eells, 1951; Lucas, 1953; McNemar, 1942). Davis further hypothesized that when cultural factors are controlled, average, real intellectual ability is at the same level for all economic groups. Eells (1951) suggested that finding real intellectual ability where it was not previously noticed was the central responsibility for intelligence testing. His emphasis was on the fact that if good tests of basic problem solving ability could be developed and these tests could measure ability to solve real life problems of the kind that are important, school authorities could use such tests as a basis for curriculum planning and as a basis for educational evaluation.

The Davis Eells Games were published in 1953. They were developed to measure basic intellectual potential which was free of socio-economic cultural bias. These tests have gone through some revealing studies since they were published, and they have been demonstrated to be not free from the bias which the authors had hoped to avoid.

---

*Reprinted by permission of the publisher, Clinical Psychology Publishing Company, Inc.

The late Irving Lorge (1952) in an incisive critique of the movement for cultural free tests points out that the efforts for development of such tests are motivated by the desire to show that there are no real differences between groups. He cites evidence from ability tests which shows over and over again that men and boys do less well than women and girls on certain types of test items. Since group means of male and female subjects are hypothesized to be equal, test authors have included enough items favoring men as well as women so that the resulting test has added bias and taken away bias to accomplish the original motive-equal means. Lorge feels that to deny differences between groups is to build a house on a shifting foundation in measurement. To make unbiased tests of ability is to try to reduce group differences, which may be, and probably are real, to zero. If tests can be developed which show no difference between groups, they are not biased—no difference, no bias. Culture-fair tests therefore often are tests measuring single types of ability. With tests measuring several types of ability, culture-fair tests must achieve this by subtracting out of the tests the items which differentiate between cultural groups. The result is development of culture-fair tests that reduce the uncommon characteristics of two groups by eliminating them; thus we often have tests with no verbal items, no verbal instructions, and which are abstract but concerned with figural abstractions rather than verbal ones. Lorge raises the issue that if such tests can be developed, what do we have when finished. The problem of establishing their validity still remains and as long as we have performance on learning tasks and teacher judgment through grades (which necessarily involve culture) what good are tests which predict these criteria less well than traditional tests of mental ability?

Lorge would have psychologists measure difference with as great a variety of tasks as possible. When differences can be reduced by changes in opportunity, credit should be given to the tests which showed an initial difference. He would reinforce the movement in differential psychology and attempt to appraise the interaction of endowment and opportunity. The task for the development of culture-fair tests is not only to reduce differences resulting from socio-economic status. In many parts of the United States and in other English-speaking countries, culture-fair tests would offer a great advantage in evaluating persons from other cultural and racial groups. Testing of Indian children in the Southwest United States as well as the problems in testing children of Mexican background has occupied a few psychologists for some time. Testing African natives is the particular concern of the South African whites who wish to use the natives in industry. The Canadian provinces and the United States are interested in evaluating the abilities of Eskimo and Indian children for educational programs. The great influx of migrants in the last few years to Australia has increased need for the use of tests which will evaluate basic intellectual endowment and contribute to the knowledge or prediction of the success of people from different cultural backgrounds in educational and industrial endeavors.

EXAMPLES OF CULTURE-FAIR TESTS

Davis Eells Games (1953), World Book Company

This test was developed to measure ability of children of differing socio-economic levels. It is composed of a number of items which require no reading nor attention to instructions written on the test forms. Several studies (Cooper, 1958; Richie, 1954; Rosenblum, 1955) have questioned the cultural bias of the test and some of the initial claims for socio-economic fairness are no longer made. The test may have value for use with poor readers (Justman, 1955), but Smith (1956) has indicated that auding ability (ability to understand spoken language) is a major source of bias in the test.

IPAT—A Culture-Free Intelligence Test. Cattell, R. B. Psychological Corporation

This is a test containing figure analogies and figure reasoning items (Cattell, 1940). There are three levels; I, 4–8 years, II, 8–12 years and III, adults. Marquardt (1955) demonstrated that with children from low, middle and high socio-economic groups IPAT Level I was as influenced by socio-economic status as the Stanford Binet but this was not true of Levels II and III. Marquardt ignores the fact in her conclusion that the items on the lower end of the Stanford Binet Scale are not heavily weighted with school learning and achievement and this may have accounted for the similar variability on the IPAT and the Binet. As the items on the Stanford Binet become more difficult, they are more heavily weighted with achievement and one would expect greater discrepancy between this and the IPAT.

Anastasi (1953) tested Puerto Rican children from bi-lingual homes with the IPAT and found that the over-all performance of this group was considerably lower than that reported on the norming sample by Cattell. An analysis of variance of the results showed that there was significant variance attributed to the subjects as well as to the test session. She concluded that there was marked improvement of performance from first to second testing regardless of whether the test was given in English or Spanish. The discrepancy between the bi-lingual performance and the performance of the norming sample was attributed to low socio-economic status, bi-lingualism, lack of test sophistication and poor emotional adjustment to school.

The IPAT was used by Keehn (1955) with Lebanese children in order to determine how well the results agreed with teachers' judgments of intelligence. The Progressive Matrices, a French Dominoes Test and Number series were also administered. Correlation of test score with estimates of intelligence as seen by teachers ranged from −.20 to .52. A factor analysis showed that all tests had saturation on a single factor presumed to be by the authors. Although the tests were heavily loaded on a single factor, they were only slightly correlated with either academic marks or teacher judgments. These results remind one of the arguments offered by Lorge for continuing the bias in tests or determining what so-called culture-fair tests are really measuring. It may be that what is involved in the IPAT as well as the other tests which were used has little relationship to performance in Lebanese schools.

Raven's Progressive Matrices. Raven, J. C. H. K. Lewis & Co., London and Psychological Corporation, New York

The progressive matrices were developed to be a test of "g." They contain three sets of colored matrices which require increasingly difficult figure reasoning abilities. Factorially they measure complex spatial ability and reasoning by analogy. The test has its rationale in Spearman's cognitive principles and the manual reports a "g" saturation of .82. Martin (1954) administered the Progressive Matrices and the Wechsler Intelligence Test for Children (WISC) to 100 Indiana school children between 9 and 10 years. The IQs ranged from 74 to 141 on the WISC with a mean of 107. The correlation between the WISC and the Progressive Matrices were from .83 for the Performance Scale, .84 for the Verbal Scale and .91 for the Full Scale. These correlations are close to the estimated reliability for the WISC and indicate that the tests may be measuring some common ability. These results do not tell us much about the use of the test with various socio-economic groups or with other cultural groups.

Barratt (1956) administered the Progressive Matrices and the WISC to the same children but he reports correlations from .70 to .75 between the two tests. These correlations are considerably lower than those reported by Martin.

Ninety Navajo children attending the U.S. Indian school in Alburquerque were given the Progressive Matrices and the Goodenough Draw a Man (Norman, 1955). The results of this study showed that performance on the Progressive Matrices was consistently inferior to that on the Draw a Man. Other native populations are reputed to have equally poor scores on the Progressive Matrices. Raven in correspondence with Norman, the author of this study, states that African children in French-African colonies seem to "think" differently from Europeans. When they acquire the European's ways of thinking, they begin to perform the matrices test in a more equivalent fashion.

A Semantic Test of Intelligence. Rulon, P. J. Harvard University

At the 1952 Invitational Conference on Testing Problems, Philip Rulon (1952) introduced basic test item types for a test of intelligence which reduced common verbal symbols to a minimum and attempted by the test items to imitate semantic relationships of symbols and concepts. The test requires no understanding of any language and is administered in pantomine. Little research is available on the use of this instrument with various socio-economic groups of children of other cultures. It is included in the list of culture-fair tests because it represents another approach to the problem of developing test items free from bias.

Goodenough Draw a Man. Goodenough, F. (1926)

While the Draw a Man test is not commonly used as a measure of intelligence in school children, some research has been completed to determine whether what is required to complete this test (drawing the human figure) is affected by culture. Britton (19e4) studied social class influences on the test and found that while IQ scores for the DAM were considerable lower than those for verbal tests commonly used in schools, the correlation with socio-economic status was .11. The DAM was administered to children in Lebanon and the scores show that the IQs decline with age from 5 to 10 years except in the school where education was the most similar to that of Western children. The results also showed differences between high and low status Armenian children.

Gestalt Continuation Test. Hector, H. (1960)

This test is in a developmental phase in South Africa and attempts to provide a task for illiterate testees who have had no previous experience with paper and pencil. It also assumes that the ability to trace sequences of angular patterns and continue them reflects an individual's degree of intelligence in the sense of general adaptability. Correlations for 152 illiterates between the Gestalt Continuation Test and Biesheuvel Adaptability Battery were from .38 to .48. The reliability is estimated at .74 to .76. The task requires the continuation of a geometric pattern of straight lines. It is scored either by counting the number of gestalts completed correctly or by counting the number of lines in the longest correct sequence (Tekane, 1960).

7 Squares Test. Hector, H. (Bradley, 1960)

Bradley used the 7 Squares Test devised by Hector to determine whether education of natives affected ability to make meaningful arrangements of 7 black squares. The author found that education had little effect, but suggests the use of this test is still in an experimental stage.

SUMMARY OF THE ATTEMPTS TO PRODUCE CULTURE-FAIR TESTS

From the list of available culture-fair tests we see that there has been an attempt to translate verbal material into pictures which should have equal difficulty for high and low socio-economic groups and attempts to use figural reasoning and figure analogies to be measures of ability. The use of drawings of the human figure has also been explored as well as some new tests to continue gestalt patterns and to produce meaningful representations from abstract materials. Thus far the research on all of these instruments has shown that the results are affected not only by socio-economic status, but by ethnic and cultural origins. What, if anything, can be said about the possibilities of measurement without cultural bias. It would have to be re-stated that these results support Lorge's contentions mentioned earlier and certainly they support Dyer's comments on measurement of human ability (1960). Dyer contends that since any ability test is made up of a series of pieces of the environment to which the pupil is expected to react in one way or another, it is impossible to sample a common denominator of all cultures. Dyer suggests that while it theoretically is possible to find test items which might be pretty comparable to all the sub-cultures of a cultural group, they might when completed predict very little in the way of meaningful validity criteria. He suggests that those psychologists who are interested in improving the lot of the culturally underprivileged should direct their attentions not to changing the tests, but to improving the quality of educational opportunity. The work of the New York City Schools in replacing cultural experiences where they were missing for Puerto Rican and Negro pupils and finding that the test scores improved as the students began to achieve more in school is a good example of what is implied in Dyer's point of view.

TESTING ACTIVITIES IN VARIOUS PARTS OF THE ENGLISH-SPEAKING WORLD WHICH HAVE IMPLICATIONS FOR THE CULTURE-FAIR TESTING MOVEMENT

South Africa

The tests, the Gestalt Continuation Test and the 7 Squares Test have already been mentioned as examples of the type of material which is being produced in South Africa for testing illiterates. Dr. Simon Biesheuvel who is director of personnel research of the South African Council for Scientific and Industiral research has been working in this special testing field for a number of years. His work has been directed toward evaluating the hundreds of thousands of black workers who show up regularly for work in the mines. His responsibility is not only to make some prediction about how well they will perform on the job, but also to select those men who show some aptitude for supervisory activities.

The workers are assigned to training courses and the personnel research group administers tests designed to classify the workers into non-mechanical duties, mechanical duties and supervisory duties. Thes tests are administered by means of silent pictures. Dr. Biesheuvel found that the men were confused by still-life pictures, but that silent motion pictures were most useful in communicating the task demanded by the test. As he takes the test, the worker gets the idea of starting and stopping with instructions, the idea of speed and accuracy, and some understanding of the task involved. By doing so, he demonstrated his degree of adaptability by transferring his experience in the testing situation to other tasks. The men who perform best on the adaptability tests are given leadership tests which involve putting small groups of men through physical tasks in which they have to work as a team and in which it is possible for a man to show whether he has the capacity to direct the work of others.

Biesheuvel has not tried to compare the performance of these workers with performance of workers from other cultures. He feels strongly that there are no culture-free tests and that even concepts like straight lines have cultural implications and values. Their work has been to construct tests which solve the task at hand—to locate the best workers for the mines and find those with supervisory ability. They have been quite successful, but they do not generalize the usefulness of their instruments beyond these results.

United States

Aside from the limitations or even deterioration of measured ability in our culture, certain special ethnic groups in the United States demonstrate dramatically special testing problems. A year ago last summer I had an opportunity to discuss some problems in Indian education with Dr. A.A. Wellck, Director of the University of New Mexico Counseling Center, and Mr. Herbert Blatchford, Consultant to the New Mexican Department of Education, who is stationed in Gallup, New Mexico, the Indian Capitol of the U.S. Mr. Blatchford is a Navajo and it is partly for this reason that he is assigned to working with Navajo children. The Navajos present special problems to education in New Mexico. The Navajos have stubbornly maintained their special culture for centuries. The Pueblo Indians, Hopis and Zunis have accommodated to the teaching of the mission fathers, and participate more fully in what amounts to Spanish-American general culture. On the other hand, the Navajos who refer to themselves as the "Denay," which means the chosen people, have resisted erosion of their old ways.

One of their particular problems in school is their slow work pace. Navajo children who seem perfectly happy and well adjusted in school tend to meet any scholastic assignment as if there were all the time in the world. If they are given any speeded test, even with exhortations to work as fast as they can, they proceed dutifully, but at a more leisurely pace. For example, their scores on a California Test of Mental Ability (CTMM) or Otis (Higher Form) are always markedly depressed because they do not finish. They do better on a test such as the School and College Ability Test (SCAT) which is relatively unspeeded, but it is apparent that no existing test is satisfactory. Even the WISC presents a picture which seems to be markedly out of proportion to what observers feel is their true potential. The Navajo children earn few time bonus points on WISC performance scores even though they may completely understand what they are supposed to do and proceed skillfully. Their familiarity with objects presented is usually as great as that of the Pueblos or Hopis, but their work pace results in lower scores. In this case, deliberateness and inability to accept speed make the existent measurement devices more unsuitable for them than for other Southwest Indians.

Mr. Blatchford uses the School and College Ability Tests, and feels that they predict pretty well the degree to which the Navajos will succeed in school. These tests are not only heavily culture bound, but they involve speed and previous achievment. However, as Mr. Blatchford puts it, "We are interested in what makes these Indians unique, but when it comes to determining how they will do in school, we need measures of scholastic potential, not culture-fair tests."

Dr. A.A. Wellck, Director of Counseling and Testing, from the University of New Mexico is responsible for the state testing program and for the compilation of measurement data throughout New Mexico. He concurs with Mr. Blatchford in his views on the limitations of so-called culture-fair tests and also states that no culture-fair tests are used in the state testing program in New Mexico even though there is a very high percentage of Spanish-American and Indian children attending schools in the state. The experience of specialists in New Mexico is that the culture-fair tests have little value and that scholastic predictors are the most usable sources of information for educational application.

Dr. H. T. Manuel of the University of Texas is presently revising and standardizing the successors to the Cooperative Inter-American Tests published by Educational Testing Service in 1950. This work is financed largely by the U. S. Office of Education. The tests in preparation are scholastic ability tests and reading tests for use from the primary grades to the first year of college. While these tests are not designed to be culture-fair in the sense that is usually meant by the term, they offer another approach to the problem of measuring people from different ethnic and cultural backgrounds. This approach is to translate material into the native tongue and then pre-test, conduct item studies, formulate final editions and standardize the tests.

Dr. Pablo Roca who was formerly Technical Director of the Department of Education in Haito Rey, Puerto Rico, presently with the U. S. Office of Education, has just published under the auspices of the Psychological Corporation, a Spanish edition of the Wechsler Intelligence Test for Children. This approach is essentially the same as that undertaken by Manuel, and represents a translation of existing English language test material and the subsequent standardization of the items on a different cultural population.

Another attempt at evaluating learning ability of children from different cultural groups which is at the same time a departure from the approaches described thus far is the unpublished work of Arthur R. Jensen at the University of California in Berkeley. He located four groups of children—high and low IQ Mexican-Americans, and high and low IQ Anglo-Americans by means of the California Test of Mental Maturity. The children comprised an unselected population from fourth and fifth grades in eastern Contra Costa County in California. Learning tasks were administered to the four groups of children. The tasks were composed of recall of familiar objects, serial learning, and paired associates learning. The child responded in either English or Spanish. He found a significant nationality x IQ interaction with the low IQ Mexican-American children performing better than the low IQ Anglo-Americans, while there was little difference at the high IQ levels. The same tasks were administered two weeks later and the results showed that the reliabilities of the tests were substantial. He concludes that the development of a complete battery of direct learning tests should have promise for improving the assessment of learning ability and the diagnosis of educational disabilities, especially in ethnic and cultural groups.

Jensen's procedure is comparable to an approach suggested by Sorenson (1963) where the time spent in learning and the number of errors recorded in a programmed learning task could replace traditional IQ tests as measures of intelligence.

Canada

In the Province of British Columbia,[1] regular testing in the schools includes children who are Chinese, Japanese, Indian and Eskimo as well as "white." The performance of these ethnic groups of children must be interpreted in terms of selective immigration and does not offer much in the way of information about the fairness of existing tests for these groups. Recently in this province the recording of racial origin of children has been frowned upon

[1]The author is indebted to Dr. Clifford Conway, Director, Division of Tests Standards and Research, Province of British Columbia, for this information.

as an aspect of segregation. As a result there is no indication on school records as to the cultural or ethnic background of the child. This makes it relatively impossible to gather any data about how well particular children perform in intelligence tests or school tasks. Children from different cultural groups are incorporated into regular classes and teachers are instructed not to segregate the pupils into special classes or to treat them differently in any way. Indian and Eskimo children attend public schools, private and residential schools. The efforts of those charged with the responsibility of Indian Education (Renaud, 1958) are directed toward acculturation of these youngsters. The success of the acculturation program can be measured by the degree to which the gap between the "whites" and the ethnic groups closes as they proceed through the school grades. Snider (1961) studied acculturated Indian high school students in northern Idaho. His findings demonstrate that the performance of the acculturated group was comparable to the performance of other children with whom they went to school, and in some learning areas there were no significant differences between the two groups.

These data offer little in the way of enlightenment about the use of culture-fair measurements to evaluate Indian and Eskimo learning potential in Canada. While non-verbal tests are frequently used, they are selected because they minimize reading handicap rather than because they offer common cultural denominators which would make them fair measures for these pupils.

The efforts of educators in Canada have been to look at the Indian and Eskimo as he compares to others in his own tribe or ethnic group as well as to compare him with children not of his ethnic group but of the same age. Here again the need is enunciated for a wide a variety of measures resulting in as broad a description of the pupil as possible. No one test is believed to do the job of measuring native potential and these educators are aware of the limitation of the tests which they use. They deal with cultural handicaps not by trying to perpetuate their effect on education, but to reduce them so pupils thus handicapped can profit more from instruction.

Australia

Even though there are a great variety of racial, ethnic and cultural groups in Australia, little work has been done at a national level with tests designed to be culture-free. Mr. S. S. Dunn, who is the Assistant Director of the Australian Council for Educational Research and in charge of the Test Division, writes that there has been little work on the topic. A few small studies have been conducted in which such tests as the Progressive Matrices have been used with New Australians and Australian aborigines, but the results are inconclusive. Mr. Dunn writes that "to prepare a culture-free test, one must assume that you can find a content that is equally familiar in all cultures, an impossibility, or that one can divorce the quality of thought processes in problem solving from familiarity with content." He goes on to say that "In my opinion quality of thinking cannot be divorced from familiarity with the content area in which the thinking takes place. Thus, a non-verbal test which uses such non-verbal symbols as triangles, squares, etc., is not culturally free when used to test, say, two races, one of which is far more familiar with the symbols than the other." Empirically, researchers have found that Asian students do less well on Progressive Matrices than one would expect from their scholastic results. Even though the test is completely abstract in content, it is not a "fair" test for the Asian students.

Overview of Work in Progress

These comments certainly confirm the fact that measurement specialists in different parts of the world are in essential agreement about the value and use of culture-fair tests. From these major sources of professional opinion and action in measurement, one must conclude that culture-fair tests as they are now described may have value in assessing certain aspects of the cognitive abilities of those tested, but they lose meaning when scores from one cultural group are compared with scores from another. The approach of those responsible for evaluating abilities of people from a complex culture is to design tests with specific predictive potential in mind and then to test their validity against the criterion. This is the approach in South Africa. Translation of English language tests into other languages and then standardizing them is another approach. Omitting the goal of fairness in testing and evaluating students on how well they will succeed in specific scholastic tasks is still another approach. Finally it has also been noted that measuring the ability to learn new tasks has potential in evaulating the degree to which students may succeed in subsequent learning situations.

SUMMARY AND CONCLUSION

There is a paradox in the theory and practice of educators who would, on the one hand speak up for the need to understand individual differences, and on the other hand continue to support educational programs which sublimate such differences to single standard evaluations of accomplishment. John H. Niemeyer, writing in the September 12, 1959, issue of *The Saturday Review*, estimates that perhaps one-half of the pupil population of the nation is culturally deprived. "It is these young people," states Mr. Neimeyer, "whom our schools, staffed generally with teachers whose eyes are focused on an Anglo-Saxon middle class way of life and who utilize educational procedures geared to that way of life, are leaving almost entirely untapped." In the current emphasis in education on academic excellence, one must remember that large numbers of youth come from backgrounds where cultural deprivations exist; cultural deprivations which have a decided negative effect upon effective intellectual learning. The New York City program, Higher Horizons, has shown that by removing some of the cultural deficiencies, children who otherwise would have dropped out of high school or not succeeded beyond graduation have a much greater chance of developing into educated citizens. Such new programs in education show that there is promise in programs of acculturation with the resultant improvement in the youngster's ability to profit from education. Such programs do not provide, however, much information as to how to locate those students who have ability to profit from such educational and cultural opportunity when their test scores are far below average because of cultural interaction with the test material.

The tests now used to measure scholastic potential can predict traditional school success quite adequately. Many of them have been continually improved over the years so correlations between scholastic ability and achievement are quite high. What has happened has been that as education has become more and more standardized, ability tests have become more and more refined to predict this common standard. There is a single criterion for educational success in most courses taught in school. To the extent that these criteria have factors in common with ability tests, the prediction is good and the validity of the ability test is established.

Such comments lead next to the question of what happens when the common standard for achievement is changed. The National Science Foundation, interested in improving instruction in the physical and biological sciences, contracted with Educational Testing Service to develop achievement tests to measure performance in the new science curricula. One interesting finding (Ferris, 1961) was that scores on the School And College Ability Tests (SCAT) do not predict scores on the new physical science achievement tests as well as they predict scores on other achievement tests. This finding is especially interesting since the achievement tests were designed to measure anticipation and thinking in science problems. Ferris reports that many students below the 75 percentile on SCAT were able to ahcieve as well as, or better than, students above this cut-off point. Ferris believes that a type of ability is measured by the achievement tests which is not being measured by the traditional scholastic aptitude tests. Further efforts of this type which change educational curricula and subsequently or concomitantly investigate the degree to which these new learnings can be predicted by existing or newly-developed ability tests are extremely important. Such efforts involve proposed changes in curricula which can be described and implemented into the school setting. They provide some encouragement for a wider variety of achievement and success for some students who might get passed over by the more traditional educational programs.

The problem in developing culture-fair tests lies, just as in test development problems of any type, in deciding on what types of items and cognitive abilities such tests should include. After the test development process has been concluded the tests must be validated against acceptable criteria. If there are educational criteria which can be established, which are different from the traditional ones, as in the case of the Physical Science Study Committee work by Ferris, it may be possible to validate revised ability tests against new educational criteria. If such criteria do not exist, the problem of obtaining meaningful validity information still remains. There is nothing wrong with developing ability tests which are reliable and which can be shown to measure important individual differences. Such a task is descriptive of the work of Raven, Cattell, Davis and Eells reported previously. These tests seem to have fair reliability and validity for measuring individual differences of the particular behavioral tasks involved, but research has shown that the predictive validity in estimating school achievement is fairly weak. Some new way of classifying or evaluating the usability of such tests as the Progressive Matrices or the IPAT and the others which have been mentioned is necessary, and new criteria against which to validate the tests may also be necessary.

Haggard (1952) summarizes the test development problems for culture-fair tests and lists four areas which need research consideration: (1) existing tests have measured only a very narrow range of mental abilities, namely those related to verbal or academic success, and have ignored many other abilities and problem-solving skills, which are perhaps more important for adjustment and success—even in a middle class society; (2) existing tests have failed to provide measures of the wide variety of qualitative differences in the modes or processes of solving mental problems; (3) even culture-fair tests have ignored the differences in cultural training and socialization on the repertoire of experience of not only different cultural groups, but on the sub-groups of culture as well; (4) mental functioning has been considered in isolation and must be related to culturally determined personality and values of the individual.

A review of the item types of culture-fair tests would certainly support Haggard's contention that only a narrow range of abilities has been provided for. Test developers have substituted abstract figural reasoning for abstract verbalreasoning items. Often spatial abilities predominate and determine the fdegree to which a student is able to perform well on these tests. In other cases, items which favor a lower cultural group have been included in order to make the test less biased. Items measuring social intelligence—as often factored mental ability (Thorndike, 1926)—are added to the Davis Eells Tests in order to make them more fair for lower socioeconomic groups. Anastasi (1961), however, suggests that all cultural groups on which test information is obtained should be tested by as wide a variety of tests as possible. It is an obvious fact that groups do not occupy the same relative position when compared in different intellectual traits. She goes on to suggest that some meaningful classification of tests by the factors which the tests are measuring would be most useful.

If one refers to Guilford's Structure of Intellect (1956; 1958), the variety of test item types used on the many culture-fair tests take on new meaning. First of all it becomes possible to suggest a position for each of the tests in terms of Guilford's three classifications of intellectual activities—operations, products, and contents. Thus the more traditional ability tests—those not designed to be culture-fair—can be (if the factor structure of the test is known) arranged in this matrix according to the abilities which are being measured. The culture-fair tests, if their factor structure is known, could also be arranged in this matrix. What would result would be some overlapping of intellectual factors measured by some of the culture-biased and culture-fair tests. In most cases there would be little overlap since it is hypothesized that culture-fair tests as they are now designed are measuring different intellectual abilities from the abilities measured by conventional ability tests.

If the existing culture-fair tests could be adminsitered in batteries with tests of reference factors (French, 1951), information could be given about the types of intellectual abilities that they are measuring. This would add greatly to our knowledge of the uniqueness or commonness of the culture-fair materials.

An extension of this approach would also be useful and contribute to our knowledge of cutural differences as they vary with performance on intellectual tasks. Such a study would be patterned after the work of Swineford (1948) who studied general, verbal and spatial factors as they differ in performance of boys and girls, change with increase in mental maturity, vary with bright and dull pupils, and predict success in school performance.

Tests with items having symbols and semantics which are common to a variety of cultures, measuring a number of the established factors, could be placed with tests of reference factors in a battery. This battery could be then administered across sub-cultural groups within a given culture, and across distinct cultural or ethnic groups. The results would add greatly to our enlightenment of how these groups differ. Prediction of success in a variety of educational tasks and life situations for that particular cultural or ethnic group from a combination of tests would then increase our knowledge of how valid such batteries are as predictors of useful, practical criteria for that culture.

REFERENCES

Anastasi, Anne, and I. Cruz. 1953. "Language Development and Non-Verbal IQ of Puerto Rican Children in N $$,York City," *J. Abnorm. Soc.Psychol.,* 54, 357–366.

Anastasi, Anne, and F. A. Cordova. 1953. "Some Effects of Bilingualism upon the Intelligence Test Performance of Puerto Rican Children in New York City," *J. Educ. Psychol.,* 44 1–19.

Anastasi, Anne. 1958. *Differential Psychology.* New York: Macmillan.

Anastasi, Anne. 1961. "Psychological Tests: Uses and Abuses," *Teachers Coll. Rec.*, 62, 389–393.

Barratt, E. S. 1956. "The Relationship of the Progressive Matrices and the Columbia Mental Maturity Scale to the WISC," *J. Consult. Psychol.*, 20, 294–296.

Bradley, D. J. 1960. "The Ability of Black Groups to Produce Recognizable Patterns on the 7-Squares Test," *J. Nat. Inst. Personnel Res.* 8, 142–144.

Britton, J. H. 1954. "Influence of Social Class upon Performance on the Draw A Man Test," *J. Educ. Psychol.*, 45, 44–51.

Burke, H. R. 1958. "Raven's Progressive Matrices—A Review and Cricital Examination," *J. Genet. Psychol.*, 93, 199–228.

Cattell, R. B. 1940. "A Culture-Free Intelligence Test," *J. Educ. Psychol.*, 31, 161–179.

Coleman, W., and Annie W. Ward. 1953. "A Comparison of the Davis Eells and Kuhlman Finch Scores of Children from High and Low S-E Status," *J. Educ. Psychol*, 46, 465–469.

Cooper, J. G. 1958. "Predicting School Achievement for Bi-lingual Pupils," *J. Educ. Psychol.*, 49, 34–36.

Davis, A. 1948. *Social Class Influences upon Learning.* (The Inglis Lecture, 1948) Cambridge, Mass.: Harvard Univer. Press.

Davis, A., and K. Eells. 1953. *Manual for the Davis Eells Test of General Intelligence.* Yonkers on Hudson, New York: World Book Co.

Davis, A. 1951. "Socio Economic Influences upon Children's Learning," *Proceedings of Midcentury White House Conference on Children and Youth.* Report of conference sessions, Washington, D. C., December 3–7, 1950. Raleigh, North Carolina: Health Publications Institute, Inc.

Dennis, W. 1957. "Performance of Near Eastern Children on the Draw a Man Test," *Child Develpm.*, 28, 427–30.

Dyer, H. 1960. "A Psychometrician Views Human Ability," *Teachers Coll. Rec.*, 61, 394–403.

Eells, K. 1951. *Intelligence and Cultural Differences.* Chicago: Univer. of Chicago Press.

Ferris, F. L. 1961. "Some New Science Curricula and Their Measurement," *Proceedings of the Western Regional Conference on Testing Problems.* Los Angeles: Educational Testing Service.

French, J. W. 1951. "The Description of Aptitude and Achievement Tests in Terms of Rotated Factors," *Psychometr. Monogr.*, No. 5.

Geist, H. 1954. "Evaluation of Culture-Free Intelligence," *Calif. J. Educ. Res.*, 5, 209–214.

Goodenough, Florence. 1926. *The Measurement of Intelligence by Drawings.* Yonkers, New York: World Book Co.

Guilford, J. P. 1956. "The Structure of Intellect," *Psychol. Bull.*, 53, 267–293.

Guilford, J. P. 1958. "New Frontiers of Testing in the Discovery and Development of Human Talent," *Proceedings of the Seventh Annual Western Regional Conference on Testing Problems.* Los Angeles: Educational Testing Service.

Haggard, E. A. 1952. "Techniques for the Development of Unbiased Tests," *Proceedings Invitational Conference on Testing Problems.* Princeton, New Jersey: Educational Testing Service.

Hector, H. 1960. "Results from a Simple Gestalt Continuation Test Applied to Illiterate Black Mineworkers," *J. Nat. Inst. Personnel Res.*, 8, 145–147.

Indian and Eskimo Welfare Commission. 1958. *Residential Education for Indian Acculturation.* Ottowa, Ontario: Oblate Fathers in Canada.

Justman, J., and Miriam Aronow. "The Davis Eells Games as a Measure of the Intelligence of Poor Readers," *J. Educ. Psychol.* 46, 418–22.

Keehn, J. D., and E. Prothro. 1955. "Non-Verbal Tests as Predictors of Academic Success in Lebanon," *Educ. Psychol. Measmt.*, 15, 495–498.

Knief, Lotus, and J. B. Stroud. 1959. "Intercorrelations among Various Intelligence Achievement, and Social Class Scores," *J. Educ. Psychol.*, 50, 117–120.

Lorge, I. 1952. "Difference of Bias in Tests of Intelligence," *Proceedings Invitational Conference on Testing Problems.* Princeton, New Jersey: Educational Testing Service.

Lucas, C. M. 1953. *Survey of the Literature Relating to the Effects of Cultural Background on Aptitude Test Scores.* Research Bulletin. Princeton, New Jersey: Educational Testing Service.

McNemar, Q. 1942. *The Revisions of the Standford Binet Scale.* Boston: Houghton-Mifflin.

Marquardt, Dorothy I., and Lois L. Bailey. 1955. "An Evaluation of the Culture-Free Test of Intelligence," *J. Genet. Psychol.*, 87, 353–358.

Martin, A. W., and J. E. Weichers. 1954. "Raven's Colored Progressive Matrices and the Wechsler Intelligence Scale for Children," *J. Consult. Psychol.*, 18, 143–4.

Norman, R. D. and Katherine L. Midkiff. "Navajo Children on Raven Progressive Matrices and Draw a Man Test," *Southwest J. Anthrop.*, 10, 129–136.

Raven, J. C. 1951. *Guide to Using Progressive Matrices.* London: H. K. Lewis.

Renaud, A. 1958. "Indian Education Today," *Anthropologica*, 6, 15–22.

Richie, Alice. 1954. "A Comparison of the Kuhlman Anderson with the Davis Eells Intelligence Tests in a Fifth Grade," *Calif. J. Educ. Res.*, 5, 186.

Roca, P. 1961. *Escala De Intelligencia Wechsler Para Ninos.* New York: Psychological Corp.

Rosenblum, S., J. E. Keller, and N. Papnia. 1955. "Davis-Eells Test Performance of Lower Class Retarded Children," *J. Consult. Psychol.*, 19, 51–4.

Rulon, P. J. 1952. "A Semantic Test of Intelligence," *Proceedings Invitational Conference on Testing Problems.* Princeton, New Jersey: Educational Testing Service.

Sawrey, J. M. 1955. "The Predictive Effectiveness of Two Non-Verbal Tests of Intelligence in First Grade," *Calif. J. Educ. Res.*, 5, 133.

Smith, T. W. 1956. *Auding and Reading Skills as Sources of Cultural Bias in the Davis Eells Games and California Test of Mental Maturity.* Unpublished doctoral dissertation, Univer. of Southern California.

Snider, J. G. 1961. "Achievement Test Performance of Acculturated Indian Children," *Alberta J. Educ. Res.*, 7, 39–41.

Sorenson, A. G. 1963. "The Use of Teaching Machines in Developing an Alternative to the Concept of Intelligence," *Educ. Psychol. Measmt.*, 23, 323–30.

Swineford, Frances. 1948. "A Study in Factor Analysis: The Nature of the General, Verbal and Spatial Bi-factors," *Supplementary Educational Monographs*, Univ. of Chicago Press, 67.

Tekane, I. 1960. "A New and Objective Scoring Method for the Gestalt Continuation Test," *J. Nat. Inst. Personnel Res.*, 8, 148–150.

Thorndike, E. L. 1926. *The Measurement of Intelligence.* New York: Teachers Coll., Columbia Univer.

Woods, W. A. and R. Toal. 1957. "Subtest Disparity of Negro and White Groups Matched for IQ's on the Revised Beta Test." *J. Consult. Psychol.*, 21, 136–8.

Joel T. Campell

23 / Testing of Culturally Different Groups *

Tests that predict academic performance have won an accepted place in American education at all levels from preprimary grades to advanced graduate work. Use of the tests under different circumstances and with different groups showed that some groups consistently received lower average scores than did others. Thus, in repeated studies with different tests, Negroes receive lower scores than white people, Northern whites score higher than Southern whites, children from higher socioeconomic groups achieve better scores than do children from lower socioeconomic groups.

These facts have led to a number of questions about education, the acquisition of intelligent behavior, and the inherent and acquired characteristics of racial and cultural groupings. This paper is intended to explore the current status of some of these questions, to identify the areas where research evidence is incomplete, and to suggest a research program to fill some of the deficiencies.

RACIAL DIFFERENCES AND ENVIRONMENTAL STIMULATION

Most of the studies on differences in tested intelligence of racial groups have been done within the framework of controversy. Those who held that genetic factors accounted for the differences between racial groups, and those who held that socioeconomic and educational factors were responsible, accumulated data and published studies to support their respective positions. This extensive literature has been reviewed recently by Dreger and Miller (1960) and by Shuey (1958). Shuey concludes that the data "all point to the presence of some native differences between Negroes and whites as determined by intelligence tests." Dreger and Miller, who admit an environmentalist bias, say that ". . . a number of differences attributed in time past to heredity have been shown to be the result of social class determination. It is not clear whether some differences adumbrated here, specifically in the intelligence and temperament realms, are genetically based or not."

Lucas (1953) surveyed the literature relating to the effects of cultural background on aptitude test scores. He pointed out that "intelligence (and aptitude) is a psychological construct that has been inferred from observable

*This study was made in 1964. Reprinted by permission of the College Entrance Examination Board and Educational Testing Service.

268

operations; it does not have an independent existence. . . . The task of finding operations common to many cultures, to which one can anchor the construct and still define it as intelligence, appears to be a weighty task. . . . On the other hand, perhaps intelligence in Culture A is not intelligence in Culture B and so on, and a better way of regarding intelligence would be Culture A Intelligence, Culture B Intelligence, and so on."

Anastasi (1958) has commented on the difficulty, if not the impossibility, of obtaining conclusive evidence on the issue, in view of the complex way in which racial, social, cultural, and educational variables are interrelated. It is clear that one racial group, the Negroes, has had disadvantages resulting from discrimination in employment, in housing, and in education. The economic disadvantages affect the probability that the child will have books and toys available for early learning experiences; inadequate housing may mean that there is no space for doing homework; education frequently has been inferior, whether in segregated schools in the South or in the split-shift slum schools of the North. All of these thing directly or indirectly affect test performance. Burt has commented, "There can be no question that environmental conditions may influence the results obtained with intelligence tests of the usual kind. How great that influence is will depend on the style of test employed and the type of child examined" (Burt & Howard, 1957).

The demonstration experiments of Moore (1960), involving use of a specially equipped typewriter to teach nursery school children to read and to type, may indicate that even the more privileged children do not receive the type of environmental stimulation which would result in maximal intellectual development.

At the other extreme, there is evidence that severe environmental deficit in infancy will result in severe retardation (Dennis, 1960) or possibly even death (Spitz, 1955).

Cultural deficit has been shown to be important even at the adult level for those diagnosed as mentally deficient. Mundy (1957) matched two groups of 28 institutionalized women on Wechsler Verbal, Performance and Total scores and on Raven's matrices. One group was retained in the institution, while women from the other group were placed in jobs in the community. Testing after two years showed that the "ordinary life" group received higher mean scores than the institutional group on all tests.

From animal psychology studies has come evidence that early environment affects later learning ability and other behavior for dogs, rats, rhesus monkeys, and other animals (Hebb, 1949). For example, Cooper and Zubek (1958) raised rats from bright and dull strains in enriched environment, deprived environment, and normal laboratory environment. Rats from both strains did almost equally well when raised in the enriched environment, almost equally poorly when raised in the deprived environment. Only those raised in the normal laboratory environment showed a clear differentiation in maze learning. Calhoun (1963) has shown that abnormal behavior in rats can result simply from overcrowding within a restricted space, even though food and water are plentiful. Behavior disturbances "ranged from sexual deviation to cannibalism and from frenetic overactivity to a pathological withdrawal."

Hahggard (1954) assessed the effect of practice and of motivation on the testing of children of high and low socioeconomic status. He found that three practice sessions improved the retest performance of high status children, but not of low status. "Motivation," provided in the form of theater passes for good performance (actually given to all children), was not effective when given during practice sessions, but was effective in improving retest performance when given during the retest session.

Quite likely, some of the reported differences are due to test-taking motivation, although this factor alone cannot account for all differences.

It should be mentioned specifically, perhaps, that despite differences in *central tendency* of test scores among various groups, individuals from all groups may be found throughout the range of scores. Jenkins (1948), for example, cites cases of Negroes with tested IQ's as high as 200.

CULTURE-FREE OR CULTURE-FAIR TESTS

Attempts to measure the intelligence of different cultural groups forced the realization that tests were based on cultural content. Thus, comparison in test results between children from different groups might show differences either because the basic capacity was unequal or because one group had more opportunity to learn the performance required or more motivation to perform well on the test. Numerous efforts were made to contruct "culture-free" tests. Dyer has commented, "So-called 'culture-free' tests are built on one of two assumptions: (1) either the learning required to perform acceptably on the test is commonly and equally available to all people of all cultures, or (2) the stimulus material on the test is completely novel to all people of all cultures. Both assumptions are patently false" (Tumin, Ed., 1963).

Hudson (1960, 1962) illustrates that much of what we tend to take for granted in our culture is actually learned. Testing the pictorial depth perceptions of groups in Africa, he showed that those in school, both black and white, interpreted pictures as two-dimensional scenes.

Similarly, McFie (1961) found that nonverbal test scores of Africans improved after they had had two years of technical institute training. He concluded that visual perception can be trained at the young adult level, even when it is not a part of the native culture. Lloyd and Pigeon (1961) made a deliberate effort to coach children in Africa on nonverbal test material. Children from European and African origin showed improvement, while children of Indian origin did not. The reason for the difference was not apparent.

Eells, Davis, Havighurst, Herrick, and Tyler (1951) made a study of item response differences between high and low socioeconomic status groups. Following this, Davis and Eells devised a test which was intended to minimize class differences in test performance. However, subsequent studies have indicated that the Davis-Eells test is also affected by social class status, and does not predict school achievement as well as do the more traditional tests (Knief, 1957; Tate & Voss, 1956; Russell, 1956).

There are few studies which show Negroes, or other persons from deprived backgrounds, doing better on other types of tests than they do on verbal and mathematical tests. Those few studies which do exist give results which differ from one sample to another. Thus, Woods and Toal (1957), using the Revised Beta test, conclude that Negroes do better on tests of perceptual speed and accuracy. In contrast, Davidson, Gibby, McNeil, Segal, and Silverman (1950), using the Wechsler-Bellevue scale on psychoneurotic patients at a Veterans Administration hospital, conclude that Negroes do not do as well as whites on the psychomotor speed factor! Teahan and Drews (1962) compared Northern and Southern Negro children on the WISC. They found the following results:

	Southern
Verbal mean score	80.29
Performance mean score	68.83
	Northern
Verbal mean score	87.42
Performance mean score	88.38

Stake (1961) found that Negro children in Atlanta did slightly better than white children on two rote memory tasks. They did almost as well as the white children on tests of perceptual speed and spatial relations. There also was lower relationship between race and learning tasks of new materials than there was between race and the usual type intelligence tests. However, these variables were not as effective in predicting school grades of the total group as were the tests involving verbal and arithmetic components. He did not, however, compute these relationships for the Negro group separately. Stake's findings on rote memory are substantiated in a study by Semler and Iscoe (1963), who found learning rate not related to race and only slightly to WISC scores.

The general conclusion must be that it does not appear to be promising to attempt to find a test (a) on which Negroes and others from deprived backgrounds will do better than they do on verbal and mathematical tests and (b) which will predict performance in higher education.

HOW WELL DO TESTS PREDICT COLLEGE PERFORMANCE OF STUDENTS OF LOWER SOCIOECONOMIC STATUS?

Even though test scores and socioeconomic status are related, the question remains as to how well this score predicts academic achievement for the lower socioeconomic group and whether there is a more valid method of selecting students for college.

A recent study by Clark and Plotkin (1963) has received wide publicity. It concluded that verbal and quantitative tests do not predict the academic achievement of Negro students in integrated schools and should, therefore, receive close attention. The sample on which this study was based was composed of those

(1) who had submitted a precollege information form to the National Scholarship Service and Fund for Negro Students (NSSFNS) in connection with a request for counselling or financial assistance;

(2) who completed a questionnaire on postcollege adjustment;

(3) for whom a college transcript was available.

Of 1,519 students, transcripts were received for 1,281 and questionnaires from 545. Analysis was based on 509 complete data cases, although some data is given for the nonrespondent group. In some places in the report, it is difficult to tell which group is involved.

Clark and Plotkin draw several conclusions from their study. Among these are the following:

(1) Test scores, including scores on the SAT, do not predict effectively the performance of Negro students in integrated colleges.

(2) Negro students from the South have better academic performance than those from the North.

Concerning the first point, at least some of the data which they present appears to lead to contrary conclusions. They distinguish three groups: Group B, successful completion of college with B- average or better; Group C, successful completion with C+ or lower average; and Group DNC, who did not complete the course.

The following data are presented:

	SAT Median Scores	
Group	Verbal	Mathematics
B	534	477
C	496	481
DNC	475	537

It is not clear whether SAT scores were available for all 509 cases, or, if not, what N this comparison is based on. For the larger group of both respondents and nonrespondents, the following information is given:

	SAT Verbal	SAT Mathematics
Received degree	507	473
Did not receive degree	453	476

These probably are medians also, but this was not explicitly stated, nor is the N given. From these two tables, it appears that the verbal score differentiates the Negro students on academic performance, while the mathematics score has an inverse relationship. Wothout more knowledge of such group characteristics as sex composition, college concerned, and so on, it appears futile to speculate on reasons for this pattern.

Data are also presented for one specific subgroup, those students who were recruited in an intensive program in Southern high schools during the years 1953 to 1955. In this program the top 10 percent of graduating classes in 45 Southern and border cities were tested with a special form of the PSAT. Of these, half met the minimal standards required by NSSFNS (Plaut, 1957). Scores received on this test by those who reappeared in Clark and Plotkin's study were as follows:

Respondents Only	PSAT Medians	
Group	Verbal	Mathematical
B	379	358
C	391	371
DNC	360	340
Total Goup		
Received degree	381	361
Did not receive degree	377	352

Again, the N's are not given for either group, although they state that the differences are not significant.

There are some limitations inherent in the design of their study which affect the generalization which can be drawn from it. The group to whom they sent questionnaires included everyone who had *applied* for scholarship assistance from the National Scholarship Service and Fund for Negro Students (NSSFNS) and who later attended an integrated college. This included those who were assisted and those who did not qualify, for whatever reason. It seems possible that this introduced a biasing factor into the sample, since students from the North might be able to attend a state or municipal college, or even a nearby private college, without financial assistance, while few students from the South were likely to be able to attend an integrated college, during this time period, unless they qualified for financial assistance. This probably means that those from the South were better qualified than those from the North, merely by selection.

A second factor is that of the college attended. The colleges attended vary widely in degree of selectivity. It is not unlikely that those admitted to the more selective and academically more stringent colleges were the better students of the group, and that, in general, those students who did not measure up to that level went to the less selective colleges. Since the same credence was given to grades achieved and to graduation regardless of the college attended, this pattern, if it in fact existed, would reduce the apparent relationship between test score and college success.

Results from other sources indicate that selection tests are valid predictors for students attending predominantly Negro colleges. Hills, Klock, and Lewis (1963) have reported the correlation of SAT verbal and mathematics scores with first year average grades from freshmen entering both the white and Negro colleges in the Georgia State University system. The ranges of the resulting validity coefficients are shown separately for men and women in the following table.

Range of Correlation Coefficients Between SAT Scores
and First Year Average Grades

	N's		Verbal		Mathematical	
			Male Students			
Negro colleges	97	119	.29	.55	.29	.54
White colleges	96	1055	.18	.54	.02	.53
			Female Students			
Negro colleges	131	202	.51	.51	.40	.44
White colleges	64	709	.44	.56	.21	.58

(In the table above, the validity of .75 for the mathematics test on 12 female students at Georgia Tech has been disregarded.) The size of the validity coefficients for the Negro colleges is the more striking since the standard deviations of the SAT scores for white students range from 85.7 to 100.4 while for Negro students it ranges from 40.7 to 51.5.

These results are consistent with the results obtained by Lowry (1957) who found the predictive validity of the ACE, Iowa High School Content and Cooperative Reading Comprehension tests for various groups in a private liberal arts college for Negroes. The validity coefficients ranged from .39 to .83.

An unpublished study from Fisk University shows validity for the SAT against first year grades to be .49 for males and .57 for females on the verbal section and .61 for males and .59 for females for the mathematical section.

On the other hand, Roberts (1950) found that Northern Negro women did better on both the ACE and first year achievement than did Southern Negro women attending Fisk University. By the senior year, however, the achievement differences between the two groups had disappeared for those of higher socioeconomic status, although the difference increased for those of lower socioeconomic status.

It may be that a four-year period is sufficient for a person who does not perform well on a paper and pencil test due to inferior learning opportunities to overcome that handicap when given the stimulation of a good college program.

No studies have been found which would show other types of tests or selection methods to have greater validity. A hypothesis would seem to be that the developed verbal and mathematical skills measured by such tests as the ACE and SAT are necessary for effective college learning, at least as the college programs are now organized and conducted.

EFFECT OF CULTURAL ENRICHMENT OR EDUCATIONAL "PUSH"

Whether or not there is a genetic difference between the potential of racial groups, there is evidence that increased emphasis on educational achievement will result in increased gain in educational achievement. Most of the studies which have been done appear to be demonstrations that change as many elements as possible, rather than control experiments to see what factors will create change. That is, instead of varying one condition and evaluating the effect of that one factor, the typical study changes several factors simultaneously so that it is not possible to tell whether one factor is responsible for the change or whether a combination is necessary. For example, a study involving seventh grade students modeled in part after the New York City Higher Horizons Program involved four features:

(1) An in-service reading skills instruction program for teachers

(2) A program of increased teacher-parent relationships designed to improve student motivation and study conditions

(3) A program of group guidance designed to heighten occupational awareness and to lift self-concepts

(4) A program of cultural enrichment.

This program resulted in a measured gain in reading level of 1.5 years between September and May where .8 years is the expected gain rate (Brazziel & Gordon, 1963). Similarly, the Demonstration-Guidance project and the Higher Horizons project in New York City included a variety of activities and efforts to upgrade the young people. They achieved successful results but there is no way of telling which facets of the program were essential, which were helpful but not essential, and which factors had no effect.

At the elementary level, a six-weeks project to improve reading and number readiness for first grade students was carried out at a school in Tennessee (Brazziel & Terrell, 1962). This project involved weekly meetings with parents, having the children watch a daily thirty-minute educational television program at home, and the use of readiness readers designed to develop perception, vocabulary, work reasoning, and the ability and will to follow directions. In addition, each week the children were given a test on some phase of readiness. Scores on the Metropolitan Readiness Tests at the end of the six-week period showed that the experimental group was significantly higher than the three control groups in both number and reading readiness. On total score, the experimental group was also higher than the classes taught by the experimental group and control group teachers the year before. No indication is given as to the activities of the control groups during the six-week period.

Lee (1951) has shown that Negro children in the Philadelphia schools who had gone to kindergarten achieved higher scores on the Philadelphia Tests of Mental and Verbal Ability than those who had not. This result could be due to selective factors or to the stimulating effect of kindergarten training. He also showed that Southern-born Negro students had lower IQ scores at the time of entering Philadelphia schools than Philadelphia-born children at the same grade level. However, the Southern-born children had consistent year-to-year increases in mean IQ, where the Philadelphia-born children showed no such increase. These results were based on retests of the same children. Klineberg (1935) found a similar relationship between intelligence test score and length to residence in New York City, but his results were subject to the criticism that the comparisons involved different individuals.

From these two studies, it appears that the large-city school or the city environment has a stimulating effect reflected in IQ scores, which had not been elicited in the South. This does *not* necessarily mean that these students were brought up to their maximum potential.

At the college level, Roberts (1946, 1950) retested women students at Fisk University with alternate forms of the ACE over a four-year period. Students from the North were consistently higher than those from the South in test performance, even when matched on socioeconomic status. The average test performance of all groups increased substantially.

The findings in the studies cited above contrast with other studies in which IQ's tend to decrease over a period of time. Thus, Sherman and Key (1932) found that the average Pintner-Cunningham IQ score of white children between the ages of 6 and 8 in isolated mountain areas was 84, while for those 10 to 12 it was 53. They comment, ". . . the young children of the various Hollows do not differ greatly in intelligence, whereas great differences are found between the older children of the different Hollows. The only plausible explanation of the increasing difference with increasing age is that children develop only as the environment demands development."

It has been shown (Gilliland, McBath, Pfaff, 1951) that at the infant level, Negro children score as well as whites on infant intelligence tests. This finding would be consistent with an environmental interpretation that Negro children with genetic capacity equal to whites have their achievement limited by cultural deprivation. However, in view of Bayley's (1949) finding that tests given at the infant level have very low and occasionally negative correlations with tests given more than one year later, some caution must be used in making an interpretation.

In the area of achievement measures, Findley (1956) found that the differences between white and Negro children increased from the early to the late years. His study, which involved testing all children in the Atlanta school system at grades 4, 6, and 8 with tests of reading and arithmetic, showed increasing disparity between whites and Negroes with longer educational exposure. A different set of tests was used for the 12th grade, but the general pattern of increasing spread between whites and Negroes appeared to hold.

Similar results were formed by Osborne (1960) in retests of the same individuals at 6th, 8th, and 10th grade levels with the California Mental Maturity, reading and arithmetic tests. Similarly, Tomlinson (1944) found that the mean Stanford-Binet IQ of 4 to 5 year old Negro children was 92.5, while their older siblings had a mean IQ of 86.7.

A possibility which cannot be ignored is that the stimulating effects of remediation come from the "Hawthorne-like" effects of being an experimental group, rather than from the specific training involved. Thus, Entwisle (1961) found that a pseudo-training group learned almost as much as a group actually given additional training.

CONCLUSIONS

It seems apparent from the studies mentioned earlier that several conclusions may be drawn. Among these are:

1. There is a possibility that genetic factors are involved in test performance differences among racial groups.

2. Environmental effects are almost certainly involved in test performance differences among racial groups.

3. Cultural deprivation will lead to a decrease in tested intelligence for both Negro and white groups from early to late years.

4. Remedial efforts can improve test performance at least up through high school.

5. The limits of improvement have not been established.

6. The effectiveness of specific elements in remediation has not been established.

7. The maximum age at which remediation can be accomplished has not been established.

8. Paper and pencil tests of verbal and arithmetic ability are effective predictors of college performance, whether in predominantly white or predominantly Negro colleges.

9. Other types of tests have not been shown to be as effective in prediction.

ADDITIONAL RESEARCH NEEDED

The available literature indicates that answers to some important questions are not presently available. Research in these areas, therefore, might be undertaken profitably. Some of these possibilities will be discussed below.

1. Would "coaching" for the Scholastic Aptitude Test be effective with a culturally deprived group? If so, would the "coached" test score be more or less predictive of college performance than uncoached scores? Previous studies have shown that coaching is not effective, but these studies have been done with groups who have had good learning conditions. It may be that those whose learning possibilities have been restricted could profit from short-term coaching.

2. For culturally deprived groups, would nonverbal tests or tests involving a learning task be more predictive of college performance than the verbal or mathematical tests? Evidence available indicates that the customary verbal or mathematical test predicts school performance better than other types of tests. However, the evidence available is incidental to other studies rather than resulting from a systematic effort to find the most effective predictor for culturally deprived groups. A systematic effort might yield more fruitful results.

3. How does prediction of four-year college performance differ from prediction of first-year college performance? The Roberts study previously mentioned indicated that Southern Negro women from the upper socioeconomic group did as well over a four-year period as Northern Negro women, but not during the first year. Whether this phenomenon will hold with other groups and in other colleges should be investigated.

4. With culturally deprived groups, is precollege remediation training (not test coaching) effective in reducing the handicap? What length and type of training is required to effect remediation? A number of projects have been undertaken at the junior high school and early high school level to effect remediation, but none have been found at the high school graduate, pre college level. The effect of remediation efforts at this level should be investigated.

5. Over how long a period will the effects of remediation efforts persist? Whether remediation efforts at the various age levels have permanent effects or are relatively transitory has not been established.

6. Are there differences in the factor structure of abilities for deprived and advantaged groups? The Hudson studies would indicate that a different structure should be found for groups with dissimilar backgrounds. The variation in the levels of correlation that Stake found between race and different tests is an additional indication. Systematic investigation of the factor structures of groups from different backgrounds might give additional insight on the acquisition of abilities.

7. The increase in achieved knowledge which is possible for individuals of college age from deprived backgrounds should be investigated.

8. What factors are most advantageous in the acquisition of knowledge at the college level? Will improvement in library resources have more effect than strengthening the faculty, or vice versa? The upgrading program undertaken by one group of Negro colleges might offer an opportunity to evaluate such factors, with possibly a comparison group of predominantly white or integrated colleges.

9. What are the college environment characteristics of the colleges with the largest achieved gain and those with the smallest achieved gain and do these differ for advantaged and deprived groups?

10. What would be the effect of using a criterion of amount of gain in achieved knowledge, rather than level of achievement, for college graduation? What types of predict on instuuments would be most effective? Would the same prediction instruments be effective for culturally advantaged and culturally disadvantaged groups?

REFERENCES

Anastasi, Anne. 1958. *Differential Psychology.* 3d ed. New York; Macmillan.

Bayley, Nancy. 1949. "Consistency and Variability in the Growth of Intelligence from Birth to Eighteen Years," *J. Genet. Psychol.,* 75, 165–196. Cited by L. Cronbach, *Essentials of Psychological Testing.* 2d ed. New York: Harper, 1960.

Board of Education of the City of New York. "Demonstration Guidance Project—Jun or High School 43, Manhattan and George Washington High School." Fifth Annual Progress Report, 1960–61.

Board of Education of the City of New York. "The Higher Horizons Program." First Annual Progress Report, 1959–60.

Brazziel, W. F., and Margaret Gordon. 1963. "Replications of Some Aspects of the Higher Horizons Program in a Southern Junior High School," *J. Negro Educ.,* 32, 107–113.

Brazziel, W. F., and Mary Terrell. 1962. "An Experiment in the Development of Readiness in a Culturally Disadvantaged Group of 1st Grade Children," *J. Negro Educ.,* 31, 4–7.

Burt, C., and Margaret Howard. 1957. "Heredity and Intelligence: A Reply to Criticisms," *Brit. J. Stat. Psychol.,* 10, 33–63.

Clark, K. B., and L. Plotkin. 1963. *The Negro Student at Integrated Colleges.* New York: National Scholarship Service and Fund for Negro Students.

Cooper, R. M., and J. P. Zubek. 1958. "Effects of Enriched and Restricted Early Environments on the Learning Ability of Bright and Dull Rats," *Canad. J. Psychol.,* 12, 159–164.

Davidson, K. S., R. G. Gibby, E. B. McNeil, S. J. Segal, and H. Silverman. 1950. "A Preliminary Study of Negro and White Differences on Form I of the Wechsler-Bellevue Scale," *J. Consult. Psychol.,* 14, 489–491.

Dennis, W. 1960. "Causes of Retardation Among Institutional Children: Iran," *J. Genet. Psychol.,* 96, 47–59.

Dreger, R. M., and K. S. Miller. 1960. "Comparative Psychological Studies of Negroes and Whites in the United States," *Psychol. Bull.,* 57, 361–402.

Entwisle, Doris R. 1961. "Attensity: Factors of Specific Set in School Learning," *Harv. Educ. Rev.,* 31, 84–101.

Eells, K., A. Davis, R. J. Havighurst, V. E. Herrick, and L. Cronbach. 1951. *Intelligence and Cultural Differences.* Chicago: Univer. Chicago Press.

Findley, W. G. 1956. *Learning and Teaching in Atlanta Public Schools—1955–56.* Statistical Report. Princeton, N. J.: Educational Testing Service.

Gilliland, A. R., Mary McBath, and Jeanne Pfaff. 1951. "Socio-Economic Status and Race as Factors in Infant Intelligence Test Scores," *Child Develpm.,* 22, 271–273.

Haggard, E. A. 1954. "Social Status and Intelligence: An Experimental Study of Certain Cultural Determinants of Measured Intelligence," *Genet. Psychol. Monogr.,* 49, 141–186.

Hebb, D. O. 1949. *The Organization of Behavior.* New York: Wiley & Sons.

Hills, J. R., J. C. Klock, and Sandra Lewis. 1961–1962. *Freshman Norms for the University System of Georgia.* Atlanta: Office of Testing and Guidance, Regents of the University System of Georgia.

Hudson, W. 1960. "Pictorial Depth Perception in Sub-Cultural Groups in Africa," *J. Soc. Psychol.,* 52, 183–208.

Hudson. W. 1962. "Pictorial Perception and Educational Adaptation in Africa," *Psychol. Africana,* 9, 226–239.

Jenkins, M. D. 1948. "The Upper Limit of Ability Among American Negroes," *Sci. Mon. N.Y.,* 66, 399–401.

Klineberg, O. 1935. *Negro Intelligence and Selective Migration.* New York: Columbia Univer. Press.

Knief, Lotus Mae. 1957. "An Investigation of the Cultural Bias Issue in Intelligence Testing," *Dissertation Abstracts,* p. 1951. State Univer. of Iowa.

Lee, E. S. 1951. "Negro Intelligence and Selective Migration: A Philadelphia Test of the Klineberg Hypothesis," *Amer. Sociol. Rev.,* 16, 227–232.

Lloyd, F., and D. A. Pidgeon. 1961. "An Investigation into the Effects of Coaching on Non-Verbal Test Material with European, Indian, and African Children," *Brit. J. Educ. Psychol.,* 31, 145–151.

Lowry, Carmen E. 1957. "Prediction of Academic Success in a Private Liberal Arts College for Negroes," *Dissertation Abstracts,* p. 2500. Univer. of Texas.

Lucas, C. M. 1953. "Survey of the Literature Relating to the Effects of Cultural Background on Aptitude Test Scores." Research Bulletin 53-13. Princeton, N. J.: Educational Testing Service. (Multilithed Report.)

McFie, J. 1961. "The Effect of Education on African Performance on a Group of Intellectual Tests," *Brit. J. Educ. Psychol.,* 31, 232–240.

Moore, O. K. 1960. "Orthographic Symbols and the Preschool Child—A New Approach." Paper prepared for the 3rd Minnesota Conference on Gifted Children, October.

Mundy, Lydia. 1957. "Environmental Influence on Intellectual Functions as Measured by Intelligence Tests," *Brit. J. Med. Psychol.,* 30, 194–201.

Osborne, R. T. 1960. "Racial Differences in Mental Growth and School Achievement: A Longitudinal Study," *Psychol. Rep.,* 7, 233–239.

Plaut, R. L. 1957. *Blueprint for Talent Searching.* New York: National Scholarship Service and Fund for Negro Students.

Roberts, S O. 1946. "Socio-Economic Status and Performance of Negro College Women, North and South, on the ACE," *Amer. Psychologist,* 1, 253. (Abstract)

Roberts, S. O. 1950. "Socio-Economic Status and Performance over a Four-Year Period on the ACE of Negro College Women from the North and South," *Amer. Psychologist,* 5, 295. (Abstract)

Russell, I. L. 1956. "The Davis-Eells Test and Reading Success in the First Grade," *J. Educ. Psychol.,* 47, 269–270.

Semlar, I. J., and I. Iscoe. 1963. "Comparative and Developmental Study of Learning Abilities of Negro and White Children under Four Conditions," *J. Educ. Psychol.,* 54, 38–44.

Sherman, M., and Cora B. Key. 1932. "The Intelligence of Isolated Mountain Children," *Child Develpm.,* 3, 279–290.

Shuey, Audrey M. 1958. *The Testing of Negro Intelligence.* Lynchburg, Va.: J. P. Bell.

Spitz, R. A. 1955. "Reply to Dr. Pinneau," *Psychol. Bull.,* 52, 453–458.

Stake, R. E. 1961. "Learning Parameters, Aptitudes and Achievements," *Psychometric Monogr. No. 9.* Chicago: Univer. of Chicago Press.

Tate, M. W., and C. E. Voss. 1956. "A Study of the Davis-Eells Test of General Intelligence," *Harv. Educ. Rev.,* 26, 374–387.

Teahan, J., and Elizabeth Drews. 1962. "A Comparison of Northern and Southern Negro Children on WISC," *J. Consult. Psychol.,* 26, 292.

Tomlinson, H. 1944. "Differences Between Pre-school Negro Children and Their Older Siblings on the Stanford-Binet Scales," *J. Negro Educ.,* 13, 474–479.

Tumin, M. M. (ed.). 1963. *Race and Intelligence.* New York: Anti-Defamation League of B'nai B'rith.

Woods, W. A., and R. Toal. 1957. "Subtest Disparity of Negro and White Groups Matched for IQ's on the Revised Beta Test," *J. Consult. Psychol.,* 21, 136–138.

Martin Deutsch
Joshua A. Fishman
Leonard Kogan
Robert North
Martin Whiteman

24 / Guidelines for Testing Minority Group Children * †

INTRODUCTION

American educators have long recognized that they can best guide the development of intellect and character of the children in their charge if they take the time to understand these children thoroughly and sympathetically. This is particularly true with respect to the socially and culturally disadvantaged child.

Educators must realize that they hold positions of considerable responsibility and power. If they apply their services and skills wisely they can help minority group children to overcome their early disadvantages, to live more constructively, and to contribute more fully to American society.

Educational and psychological tests may help in the attainment of these goals if they are used carefully and intelligently. Persons who have a genuine commitment to democratic processes and who have a deep respect for the individual, will certainly seek to use educational and psychological tests with minority group children in ways that will enable these children to attain the full promise that America holds out to all its children.

Educational and psychological tests are among the most widely used and most useful tools of teachers, educational supervisors, school administrators, guidance workers, and counselors. As is the case with many professional tools, however, special training and diagnostic sensitivity are required for the intelligent and responsible use of these instruments. That is why most colleges and universities offer courses in educational and psychological testing. It is also the reason for the growing number of books and brochures designed to acquaint educators and their associates with the principles and procedures of proper test selection, use and interpretation.[1]

*Prepared by a Work Group of the Society for the Psychological Study of Social Issues (Division 9 of the American Psychological Association), Martin Deutsch, Joshua A. Fishman, *Chairman,* Leonard Kogan, Robert North, and Martin Whiteman.
†Reprinted by permission of Dr. Martin Deutsch, the major author, and the Society for the Psychological Study of Social Issues.
[1]See, for example, Katz (1958), Froelich and Hoyt (1959), Cronbach (1960), Anastasi (1961), Thorndike and Hagen (1961).

Responsible educational authorities recognize that it is as unwise to put tests in the hands of untrained and unskilled personnel as it is to permit the automobile or any highly technical and powerful tool to be handled by individuals who are untrained in its use and unaware of the damage that it can cause if improperly used.

The necessity for caution is doubly merited when educational and psychological tests are administered to members of minority groups. Unfortunately, there is no single and readily available reference source to which test users can turn in order to become more fully acquainted with the requirements and cautions to be observed in such cases. The purpose of this committee's effort is to provide an introduction to the many considerations germane to selection, use and interpretation of educational and psychological tests with minority group children, as well as to refer educators and their associates to other more technical discussions of various aspects of the same topic.

The term "minority group" as we are using it here is not primarily a quantitative designation. Rather it is a status designation referring to cultural or social disadvantage. Since many Negro, Indian, lowerclass white, and immigrant children have not had most of the usual middle-class opportunities to grow up in home, neighborhood, and school environments that might enable them to utilize their ability and personality potentials fully, they are at a disadvantage in school, and in after-school and out-of-school situations as well. It is because of these disadvantages, reflecting environmental deprivations and experiential atypicalities, that certain children may be referred to as minority group children.

The following discussion is based in part on some of the technical recommendations developed for various kinds of tests by committees of the American Psychological Association, the American Educational Research Association, and the National Council on Measurement in Education (1954, 1955). Our contribution is directed toward specifying the particular considerations that must be kept in mind when professional educators and those who work with them use educational and psychological tests with minority group children.

CRITICAL ISSUES IN TESTING MINORITY GROUPS

Standardized tests currently in use present three principal difficulties when they are used with disadvantaged minority groups: (1) they may not provide reliable differentiation in the range of the minority group's scores, (2) their predictive validity for minority groups may be quite different from that for the standardization and validation groups and (3) the validity of their interpretation is strongly dependent upon an adequate understanding of the social and cultural background of the group in question.

1. Reliability of Differentiation

In the literature of educational and psychological testing, relatively little attention has been given to the possible dependence of test reliability upon subcultural differences. It is considered essential for a test publisher to describe the reliability sample (the reference group upon which reliability statements are based) in terms of factors such as age, sex, and grade level composition, and there is a growing tendency on the part of test publishers to report subgroup reliabilities. But to the best of our knowledge, none of the test manuals for the widely used tests give separate reliability data for specific minority groups. Institutions that use tests regularly and routinely for particular minority groups would do well to make their own reliability studies in order to determine whether the tests are reliable enough when used with these groups.

Reliability Affected by Spread of Scores

In addition to being dependent on test length and the specific procedure used for estimating reliability (e.g., split-half or retest), the reliability coefficient for a particular test is strongly affected by the spread of test scores in the group for which the reliability is established. In general, the greater the spread of scores in the reliability sample, the higher the reliability coefficient. Consequently, if the tester attempts to make differentiations within a group which is more homogeneous than the reference or norm group for which reliability is reported, the actual effectiveness of the test will find to be lower than the reported reliability coefficient appears to promise. For many tests, there is abundant evidence that children from the lower-socio-economic levels commonly associated with minority group status tend to have a smaller spread of scores than do children from middle-income families, and such restriction in the distribution of scores tends to lower reliability so far as differentiation of measurement with such groups is concerned.[2]

Characteristics of Minority Group Children that Affect Test Performance

Most of the evidence relating to the contention that the majority of educational and psychological tests tend to be more unreliable, i.e., more characterized by what is technically called "error variance," for minority group children, is indirect, being based on studies of social class and socioeconomic differences rather than on minority group performance *per se*. Nevertheless, the particular kinds of minority groups that we have in mind are closely associated with the lower levels of socio-economic status. The results of studies by Warner, Davis, Deutsch, Deutsch and Brown, Havighurst, Holl-

[2]See Anastasi (1958) and Tyler (1956).

ingshead, Sears, Maccoby, and many others are cases in point. Many of these studies are discussed by Anastasi (1958), Tyler (1956) and Deutsch (1960). For children who come from lower socio-economic levels, what characteristics may be expected to affect test performance in general, and the accuracy or precision of test results in particular? The list of reported characteristics is long, and it is not always consistent from one investigation to another. But, at least, it may be hypothesized that in contrast to the middle-class child the lower-class child will tend to be less verbal, more fearful of strangers, less self-confident, less motivated toward scholastic and academic achievement, less competitive in the intellectual realm, more "irritable," less conforming to middle-class norms of behavior and conduct, more apt to be bilingual, less exposed to intellectually stimulating materials in the home, less varied in recreational outlets, less knowledgeable about the world outside his immediate neighborhood, and more likely to attend inferior schools.

Some Examples

Can it be doubted that such characteristics—even if only some of them apply to each "deprived" minority group—will indeed be reflected in test-taking and test performance? Obviously, the primary effect will be shown in terms of test validity for such children. In many cases, however, the lowering of test validity may be indirectly a result of lowered test reliability. This would be particularly true if such characteristics interfere with the consistency of performance from test to retest for a single examiner, or for different examiners. Consider the following examples and probable results:

Example: A Negro child has had little contact with white adults other than as distant and punitive authority figures. *Probable Result:* Such a child might have difficulty in gaining rapport with a white examiner or reacting without emotional upset to his close presence. Even in an individual testing situation, he might not respond other than with monosyllables, failing to give adequate answers even when he knows them. The examiner, reacting in terms of his own stereotypes, might also lower the reliability and validity of the test results by assuming that the child's performance will naturally be inferior, and by revealing this attitude to the child.

Example: Children from a particular minority group are given little reason to believe that doing well in the school situation will affect their chance for attaining better jobs and higher income later in life. *Probable Result:* Such children will see little purpose in schooling, dislike school, and will reject anything associated with school. In taking tests, their primary objective is to get through as rapidly as possible and escape from what for them might be an uncomfortable situation. Their test performance might, therefore, be characterized by a much greater amount of guessing, skipping, and random responses that is shown by the middle-class child who never doubts the importance of the test, wants to please his teacher and parents, and tries his best.

Special Norms Often Needed

When the national norms do not provide adequate differentiation at the lower end of the aptitude or ability scale, special norms, established locally, are often useful. For instance, if a substantial number of underprivileged or foreign-background pupils in a school or school district rank in the lowest five percent on the national norms, local norms might serve to provide a special scale within this range. If the score distribution with the first few percentiles of the national norms is mainly a function of chance factors, however, a lower level of the test or an easier type of test is needed for accurate measurement of the low-scoring children.

Responsibilities of Test Users

The sensitive test user should be alert to reliability considerations in regard to the particular group involved and the intended use of the tests. In assessing reports on test reliability provided by test manuals and other sources, he will not be satisfied with high reliability co-efficients alone. He will consider not only the size of the reliability samples, but also the nature and composition of the samples and the procedures used to estimate reliability. He will try to determine whether the standard error of measurement varies with score levels, and whether his testing conditions are similar to those of the reliability samples. He will ask whether the evidence on reliability is relevant to the persons and purposes with which he is concerned. He will know that high reliability does not guarantee validity of the measures for the purpose in hand, but he will realize that low reliability may destroy validity.

The examiner should be well aware that test results are characteristically influenced by cultural and subcultural differentials and that the performance of under-privileged minority group children is often handicapped by what should be test-extraneous preconditions and response patterns. He should not necessarily assume that the child from a minority group family will be as test-sophisticated and motivated to do his best as are the majority of environment-rich middle-class children.

If the examiner finds—and this will be typical—that the reliability sample does not provide him with information about the reliability of the test for the kind of children he is testing, he should uge that the test results not be taken at face value in connection with critical decisions concerning the children. Very often, careful examination of responses to individual test items will indicate to him that the apparent performance of the child is not adequately reflecting the child's actual competence or personality because of certain subcultural group factors.

II. Predictive Validity

Of course, if an individual's test scores were to be used only to describe his relative standing with respect to a specified norm group, the fact that the individual had a minority-group background would not be important. It is when an explanation of his standing is attempted, or when long-range predictions enter the picture (as they usually do), that background factors become important.

For example, no inequity is necessarily involved if a culturally disadvantaged child is simply reported to have an IQ of 84 and a percentile rank of 16 on the national norms for a certain intelligence test. However, if this is interpreted as meaning that the child ranks or will rank no higher in learning ability than does a middle-class, native born American child of the same IQ, the interpretation might well be erroneous.

Factors Impairing Test Validity

Three kinds of factors may impair a test's predictive validity. First, there are test-related factors—factors or conditions that affect the test scores but which may have relatively little relation to the criterion. Such factors may include test-taking skills, anxiety, motivation, speed, understanding of test instructions, degree of item or format novelty, examiner-examinee rapport, and other general or specific abilities that underlie test performance but which are irrelevant to the criterion. Examples of the operation of such factors are found in the literature describing the problems of white examiners testing Negro children (Dreger and Miller, 1960), of American Indian children taking unfamiliar, timed tests (Klineberg, 1935), and of children of certain disadvantaged groups being exposed for the first time to test-taking procedures (Haggard, 1954).

It should be noted that some test-related factors may not be prejudicial to disadvantaged groups. For example, test-taking anxiety of a disruptive nature (Sarason et al., 1960) may be more prevalent in some middle-class groups than in lower-class groups. In general, however, the bias attributable to test-related factors accrues to the detriment of the culturally disadvantaged groups.

The problem of making valid predictions for minority group children is faced by the Boys' Club of New York in its Educational Program,[3] which is designed to give promising boys from tenement districts opportunities to overcome their environmental handicaps through scholarships to outstanding schools and colleges. Although the majority of the boys currently enrolled in this program had mediocre aptitude and achievement test scores up to the time

---

[3]Information about this program is obtainable from The Boys Club of New York, 287 East 10th Street, New York, N.Y.

they were given scholarships, practically all of the boys have achieved creditable academic success at challenging secondary boarding schools and colleges. In this program, normative scores on the Otis Quick-Scoring Mental Ability Test and the Stanford Achievement Test are used for screening purposes, but they are regarded as minimal estimates of the boys abilities. The Wochsler Intelligence Scale for Children (WISC) is frequently used in this program to supplement the group tests. The boys typically score 5 to 10 points higher on the WISC than on the Otis, probably because the WISC gives less weight to educational and language factors.

Interest and Personality Inventory Scores

When standardized interest inventories are used, special caution should be observed in making normative interpretations of the scores of culturally disadvantaged individuals. When a child has not had opportunities to gain satisfaction or rewards from certain pursuits, he is not likely to show interest in these areas. For example, adolescent children in a particular slum neighborhood might rank consistently low in scientific, literary, musical, and artistic interests on the Kuder Preference Record if their home and school environments fail to stimulate them in these areas. With improved cultural opportunities, these children might rapidly develop interests in vocations or avocations related to these areas.

Scores on personality inventories may also have very different significance for minority group members than for the population in general (Auld, 1952). Whenever the inventory items tap areas such as home or social adjustment, motivation, religious beliefs, or social customs, the appropriateness of the national norms for minority groups should be questioned. Local norms for the various minority groups involved might again be very much in order here.

Predicting Complex Criteria

A second class of factors contributing to low predictive validity is associated with the complexity of criteria. Criteria generally represent "real life" indices of adjustment or achievement and therefore they commonly sample more complex and more variegated behaviors than do the tests. An obvious example is the criterion of school grades. Grades are likely to reflect motivation, classroom behavior, personal appearance, and study habits, as well as intelligence and achievement. Even if a test measured scholastic aptitude sensitively and accurately, its validity for predicting school marks would be attenuated because of the contribution of many other factors to the criterion. It is important, therefore, to recognize the influence of other factors, not measured by the tests, which may contribute to criterion success. Since disadvantaged groups tend to fare poorly on ability and achievement tests (Anastasi, 1958; Tyler, 1956; Masland, Sarason, and Gladwin, 1958; Eels et al., 1951;

Haggard, 1954), there is particular merit in exploring the background, personality, and motivation of members of such groups for compensatory factors, untapped by the tests, which may be related to criterion performance.

In some instances, such as in making scholarship awards on a statewide or national basis, test scores are used rigidly for screening or cut-off purposes to satisfy demands for objectivity and "impartiality." The culturally disadvantaged child (quite possibly a "diamond-in-the-rough") is often the victim of this automatic and autocratic system. Recourse lies in providing opportunities where the hurdles are less standardized and where a more individualized evaluation of his qualifications for meeting the criterion may prove to be fairer for him.

For example, the following characteristics that may be typical of minority group children who have above-average ability or talent are among those cited by DeHaan and Kough (1956), who have been working with the North Central Association Project on Guidance and Motivation of Superior and Talented Secondary School Students:

> They learn rapidly, but not necessarily those lessons assigned in school.
> They reason soundly, think clearly, recognize relationships, comprehend meanings, and may or may not come to conclusions expected by the teacher.
> They are able to influence others to work toward desirable or undesirable goals.

Effects of Intervening Events on Predictions

A third set of contributors to low criterion validity is related to the nature of intervening events and contingencies. This class of conditions is particularly important when the criterion measure is obtained considerably later than the testing—when predictive rather than concurrent validity is at stake. If the time interval between the test administration and the criterial assessment is lengthy, a host of situational, motivational, and maturational changes may occur in the interim. An illness, an inspiring teacher, a shift in aspiration level or in direction of interest, remedial training, an economic misfortune, an emotional crisis, a growth spurt or retrogression in the abilities sampled by the test—any of these changes intervening between the testing and the point or points of criterion assessment may decrease the predictive power of the test.

One of the more consistent findings in research with disadvantage children is the decline in academic aptitude and achievement test scores of such children with time (Masland, Sarason, and Gladwin, 1958). The decline is, of course, in relation to the performance of advantaged groups or of the general population. It is plausible to assume that this decline represents the cumulative effects of diminished opportunities and decreasing motivation for acquiring academic knowledge and skills. When such cumulative effects are not taken into consideration, the predictive power of academic aptitude and achievement tests is impaired. If it were known in advance that certain individuals or groups would be exposed to deleterious environmental conditions, and if allowances could be made for such contingencies in connection with predictions, the test's criterion validity could be improved.

Looking in another direction, the normative interpretation of the test results cannot reveal how much the status of underprivileged individuals might be changed if their environmental opportunities and incentives for learning and acquiring skills were to be improved significantly. In the case of the Boy's Club boys mentioned above, estimates of academic growth potential are made on the basis of knowledge of the educational and cultural limitations of the boys' home and neighborhood environment, observational appraisals of the boys' behavior in club activities, and knowledge of the enhanced educational and motivational opportunities that can be offered to the boys in selected college preparatory schools. With this information available, the normative interpretation of the boys' scores on standardized tests can be tempered with experienced judgment, and better estimates of the boys' academic potential can thus be made.

In situations where minority group members are likely to have to continue competing with others under much the same cultural handicaps that they have faced in the past, normative interpretation of their aptitude and achievement test scores will probably yield a fairly dependable basis for short-term predictive purposes. When special guidance or training is offered to help such individuals overcome their handicaps, however, achievement beyond the normative expectancies may well be obtained, and predictions should be based on expectancies derived specifically from the local situation. In this connection, it should be recognized that attempts to appraise human "potential" without defining the milieu in which it will be given an opportunity to materialize are as futile as attempts to specify the horsepower of an engine without knowing how it will be energized.

"Culture Fair" and "Unfair"—in the Test and in Society

The fact that a test differentiates between culturally disadvantaged and advantaged groups does not necessarily mean that the test is invalid. "Culturally unfair" tests may be valid predictors of culturally unfair but nevertheless highly important criteria. Educational attainment, to the degree that it reflects social inequities rather than intrinsic merit, might be considered culturally unfair. However, a test must share this bias to qualify as a valid predictor. Making a test culture-fair may decrease its bias, but may also eliminate its criterion validity. The remedy may lie in the elimination of unequal learning opportunities, which may remove the bias in the criterion as well as in the test. This becomes more a matter of social policy and amelioration rather than a psychometric problem, however.

The situation is quite different for a test that differentiates between disadvantaged and advantaged groups even *more* sharply than does the criterion. The extreme case would be a test that discriminated between disadvantaged and advantaged groups but did not have any validity for the desired criterion. An example of this would be an academic aptitude test that called for the identification of objects, where this task would be particularly difficult for disadvantaged children but would not be a valid predictor of academic achievement. Here, one could justifiably speak of a true "test bias." The test would be spuriously responsive to factors associated with cultural disadvantage but unrelated to the criterion. Such a test would not only be useless for predicting academic achievement, but would be stigmatizing as well.

While certain aptitude and ability tests may have excellent criterion validity for some purposes, even the best of them are unlikely to reflect the true *capacity for development* of underprivileged children. For, to the extent that these tests measure factors that are related to academic success, they must tap abilities that have been molded by the cultural setting. Furthermore, the test content, the mode of communication involved in responding to test items, and the motivation needed for making the responses are intrinsically dependent upon the cultural context.

Elixir of "Culture-Fair" Tests

The exilir of the "culture-fair" or "culture-free" test has been pursued through attempts to minimize the educational loading of test content and to reduce the premium on speed of response. However, these efforts have usually resulted in tests that have low validities for academic prediction purposes and little power to uncover hidden potentialities of children who do poorly on the common run of academic aptitude and achievement tests.

In spite of their typical cultural bias, standardized tests should not be sold short as a means for making objective assessments of the traits of minority-group children. Many bright, non-conforming pupils, with backgrounds different from those of their teachers, make favorable showings on achievement tests, in contrast to their low classroom marks. These are very often children whose cultural handicaps are most evident in their overt social and interpersonal behavior. Without the intervention of standardized tests, many such children would be stigmatized by the adverse subjective ratings of teachers who tend to reward conformist behavior of middle-class character.

III. The Validity of Test Interpretation

The most important consideration of all is one that applies to the use of tests in general—namely, that test results should be interpreted by competently trained and knowledgeable persons wherever important issues or decisions are at stake. Here, an analogy may be drawn from medical case history information that is entered on a child's record. Certain features of this record, such as the contagious-disease history, constitute factual data that are easily understood by school staff members who have not had medical training. But other aspects of the medical record, as well as the constellation of factors that contribute to the child's general state of health, are not readily interpretable by persons outside the medical profession. Consequently, the judgment of a doctor is customarily sought when an overall evaluation of the child's physical condition is needed for important diagnostic or predictive purposes. So, too, the psychological and educational test records of children should be interpreted by competently trained professional personnel when the test results are to be used as a basis for decisions that are likely to have a major influence on the child's future.

There are several sources of error in test interpretation stemming from a lack of recognition of the special features of culturally disadvantaged groups. One of these may be called the "deviation error." By this is meant the tendency to infer maladjustment or personality difficulty from responses which are deviant form ths viewpoint of a majority culture, but which may be typical of a minority group. The results of a test might accurately reflect a child's performance or quality of ideation, but still the results should be interpreted in the light of the child's particular circumstance in life and the range of his experiences. For example, a minister's son whose test responses indicate that he sees all women as prostitutes and a prostitute's son whose test responses give the same indication may both be accurately characterized in one sense by the test. The two boys may or may not be equally disturbed, however. Clinically, a safer inference might be that the minister's son is the one who is more likely to be seriously disturbed by fantasies involving sex and women.

There is evidence to indicate that members of a tribe that has experienced periodic famines would be likely to give an inordinate number of food responses on the Rorschach. So too might dieting Palm Beach matrons, but their underlying anxiety patterns would be quite different than those of the tribesmen. Or, to take still another example, the verbalized self-concept of the son of an unemployed immigrant might have to be interpreted very differently from that of a similar verbalization of a boy from a comfortable, middle-class, native-American home.

A performance IQ that is high in relation to the individual's verbal IQ on the Wechsler scales *may* signify psychopathic tendencies but it also may signify a poverty of educational experience. Perceiving drunken males beating up women on the Thematic Apperception Test may imply a projection of idiosyncratic fantasy or wish, but it may also imply a background of rather realistic observation and experience common to some minority group children.

For children in certain situations, test responses indicating a low degree of motivation or an over-submissive self-image are realistic reflections of their life conditions. If these children were to give responses more typical of the general population, they might well be regarded as sub-group deviants. In short, whether test responses reflect secondary defenses against anxiety or are the direct result of a socialization process has profound diagnostic import so that knowledge of the social and cultural back ground of the individual becomes quite significant.

What Does the Test Really Measure

A second type of error, from the viewpoint of construct and content validity,[4] might be called the "simple determinant error." The error consists in thinking of the test content as reflecting some absolute or pure trait, process, factor, or construct, irrespective of the conditions of measurement or of the population being studied. Thus, a fifth-grade achievement test may measure arithmetical knowledge in a middle-class neighborhood where most children are reading up to grade level, but the same test, with the same content, may be strongly affected by a reading comprehension factor in a lower-class school and therefore may be measuring something quite different than what appears to be indicated by the test scores.

Generally, the test-taking motivation present in a middle-class group allows the responses to test content to reflect the differences in intelligence, achievement, or whatever the test is designed to measure. On the other hand in a population where test success has much less reward-value and where degree of test-taking effort is much more variable from individual to individual, the test content may tap motivation as well as the trait purportedly being measured.

Caution and knowledge are necessary for understanding and taking into account testing conditions and test-taking behavior when test results are being interpreted for children from varying backgrounds. A child coming from a particular cultural subgroup might have very little motivation to do well in most test situations, but under certain conditions or with special kinds of materials he might have a relatively high level of motivation. As a result, considerable variability might be evident in his test scores from one situation to another, and his scores might be difficult to reconcile and interpret.

How a question is asked is undoubtedly another important factor to consider in interpreting test results. A child might be able to recognize an object, but not able to name it. Or, he might be able to identify a geometric figure, but not able to reproduce it. Thus, different results might be obtained in a test depending upon whether the child is asked to point to the triangle in a set of geometric figures or whether he is required to draw a triangle.

---

[4]For a discussion of various types of test validity, see Anastasi (1961), Cronbach (1960), Guilford (1954), Thorndike and Hagen (1961), Lindquist (1950).

Response Sets May Affect Test Results

In attitude or personality questionnaires, response sets[5] such as the tendency to agree indiscriminately with items, or to give socially desirable responses, may contribute error variance from the viewpoint of the content or bahavior it is desired to sample. To the extent that such sets discriminate between socially advantaged and disadvantaged groups, the target content area may be confounded by specific test format. Thus, a scale of authoritarianism may be found to differentiate among social classes, but if the scale is so keyed that a high score on authoritarianism is obtained from agreement with items, the social class differences may be more reflective of an agreement set rather than an authoritarian tendency. If authoritarian content is logically distinct from agreement content, these two sources of test variance should be kept distinct either through statistical control, by a change in the item format, or by having more than one approach to measurement of the trait in question.

From the standpoint of content validity, there is a third type of error. This may be termed the "incompleteness of content coverage" error. This refers to a circumscribed sampling of the content areas in a particular domain. In the area of intelligence, for instance, Guilford (1954) has identified many factors besides the "primary mental abilities" of Thurstone and certainly more than is implied in the unitary concept of intelligence reflected by a single IQ score. As Dreger and Miller (1960) point out, differences in intellectual functioning among various groups cannot be clearly defined or understood until all components of a particular content area have been systematically measured.

Familiarity with the cultural and social background of minority-group children not only helps to avoid under-evaluating the test performance of some children, but also helps to prevent over-evaluating the performance of others. For example, children who have been trained in certain religious observances involving particular vocabularies and objects, or those who have been encouraged to develop particular skills because of their cultural orientations, might conceivably score "spuriously" high on some tests or on particular items. In other words, any special overlap between the subgroup value-system of the child and the performances tapped by the test is likely to be an important determinant of the outcome of the test.

Failure Barriers May Be Encountered

Failure inducing barriers are often set up for the minority-group child in a testing situation by requiring him to solve problems with unfamiliar tools, or by asking him to use tools in a manner that is too advanced for him. To draw an analogy, if a medical student were handed a scalpel to lance a wound, and if the student were to do the lancing properly but were to fail to sterilize

[5]For a discussion of this and related concepts, see Anastasi (1961), Cronbach (1960).

the instrument first, how should he be scored for his accomplishment? If he had never heard of sterilization, should his skillful performance with the instrument nevertheless be given a "zero" score? Similarly, if a child from a disadvantaged social group shows a considerable degree of verbal facility in oral communication with his peers but does very poorly on tests that stress academic vocabulary, can he justifiably be ranked low in verbal aptitude?

In a broad sense, most intelligence test items tap abilities involving language and symbol systems, although opportunities for developing these abilities vary considerably from one social group to another. One might reasonably expect that a child living in a community that minimizes language skills—or, as depicted by Bernstein (1960), a community that uses a language form that is highly concrete—will earn a score that has a meaning very different from that of the score of a child in a community where language skills are highly developed and replete with abstract symbolism. It is important, therefore, to interpret test results in relation to the range of situations and behaviors found in the environments of specific minority groups.

Some Suggested Remedies

While this analysis of the problems involed in the use and interpretation of tests for minority group children may lead to considerable uneasiness and skepticism about the value of the results for such children, it also points up potential ways of improving the situation. For example, one of these ways might consist of measuring separate skills first, gradually building up to more and more complex items and tests which require the exercise of more than one basic skill at a time. With enough effort and ingenuity, a sizable universe of items might be developed by this procedure. Special attention should also be given to the selection or development of items and tests that maximize criterial differentiations and minimize irrelevant discriminations. If a test is likely to be biased against certain types of minority groups, or if its validity for minority groups has not been ascertained, a distinct *caveat* to that effect should appear in the manual for the test.

Furthermore, we should depart from too narrow a conception of the purpose and function of testing. We should re-emphasize the concept of the test as an integral component of teaching and training whereby a floor of communication and understanding is established and *learning* capabilities are measured in repeated and cyclical fashion.

Finally, we should think in terms of making more use of everyday behavior as evidence of the coping abilities and competence of children who do not come from the cultural mainstream. Conventional tests may be fair predictors of academic success in a narrow sense, but when children are being selected for special aid programs or when academic prediction is not the primary concern, other kinds of behavioral evidence are commonly needed to modulate the results and implications of standardized tests.

CONCLUSION

Tests are among the most important evaluative and prognostic tools that educators have at their disposal. How unfortunate, then, that these tools are often used so routinely and mechanically that some educators have stopped *thinking* about their limitations and their benefits. Since the minority group child is so often handicapped in many ways his test scores may have meanings different from those of non-minority children, even when they are numerically the same. The task of the conscientious educator is to ponder what lies behind the test scores. Rather than accepting test scores as indicating fixed levels of either performance or potential, educators should plan remedial activities which will free the child from as many of his handicaps as possible. Good schools will employ well qualified persons to use good tests as one means of accomplishing this task.

In testing the minority group child it is sometimes appropriate to compare his performance with that of advantaged children to determine the magnitude of the deprivation to be overcome. At other times it is appropriate to compare his test performance with that of other disadvantaged children—to determine his relative deprivation in comparison with others who have also been denied good homes, good neighborhoods, good diets, good schools and good teachers. In most instances it is especially appropriate to compare the child's test performance with his previous test performance. Utilizing the individual child as his own control and using the test norms principally as "bench marks," we are best able to gauge the success of our efforts to move the minority group child forward on the long, hard road of overcoming the deficiencies which have been forced upon him. Many comparisons depend upon tests, but they also depend upon *our* intelligence, our good will, and our sense of responsibility to make the proper comparison at the proper time and to undertake proper remedial and compensatory action as a result. The misuse of tests with minority group children, or in any situation, is a serious breach of professional ethics. Their proper use is a sign of professional and personal maturity.

REFERENCES

American Educational Research Association and National Committee on Measurements Used in Education. 1955. *Technical Recommendations for Achievement Tests.* Washington, D.C., National Educational Association.

American Psychological Association. 1954. "Technical Recommendations for Psychological Tests and Diagnostic Techniques," *Psychol. Bull.,* 51, No. 2.

Anastasi, A. 1961. *Psychological Testing.* 2d ed. New York: Macmillan.

Anastasi, A. 1958. *Differential Psychology.* 3d ed. New York: Macmillan.

Auld, F. 1952. "Influence of Social Class on Personality Test Responses," *Psychol. Bull.,* 49, 318–332.

Bernstein, B. 1961. "Aspects of Language and Learning in the Genesis of the Social Process," *J. Child Psychol. Psychiat.,* 1, 313–324.

Bernstein, B. 1960. "Language and Social Class," *Brit. J. Sociol.,* 11, 271–276.

Chronbach, L. 1960. *Essentials of Psychological Testing.* 2d ed. New York: Harper.

DeHaan, R. and J. Kough. 1956. "Teachers Guidance Handbook: Identifying Students with Special Needs." Vol. I Secondary School Edition. Chicago: Science Research Associates.

Deutsch, M. 1960. *Minority Group and Class Status as Related to Social and Personality Factors in Scholastic Achievement.* (Monograph No. 2) Ithaca, New York: The Society for Applied Anthropology.

Deutsch, M. 1963. "The Disadvantaged Child and the Learning Process: Some Social Psychological and Developmental Considerations," in H. Passow (ed.), *Education in Depressed Areas.* New York: Teachers College Press.

Deutsch, M., and B. Brown. "Some Data on Social Influence in Negro-White Intelligence Differences," *J. Social Issues,* XX, No. 2, 24–35.

Dreger, R., and K. Miller. 1960. "Comparative Psychological Studies of Negroes and Whites in the United States," *Psychol. Bull.,* 57, 361–402.

Eells, K., et al. 1951. *Intelligence and Cultural Differences.* Chicago: University of Chicago Press.

Fishman, J. A., and P. I. Clifford. 1964. "What Can Mass Testing Programs Do for-and-to the Pursuit of Excellence in American Education?" *Harvard Educ. Rev.,* 34, 63–79.

Froehlich, C., and K. Hoyt. 1959. *Guidance Testing.* 3d ed. Chicago: Science Research Associates.

Guilford, J. 1954. *Psychometric Methods.* 2d ed. New York: McGraw-Hill.

Haggard, E. 1954. "Social Status and Intelligence: An Experimental Study of Certain Cultural Determinants of Measured Intelligence," *Genet. Psychol. Monogr.,* 49, 141–186.

Klineberg, O. 1935. *Race Differences.* New York: Harper.

Katz, M. 1958. *Selecting an Achievement Test: Principles and Procedures.* Princeton: Educational Testing Service.

Lindquist, E. (ed.). 1950. *Educational Measurement.* Washington: American Council of Education.

Masland, R., S. Sarason, and T. Gladwin. 1958. *Mental Subnormality.* New York: Basic Books.

Sarason, S. et al. 1960. *Anxiety in Elementary School Children.* New York: Wiley.

Thorndike, R., and E. Hagen. 1961. *Measurement and Evaluation in Psychology and Education.* 2d ed. New York: Wiley.

Tyler, L. 1956. *The Psychology of Individual Differences.* 2d ed. New York: Appleton-Century-Crofts.

GLOSSARY OF TERMS AS USED IN THE TEST

Criterion. A standard that provides a basis for evaluating the validity of a test.

Cultural bias. Propensity of a test to reflect favorable or unfavorable effects of certain types of cultural backgrounds.

Culture-fair test. A test yielding results that are not culturally biased.

Culture-free test. A test yielding results that are not influenced in any way by cultural background factors.

Error variance. The portion of the variance of test scores that is related to the unreliability of the test.

Educational loading. Weighing of a test's content with factors specifically related to formal education.

Norms. Statistics that depict the test performance of specific groups. Grade, age, and percentile are the most common type of norms.

Normative scores. Scores derived from the test's norms.

Reliability. The degree of consistency, stability, or dependability of measurement afforded by a test.

Reliability coefficient. A correlation statistic reflecting a test's consistency or stability of measurement.

Standard deviation. A statistic used to depict the dispersion of a group of scores.

Standard error of measurement. An estimate of the standard deviation of a person's scores that would result from repeated testing with the same or a similar test, ruling out the effects of practice, learning, or fatigue.

Validity. The extent to which a test measures the trait for which it is designed, or for which it is being used, rather than some other trait.

William E. Coffman
Research Adviser
Educational Testing Service

25 / Developing Tests for the Culturally Different *†

The central issue of this paper can be stated thus: Since individual differences are a function of many factors, how does one insure that in any particular test relevant factors are being measured and irrelevant ones excluded? Like the issue of essay vs. objective testing. it needs to be examined periodically in the light of technical advances in the field and of social changes taking place in the context within which the issue is imbedded.

Essentially, the issue involves values; that is why it is so persistent and so resistant to the impact of research. Proponents of different points of view tackle different kinds of problems and assemble different kinds of data. It takes a long time for the collections to begin to converge.

There are some things, however, on which we can agree now, *e.g.,* that a test which does not provide a valid prediction of some kind of significant behavior is not worth the time it takes to answer the questions. On the other hand, we can accent the proposition that pure empirical prediction, irrespective of possible indirect social effects, is indefensible. Tests should be constructed and used with indirect consequence as well as predictive effectiveness in mind. Finally, we can agree that we have an educational problem on our hands. We cannot concentrate all our efforts on making foolproof tests we have to do something about improving the sophistication of test users. However, we are concerned here with test construction, not the education of test users.

Historically, both the College Entrance Examination Board and Educational Testing Service have been aware of the significance of cultural differences in the interpretation of test scores and have mounted systematic programs of research designed to clarify such differences. Member colleges and colleges contemplating membership in the Board have been encouraged to conduct studies in which sub groups that might be expected to show different predictive relationships are treated separately: men and women, liberal arts and engineering students, independent and public school applicants—logically there is no limit to the breakdowns one might try. There are, however, limitations of a practical nature.

---

*Based on "Proceedings of the 1961 Invitational Conference on Testing Problems." Copyright, 1965, Educational Testing Service, Princeton, N.J.

†From *School and Society*, November 13, 1965. Reprinted by permission of the author and the publisher.

It is probably unrealistic to expect each college to conduct its own studies and develop separate predictive equations for every significant sub-group of the applicant population. Often, there are not enough cases available to establish a line of relationship. Inevitably, there comes a point where the test user is forced to make clinical judgments as he encounters individual cases which seem not to fit into any of his previously studied categories. This is not necessarily an undesirable practice; actually, it may be the only way to temper the impact of large-scale data processing methods on the unusual individual.

The problem may be tackled directly to eliminate irrelevant cultural differences at the point of test construction. Even it the attempt is not entirely successful, at least it may serve to identify potential problems for the test user and to provide him with some guide lines for his clinical judgments.

To a considerable extent, efforts of the College Board and ETS have been guided by rational considerations; but, particularly in recent years, systematic research has guided our efforts. To cite a few examples, the early forms of the SAT were made up of sub-tests, each containing so many questions that nobody could finish in the time allotted. Studies in the general literature of psychology show that in a speed task a rural youth is likely to respond differently than an urban youth. We therefore set about systematically to reduce the weight of the speed factor in the test.

Some parents also could pay for special coaching in preparation for the test while others could not, and the availability of practice exercises would vary widely. Therefore, we designed item types which were relatively unresponsive to special coaching experiences. And we collected data indicating that our efforts had been reasonably successful.[2] At the same time, we prepared booklets describing the test and providing enough illustrative questions to insure that candidates had opportunities to know the kinds of questions to expect.

Studies showed that familiarity with the general content of a reading passage would improve a candidate's chances of understanding the passage and answering questions about it. Other studies showed that the reading interests of candidates would determine to a considerable extent the kinds of materials they would read. Some would favor literary readings, others scientific; some would read agricultural magazines, others would read magazines aimed at the homemaker. Our studies suggested, for example, that girls were more likely to do well with material in the biological and medical sciences while boys excelled with materials in the physical sciences.[3] We, therefore, set

[2]J. W. French and R. E. Dear, "Effects of Coaching on an Aptitude Test," *Educational and Psychological Measurement,* 19: 319–329 (Autumn 1959); Donald J. Malcolm, "Summary of Studies Pertaining to the Effects of Coaching on the Performance of Students on the Scholastic Aptitude Test." (Unpublished report, ETS, March 21, 1961.)

[3]William E. Coffman, "The Effects of Lapse of Time on Item Statistics for the Contemporary Affairs Test," *The Tenth Yearbook* (National Council on Measurement in Education, Michigan State University, East Lansing, 1953), pp. 58–65.

up categories to guide our selection of reading passages which would insure a balance of content. We learned that women excelled in knowledge of words related to people while men tended to excel with vocabulary related to things.[4] And we reasoned that regional and cultural background would also be reflected in the vocabularies of different candidates. We, therefore, established categories to tuide our selection of the verbal omnibus questions in the test.

In order to increase our understanding of the cultural factors which influence test scores, we have sought out in recent years samples from widely different backgrounds and studied their responses to questions. We have studied samples from Scotland and Alberta, from Nigeria and East Africa, from the rural Midwest and New York City, and from all-Negro groups in the South.

As the questions we asked became more focused, we realized that we had methodological problems to solve. Eells and his associates at the University of Chicago had completed studies in which the chief method was that of comparing the percentage of one group marking a correct answer with the percentage of another group marking a correct answer to the same question. There were two limitations to this approach. In the first place, since all the questions in a test had been answered by the same people, it was improper to make the tests of significance as if the successive differences were based on independent samples. In the second place, the effect one wished to study—the interaction between status and test questions—might possibly be confounded with real ability differences between the groups.

We have not yet solved all the problems of sorting out the various factors contributing to differences in test performance of different groups, but we have made some progress and are continuing our studies. During the summer of 1963, Cardall[5] applied the analysis of variance design for two factor experiments with repeated measures on one factor to data from three different groups and showed how mean effects and interaction effects might be separated. She demonstrated significant interaction effects for items in the SAT across the three groups. At the same time, she pointed out that the statistical analysis did not permit us to differentiate between balance and bias in a test. We are continuing our search for such a differentiating procedure.

In the summer of 1964, Fremer[6] examined Cardall's data subjectively for evidence of balance or bias and concluded that whatever factors were causing the significant interactions were not readily apparent from an examination of

[4]William E. Coffman, "Sex Differences in Responses to Items in an Aptitude Test," *The 18th Yearbook* (National Council on Measurement in Education, Michigan State University, East Lansing, 1961) pp. 117–124.

[5]Carolyn Cardall and William E. Coffman, "A Method for Comparing the Performance of Different Groups on the Items in a Test," *Research and Development Reports*, 64–5, No. 9 (CEEB, November 1964).

[6]John Fremer, (Study in progress.)

item content. In general, the factors producing changes in the relative difficulty of questions from group to group appeared to be the result of complex factors such as those producing individual differences within groups. And since the interactions tend to be represented in the scatter plots by ellipses in which the points are distributed symmetrically, we have tended to favor interpretations in terms of balance rather than bias.

When we examine samples for whom English is a second language and where differences in culture are immediately apparent, as with our African samples, however, both mean differences across all items and interaction effects indicating changes in the relative difficulty of items are dramatic. Details of our findings have been presented elsewhere.[7] Essentially, the differences are attributable to the fact that English was a second language and that the individuals in the sample had grown up in a rural tropical society rather than in an industrialized country located in the North Temperate Zone.

The data from our African studies led us to become concerned about other College Board candidates for whom English is not a native language. Studies by Howell[8] have provided evidence from which we have developed a frame of reference for interpreting scores of such candidates. In the booklet describing the Scholastic Aptitude Test, the student is informed of special provisions for interpreting the scores of candidates whose native language is not English, and a special guide has been prepared to alert admissions officers in colleges to the need for making such provisions.

Our studies have shown generally that responses to the questions in the mathematical sections of the SAT are relatively unaffected by differences in cultural background. Unlike the verbal aptitude score, which reflects many and varied influences within a culture, the mathematical skills and abilities are generally developed in school. Such differences as do appear are likely to be reflections of curricular differences across schools rather than linguistic, geographic, or socio-economic differences, except as these may be indirectly reflected in school practices.

In fact, the curricular developments in secondary schools at the present time are generating groups of "culturally different" candidates so far as tests of academic achievement are concerned; and much of our research and development efforts during the past several years has been devoted to dealing with problems arising from this source.

The problem of validation of an achievement test is somewhat different from that for an aptitude test. While it is true that the College Board Achieve-

---

[7]William E. Coffman, "Evidence of Cultural Factors in Responses of African Students to Items in an American Test of Scholastic Aptitude." *Research and Development Reports,* RM—63–6 (CEEB. June 1963).

[8]John J. Howell, "College Board Scores of Candidates of Non-English Language Background Tested at Foreign Centers," *Research and Development Reports,* 64–5, No. 2 (CEEB, August 1964).

ment Tests have proved useful in predicting performance in college, there are those who will argue, with justification, that the tests should be considered assessments rather than predictors. As an assessment, the validity of an achievement test rests on the judgments of competent authorities that the test requires the candidate to perform a representative sample of the tasks toward which the instruction of the school has been directed.

But how shall one decide who are competent authorities and what can be done about providing those authorities, once identified, with the data necessary to arrive at sound judgment? In the selection of committees of examiners, in the developing of specifications for each new test, in the detailed test analysis prepared following the administration of each new test, and in special research studies undertaken from time to time, both ETS and the College Board are seeking to answer this question.

To guide committees of examiners, surveys of curricular practices have been conducted. Thus, a study of the preparation of mathematics candidates provided one basis for changes in the mathematics achievement tests during the current academic year.[9] Many similar studies have guided committees in mathematics and in other fields over the years.

We have also made systematic comparisons of the performance of candidates with different curricular backgrounds. Several years ago, for example, we began offering a special examination for candidates who had studied the PSSC[10] physics course after studies had indicated that such students were at a disadvantage on the regular physics test. At the same time, we set about designing a test which would be appropriate for all groups of physics students. Now we are again offering a single physics achievement test.

More recently, recognizing the primary place of expert judgment in determining the appropriateness of achievment tests, we have assembled and analyzed the judgment of teachers of various courses with respect to the appropriateness of questions in the College Board tests.[11] Finally, we have undertaken a study of the relationship between curricular background and test performance which involved all of the College Board Achievement Tests. We hope that the data will provide us with a vastly richer frame of reference for building specifications to insure that the tests reflect accurately the learning of all candidates.

To summarize: First, since tests scores are often misinterpreted or used in ways which reflect unfavorably on the culturally different, whenever possible without serious reductions in validity, differences should be eliminated at

[9]Donald J. Malcolm, "Preparation in Mathematics of Candiates Who Take the Intermediate or Advanced Mathematics Test," *Research and Development Reports,* TDR–63–4 (CEEB, June 1963).

[10]Physical Sciences Study Committee.

[11]Donald J. Malcolm, "Study of the Relevance of Items in CEEB Science Tests for Special Curricula," *Research and Development Reports,* RB–61–20 (CEEB, November 1961).

the point of test construction. Second, if the test is a predictor and if subgroups of sufficient size are available, the validity of a test should be determined separately for each sub-group. Third, if cultural differences remain after careful test construction, the fact should be communicated to test users with guides to proper interpretation of test scores for those who are culturally different. Finally, when assessments rather than predictions are involved, the basis of comparison should be expanded to include the judgments of different groups of experts as well as differences in responses to test items by different groups of test takers.

VI / THE TEACHER AND CULTURE

26 / The Remarkable Culture of the American Educators *

Few more fascinating cultures exist than that of the American Educators," said the anthropologist to his colleague.

The two anthropologists were deep in their favorite leather chairs at the Explorers' Club. They had been trading information on tribal customs they had found at the far ends of the earth. The roaring blaze in the great stone fireplace was fed steadily with massive logs. From the paneled walls, masks used in primitive ceremonials stared down unblinkingly.

"As you well know," continued the speaker, "some of America's greatest anthropologists have applied the anthropological approach to American society as a whole. Others have studied isolated American sub-cultures, such as hill people of the Appalachians. But, until my study, occupational sub-cultures in modern American were uncharted anthropologically."

"How did you happen to choose the American Educators as the occupational sub-culture to be studied?"

"The same three standards I used in choosing South Seas cultures for inclusion in my recent book."

"Check my memory," said his companion, his eyes wandering to the primitive masks. "The tribe must have a special language for in-group communication."

"Right. The vocabulary and sentence structure of the upper class of the American Educators are particularly remarkable."

"The tribe must manifest characteristic in-group behavior."

"Right again. In local communities the American Educators, except for their gregarious upper middle class, are regarded as strange and special creatures. This, along with the rituals of their upper class, may help explain the absorption of the American Educators in talking to themselves through manuscripts, magazines, and meetings."

"Third, the tribe must be suspicious of the out-group."

"Remarkable memory! 'Lay public' is the word this culture uses for the out-group. Roughly translatable as 'foreigners.' "

His companion lit a pipe. "You mentioned classes among the American Educators. What is their class system?"

"As a fellow anthropologist, you are of course familiar with the five

*From *Educational Leadership,* January 1950. Reprinted with permission of the author and the Association for Supervision and Curriculum Development. Copyright 1950 by the Association for Supervision and Curriculum Development.

(sometimes six) social classes documented by many able students of American society. A disreputable lower-lower class. A poor but honest upper-lower class. A solid, substantial lower-middle class. An energetic, influential upper-middle class. A prestige-bearing, established upper class. Approximately so, Herbert?"

"Over-simplified by you for the purpose of summary, of course."

The student of life among the American Educators leaned forward earnestly and tapped his listener's knee as he continued. "Herbert, I have made a tremendous discovery. The American Educators have an *educational* class system which parallels the *social* class system of their country!"

"How does one recognize an upper class American Educator?" asked Herbert, thoughtfully blowing pipe smoke at a particularly hideous tribal mask. "Upper *educational* class, that is."

"I found the habitat of the upper class American Educators in the universities," responded and the anthropologist enthusiastically. Here the member of the upper educational class weaves elaborate theories, engages in research, initiates acolytes to the upper class, produces tomes, and disputes the findings of other members of the upper class. It is believed in this class that the more incomprehensible the language and the fewer the readers, the more the result is to be judged profound and thus worthy of respect. Over the years, knowledge gathered by the upper class trickles down to the masses. The cultural lag is estimated at fifty to seventy-five years.

"The upper educational class is separated from the other classes by an extraordinary caste-like barrier termed Ph.D. and Ed.D. But so honorable is this caste-like distinction that it is now almost a requirement for upper-middle class membership. The upper educational class is in great demand for ceremonial occasions such as local institutes and state meetings required of the lower-lower and upper-upper educational classes."

"And on these occasions the upper class speeches change the behavior of these lower classes?"

"Of course not," said the student of American Educators indignantly. "Not even the upper-middle and lower-middle classes in charge of the meetings expect change to result. The upper class member is there to grace the meeting with upper class participation. I *said* these were ceremonial occasions!"

"Of course. And the other classes?"

"The upper-middle educational class," continued the enthusiastic anthropologist, "is populated largely by people high in the public school hierarchy. It also includes a few declassed university professors who have been revealed as upper-middles in upper's robes, and a handful of teachers from highly rated experimental schools. They are vigorous, energetic, and gregarious characters. They are also distinguishable by their many griefs about something they call 'the curriculum.' This curriculum (which, frankly, I don't quite understand) must be in a very bad way for they are constantly doing things to it. Indeed, the upper-middle clsss holds annual tribal gatherings in which they pray over this curriculum affair!"

"Do the two lower classes pray at these meetings too?"

"No," said the investigator. "One of the major educational class distinctions between the middle classes and the lower classes is in this matter of meeting. The lower classes do not attend such gatherings on the sea coast of New Jersey or in the metropolises or salubrious mountains. The few lower class members who do attend are definitely upward mobile. Incidentally, one important distinction between the upper-middle educational class and the lower-middle educational class is that the upper-middle has expenses paid to these tribal gatherings while lower-middle does not. Consequently, the lower-middle class is much more frequently encountered in state meetings.

"Degree of literacy also appears to be a distinction between the two middle classes. The upper-middle class contributes to magazines and yearbooks; the lower-middle class does not write for publication."

"You mentioned economic considerations. Is the upper class much more prosperous than the upper-middle educational class?"

The explorer of the folkways of the American Educators was genuinely shocked. "Indeed not! Surely, Herbert, you know that money isn't an infallible index to social position. The way one's culture *regards* one is important. Reputation! Many upper-middle Educators are more prosperous than many upper Educators. Upper-middles have been known to give up crass material advantages to join the uppers in university meccas. Similarly, when some uppers have shifted their class position to upper-middle, income was gained but face was lost."

"And the lower classes?" asked Herbert, watching the primitive masks through narrowed eyes. He had the illusion that they were winking at him.

"The upper-lower educational class is made up of garden variety Educators who are regarded as the backbone of the American Educator tribe. All of the class members above them admire and extol upper-lowers. However, none wishes to be one again. The upper-lowers attend workshops, take courses, try experiments, study child development, serve on committees, keep anecdotal records. They try to interpret what the three classes above them advocate. This is no easy task as you can plainly see. When an upper-lower achieves a fine interpretation, the upper-middles or an upward mobile lower-middle generously translates it back into the special tribal language at the tribal gatherings. Yes, upper-lowers are quite different from lower-lowers—" He shuddered.

"Yes?"

"On one thing all of the other educational classes are agreed. They deplore the attitudes and behavior of the lower-lower educational class. As a matter of fact, the uplift of the lower-lowers is the major work of the middle classes. The middle classes try to make upper-lowers out of lower-lowers. (Some 'superintendents' are among the lower-lowers. I am not yet certain what a 'superintendent' really is. It seems to be a kind of businessman.) Lower-lowers resist all new and educationally moral ideas. They simply put in their time. They have a peculiar unofficial slogan. 'Friday, thank God.' They are not upward mobile. One informant refers to them as the Dead End Kids of American education. Apparently they have few middle class virtues."

"A remarkable culture!" said Herbert.

"Let me illustrate," said the indefatigable anthropologist. "Curriculum Director Joseph Doakes, who is lower-middle educational class, plans to attend a Denver convention of an organization mysteriously initialled ASCD, which is basically upper-middle with some upper and some lower-middle members. Now Doakes. . . ."

On the paneled walls, the masks used in primitive ceremonials were smiling at each other.

Samuel Tenenbaum*

27 / The Teacher, the Middle Class, the Lower Class†

I live on the West Side of Manhattan in a rather solid middle-class house with doorman and all. My neighbors have been complaining for a long time that the neighborhood has been running down. But the building I live in has held like a bastion, a strong fifteen-story fortress. My neighbors felt safe and protected once within its high walls, until a hotel on the opposite side of the street began to be used by the city relief agency to house indigent families. The hotel, a great affair, once magnificient, in bygone days probably catered to people of substance. This is the way, I suppose, of an American city. It represents the great human flow and ebb, the tidal waves of a dynamic culture that pushes people and fortunes around endlessly.

But this is not really my story. I meant to speak of how these lower-class people affected us, the middle-class in our house; and what I myself learned in terms of my own feelings as a teacher. If I am a little roundabout, forgive me.

First of all, in what seemed almost overnight (and in actuality was not more than a month), this once great hotel was seething with life and ferment and energy. This comparatively quiet block took on all the aspects of a slum block and some of the aspects of a perpetual carnival. Hordes of children, like milling cattle, cluttered the once empty street; children of all ages, from one year to—well, they looked like eighteen and twenty. Boys and girls mixed in packs, and it was difficult to think of them as single, individual children. They shouted, they screamed, they pushed, they fought. In the midst of play, they would suddenly get into individual fights and collective fights. Violence, aggression, play, and friendliness seemed all mixed up. Every wall on the block was used, either to play ball on or to throw things on. The streets became cluttered with debris, especially broken glass. Where they got all the glass to break is beyond me. The area around this hotel became one vast accumulation of litter. Also, it was quite common for children to throw things from the windows at passersby. The parents apparently did not object, for I never saw a parent reprimand a child for this. The children resembled an uncontrolled, undisciplined herd, doing what they wished, with neither mother nor father

*Mr. Tenenbaum is an associate professor of education at Long Island University. He is the author of *Why Men Hate* and *William Heard Kilpatrick: Trail-Blazer in Education,* and has contributed extensively to professional and general publications.

†From *Phi Della Kappan,* November 1963. Reprinted by permission of Ohi Della Kappan, publisher.

in sight to curb, admonish, or chastise. In fact, when these lower-class children moved in, some of the motherly women in our building occasionally attempted to discipline a child, invariably with frightening results. A cluster of febrile humanity arose like spontaneous combustion to repel the invader, and these well-intentioned women felt lucky if they escaped unharmed. Such incidents only increased my neighbors' sense of helplessness and fear. In the end, my middle-class neighbors, through painful experience, learned to look on aloofly and distantly as children of six and seven smoked and young boys and girls openly engaged in physical contact. Attracted by such scenes, almost glued to them, these neighbors of mine expressed by bodily demeanor and by speech their shock and disapproval.

The parents of the children themselves acted strangely. In all states of undress, they hung out of windows, while below mixed adult groups and groups including children, congregated, drinking beer, joshing, pushing each other about and carrying on in a merry and boisterous way through all hours of the night.

The tenants of our building, guarded more carefully than ever by door-men, made it a point never to loiter outside (which seemed to them a confession of idleness and lack of industry). They were in the habit of going in and out of the building with scarcely anyone seeing or hearing them; they were quiet, inconspicuous, and rarely communicated with neighbors, even though they may have lived together for a quarter of a century.

In contrast, the welfare families lived outside, on the street, conspicuously, loudly, openly. Their social life centered almost exclusively around those who happened to live in the same building. That did not mean it was a serene kind of neighborliness. We never knew when a fist fight or some loud fracas would start and it was not unusual for the occupants of our building to be awakened by a horrible commotion—even the firing of bullets—at 2 or 3 o'clock in the morning. Some of my neighbors were infuriated by such behavior and indignantly called the police, demanding that something be done immediately.

There was one type of behavior, however, that affected my neighbors beyond all others. I cannot say that they liked to see children smoking or engaged in open sex play; it violated their sense of morality. But they could somehow stand that. What they couldn't stand, what frightened them, was the violent, hostile way in which lower-class families found their amusement. An almost palpable atmosphere of aggression and violence hovered over the street. The children would attack an automobile—literally attack it as locusts attack a field—climb on top of it, get inside, and by combined, co-operative effort shake and tug until they left it a wreck. The older men would strip the tires from a car and sell them. A three-wheeled delivery bicycle from a local merchant provided a special holiday. The children gathered from nowhere and everywhere, piled on the delivery bicycle, and drove it up and down the street loaded down with humanity. When they made no dent in the vehicle by this misuse, in disgust they poked at it and pushed it in an effort to make it come apart. I have never seen young people work so assiduously as they did riding, pushing, and shaking the cart. They didn't give up until it was completely destroyed. I have seen children, several of whom could not have been more than seven or eight years old, at this job of destruction past 10 p.m.; and they all appeared to be having the merriest time. Even their innocent, friendly play was violent. Suddenly, strong, tall, gangling adolescent boys would dash pell-mell down the street, like stampeding cattle, shrieking and screaming, pushing, shoving, mauling each other.

Of course, this hotel where they lived was not meant for families with many children. Since it was enormous in size, at least fifteen stories high, it probably represented the most concentrated slum of all times, greater than could possibly prevail in Harlem. You might say as I did: "What can you expect? Children have to play. Here they are growing up without a mother, or a mother who never seems to make her presence felt, like animals, without love or warmth, pushing out for some sort of life on the street. Are not these unfortunate children more sinned against than sinning?"

So I spoke to my neighbors. Yet I knew that was not the whole truth. Nearby, within a few blocks, were two magnificent parks: Riverside Drive and Central Park. There they could have green fields and space and freedom. Yet none made a move to play there. Although I believe I understand many other facets of their conduct, this aspect remains a mystery I cannot fathom.

Broadly, this gives you some notion of what happened to a quiet, respectable block when invaded by the lower classes. What happened to my neighbors? First there was general, immediate, universal consernation and some took direct action. Posthaste some moved out; they wouldn't live, they said, with such trash. A second group remained. This group didn't mind the shenanigans, the broken glass, the commotion, but they experienced an awful fear of personal attack. Many of them became so frightened by the invaders that they stayed home at night. The sense of physical peril was probably the most frightening and demoralizing aspect of the situation, though I never heard of anyone being molested or attacked. There was a great deal of damage to parked cars, and we soon learned to avoid that side of the street. It was peculiar to see the gaping empty spaces near the hotel curb, when all around were cars choking for an inch of space.

After the first shock had passed, the tenants of our building took action. The middle class is not without power, which it exercises in its own way (generally of course polite, proper, and without violence). A committee got up a petition and collected signatures asking that a policeman be stationed on our street twenty-four hours a day. A tenant with political connections began to put them to work. I hear that the matter has reached the mayor himself, and that the welfare agency plans to remove families with children from the hotel since, after the petition, the Powers-That-Be agreed that it is an improper place for them.

But these lower-class people are still across the street and the fear remains. Even worse, my middle-class neighbors are convinced that these new people are trash, some monstrous excretion of mankind, a lower order of animal, apart from the human species. So long as such attitudes persist, these unfortunate newcomers—poverty-stricken, ignorant, addicted to vice, drink, violence, and brutality—will never be understood in terms of what causes such living: their bleak, helpless, and hopeless state, their lack of identity and purpose. My middle-class neighbors will piously continue to stay aloof, judging them; and this judgmental attitude itself makes the gulf wider. It is inconceivable that our middle-class house will ever join in friendship or good will to these lower-class invaders.

What I was witnessing had enormous meaning for me as a student of education and as one who teachers future teachers. I thought I knew the problem of the lower-class student; it is all explained in the textbook. Like other instructors, I have discussed the problem in polite, academic terms. But this experience made me see clearly and vividly, as nothing else has, how farfetched and remote is our present school system for these children—in philosophy, methodology, approach, values, and meaning.

In contrast to the lower-class children, how preciously kept is each child in our house; how carefully clothed; how carefully guarded; how often admonished by parents, grandparents, relatives, and friends. In the elevator, the icy tone of the father to his seven-year-old son: "Is that hat glued on to your head, John?" How quickly and politely that hat comes off. How often are they shown pride and love. "My son is the valedictorian of his class. He plans to go to Harvard, get his Ph.D., and teach chemistry." Even our doorman, hard and brusque and violent with lower-class children, takes on a different tone and manner with the building children; to them he is gentle and tender and protective. The children themselves for the most part are loving and lovable. As they imbibe attention and love, as these qualities are poured into them, they have them to give out. If at times the children become rambunctious, the doorman finds it sufficient to threaten them with parental disclosure and they fall in line. There is no discipline problem. From infancy on, they experience discipline.

These children have pride and are conscious of family position. Even if you are a stranger, they will inform you that their father, a lawyer, is involved in some famous current trial; or he has been called to Washington on an important mission; or that their father or grandfather owns this well-known establishment or business. And they tell you with equal pride what they themselves plan to be; and they act as if they have already achieved it and have a right to all the honors thereof.

On school holidays our building takes on a festive air as the children come home from out-of-town schools and colleges. You see a little boy with a ramrod figure sporting a magnificient uniform; he attends a military academy. Parents take special pride in introducing children all around. For these holidays parents have a well-planned schedule—theaters, lunches downtown, visiting and inter-visiting, parties that their children give and parties that they go to. The building is full of young people coming and going; it is really most pleasant and exciting.

Yes, the children in this middle-class building are solicitously nurtured. Just as the parents seem to have purpose and direction for themselves, so the children seem also to have imbibed purpose and direction. Some of them, still in elementary school, speak of college and careers. Coming home in the afternoon, they hold their books tightly and neatly; for it is obvious that for them books represent important and powerful tools for the future.

What a stark contrast are these children on the opposite side of the street! These children seem to have no purpose, no objective; they seem to live for the moment, and the big objective is to make this moment pass away as amusingly and excitingly as possible. And no matter what, they seem a lot more bored and idle than the middle-class children. They hang around, in gangs or small groups, and in boredom they poke at one another or get into mischief; they are ready for any or everything, but mostly nothing happens and there they are, hanging around in idleness.

Even when playing near the house, the children in our building go to the parks already referred to, and they participate in organized games, or if not, they telephone to a friend or friends to meet and play together. In contrast, the children on the opposite street have many of the characteristics of neglected alley cats, growing up in a fierce, hostile jungle. The children from the two sides of the street never mix. Since the invasion of this new element, the children in our building are more closely supervised than ever; they are so apart in thinking and feeling that functionally they are like two different species.

As I saw these two groups first-hand, I understood how easily middle-class children fit conventional school systems; how almost from infancy they have been trained for the role of a good, conforming member of this institution; and how easily and naturally their middle-class teachers would respond with understanding and affection.

Also, I could see how wrong, how incongruous and meaningless this school was for lower-class children; how their very being was an irritant to it, and it to them; how ill-prepared they were for the demands of the school; how what they were and how they lived would elicit from their middle-class teachers scorn, resentment, rejection, hostility, and—worst of all—how these children would create in their teachers fear, a physical, sickening fear, as thirty or forty of them crowded together in one room hour after hour, day after day. This was the most demoralizing feature of all. For once fear sets in, you can no longer understand, apprecaite, or help; what you want is distance, separation, safety; or if this is impossible, you want the backing of superior strength or a counter fear; and one cannot educate or help another human being through force or fear.

As I thought of what was happening to my block, I was astonished to realize how in nearly all respects our teachers respond to lower-class children just as my house neighbors do. They cannot understand their idleness, their purposelessness, their lack of ambition. They regard such traits as some congenital evil. Like my neighbors, they are indignant and shocked by their sexual frankness, and are astonished and chagrined by parental indifference to children's progress in school. When parents do come to school they may even side with the child against the teacher. Like my neighbors, teachers remain in a perpetual state of fear of these children, at their acting out, their defiance of discipline, their destructiveness and vandalism. "Look at what they did!" a teacher will say, pointing to a desk ripped open or shattered panes of glass, speaking as if some holy altar had been violated. Looking at these lower-class children distantly, unapprovingly, and judgmentally, as my neighbors did, many teachers feel trapped, frightened, helpless. Like my neighbors, when a child gets into trouble with the law, they often take a smug satisfaction in the tragedy, as if their original judgment had been vindicated. "I knew he would come to a bad end." Middle-class virtue is written all over them.

A good case can be and has been made that the only purpose of our educational system is to inculcate middle-class values, to create a middle-class person; and its purpose is not at all to transmit knowledge and subject matter. If this is true, and I am beginning to feel that it is, the main task of our schools, to repeat, is to train children in the proprieties, the conventions, the manners, the sexual restraints, the respect for private property of the middle class; and also to promote such middle-class virtues as hard work; sportsmanship, and ambition—especially ambition. The aim becomes to create a gentleman, a person striving for high achievement, so that he can attain the middle-class ideal; money, fame, a lavish house in the suburbs, public honors etc.

I now perceive more clearly why lower-class children are such problems in school, why they do so poorly, why they are so alien to this institution, why they stand out like sore thumbs. Bluntly put, they don't fit in at all with what the schools and teachers demand, want, and expect.

I now understand why even bright lower-class children do not do nearly as well in school as middle-class children of equal and even lower ability; why bright lower-class children drop out of school even when intellectually capable of doing the work. They never feel part of the institution, their school is not theirs, their team is not theirs, their classmates are not theirs.

Just as the children in my building did not mix with the children on the hotel side of the block, so they do not mix in school. But here in school middle-class children are on home ground; it is *their* school, *their* teachers, *their* clubs, *their* team, *their* classmates. Parents of lower-class children also feel strange and remote from the institution, frightened by its conventions. Sometimes a lower-class child, through the influence of some good, loving, middle-class person, generally a teacher, begins to aspire to middle-class status. The parents, instead of reinforcing middle-class values, may resent these new feelings in the child and fear that he is being alienated from them; they will try to keep the child in their own class. I know a fine and able student who applied for a scholarship and was accepted by a prestige college. Her father, a laborer, was incensed at the whole idea. We were turning his daughter's head. A good girl should get a job, come home, help her mother, and get married. When he was told that college and marriage are not incompatible, he showed every doubt that the two go together. Then he took another tack. Deep study in college, he said, affects the head, and his daughter had fragile health; he didn't want her to become rattle-brained. Finally, he trotted out his last argument: he wasn't going to have his daughter gallivanting off mixing with those snobs and good-for-nothings. The father won out.

It also happens, undoubtedly with greater frequency in America than in another major culture, that a lower-class child does break out of his group to enter the middle class. A play, "The Corn Is Green," deals with this theme. It is the true account of a Welsh boy whose teacher, Miss Cooke, out of dedication and devotion, held the youth steadfast in his studies. After many trials, the young man passed his examinations and won an Oxford scholarship. The son of a nursemaid and a seaman, he became an eminent playwright, actor, and director, and, incidentally, the author of "The Corn Is Green."

It sometimes happens that a member of the middle class will flunk out of his class also, although this is quite rare, as a review of your own experience will indicate. Middle-class parents will go to any extreme to save their children for middle-class status. How would an eminent and respected professional person regard his son who worked as a janitor or as a laborer, although the young man might be quite happy with his work and the work right for him? Middle-class parents attempt all kinds of shenanigans to keep their off-spring in their class. We all know of the student who fails at a good university, whereupon the parents find a mediocre school where he can obtain the degree. The parents rejoice, for the boy is now a college graduate; he has achieved middle-class status and need not disgrace the family.

I am beginning to feel that if we want to help lower-class children we will have to reorient our thinking and philosophy. We will have to adopt fundamental reforms, radical and crucial in nature, so that the school as an institution will be more nearly in conformity with the cultural and behavioral patterns of this class. I am beginning to think that it might be best if we would enlist in this task the more able and brighter lower-class members, with the hope that they will be better able to cope with the lower-class child. Little good can come to any child when a teacher relates to him with fear and condemnation.

What has long been a national fetish, almost religious in fervor, is the effort to shape all children, regardless of their state or condition, in the middle-class mold. It would appear that the chief end of man is to glorify the middle class. When teachers fail at this task, they regard themselves and the school as failures. I believe that until now we have done a remarkable job in converting this "melting pot" material into a sort of middle-class stew, although frequently of questionable taste and quality.

I raise this question: Should all people strive to become middle-class? Hasn't our middle-class culture produced a society with more than its share of tensions, anxieties, neuroses, and psychoses? How many souls have been blighted, twisted, and distorted by its impossible demands! Middle-class culture, it is true, stresses ambition and achievement, but does it not leave altogether too many of us feeling and thinking of ourselves as failures, even when we have striven mightily and have done our best? And how many, after high achievement, still feel discontented, unhappy, striving ever higher? For there is no end goal to achievement; the goal is almost by definition unattainable. As a clinical psychologist who has seen men and women in travail, I can only say that I have nothing but sympathy for the middle-class child; the demands made on him by parents and his sub-culture are often unbearable. I think of him as frequently caught in a vortex, the victim of uncontrollable forces, so strong that they may destroy him.

In our sanctimonious way, we have assumed that this, our middle-class culture, represents the best of all possible worlds. We have never examined lower-class culture with the view of asking: Is there perhaps something in another way of life to alleviate our own sickness? Like my house neighbors, we have regarded every deviation with moral condemnation. Even if all these feelings about middle-class values are right, even if we should continue to force lower-class children into middle-class molds, shouldn't we recognize that for some children this can never be achieved? It isn't for them, as a duck isn't for running a race with a rabbit. In this world isn't there a need and an honorable place for carpenters, plumbers, and yes, laborers? Aren't we doing infinite harm to children by our insistence that they be something they cannot be, and then making them feel like failures because they have not achieved what they cannot achieve? Wouldn't it be better if we found out what they *can* be, and then set about changing our schools so that we can help them, not to become middle-class, but to become the best selves they are capable of becoming?

Ronald Shinn

28 / Cultural Conflict in the Classroom: Emphasis on Teachers as Classroom Communicators

An imposing array of research contends there is a high degree of correlation between public school teachers of middle-class heritage and the inability to relate to children from diverse sub-cultures. Furthermore, teachers who adhere to middle-class values are often linked with attributing to the dropout statistics of children from the dominant culture. It is understandable that educators are somewhat defensive in discussing their role in the classroom because invariably they are confronted with this kind of research which by itself not only depicts them as "monsters" but is a gross simplicity of teaching in public schools. This article will attempt to come to grips with the dynamics of teaching relative to the problem of cultural conflict in the classroom. Identifying and examining the correlation of the social class values of teachers to their teaching behavior should be construed as a step toward the understanding of how problems pertaining to cultural conflict enter into the teacher-pupil relationships and not necessarily its resolution.

SOME DIFFICULTIES BECAUSE OF THE NOTION OF CULTURAL TRANSMISSION

As a cultural transmitter, teachers are expected to convey and cultivate the beliefs and values of the dominant culture. Acculturation is accentuated to such an extent that children from diverse sub-cultures are adversely affected because of their nonconformity to a school curriculum based on dominant cultural criteria. It does not necessarily follow that educators are not well intentioned but perhaps in attempting to fulfill their role as an agent of the culture they have become cultural transmitters.

School curricula that is characterized by strict adherence to such measures as culturally biased tests as well as the promulgation of values related to hygiene, dress, and high achievement orientation could easily obscure the academic potential and social worth of not only ethnic minorities, but any youth who is a poor "cultural fit." Irrespective of the cultural origin of any youth, he must be afforded the opportunity to assert pride in his heritage. This is not easy for the culturally different, because there is little latitude for examination of any subject of a nondominant cultural origin. Furthermore, he might be subjected to negative psycho-educational experiences by being placed in mentally retarded classes and programs of a vocational nature because ethnic minorities are thought to be "culturally deprived." No culture is better or superior than the other and so often we mistake socioeconomic deprivation as the cultural antecedents that affect learning in the schools. Children from poverty backgrounds come to school with many psycho-educational difficulties in contrast to their counterparts from suburbia. However, this should not deter educators from fully extending themselves in meeting this challenge. Frank Riessman (1964) points out how educators are prone to overlook the positives of disadvantaged groups by building educational programs exclusively around the weaknesses or deficits. He goes on to cite Irving Taylor who likens the mental style of the socioeconomically disadvantaged to that of the mental style of one type of highly creative persons, thus necessitating the need of schools to provide for these unique, untapped resources of creativity.

Another factor to consider according to George Spindler (1965) is the transmission of conflicts and discrepancies interwoven into the very fabric of the American value system. The transformation from traditional to emergent values is the basis for the culturally patterned contradictions. Spindler cites specific examples for these social anomalies: We place a traditional value on thrift yet we stress keeping up good appearances at all costs; we believe success to be derived by hard work yet we emphasize social contacts as means in getting ahead; and we deny sexuality but deluge the mass media, dress, and imagery with sex. As a cultural transmitter, teachers probably have internalized these conflicts and probably will transmit them to the children. He manifests this conflict between ideal and real by professing one thing and doing another. It is not that he is lacking good intentions or is not generous but reflects the discrepancy between ideal in our culture and consequently defeats his professed aims. Consider the following:

Teacher: Class, today we shall discuss your opinions and concerns about lowering the voting age to 18.

Student: I feel that if young people are old enough to serve in the Armed Forces, they are old enough to vote.

Teacher: Don't you feel that the basic focal point is whether or not young people of 18 years of age have garnered enough experiences and insights to vote intelligently?

Student: It has been demonstrated time after time that adults have often voted along emotional lines as opposed to an evaluation of the party platform of the various candidates.

Teacher: I suppose you are right, but in light of the kinds of social problems teenagers have been involved in the past, lowering the voting age to 18 may not be a good idea. Mindful, I am not opposed to you voting, but I am saying youngsters should be given the opportunity to mature fully without adding on to their problems by thrusting this kind of responsibility upon them.

The teacher defeated his pupose of an open class discussion of this voting concern by closing off alternative avenues for student exploration. Not only did he dominate the discussion with his version of the problem, but devastatingly conveyed his lack of confidence in their abilities to think out the problem. Although this teacher is of a democratic orientation and felt the students had the necessary repertoire of problem-solving skills to delve into this kind of a problem, he could not relinquish his own feelings about the inadequacies of youth.

The notion of cultural transmission can also eradicate all traces of rapport between teacher and students if not checked. The teacher's over-riding concern about what children should emulate and become might easily detract emphasis on relating to students in a warm interpersonal manner. There is also the danger of not utilizing the general knowledge of the peer group and the obfuscation of the value of social network of the students in terms of cultivating rapport. Perhaps the problem of rapport is more fundamental than previously addressed and is the antithesis of the fixation toward the development of a cultural mold which defies such basic questions of concern as to who is this student, where is he and where does he want to go?

It would appear that schools subscribing to the notion of cultural transmission are enjoined from establishing a working relationship with their immediate communities. In a large sense, educators would tend to view themselves as the "regulators" of society as evidenced by their haughtiness in talking *down* to parents in parent-teacher conferences and concern in contacting parents of children only when there are problems to discuss rather than when compliments are due. Furthermore, much can be said about the reluctance of educators of all levels going out to the communities contiquous to the institutions and sharing their talents and insights to effectuate social and environmental changes. Schools cannot operate in a vaccuum. Open communication and interaction between the school and community is vital if there is to be a joint venture in the education of youngsters.

THE TEACHER AS A CLASSROOM COMMUNICATOR

The simplest definition of communication is the act of sending information from one system to another (Cherry, 1957). The transmission-belt theory of communication (Fearing, 1962) assumes a simple linear, one-directional relationship between the source and destination, subject to interferences or disturbances analogous to malfunctions or imperfections that distort the signals enroute over a message-relay system, i.e., telegraph, telephone, radio broadcast, etc. The following paradigm depicts the transmission-belt theory model of communication:

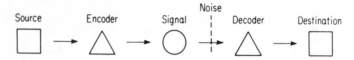

In human communication, the transmission-belt theory is grossly inadequate. Communication behaviors of humans demand a two-way relationship. Dissimilar to the receiver (decoder) in the mechanical model, human beings are not devoid of feelings, perceptions and predilections of how the universe of events should be organized and function. Feedback ensues after reception of the intended message, but it is transposed into a variety of forms, some of which may not resemble the form of the initial signals transmitted but are important cues relating to the reception and reaction to the message, i.e., boredom, hostility, indifference, daydreaming, etc. The two-way flow communication is illustrated by the following paradigm:

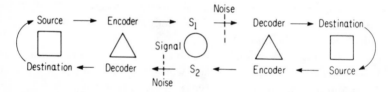

It would appear that instructors who ascribe to the transmission belt communication model are engendering miscommunication in their classrooms. Perhaps we may never be entirely free from miscommunication. Our attitudes, values and beliefs not only shapen our social universe, but affect the way we receive and interpret messages. Misunderstandings and confusion may stem from the failure of the teacher to bridge the gap that exists between his experiences and those of students. Tillman Jackson (1968) cogently illustrates this in the following excerpt:

> Teachers face classes composed of individuals, each having his own unique background of experiences. Teachers seldom have sufficiently acquainted themselves with the anthropological, sociological and cultural differences. Too frequently, the values which they attempt to promote in their classrooms are in conflict with the realisms to which students have adapted.

The notion of the teacher as a classroom communicator would necessitate the utilization of the two-way flow communication model to deal with the problem of cultural conflict. By being open to student feedback and assessing the verbal and nonverbal cues for possible misunderstandings, instructors become cognizant that communication skills are as important as knowledge and empathy toward students from diverse subcultures relative to the development of a positive social-emotional climate in classrooms. The inherent danger of not dealing with students' internal frame of references is the orientation toward a teaching modality characterized by the consistent behavior of talking *at* students. This kind of teaching behavior not only defies making the subject matter interesting and relevant, but impedes the development of warm interpersonal relationships between the teacher and students. A white teacher of middle-class orientation may be enjoined from relating to children in general, not necessarily because of his background, but because of his unwillingness to implement a two-way communication system in the classroom in terms of eliciting student participation, the sharing of ideas, and the clarification of misunderstood ideas and concepts.

A teacher's perception of a discipline problem stemming from a cultural conflict in the classroom may instead trace its roots to the misunderstandings and ignorance on the part of the instructor relative to the kinds of experiences and expectations that children bring with them to school. Again, the teacher must possess the basic communication skills to be able to probe into the private world of this individual child. In an elementary school, a teacher recently told the story of a little girl of Mexican-American descent who happened to come from a background of extreme poverty. In the beginning of school, this child of approximately nine years of age, Mary, refused to take her spot in the proper alphabetical sequence in the lunch line procession to the cafeteria. It turned out that she would claw and kick her way to the very front of the line and totally disrupt this traditional procedure of approaching the cafeteria at lunchtime. The teacher's first inclination was to punish this child for this kind of unacceptable behavior. Somehow, she felt that there must be more than this child's adverse reaction to her and her authority and decided to ask Mary in a variety of ways what seemed to be the problem. It seems that eventually the teacher was able to piece the story together and what she came up with was that Mary had barely enough to eat at home because there was little food to be eaten and often what little she had would be partially consumed by the older and stronger siblings. As a result, Mary had to reassure herself that she would get enough to eat at school by being the first in line so she would receive her food before anyone. The third week of school had gone by and one day Mary was back in her proper alphabetical order. Mary's response when questioned as to why, was, "I know that I will get enough to eat now, but I also know you love me very much and care about me."

Frequently, student-teachers approach their supervisors voicing these concerns: "How can I best relate the subject matter to the students?" and "I don't seem to be communicating with the class." It would seem that the task of teacher educators, as stressed by Minnis and Shrable (1968) is to "translate teaching concerns into competence, the particular area of competence being a set of attitudes and overt behavior to be enacted in the public school classroom." Social scientists, such as Amidon and Flanders (1961), in the area of teacher-pupil interactions present evidence which incorporates the attributes of the two-way flow communication model as part of the conditions necessary for a social climate conducive to desirable pupil attitudes and superior patterns of work.

It would appear instructional models in terms of the shaping of specific classroom skills and teacher behavior patterns relevant to effective teaching might be invaluable as training protocols. In regard to facilitating teachers to become classroom communicators, we might consider the study of Shinn (1970) in which he reported success in altering the teaching behavior of student teachers in oral communication competence at the .05 level of statistical significance.

CONCLUSION

It cannot be denied that one's social background is influential in the way one perceives the social universe. After all, one can only live his life and no one else's. Perhaps what is of critical concern in teaching is not the particular set of values that one adheres to but the ability to relate to children irrespective of their backgrounds. We are not about to make a black teacher white or the converse of a white teacher. To be effective, teachers, like anyone else, have to be themselves. In essence, they have to be real. Artificiality soon manifests itself when teachers are no longer able to involve the universals that cut cross-cultures into their teaching: respect, fair play, trust, love, and empathy.

The notion of cultural transmission has too many limitations. Children should be afforded the opportunity to develop awareness and pride of their respective cultures. The notion of the teacher as a classroom communicator has not only an air of openness and freedom about it but addresses itself to more fundamental concerns as to who is this child, where is he, and how can I help him get where he wants to go?

In the final analysis, you teach what you are. If you enjoy helping children, you will spare no efforts to find out how you can continually improve your teaching. If not, there will always be conflict in your classroom. You cannot get more out of teaching than what you put into it.

BIBLIOGRAPHY

Amidon, Edmund J., and Ned A. Flanders. 1961. "The Effects of Direct and Indirect Teacher Influence on Dependent-Prone Students Learning Geometry," *Journal of Educational Psychology*, 52:6, 286–291.

Cherry, Colin. 1957. *On Human Communication.* Massachusetts Institute of Technology and Chapman and Hall, 31–32.

Fearing, Franklin. 1962. "Human Communication," *Audiovisual Communication Review,* 10:5, 78–108, September-October.

Jackson, Tillman V. 1968. "Communication and the Classroom Teacher," *Improving College and University Teaching,* 16:1, 50–52, Winter.

Minnis, Douglas, and Kenneth Shrable. 1968. "Micro-Teaching and Interaction Analysis in a Teacher Education Program." Davis: University of California, Davis (mimeographed report).

Riessman, Frank. 1970. "The Overlooked Positives of Disadvantaged Groups," in R. Shinn (ed.), *The School and the Culturally Different.* New York: Simon and Schuster, Inc.

Shinn, Ronald. 1970. "Sensitivity Instructional Model and the Teacher as a Classroom Communicator." Paper presented at the California Educational Research Association, San Francisco, California, February 13. To be published as a research booklet by Educational Technology Publications.

Spindler, George D. 1965. "The Transmission of American Culture," in G. Spindler (ed.). *Education and Culture.* New York: Holt, Rinehart and Winston, Inc.

VII / THE SCHOOL AS A SOCIO-CULTURAL SYSTEM

Glen H. Elder, Jr.*

29 / Peer Socialization in School†

Although the student group is a valuable educational resource, it remains an untapped potential in the curriculum of most primary and secondary schools. Recognition of this potential is frequently obscured by concern over the peer group's contrainfluence on student achievement and conduct. Considering the influence of peer groups on the social development of youth, Bronfenbrenner concludes that it is

> ... questionable whether any society, whatever its social system, can afford largely to chance the direction of this influence, and realization of its high potential for fostering constructive development both for the child and society.[1]

The primary objective of this article is to examine structures and interaction patterns in the classroom which promote the utilization and development of student resources within the peer-group setting.[2] Unlike the stress on social adjustment and conformity in earlier writings in education, the following discussion emphasizes the development of individual talents as well as social responsibility, cooperation, and tolerance through processes of social exchange, observational learning, and social reinforcement.

The first part of the article—on socialization as a transactional process —establishes a perspective for the analysis of classroom socialization.[3] This section is followed by an examination of the learning experiences afforded by inter-age and interracial relationships. The article is primarily restricted to children in elementary school for reasons of available data and brevity.

SOCIALIZATION AS A TRANSACTIONAL PROCESS

Socialization entails social learning which prepares the individual for membership in society and in groups within the society; it facilitates transitions

*Glen H. Elder, Jr., Associate Professor of Sociology, University of North Carolina at Chapel Hill

†From *Educational Leadership*, Vol. 26, No. 5 (February 1969), pp. 465–473. Copyright, February 1969, by the Association for Supervision and Curriculum Development. Reprinted by permission of the author and the Association for Supervision and Curriculum Development.

[1]Urie Bronfenbrenner, "Responses to Pressure from Peers vs. Adults Among Soviet and American School Children," *International Journal of Psychology*, 2: 206 (1967).

[2]A longer version of this paper has been written by the author: Department of Sociology, Alumni Building, University of North Carolina, Chapel Hill.

[3]For a recent review of peer socialization in the elementary schools see: John C. Glidewell, Mildred B. Kantor, Louis M. Smith, and Lorene H. Stringer, "Socialization and Social Structure in the Classroom," in Martin and Lois Hoffman, *Review of Research in Child Development*, 2: 221 –56 (1966), Russell Sage Foundation.

from one status to another by conditioning behavior for the new requirements of specific roles and group life. Such learning is influenced by the degree of coordination among socializing agents in goals and practices, and by particular training techniques and ecological contexts.

There are three *time emphases* in the socialization of children: (a) on the past—molding the young in the image of the older generation by transmitting the cultural heritage and by reinforcing traditional behavior: (b) on the present —orienting the child toward the standards of membership and role performance in his current groups, such as the family, age-group, and classroom; and (c) on the future—preparing the child for the anticipated requirements of future roles, groups, and transitions.

Socialization agencies are concerned to some extent with all three emphases, especially the contemporary demands of group membership, but schools in particular have major responsibilities in the preparatory task. In American society, the dominant time-perspective—toward the future is most characteristic of the middle class, while an emphasis on the past and present is found in the upper and lower classes respectively.[4]

The influences to which a child is exposed include explicit training and a broad range of social conditioning which might be described as the unconscious patterning of behavior. Instruction and learning through observation are potential examples of these two types of influences.

Socialization is most commonly viewed as a one-way process which stresses the effect of the social agent on the child. Reliance on this framework has had the unfortunate effect of obscuring a basic source of socialization for authority figures—the young. Like parents, teachers partly learn their role, develop teaching skills, and acquire language patterns from the young.[5] A transactional perspective is sensitive to the way in which students socialize their teachers and each other, as well as to the influence of teacher on students.[6] Student and teacher are defined in terms of each other and behavior is a consequence of the reciprocal influence of each person on the other in a particular situation. A satisfying social exchange in this relationship generally creates conditions favorable to similar transactions among students in the classroom. Elementary school classrooms, in which the teacher encourages student participation in problem solving and decision making, are generally distinguished by a high level of interaction and cooperation among students, minimal conflicts, tolerance for divergent opinions, and responsible initiative in school work.[7]

---

[4]See: Florence R. Kluckhohn and Fred L. Strodtbeck, *Variations in Value Orientations* (Evanston, Illinois: Row Peterson and Company, 1961), pp. 27–28.

[5]On language patterns, see: Emil J. Haller, "Pupil Influence in Teacher Socialization: A Socio-Linguistic Study," *Sociology of Education*, 40: 316–33 (Fall 1967).

[6]For a thoughtful analysis of classroom behavior from a transactional perspective, see: Ira J. Gordon, *Studying the Child in School* (New York: John Wiley , Sons, Inc., 1966).

[7]Glidewell *et al., op. cit.,* p. 232.

In a teaching relationship that is truly reciprocal, the teacher at times is also a student, and the student—especially in adolescence—is also an instructor. The teaching role of the child is especially relevant to the situation of youth in a rapidly changing society, for as Erikson observes,

> . . . no longer is it merely for the old to teach the young the meaning of life, whether individual or collective. It is the young who, by their responses and actions, tell the old whether life as represented by the old and as presented to the young has meaning.[8]

Teaching becomes effective when the materials presented possess or acquire such meaning for the learner. Since teachers typically have relatively limited authority, this restricts the authority which they can reinvest in their students and contributes to the negligible control which students exercise over their education.[9] This handicap to meaningful teacher-student exchange is seen on all levels of formal education.

Up to mid-adolescence, the presence of children in school is a compulsory requirement, and thus the principles which govern social exchange in a voluntary relationship are not entirely applicable to teacher-student transactions.[10]

Nevertheless, it is apparent that social exchange with teachers is not a profitable experience for many students, and although restraints may keep their bodies in school, aggressive or passive responses to injustice and relative deprivation diminish the value of classroom experiences for other students. These consequences suggest that an equitable exchange of services, knowledge, and rewards should be an intrinsic objective in teacher-student transactions.

Teaching opportunities provide a basis for social exchange among students. The child who excels in a particular subject has the opportunity to gain competence and a sense of social responsibility by tutoring a slower student. Thus the slower student gains encouragement, understanding, and academic assistance from a person who is not socially removed by a large age difference and evaluative authority. The learning benefits achieved by students in the teaching role generally affirm the principle that teaching is a valuable developmental experience. Student tutors gain as much or even more in academic learning than the students they work with.[11] When students are used as instructors of other students, aptitude heterogeneity within the classroom may be transformed from a teaching handicap to an educational asset. Both age

---

[8]Erik H. Erikson, "Youth: Fidelity and Diversity," *Daedalus*, 91: 24 (Winter 1962).

[9]James G. Anderson, "The Authority Structure of the School: System of Social Exchange," *Educational Administration Quarterly*, 3: 145 (Spring 1967).

[10]On social behavior as exchange, see: George C. Homans, *Social Behavior: Its Elementary Forms* (New York: Harcourt, Brace & World, Inc., 1961).

[11]Robert D. Cloward, "Studies in Tutoring," *Journal of Experimental Education*, 36: 14–25 (Fall 1967); and Glen H. Elder, Jr., "Age Integration and Socialization in an Educational Setting," *Harvard Educational Review*, 37: 594–619 (Fall 1967).

and ability groupings can be viewed as consequences of a teacher-centered model of instruction. Such groupings facilitate the instructional task for the adult teacher, but limit teaching-learning possibilities within the student group. Systematic incorporation of tutoring relationships in the curriculum may help to reduce student indifference associated with the passive role of the learner.

SOCIALIZATION IN THE CLASSROOM

Socialization is a continuing process for the individual. Thus an understanding of peer influences and learning at one point in time requires an examination of the student's past, especially of his reinforcement history in family and classroom experiences.

One of the first tasks the child faces as he enters a new classroom in elementary school is to gain an understanding of his rôle, of where he stands in relation to classmates and the teacher. This cognitive map or perspective is associated with the child's developing status as defined by his peers.

In the first few days or weeks of class, students tend to sort themselves out on three status dimensions: (a) liking or social acceptance, (b) the ability to influence other students, and (c) competence in schoolwork.[12] One should note here the resemblance between these status dimensions among children in the classroom and those in the larger society, such as prestige, power, and wealth or accomplishment. Accuracy of the student's perception of his classroom status is generally greater among children of high versus low status (defense mechanisms are a factor here) and in classrooms with a clear status hierarchy. This determinant of status perception is likewise operative in the larger community.

In the elementary school, a child's status on these dimensions remains moderately stable from one grade to another. Although a causal sequence among these status factors cannot be confidently determined, the success of a child in working out friendships or accepting relationships with other students appears to have a very significant effect on his perceived ability to influence his classmates and to achieve.

The peer system in most elementary school classrooms includes several subgroups, some dyads, and a few isolates. While there is little need to recite the widely recognized consequences of social rejection, studies of peer-group socialization have found that these effects vary in relation to the status structure of the classroom. Possession of low status in the eyes of classmates is most strongly correlated with negative attitudes toward school, low self-esteem, and underutilization of mental ability when this status is correctly perceived by the

[12]This paragraph and the next are indebted to a review of research by Glidewell et al., op. cit.

student.[13] As noted earlier, clarity of the status structure increases the accuracy of this perception. More detailed information on the determinants and content of social exchange in elementary school classrooms is needed.

Conditions which foster beneficial exchange and learning among students are also those which lessen prejudice: equal status in the situation, pursuit of common goals, cooperative interdependence, and support from the main authorities, structures, and norms.[14] As individuals interact with one another under favorable conditions, they are likely to acquire common perspectives and more positive feelings toward each other.

While status equality and similarity in values, background, or skin color are significant bases of interpersonal attraction, there are tasks within the classroom which bring together children who would not ordinarily choose each other—such as the bright and dull, or older and younger students. The tutoring relationship is a good example. Rewards for tutor and learner are contingent on cooperative rather than competitive interdependence. Relatively equal rewards for progress on the teaching-learning task serve to reinforce cooperative behavior.

SCHOOL COMPOSITION, STUDENT RELATIONSHIPS, LEARNING

Social stratification and segregation in a complex society limit a child's knowledge and understanding of himself and of others from different life situations. In schools, the composition of the student body on sex, race, and family status specifies a particular type of learning environment, as do age-grades and ability groups. If the social composition of the classroom resembles that of the larger community and society, children have the opportunity to acquire an understanding and appreciation of social and cultural variation through observation, exchange, and instruction. Instead of reinforcing uniformity in the children of diverse groups in society, schools could utilize this diversity for broadening the knowledge and understanding of the students. Age-heterogeneous and inter-racial relationships are two examples of such diversity. The educational and social relevance of these experiences are suggested by the results of several recent studies.

Cross-Age Relations

At the University of Michigan's Institute for Social Research, a series of exploratory investigations have been conducted on relationships between chil-

[13] Richard G. Schmuck, "Some Relationships of Peer Liking Patterns in the Classroom to Pupil Attitudes and Achievement," *School Review,* 71: 337–59 (1963).
[14] Gordon W. Allport, *The Nature of Prejudice* (New York: Doubleday Anchor, 1958), p. 267.

dren of different ages in two elementary schools and in a summer camp for children from 4 to 14 years of age.[15] The main objectives of the project are to develop and implement a constructive program of cross-age interaction, and to assess the impact of inter-age perceptions and attitudes on both younger and older children.

The inter-age program among elementary school children included the following elements. Children in the sixth grades were assigned as academic assistants in the first four grades, where they helped the children with their course work. The effectiveness of the older students and the response of the younger children were contingent on the following training procedures.

The teachers were first oriented to the potential of cross-age interaction among students and teachers. The use of academic assistants was described as requiring the teacher to "lend the resources" of his children. At several points during the school day, older children were given special training in relating to younger children, and in teaching content material. In order to counter peer-group norms which did not reward interaction with younger children, the investigators asked a small group of seventh graders, who had high status among their peers and were experienced in working as helpers, to talk to the sixth graders about the benefits of the helping relationship.

The importance of these training procedures was reinforced many times in initial sessions with the older helpers. When asked, "What sorts of things have you observed at school or at home between youngers and olders?" the children reported few constructive encounters. It was commonly that "some bigger kids" were taking something away from, bossing, or shoving "little kids." One potential source of this dominance pattern is the process by which children learn agenorms in the family. The behavior of younger children is frequently derogated when adults attempt to reinforce age-appropriate behavior in their offspring.[16] "Don't act like your little brother" is a mild example of this practice.

The results of this experiment in cross-age interaction show that younger boys and girls perceive older children positively when the latter include them in activities, display friendliness, or offer help and recognition. The younger children tended to learn how to cope with adults and older children; became aware of the abilities, freedoms, and limitations of older children; developed conceptions of the meaning of different levels of "grown-upness"; and gained

[15]Peggy Lippitt and John E. Lohman, "Cross-Age Relationships: An Educational Resource," *Children,* 12: 113–17 (1965); Jeffery W. Eiseman and Peggy Lippitt, "Olders-Youngers Project Evaluation." Report prepared for the Stern Family Fund and the Detroit Board of Education, 1966; and Ronald Lippit *et al.,* "Implementation of Positive Cross-Age Relationships." Chapter 5 in unpublished manuscript, 1966.

[16]For a more detailed discussion of this point, see: Glen H. Elder, Jr., "Age Groups, Status Transitions, and Socialization." Prepared for the Task Force on Environmental Aspects of Psycho-Social Deprivation, National Institute of Child Health and Human Development, June 19, 1968.

an opportunity for greater reciprocity and autonomy than is possible in relations with an adult teacher.

The ability of the older children to communicate with younger children, coupled with their other services, greatly enriched the educational experience of both groups. Most of the older students were enthusiastic about the program, especially the low-achievers from low-status families, whose desire to learn and relation to authority figures in the school generally improved. The older children were given a chance to assume responsibility; to test and evaluate their knowledge, teaching, and social skills; and to work through personal problems encountered with age-mates and siblings.[17] In a number of cases, attitudes and skills acquired in the cross-age experience were transferred to relationships in the family.

Similar opportunities for cross-age interaction and exchange are available in nongraded elementary schools, but competent research on these processes is sadly lacking.[18] One searches in vain among countless reports on the nongraded school for any sophisticated examination of cross-age interaction, or even for any recognition of its educational potential. Reliable evidence on the academic effects is also lacking. In view of the social learning potential of age-heterogeneous groups, the need for well-designed research on cross-age interaction in this setting is compelling.

Interracial Friendships and Learning

The accumulation of research findings on interracial contact provides a preliminary appraisal of the social and academic effects of desegregated schools and classrooms. In the nationwide Coleman study,[19] academic performance and a sense of mastery among Negro students were related to the proportion of white students in their schools. Much of this effect is a consequence of the higher social class background and scholastic ambitions of the white students. More recently, studies supported by the U.S. Commission on Civil Rights show that close friendships with white students have a positive effect on the academic performance and attitudes of Negro students over and above the influence of student social class.[20]

[17]The results of this research are similar in many respects to the findings of a study of cross-age interaction in an adult-adolescent school. See: Glen H. Elder, Jr., "Age Integration and Socialization in an Educational Setting," *op. cit.*

[18]John I. Goodlad and Robert H. Anderson, *The Non-Graded Elementary School* (rev. ed; New York: Harcourt, Brace & World, Inc.; 1963); and Frank R. Dufay, *Ungrading the Elementary School* (New York: Parker Publishing Company, 1966).

[19]James S. Coleman *et al, Equality of Educational Opportunity* (Washington, D.C.: Superintendent of Documents, U.S. Government Printing Office, 1966).

[20]U.S. Commission on Civil Rights, *Racial Isolation in the Public Schools* (Washington, D.C.: Superintendent of Documents, U.S. Government Printing Office, 1967), Volume 2. Findings reported in the following paragraphs were drawn from this volume.

Although observational research is needed to fill in the intervening processes through which interracial friendships have their effect, a clue to such processes is suggested by available data on classroom social structure; emotional acceptance is related to leadership status, self-esteem, and the utilization of abilities. Among Negro students in the study, possession of close white friends was correlated with their involvement in extracurricular activities and a preference for desegregated schools regardless of the racial composition of the classroom.

On the other hand, interracial tension—which was inversely related to the length of time students were enrolled in a desegregated school—had a negative effect on the attitudes and performance of Negro students. Desegregated schooling in childhood has also been found to be related to positive interracial attitudes among Negro adults.

The interracial consequences of desegregated schooling and close Negro friends were similar among white students. White students with close Negro friends were less likely than other white students to prefer an all-white school, regardless of the proportion of Negro students in their classroom. Length of time in a desegregated school—a crude index of exposure to the socializing influence of a biracial setting—was related both to having Negro friends and to a preference for desegregated schooling.

These limited findings are a mere steptoward an understanding of interracial contact and learning in the schools. Classroom observations and laboratory research,[21] in particular, are needed to supplement the findings of survey research.

The educational resources present among students in a classroom may either be utilized within the curriculum or ignored. The challenging task for teachers with biracial or age-heterogeneous classrooms is to use these resources creatively in furthering the social and academic learning of their students.

What task in the classroom can effectively bring children differing in age, race, and aptitude together for exchanging services, ideas, and experiences in a mutually rewarding relationship? Equally important, what conditions sustain an equitable social exchange between teacher and students?

[21]An example of the kind of experimental work needed is described in: Irwin Katz, "The Socialization of Academic Motivation in Minority Group Children," in David Levine (ed.), *Nebraska Symposium on Motivation* (Lincoln: University of Nebraska Press, 1967), 15, 133–191.

Talcott Parsons*
Harvard University

30 / The School Class as a Social System: Some of Its Functions in American Society †

This essay will attempt to outline, if only sketchily, an analysis of the elementary and secondary school class as a social system, and the relation of its structure to its primary functions in the society as an agency of socialization and allocation. While it is important that the school class is normally part of the larger organization of a school, the class rather than the whole school will be the unit of analysis here, for it is recognized both by the school system and by the individual pupil as the place where the "business" of formal education actually takes place. In elementary schools, pupils of one grade are typically placed in a single "class" under one main teacher, but in the secondary school, and sometimes in the upper elementary grades, the pupil works on different subjects under different teachers: here the complex of classes participated in by the same pupil is the significant unit for our purposes.

THE PROBLEM: SOCIALIZATION AND SELECTION

Our main interest, then, is in a dual problem: first of how the school class functions to internalize in its pupils both the commitments and capacities for successful performance of their future adult roles, and second of how it functions to allocate these human resources within the role-structure of the adult society. The primary ways in which these two problems are interrelated will provide our main points of reference.

First, from the funtional point of view the school class can be treated as an agency of socialization. That is to say, it is an agency through which individual personalities are trained to be motivationally and technically adequate to the performance of adult roles. It is not the sole such agency; the family, informal "peer groups," churches, and sundry voluntary organizations all play a part, as does actual on-the-job training. But, in the period extending from entry into first grade until entry into the labor force or marriage, the

*I am indebted to Mrs. Carolyn Cooper for research assistance in the relevant literature and for editorial work on the first draft of this paper.

†From *Harvard Educational Review,* Vol. 29, No. 4 (Fall 1959), pp. 297–318. Copyright 1959 by President and Fellows of Harvard College. Reprinted by permission of the publisher.

school class may be regarded as the focal socializing agency.

The socialization function may be summed up as the development in individuals of the commitments and capacities which are essential prerequisites of their future role-performance. Commitments may be broken down in turn into two components: commitment to the implementation of the broad *values* of society, and commitment to the performance of a specific type of role within the *structure* of society. Thus a person in a relatively humble occupation may be a "solid citizen" in the sense of commitment to honest work in that occupation, without an intensive and sophisticated concern with the implementation of society's higher-level values. Or conversely, someone else might object to the anchorage of the feminine role in marriage and the family on the grounds that such anchorage keeps society's total talent resources from being distributed equitably to business, government, and so on. Capacities can also be broken down into two components, the first being competence or the skill to perform the tasks involved in the individual's roles, and the second being "role-responsibility" or the capacity to live up to other people's expectations of the interpersonal behavior appropriate to these roles. Thus a mechanic as well as a doctor needs to have not only the basic "skills of his trade," but also the ability to behave responsibly toward those people with whom he is brought into contact in his work.

While on the one hand, the school class may be regarded as a primary agency by which these different components of commitments and capacities are generated, on the other hand, it is, from the point of view of the society, an agency of "manpower" allocation. It is well known that in American society there is a very high, and probably increasing, correlation between one's status level in the society and one's level of educational attainment. Both social status and educational level are obviously related to the occupational status which is attained. Now, as a result of the general process of both educational and occupational upgrading, completion of high school is increasingly coming to be the norm for minimum satisfactory educational attainment, and the most significant line for future occupational status has come to be drawn between members of an age-cohort who do and do not go to college.

We are interested, then, in what it is about the school class in our society that determines the distinction between the contingents of the age-cohort which do and do not go to college. Because of a tradition of localism and a rather pragmatic pluralism, there is apparently considerable variety among school systems of various cities and states. Although the situation in metropolitan Boston probably represents a more highly structured pattern than in many other parts of the country, it is probably not so extreme as to be misleading in its main features. There, though of course actual entry into college does not come until after graduation from high school, the main dividing line is between those who are and are not enrolled in the college preparatory course in high school; there is only a small amount of shifting either way after about the ninth grade when the decision is normally made. Furthermore, the evidence seems to be that by far the most important criterion of selection is the record of school performance in elementary school. These records are evaluated by teachers and principals, and there are few cases of entering the college preparatory course against their advice. It is therefore not stretching the evidence too far to say broadly that the primary selective process occurs through differential school preformance in elementary school, and that the "seal" is put on it in junior high school.[1]

The evidence also is that the selective process is genuinely assortative. As in virtually all comparable processes, ascriptive as well as achieved factors influence the outcome. In this case, the ascriptive factor is the socio-economic status of the child's family, and the factor underlying his opportunity for achievement is his individual ability. In the study of 3,348 Boston high school boys on which these generalizations are based, each of these factors was quite highly correlated with planning college. For example, the percentages planning college, by father's occupation, were: 12 per cent for semi-skilled and unskilled, 19 per cent for skilled, 26 per cent for minor white collar, 52 per cent for middle white collar, and 80 per cent for major white collar. Likewise, intentions varied by ability (as measured by IQ), namely, 11 per cent for the lowest quintile, 17 per cent for the next, 24 per cent for the middle, 30 per cent for the next to the top, and 52 per cent for the highest. It should be noted also that within any ability quintile, the relationship of plans to father's occupation is seen. For example, within the very important top quintile in ability as measured, the range in college intentions was from 29 per cent for sons of laborers to 89 per cent for sons of major white collar persons.[2]

The essential points here seem to be that there is a relatively uniform criterion of selection operating to differentiate between the college and the non-college contingents, and that for a very important part of the cohort the operation of this criterion is not a "put-up job"—it is not simply a way of affirming a previously determined ascriptive status. To be sure, the high-

---

[1] The principal source for these statements is a study of social mobility among boys in ten public high schools in the Boston metropolitan area, conducted by Samuel A. Stouffer, Florence R. Kluckhohn, and the present author. Unfortunately the material is not available in published form.

[2] See table from this study in J. A. Kahl, *The American Class Structure* (New York: Rinehart & Co., 1953), p. 283. Data from a nationwide sample of high school students, published by the Educational Testing service, show similar patterns of relationships. For example, the ETS study shows variation, by father's occupation, in proportion of high school seniors planning college, of from 35 per cent to 80 per cent for boys and 27 per cent to 79 per cent for girls. From *Background Factors Related to College Plans and College Enrollment among High School Students* (Princeton, N.J.: Educational Testing Service, 1957).

status, high-ability boy is very likely indeed to go to college, and the low-status, low-ability boy is very unlikely to go. But the "cross-pressured" group for whom these two factors do not coincide[3] is of considerable importance.

Considerations like these lead me to conclude that the main process of differentiation (which from another point of view is selection) that occurs during elementary school takes place on a single main axis of *achievement*. Broadly, moreover, the differentiation leads up through high school to a bifurcation into college-goers and non-college-goers.

To assess the significance of this pattern, let us look at its place in the socialization of the individual. Entering the system of formal education is the child's first major step out of primary involvement in his family of orientation. Within the family certain foundations of his motivational system have been laid down. But the only characteristic fundamental to later roles which has clearly been "determined" and psychologically stamped in by that time is sex role. The postoedipal child enters the system of formal education clearly categorized as boy or girl, but beyond that his *role* is not yet differentiated. The process of selection, by which persons will select and be selected for categories of roles, is yet to take place.

On grounds which cannot be gone into here, it may be said that the most important single predispositional factor with which the child enters the school is his level of *independence*. By this is meant his level of self-sufficiency relative to guidance by adults, his capacity to take responsibility and to make his own decisions in coping with new and varying situations. This, like his sex role, he has as a function of his experience in the family.

The family is a collectivity within which the basic status-structure is ascribed in terms of biological position, that is, by generation, sex, and age. There are inevitably differences of performance relative to these, and they are rewarded and punished in ways that contribute to differential character formation. But these differences are not given the sanction of institutionalized social status. The school is the first socializing agency in the child's experience which institutionalizes a differentiation of status on nonbiological bases. Moreover, this is not an ascribed but an achieved status; it is the status "earned" by differential performance of the tasks set by the teacher, who is acting as an agent of the community's school system. Let us look at the structure of this situation.

---

[3]There seem to be two main reasons why the high-status, low-ability group is not so important as its obverse. The first is that in a society of expanding educational and occupational opportunity the general trend is one of upgrading, and the social pressures to downward mobility are not as great as they would otherwise be. The second is that there are cushioning mechanisms which tend to protect the high status boy who has difficulty "making the grade." He may be sent to a college with low academic standards, he may go to schools where the line between ability levels is not rigorously drawn, etc.

THE STRUCTURE OF THE ELEMENTARY SCHOOL CLASS

In accord with the generally wide variability of American institutions, and of course the basically local control of school systems, there is considerable variability of school situations, but broadly they have a single relatively well-marked framework.[4] Particularly in the primary part of the elementary grades, i.e., the first three grades, the basic pattern includes one main teacher for the class, who teaches all subjects and who is in charge of the class generally. Sometimes this early, and frequently in later grades, other teachers are brought in for a few special subjects, particularly gym, music, and art, but this does not alter the central position of the main teacher. This teacher is usually a woman.[5] The class is with this one teacher for the school year, but usually no longer.

The class, then, is composed of about 25 age-peers of both sexes drawn from a relatively small geographical area—the neighborhood. Except for sex in certain respects, there is initially no formal basis for differentiation of status within the school class. The main structural differentiation develops gradually, on the single main axis indicated above as achievement. That the differentiation should occur on a single main axis is insured by four primary features of the situation. The first is the initial equalization of the "contestants'·" status by age and by "family background," the neighborhood being typically much more homogeneous than is the whole society. The second circumstance is the imposition of a common set of tasks which is, compared to most other task-areas, strikingly undifferentiated. The school situation is far more like a race in this respect than most role-performance situations. Third, there is the sharp polarization between the pupils in their initial equality and the *single* teacher who is an adult and "represents" the adult world. And fourth, there is a relatively systematic process of evaluation of the pupils' performances. From the point of view of a pupil, this evaluation, particularly (though not exclusively) in the form of report card marks, constitutes reward and/or punishment for past performance; from the viewpoint of the school system acting as an allocating agency, it is a basis of *selection* for future status in society.

Two important sets of qualifications need to be kept in mind in interpreting this structural pattern, but I think these do not destroy the significance of its main outline. The first qualification is for variations in the formal organization and procedures of the school class itself. Here the most important kind

---

[4]This discussion refers to public schools. Only about 13 per cent of all elementary and secondary school pupils attend non-public schools, with this proportion ranging from about 22 per cent in the Northeast to about 6 per cent in the South. U. S. Office of Education, *Biennial Survey of Education in the United States, 1954-56* (Washington: U. S. Government Printing Office, 1959), chap. ii, "Statistics of State School Systems, 1955–56," Table 44, p. 114.

[5]In 1955–56, 13 per cent of the public elementary school instructional staff in the United States were men. *Ibid.*, p. 7.

of variation is that between relatively "traditional" schools and relatively "progressive" schools. The more traditional schools put more emphasis on discrete units of subject-matter, whereas the progressive type allows more "indirect" teaching through "projects" and broader topical interests where more than one bird can be killed with a stone. In progressive schools there is more emphasis on groups of pupils working together, compared to the traditional direct relation of the individual pupil to the teacher. This is related to the progressive emphasis on co-operation among the pupils rather than direct competition, to a greater permissiveness as opposed to strictness of discipline, and to a de-emphasis on formal marking.[6] In some schools one of these components will be more prominent, and in others, another. That is it, however, an important range of variation is clear. It has to do, I think, very largely with the independence-dependence training which is so important to early socialization in the family. My broad interpretation is that those people who emphasize independence training will tend to be those who favor relatively progressive education. The relation of support for progressive education to relatively high socio-economic status and to "intellectual" interests and the like is well known. There is no contradiction between these emphases both on independence and on co-operation and group solidarity among pupils. In the first instance this is because the main focus of the independence problem at these ages is vis-à-vis adults. However, it can also be said that the peer group, which here is built into the school class, is an indirect field of expression of dependency needs, displaced from adults.

The second set of qualifications concerns the "informal" aspects of the school class, which are always somewhat at variance with the formal expectations. For instance, the formal pattern of nondifferentiation between the sexes may be modified informally, for the very salience of the one-sex peer group at this age period means that there is bound to be considerable implicit recognition of it—for example, in the form of teachers' encouraging group competition between boys and girls. Still, the fact of coeducation and the attempt to treat both sexes alike in all the crucial formal respects remain the most important. Another problem raised by informal organization is the question of how far teachers can and do treat pupils particularistically in violation of the universalistic expectations of the school. When compared with other types of formal organizations, however, I think the extent of this discrepancy in elementary schools is seen to be not unusual. The school class is structured so that opportunity for particularistic treatment is severely limited. Because there are so many more children in a school class than in a family and they are concentrated in a much narrower age range, the teacher has much less chance than does a parent to grant particularistic favors.

[6]This summary of some contrasts between traditional and progressive patterns is derived from general reading in the literature rather than any single autoritative account.

Bearing in mind these two sets of qualifications, it is still fair, I think, to conclude that the major characteristics of the elementary school class in this country are such as have been outlined. It should be especially emphasized that more or less progressive schools, even with their relative lack of emphasis on formal marking, do not constitute a separate pattern, but rather a variant tendancy within the same pattern. A progressive teacher, like any other, will form opinions about the different merits of her pupils relative to the values and goals of the class and will communicate these evaluations to them, informally if not formally. It is my impression that the extremer cases of playing down relative evaluation are confined to those upper-status schools where going to a "good" college is so fully taken for granted that for practical purposes it is an ascribed status. In other words, in interpreting these facts the selective function of the school class should be kept continually in the forefront of attention. Quite clearly its importance has not been decreasing; rather the contrary.

THE NATURE OF SCHOOL ACHIEVEMENT

What, now, of the content of the "achievement" expected of elementary school children? Perhaps the best broad characterization which can be given is that it involves the types of performance which are, on the one hand, appropriate to the school situation and, on the other hand, are felt by adults to be important in themselves. This vague and somewhat circular characterization may, as was mentioned earlier, be broken down into two main components. One of these is the more purely "cognitive" learning of information, skills, and frames of reference associated with empirical knowledge and technological mastery. The *written* language and the early phases of mathematical thinking are clearly vital; they involve cognitive skills at altogether new levels of generality and abstraction compared to those commanded by the pre-school child. With these basic skills goes assimilation of much factual information about the world.

The second main component is what may broadly be called a "moral" one. In earlier generations of schooling this was known as "deportment." Somewhat more generally it might be called responsible citizenship in the school community. Such things as respect for the teacher, consideration and co-operativeness in relation to fellow-pupils, and good "work-habits" are the fundamentals, leading on to capacity for "leadership" and "initiative."

The striking fact about this achievement content is that in the elementary grades these two primary components are not clearly differentiated from each other. Rather, the pupil is evaluated in diffusely general terms; a *good* pupil is defined in terms of a fusion of the cognitive and the moral components, in which varying weight is given to one or the other. Broadly speaking, then, we may say that the "high achievers" of the elementary school are both the "bright" pupils, who catch on easily to their more strictly intellectual tasks, and the more "responsible" pupils, who "behave well" and on whom the teacher can "count" in her difficult problems of managing the class. One indication that this is the case is the fact that in elementary school the purely intellectual tasks are relatively easy for the pupil of high intellectual ability. In many such cases, it can be presumed that the primary challenge to the pupil is not to be his intellectual, but to his "moral," capacities. On the whole, the progressive movement seems to have leaned in the direction of giving enhanced emphasis to this component, suggesting that of the two, it has tended to become the more problematical.[7]

The essential point, then, seems to be that the elementary school, regarded in the light of its socialization function, is an agency which differentiates the school class broadly along a single continuum of achievement, the content of which is relative excellence in living up to the expectations imposed by the teacher as an agent of the adult society. The criteria of this achievement are, general speaking, undifferentiated into the cognitive or technical component and the moral or "social" component. But with respect to its bearing on societal values, it is broadly a differentiation of *levels* of capacity to act in accord with these values. Though the relation is far from neatly uniform, this differentiation underlies the processes of selection for levels of status and role in the adult society.

Next, a few words should be said about the out-of-school context in which this process goes on. Besides the school class, there are clearly two primary social structures in which the child participates: the family and the child's informal "peer group."

FAMILY AND PEER GROUP IN RELATION TO THE SCHOOL CLASS

The school age child, of course, continues to live in the parental household and to be highly dependent, emotionally as well as instrumentally, on his parents. But he is now spending several hours a day away from home, subject to a discipline and a reward system which are essentially independent of that administered by the parents. Moreover, the range of this independence gradually increases. As he grows older, he is permitted to range further territorially with neither parental nor school supervision, and to do an increasing range of things. He often gets an allowance for personal spending and begins

[7]This account of the two components of elementary school achievement and their relation summarizes impressions gained from the literature, rather than being based on the opinions of particular authorities. I have the impression that achievement in this sense corresponds closely to what is meant by the term as used by McClelland and his associates. Cf. D. C. McClelland et al., *The Achievement Motive* (New York: Appleton-Century-Crofts, Inc., 1953).

to earn some money of his own. Generally, however, the emotional problem of dependence-independence continues to be a very salient one through this period, frequently with manifestations by the child of compulsive independence.

Concomitantly with this, the area for association with age-peers without detailed adult supervision expands. These associations are tied to the family, on the one hand, in that the home and yards of children who are neighbors and the adjacent streets serve as locations for their activities; and to the school, on the other hand, in that play periods and going to and from school provide occasions for informal association, even though organized extracurricular activities are introduced only later. Ways of bringing some of this activity under another sort of adult supervision are found in such organizations as the boy and girl scouts.

Two sociological characteristics of peer groups at this age are particularly striking. One is the fluidity of their boundaries, with individual children drifting into and out of associations. This element of "voluntary association" contrasts strikingly with the child's ascribed membership in the family and the school class, over which he has no control. The second characteristic is the peer group's sharp segregation by sex. To a striking degree this is enforced by the children themselves rather than by adults.

The psychological functions of peer association are suggested by these two characteristics. On the one hand, the peer group may be regarded as a field for the exercise of independence from adult control; hence it is not surprising that it is often a focus of behavior which goes beyond independence from adults to the range of adult-*disapproved* behavior; when this happens, it is the seed bed from which the extremists go over into delinquency. But another very important function is to provide the child a source of non-adult approval and acceptance. These depend on "technical" and "moral" criteria as diffuse as those required in the school situation. On the one hand, the peer group is a field for acquiring and displaying various types of "prowess"; for boys this is especially the physical prowess which may later ripen into athletic achievement. On the other hand, it is a matter of gaining acceptance from desirable peers as "belonging" in the group, which later ripens into the conception of the popular teen-ager, the "right guy." Thus the adult parents are augmented by age-peers as a source of rewards for performance and of security in acceptance.

The importance of the peer group for socialization in our type of society should be be clear. The motivational foundations of character are inevitably first laid down through identification with parents, who are generation-superiors, and the generation difference is a type example of a hierarchical status difference. But an immense part of the individual's adult role performance will have to be in association with staus-equals or near-equals. In this situation it is important to have a reorganization of the motivational structure so that the original dominance of the hierarchical axis is modified to strengthen the egalitarian components. The peer group plays a prominent part in this process.

Sex segregation of latency period peer groups may be regarded as a process of reinforcement of sex-role identification. Through intensive association with sex-peers and involvement in sex-typed activities, they strongly reinforce belongingness with other members of the same sex and contrast with the opposite sex. This is the more important because in the coeducational school a set of forces operates which specifically plays down sex-role differentiation.

It is notable that the latency period sex-role pattern, instead of institutionalizing relations to members of the opposite sex, is characterized by an avoidance of such relations, which only in adolescence gives way to dating. This avoidance is clearly associated with the process of reorganization of the erotic components of motivational structure. The pre-oedipal objects of erotic attachment were both intra-familial and generation-superior. In both respects there must be a fundamental shift by the time the child reaches adulthood. I would suggest that one of the main functions of the avoidance pattern is to help cope with the psychological difficulty of overcoming the earlier incestuous attachments, and hence to prepare the child for assuming an attachment to an age-mate of opposite sex later.

Seen in this perspective, the socilization function of the school class assumes a particular significance. The socialization functions of the family by this time are relatively residual, though their importance should not be underestimated. But the school remains adult-controlled and, moreover, unduces basically the same kind of identification as was induced by the family in the child's pre-oedipal stage. This is to say that the learning of achievement-motivation is, psychologically speaking, a process of identification with the teacher, of doing well in school in order to please the teacher (often backed by the parents) in the same sense in which a pre-oedipal child learns new skills in order to please his mother.

In this connection I maintain that what is internalized through the process of identification is a reciprocal pattern of role-relationships.[8] Unless there is a drastic failure of internalization altogether, not just one, but both sides of the interaction will be internalized. There will, however, be an emphasis on one or the other, so that some children will more nearly identify with the socializing agent, and others will more nearly identify with the opposite role. Thus, in the pre-oedipal stage, the "independent" child has identified more with the parent, and the "dependent" one with the child-role vis-à-vis the parent.

In school the teacher is institutionally defined as superior to any pupil

---

[8]On the identification process in the family see my paper, "Social Structure and the Development of Personality," *Psychiatry,* XXI (November 1958), pp. 321–40.

in knowledge of curriculum subject-matter and in responsibility as a good citizen of the school. In so far as the school class tends to be bifurcated (and of course the dichotomization is far from absolute), it will broadly be on the basis, on the one hand, of identification with the teacher, or acceptance of her role as a model; and, on the other hand, of identification with the pupil peer group. This bifurcation of the class on the basis of identification with teacher or with peer group so strikingly corresponds with the bifurcation into college-goers and non-college-goers that it would be hard to avoid the hypothesis that this structural dichotomization in the school system is the primary source of the selective dichotomization. Of course in detail the relationship is blurred, but certainly not more so than in a great many other fields of comparable analytical complexity.

These considerations suggest an interpretation of some features of the elementary teacher role in American society. The first major step in socialization, beyond that in the family, takes place in the elementary school, so it seems reasonable to expect that the teacher-figure should be characterized by a combination of similarities to and differences from parental figures. The teacher, then, is an adult, characterized by the generalized superiority, which a parent also has, of adult status relative to children. She is not, however, ascriptively related to her pupils, but is performing an occupational role—a role, however, in which the recipients of her services are tightly bound in solidarity to her and to each other. Furthermore, compared to a parent's, her responsibility to them is much more universalistic, this being reinforced, as we saw, by the size of the class: it is also much more oriented to performance rather than to solicitude for the emotional "needs" of the children. She is not entitled to suppress the distinction between high and low achievers, just because not being able to be included among the high group would be too hard on little Johnny—however much tendencies in this direction appear as deviant patterns. A mother, on the other hand, must give *first* priority to the needs of her child, regardless of his capacities to achieve.

It is also significant for the parallel of the elementary school class with the family that the teacher is normally a woman. As background it should be noted that in most European systems until recently, and often today in our private parochial and non-sectarian schools, the sexes have been segregated and each sex group has been taught by teachers of their own sex. Given coeducation, however, the woman teacher represents continuity with the role of the mother. Precisely the lack of differentiation in the elementary school "curriculum" between the components of subject-matter competence and social responsibility fits in with the greater diffuseness of the feminine role.

But at the same time, it is essential that the teacher is not a mother to her pupils, but must insist on universalistic norms and the differential reward of achievement. Above all she must be the agent of bringing about and legitimizing a differentiation of the school class on an achievement axis. This aspect of her role is furthered by the fact that in American society the feminine role is less confined to the familial context than in most other societies, but joins the masculine in occupational and associational concerns, though still with a greater relative emphasis on the family. Through identification with their teacher, children of both sexes learn that the category "woman" is not co-extensive with "mother" (and future wife), but that the feminine role-personality is more complex than that.

In this connection it may well be that there is a relation to the once-controversial issue of the marriage of women teachers. If the differentiation between what may be called the maternal and the occupational components of the feminine role is incomplete and insecure, confusion between them may be avoided by insuring that both are not performed by the same persons. The "old maid" teacher of American tradition may thus be thought of as having renounced the maternal role in favor of the occupational.[9] Recently, however, the highly affective concern over the issue of married women's teaching has conspicuously abated, and their actual participation has greatly increased. It may be suggested that this change is associated with a change in the feminine role, the most conspicuous feature of which is the general social sanctioning of participation of women in the labor force, not only prior to marriage, but also after marriage. This I should interpret as a process of structural differentiation in that the same category of persons is permitted and even expected to engage in a more complex set of role-functions than before.

The process of identification with the teacher which has been postulated here is furthered by the fact that in the elementary grades the child typically has one teacher, just as in the pre-oedipal period he had one parent, the mother, who was the focus of his object-relations. The continuity between the two phases is also favored by the fact that the teacher, like the mother, is a woman. But, if she acted only like a mother, there would be no genuine reorganization of the pupil's personality system. This reorganization is furthered by the features of the teacher role which differentiate it from the maternal. One further point is that while a child has one main teacher in each grade, he will usually have a new teacher when he progresses to the next higher grade. He is thus accustomed to the fact that teachers are, unlike mothers, "interchangeable" in a certain sense. The school year is long enough to form an important relationship to a particular teacher, but not long enough for a highly particularistic attachment to crystallize. More than in the parent-child relationship, in school the child must internalize his relation to the teacher's *role* rather than her particular personality; this is a major step in the internalization of universalistic patterns.

---

[9]It is worth noting that the Catholic parochial school system is in line with the more general older American tradition, in that the typical teacher is a nun. The only difference in this respect is the sharp religious symbolization of the difference between mother and teacher.

SOCIALIZATION AND SELECTION IN THE ELEMENTARY SCHOOL

To conclude this discussion of the elementary school class, something should be said about the fundamental conditions underlying the process which is, as we have seen, simultaneously (1) an emancipation of the child from primary emotional attachment to his family, (2) an internalization of a level of societal values and norms that is a step higher than those he can learn in his family alone, (3) a differentiation of the school class in terms both of actual achievement and of differential *valuation* of achievement, and (4) from society's point of view, a selection and allocation of its human resources relative to the adult role system.[10]

Probably the most fundamental condition underlying this process is the sharing of common values by the two adult agencies involved—the family and the school. In this case the core is the shared valuation of *achievement*. It includes, above all, recognition that it is fair to give differential rewards for different levels of achievement, so long as there has been fair access to opportunity, and fair that these rewards lead on to higher-order opportunities for the successful. There is thus a basic sense in which the elementary school class is an embodiment of the fundamental American value of equality of opportunity, in that it places value *both* on initial equality and on differential achievement.

As a second condition, however, the rigor of this valuational pattern must be tempered by allowance for the difficulties and needs of the young child. Here the quasi-motherliness of the woman teacher plays an important part. Through her the school system, assisted by other agencies, attempts to minimize the insecurity resulting from the pressures to learn, by providing a certain amount of emotional support defined in terms of what is due to a child of a given age level. In this respect, however, the role of the school is relatively small. The underlying foundation of support is given in the home, and as we have seen, an important supplement to it can be provided by the informal peer associations of the child. It may be suggested that the development of extreme patterns of alienation from the school is often related to inadequate support in these respects.

Third, there must be a process of selective rewarding of valued performance. Here the teacher is clearly the primary agent, though the more progressive modes of education attempt to enlist classmates more systematically than in the traditional pattern. This is the process that is the direct source of intra-class differentiation along the achievement axis.

The final condition is that this initial differentiation tends to bring about a status system in the class, in which not only the immediate results of school

[10]The following summary is adapted from T Parsons, R. F. Bales *et al., Family, Socialization and Interaction Process* (Glencoe, Ill.: The Free Press, 1955) esp chap iv

work, but a whole series of influences, converge to consolidate different expectations which may be thought of as the children's "levels of aspiration." Generally some differentiation of friendship groups along this line occurs, though it is important that it is by no means complete, and that children are sensitive to the attitudes not only of their own friends, but of others.

Within this general discussion of processes and conditions, it is important to distinguish, as I have attempted to do all along, the socialization of the individual from the selective allocation of contingents to future roles. For the individual, the old familial identification is broken up (the family of orientation becomes, in Freudian terms, a "lost object") and a new identification is gradually built up, providing the first-order structure of the child's identity apart from his originally ascribed identity as son or daughter of the "Joneses." He both transcends his familial identification in favor of a more independent one and comes to occupy a differentiated status within the new system. His personal status is inevitably a direct function of the position he achieves, primarily in the formal school class and secondarily in the informal peer group structure. In spite of the sense in which achievement-ranking takes place along a continuum, I have put forward reasons to suggest that, with respect to this status, there is an important differentiation into two broad, relatively distinct levels, and that his position on one or the other enters into the individual's definition of his own identity. To an important degree this process of differentiation is independent of the socio-economic status of his family in the community, which to the child is a prior ascribed status.

When we look at the same system as a selective mechanism from the societal point of view, some further considerations become important. First, it may be noted that the valuation of achievement and its sharing by family and school not only provides the appropriate values for internalization by individuals, but also performs a crucial integrative function for the system. Differentiation of the class along the achievement axis is inevitably a source of strain, because it confers higher rewards and privileges on one contingent than on another within the same system. This common valuation helps make possible the acceptance of the crucial differentiation, especially by the losers in the competition. Here it is an essential point that this *common* value on achievement is shared by units with different statuses in the system. It cuts across the differentiation of families by socio-economic status. It is necessary that there be realistic opportunity and that the teacher can be relied on to implement it by being "fair" and rewarding achievement by whoever shows capacity for it. The fact is crucial that the distribution of abilities, though correlated with family status, clearly does not coincide with it. There can then be a genuine selective process within a set of "rules of the game."

This commitment to common values is not, however, the sole integrative mechanism counteracting the strain imposed by differentiation. Not only does the individual pupil enjoy familial support, but teachers also like and indeed "respect" pupils on bases independent of achievement-status, and peer-group friendship lines, though correlated with position on the achievement scale, again by no means coincide with it, but cross-cut it. Thus there are cross-cutting lines of solidarity which mitigate the strains generated by rewarding achievement differentially.[11]

It is only *within* this framework of institutionalized solidarity that the crucial selective process goes on through selective rewarding and the consolidation of its results into a status-differentiation within the school class. We have called special attention to the impact of the selective process on the children of relatively high ability but low family status. Precisely in this group, but pervading school classes generally, is another parallel to what was found in the studies of voting behavior.[12] In the voting studies it was found that the "shifters"—those voters who were transferring their allegiance from one major party to the other—tended, on the one hand, to be the "cross-pressured" people, who had multiple status characteristics and group allegiances which predisposed them simultaneously to vote in opposite directions. The analogy in the school class is clearly to the children for whom ability and family status do not coincide. On the other hand, it was precisely in this group of cross-pressured voters that political "indifference" was most conspicuous. Non-voting was particularly prevalent in this group, as was a generally cool emotional tone toward a campaign. The suggestion is that some of the pupil "indifference" to school performance may have a similar origin. This is clearly a complex phenomenon and cannot be further analyzed here. But rather than suggesting, as is usual on common sense grounds, that indifference to school work represents an "alienation" from cultural and intellectual values, I would suggest exactly the opposite: that an important component of such indifference, including in extreme cases overt revolt against school discipline, is connected with the fact that the stakes, as in politics, are very high indeed. Those pupils who are exposed to contradictory pressures are likely to be ambivalent; at the same time, the personal stakes for them are higher than for the others,

[11]In this, as in several other respects, there is a parallel to other important allocative processes in the society. A striking example is the voting process by which political support is allocated between party candidates. Here, the strain arises from the fact that one candidate and his party will come to enjoy all the perquisites—above all the power—of office, while the other will be excluded for the time being from these. This strain is mitigated, on the one hand, by the common commitment to constitutional procedure, and, on the other hand, by the fact that the nonpolitical bases of social solidarity, which figure so prominently as determinants of voting behavior, still cut across party lines. The average person is, in various of his roles, associated with people whose political preference is different from his own: he therefore could not regard the opposite party as composed of unmitigated scoundrels without introducing a rift within the groups to which he is attached. This feature of the electorate's structure is brought out strongly in B. R. Berelson, P. F. Lazarsfeld and W. N. McPhee, *Voting* (Chicago: University of Chicato Press, 1954). The conceptual analysis of it is developed in my own paper. " 'Voting' and the Equilibrium of the American Political System" in E. Burdick and A. J. Brodbeck (eds.), *American Voting Behavior* (Glencoe, Ill.: The Free Press, 1959).

[12]*Ibid.*

because what happens in school may make much more of a difference for their futures than for the others, in whom ability and family status point to the same expectations for the future. In particular for the upwardly mobile pupils, too much emphasis on school success would pointedly suggest "burning their bridges" of association with their families and status peers. This phenomenon seems to operate even in elementary school, although it grows somewhat more conspicuous later. In general I think that an important part of the anti-intellectualism in American youth culture stems from the importance of the selective process through the educational system rather than the opposite.

One further major point should be made in this analysis. As we have noted, the general trend of American society has been toward a rapid upgrading in the educational status of the population. This means that, relative to past expectations, with each generation there is increased pressure to educational achievement, often associated with parents' occupational ambitions for their children.[13] To a sociologist this is a more or less classical situation of anomic strain, and the youth-culture ideology which plays down intellectual interests and school performance seems to fit in this context. The orientation of the youth culture is, in the nature of the case, ambivalent, but for the reasons suggested, the anti-intellectual side of the ambivalence tends to be overtly stressed. One of the reasons for the dominance of the anti-school side of the ideology is that it provides a means of protest against adults, who are at the opposite pole in the socialization situation. In certain respects one would expect that the trend toward greater emphasis on independence, which we have associated with progressive education, would accentuate the strain in this area and hence the tendency to decry adult expectations. The whole problem should be subjected to a thorough analysis in the light of what we know about ideologies more generally.

The same general considerations are relevant to the much-discussed problem of juvenile delinquency. Both the general upgrading process and the pressure to enhanced independence should be expected to increase strain on the lower, most marginal groups. The analysis of this paper has been concerned with the line between college and non-college contingents; there is, however, another line between those who achieve solid non-college educational status and those for whom adaptation to educational expectations at *any* level is difficult. As the acceptable minimum of educational qualification rises, persons near and below the margin will tend to be pushed into an attitude of repudiation of these expectations. Truancy and delinquency are ways of expressing this repudiation. Thus the very *improvement* of educational standards in the society at large may well be a major factor in the failure of the educational process for a growing number at the lower end of the status and ability

[13] J. A. Kahl, "Educational and Occupational Aspirations of 'Common Man' Boys," *Harvard Educational Review*, XXIII (Summer 1953), pp. 186–203.

distribution. It should therefore not be too easily assumed that delinquency is a symptom of a *general* failure of the educational process.

DIFFERENTIATION AND SELECTION IN THE SECONDARY SCHOOL

It will not be possible to discuss the secondary school phase of education in nearly as much detail as has been done for the elementary school phase, but it is worthwhile to sketch its main outline in order to place the above analysis in a wider context. Very broadly we may say that the elementary school phase is concerned with the internalization in children of motivation to achievement, and the selection of persons on the basis of differential capacity for achievement. The focus is on the *level* of capacity. In the secondary school phase, on the other hand, the focus is on the differentiation of *qualitative types* of achievement. As in the elementary school, this differentiation cross-cuts sex role. I should also maintain that it cross-cuts the levels of achievement which have been differentiated out in the elementary phase.

In approaching the question of the types of capacity differentiated, it should be kept in mind that secondary school is the principal springboard from which lower-status persons will enter the labor force, whereas those achieving higher status will continue their formal education in college, and some of them beyond. Hence for the lower-status pupils the important line of differentiation should be the one which will lead into broadly different categories of jobs; for the higher-status pupils the differentiation will lead to broadly different roles in college.

My suggestion is that this differentiation separates those two components of achievement which we labelled "cognitive" and "moral" in discussing the elementary phase. Those relatively high in "cognitive" achievement will fit better in specific-function, more or less technical roles; those relatively high in "moral" achievement will tend toward diffuser, more "socially" or "humanly" oriented roles. In jobs not requiring college training, the one category may be thought of as comprising the more impersonal and technical occupations, such as "operatives," mechanics, or clerical workers; the other, as occupations where "human relations" are prominent, such as salesmen and agents of various sorts. At the college level, the differentiation certainly relates to concern, on the one hand, with the specifically intellectual curricular work of college and, on the other hand, with various types of diffuser responsibility in human relations, such as leadership roles in student government and extracurricular activities. Again, candidates for post-graduate professional training will probably be drawn mainly from the first of these two groups.

In the structure of the school, there appears to be a gradual transition from the earliest grades through high school, with the changes timed differently in different school systems. The structure emphasized in the first part of this discussion is most clearly marked in the first three "primary" grades. With progression to the higher grades, there is greater frequency of plural teachers, though very generally still a single main teacher. In the sixth grade and sometimes in the fifth, a man as main teacher, though uncommon, is by no means unheard of. With junior high school, however, the shift of pattern becomes more marked, and still more in senior high.

By that time the pupil has several different teachers of both sexes[14] teaching him different subjects, which are more or less formally organized into different courses—college preparatory and others. Furthermore, with the choice of "elective" subjects, the members of the class in one subject no longer need be exactly the same as in another, so the pupil is much more systematically exposed to association with different people, both adults and age-peers, in different contexts. Moreover, the school he attends is likely to be substantially larger than was his elementary school, and to draw from a wider geographical area. Hence the child is exposed to a wider range of statuses than before, being thrown in with more age-peers whom he does not encounter in his neighborhood; it is less likely that his parents will know the parents of any given child with whom he associates. It is thus my impression that the transitions to junior high and senior high school are apt to mean a considerable reshuffling of friendships. Another conspicuous difference between the elementary and secondary levels is the great increase in high school of organized extracurricular activities. Now, for the first time, organized athletics become important, as do a variety of clubs and associations which are school-sponsored and supervised to varying degrees.

Two particularly important shifts in the patterning of youth culture occur in this period. One, of course, is the emergence of more positive cross-sex relationships outside the classroom, through dances, dating, and the like. The other is the much sharper prestige-stratification of informal peer groupings, with indeed an element of snobbery which often exceeds that of the adult community in which the school exists.[15] Here it is important that though there is a broad correspondence between the prestige of friendship groups and the family status of their members, this, like the achievement order of the elementary school, is by no means a simple "mirroring" of the community stratification scale, for a considerable number of lower-status children get accepted into groups including members with higher family status than themselves. This stratified youth system operates as a genuine assortative mechanism; it does not simply reinforce ascribed status.

The prominence of this youth culture in the American secondary school is, in comparison with other societies, one of the hallmarks of the American

[14]Men make up about half (49 per cent) of the public secondary school instructional staff. *Biennial Survey of Education in the United States, 1954–56, op. cit.,* chap. ii, p. 7.

[15]See, for instance, C. W. Gordon, *The Social System of th High School: A Study in the Sociology of Adolescence* (Glencoe, Ill.: The Free Press, 1957).

educational system; it is much less prominent in most European systems. It may be said to constitute a kind of structural fusion between the school class and the peer-group structure of the elementary period. It seems clear that what I have called the "human relations" oriented contingent of the secondary school pupils are more active and prominent in extracurricular activities, and that this is one of the main foci of their differentiation from the more impersonally- and technically-oriented contingent. The personal qualities figuring most prominently in the human relations contingent can perhaps be summed up as the qualities that make for "popularity." I suggest that, from the point of view of the secondary school's selective function, the youth culture helps to differentiate between types of personalities which will, by and large, play different kinds of roles as adults.

The stratification of youth groups has, as noted, a selective function; it is a bridge between the achievement order and the adult stratification system of the community. But it also has another function. It is a focus of prestige which exists along side of, and is to a degree independent of, the achievement order focussing on school work as such. The attainment of prestige in the informal youth group is itself a form of valued achievement. Hence, among those individuals destined for higher status in society, one can discern two broad types: those whose school work is more or less outstanding and whose informal prestige is relatively satisfactory; and vice versa, those whose informal prestige is outstanding, and school performance satisfactory. Falling below certain minima in either respect would jeopardize the child's claim to belong in the upper group.[16] It is an important point here that those clearly headed for college belong to peer groups which, while often depreciative of intensive concern with studies, also take for granted and reinforce a level of scholastic attainment which is necessary for admission to a good college. Pressure will be put on the individual who tends to fall below such a standard.

In discussing the elementary school level it will be remembered that we emphasized that the peer group served as an object of emotional dependency displaced from the family. In relation to the pressure for school achievement, therefore, it served at least partially as an expression of the lower-order motivational system *out* of which the child was in process of being socialized. On its own level, similar things can be said of the adolescent youth culture; it is in part an expression of regressive motivations. This is true of the emphasis on athletics despite its lack of relevance to adult roles, of the "homosexual" undertones of much intensive same-sex friendship, and of a certain "irresponsibility" in attitudes toward the opposite sex—e.g., the exploitative element in the attitudes of boys toward girls. This, however, is by no means the whole

---

[16]J. Riley, M. Riley, and M. Moore, "Adolescent Values and the Riesman Typology," in S. M. Lipset and L. Lowenthal (eds.), *The Sociology of Culture and the Analysis of Social Character* (Glencoe, Ill.: The Free Press, to be published in 1960).

story. The youth culture is also a field for practicing the assumption of higher-order responsibilities, for conducting delicate human relations without immediate supervision and learning to accept the consequences. In this connection it is clearly of particular importance to the contingent we have spoken of as specializing in "human relations."

We can, perhaps, distinguish three different levels of crystallization of these youth-culture patterns. The middle one is that which may be considered age-appropriate without clear status-differentiation. The two keynotes here seem to be "being a good fellow" in the sense of general friendliness and being ready to take responsibility in informal social situations where something needs to be done. Above this, we may speak of the higher level of "outstanding" popularity and qualities of "leadership" of the person who is turned to where unusual responsibilities are required. And below the middle level are the youth patterns bordering on delinquency, withdrawal, and generally unacceptable behavior. Only this last level is clearly "regressive" relative to expectations of appropriate behavior for the age-grade. In judging these three levels, however, allowance should be made for a good many nuances. Most adolescents do a certain amount of experimenting with the borderline of the unacceptable patterns; that they should do so is to be expected in view of the pressure toward independence from adults, and of the "collusion" which can be expected in the reciprocal stimulation of age-peers. The question is whether this regressive behavior comes to be confirmed into a major pattern for the personality as a whole. Seen in this perspective, it seems legitimate to maintain that the middle and the higher patterns indicated are the major ones, and that only a minority of adolescents comes to be confirmed in a truly unacceptable pattern of living. This minority may well be a relatively constant proportion of the age cohort, but apart from situations of special social disorganization, the available evidence does not suggest that it has been a progressively growing one in recent years.

The patterning of cross-sex relations in the yough culture clearly foreshadows future marriage and family formation. That it figures so prominently in school is related to the fact that in our society the element of ascription, including direct parental influence, in the choice of a marriage partner is strongly minimized. For the girl, it has the very important significance of reminding her that her adult status is going to be very much concerned with marriage and a family. This basic expectation for the girl stands in a certain tension to the school's curricular coeducation with its relative lack of differentiation by sex. But the extent to which the feminine role in American society continues to be anchored in marriage and the family should not be allowed to obscure the importance of coeducation. In the first place, the contribution of women in various extra-familial occupations and in community affairs has been rapidly increasing, and certainly higher levels of education have served as a prerequisite to this contribution. At the same time, it is highly important that the woman's familial role should not be regarded as drastically segregated from the cultural concerns of the society as a whole. The educated woman has important functions *as wife and mother,* particularly as an influence on her children in backing the schools and impressing on them the importance of education. It is, I think, broadly true that the immediate responsibility of women for family management has been increasing, though I am very skeptical of the alleged "abdication" of the American male. But precisely in the context of women's increased family responsibility, the influence of the mother both as agent of socialization and as role model is a crucial one. This influence should be evaluated in the light of the general upgrading process. It is very doubtful whether, apart from any other considerations, the motivational prerequisites of the general process could be sustained without sufficiently high education of the women who, as mothers, influence their children.

CONCLUSION

With the general cultural upgrading process in American society which has been going on for more than a century, the educational system has come to play an increasingly vital role. That this should be the case is, in my opinion, a consequence of the general trend to structural differentiation in the society. Relatively speaking, the school is a specialized agency. That it should increasingly have become the principal channel of selection as well as agency of socialization is in line with what one would expect in an increasingly differentiated and progressively more upgraded society. The legend of the "self-made man" has an element of nostalgic romanticism and is destined to become increasingly mythical, if by it is meant not just mobility from humble origins to high status, which does indeed continue to occur, but that the high status was attained through the "school of hard knocks" without the aid of formal education.

The structure of the public school system and the analysis of the ways in which it contributes both to the socialization of individuals and to their allocation to roles in society is, I feel, of vital concern to all students of American society. Notwithstanding the variegated elements in the situation, I think it has been possible to sketch out a few major structural patterns of the public school system and at least to suggest some ways in which they serve these important functions. What could be presented in this paper is the merest outline of such an analysis. It is, however, hoped that it has been carried far enough to suggest a field of vital mutual interest for social scientists on the one hand and those concerned with the actual operation of the schools on the other.

31 / The School as a Socio-Cultural System

Suppose a social scientist from another country resided near a cluster of differential age-graded schools in a middle-income socioeconomic community. His mission was to observe school behavior for nine months. His interests in studying the schools were two-fold. (1) As an agent of the culture, the school would reflect the degree of cultural evolvement in terms of the societal ingredients that promulgate cohesion in the social universe of events, i.e., language, status and role relationships and technology; (2) the socio-cultural patterns of behavior in the school, to a large extent, mirror the norms, standards and values contained in the American society. Presumably, his studies would have revealed the following:

LANGUAGE

Formal English is stressed throughout the school curricula as the desirable mode of communication. Much credence has been placed upon the arbitrary choice of English as an appropriate vehicle of communication, and little has been done to delineate and equate the social antecedents involved. In specifics, language is not only the vehicle of communication but also a major determinant in the way one structures his universe of social events and relates it to his cognitive map. Social scientists have presented arguments to the effect that the "world view" of an individual is largely sharpened in accord with his native linguistic lexicon.[1] For example, it is reputed that the Eskimos have a minimum of three translations for snow and that certain American Indian tribes do not distinguish between blue and green but refer to these shades as turquoise. Consequently, tests administered in schools are culturally biased to the extent whereby ethnic minorities are penalized because of their different language orientations. Test makers are in disagreement as to whether culturally fair tests could be constructed and yet be valid predictors. Perhaps the concern here should be directed toward the diversification of attempts to measure and evaluate the performances of students since tests are not, in reality, the exact measurement of the abilities of the test makers but the approximation of such.[2]

It would appear the social position of students in terms of recognition

---

[1]Benjamin Lee Whorf, "Science and Linguistics," in *Readings in Social Psychology* (New York: Holt, Rinehart and Winston, 1958).

[2]Ronald Shinn, "Cultural Bias in Testing and Unemployment," *Sacramento Observer,* Vol. 7, No. 11 (April 30, 1970).

and achievement is greatly entrusted to their linguistic skills and abilities. To a large extent, the preferential-gradient scale is dependent upon the expressive sophistication of the student, almost to the extent of bordering on not *what* is said but *how* it is said. Leadership roles in the form of student body offices are attained by individuals who are linguistically adept in winning social acceptance from the various cliques and factions contained in the school populous. The range of interests among students is as diversified as those contained in their community thereby necessitating social articulation skills on the part of potential student leaders which transcends immediate social identification and interests, i.e., participation in sports, student honor societies, and other school-related activities.

Classroom behavior is centered around the oral activity of the teacher. Dr. William Floyd's research study indicated a high oral activity of teachers in regular classroom teaching. The total word count in an hour produced a teacher-pupil ratio of 71 to 29. Seven-tenths of the words spoken were by teachers and less than three-tenths spoken by students. If the "less than three-tenths" were to be divided among eighteen to thirty-four children in each class, the number of words uttered by students would be rather infinitesimal.[3] What is more apparent than conscious recognition is that through the domination of oral activity in the classroom, the teacher is exercising *social control*. The social ramifications of this kind of teaching behavior are awesome. First of all, the frequency of ideas, thoughts and concepts which the teacher transmits primarily vis-à-vis oral delivery makes him the focus of attention. He emerges as the authority and, for many students, an impossible model to emulate. Unless he is extremely careful, and in many cases it may be beyond his influence, fear, shame, and other social constraints along lines that relate to asking the right questions, expressing oneself in superlative style, conveyance of approval and acceptance of the instructor's theories, etc. could easily prevail as the dominant social climate in classrooms. This kind of social impact is not conducive for heuristic and self-initiated styles of learning. Of paramount concern, it is not conducive to the development of healthy personalities. Children need to be themselves and establish their own identities. In the process, they need reassurances and feelings of self-worth and success.

The domination of oral activity as the prominent mode of teaching could easily set the tone for classroom behavior characterized by frustration and alienation because of the built-in limitations of this kind of communication approach. Unless the transmitter (teacher) and the receiver (student) are tuned in to each other, a variety of misunderstandings, false impressions, and negative reactions could easily occur. Furthermore, if the student does not have the opportunity to clarify his interpretations and the teacher receives no direct

[3]William D. Floyd, "Do Teachers Talk Too Much?" *The Instructor,* 28:1 (August-September 1968), 53–55.

feedback upon which to evaluate the impact of his message, it augments a rift between the meeting of minds and the social distance between both parties.

The high frequency of oral activity on the part of teachers also induces social incompatibility in terms of teacher-pupil relationships by offending the "social awareness" of many students. Class presentations singularized by the predilections and experiences of the instructor have shortcomings in relating to what exists in reality and the consideration and adoption of alternative views held by the student which may be of more and/or of equal relevance. By talking *goodly,* the teacher forgets to listen and increases the probability of "rapping in splendor" which youth have identified as an innocuous approach to resolving problems and, in effect, a "mental massage."

STATUS AND ROLE

Every society has a social hierarchial structure and a particular mode of behavior ascribed to the varying levels of social position. The social structures of different societies vary. It also follows that the ways and means in which the different societies accentuate and integrate the social mechanisms to attain compatible social positions and the expectations identified with them also vary. In New Guinea, a non-technologically oriented society, the family is responsible for the socialization process of the child. Varying degrees of responsibility are shared according to the age and needs of the child beginning with the mother who absorbs the brunt of the responsibility during the child's early life.

In the American society which is in the ferment of a mechanistic age, the prime function of the family is to regulate the sexual expression of the child.[4] After birth, the child is separated from his mother and must adjust to a number of substitutes before he attends school because of the social schedule his mother must meet. In many cases, this schedule is intensified by a job she holds outside of the family. Therefore, it is the school that assumes the major responsibility for the socialization process of the child.

The school has a monopoly on the child's time and is viewed by the public as the agency that is most equipped to provide for the social and educational needs of the child. In addition to teaching, the school offers a wide range of ancillary services such as speech therapy, psychological help, contact for other specilized services, ie., medical and social welfare help, etc., free meals, if necessary, and even family-life education. The structural elements contained in the school that are most important for the socialization process of the child are as follows:

Age-grading. Very often a child proceeds from one grade to another because of an advancement of age. Because of the feeling of many educators that retainment often incurs social stigma, socio-emotional problems and the

[4]J. R. Seeley, R. A. Sim, and E. W. Loosley, *Crestwood Heights* (New York: John Wiley and Sons, Inc., 1965).

wrath of parents, the child is passed on. Also, with the coming of age is social status and role expectations in accord with a particular grade in school, of which the high schools are prominent examples. There is a great difference between the social behavior of a freshman and a senior in high school. The seniors have more latitude in dating, exclusive holds on student body offices, especially that of student body president, social events that are highlighted both in the local papers and the yearbook and, in general, possessing more prestige than the students in the lower grades. Also with the coming of age, students are able to exercise more socio-economic control in terms of obtaining money from part-time jobs for automobiles and stylish clothes, which is also tied to the prestige system.

Sex grouping. In private schools, the sexes are often separated at the onset of puberty and taught in separate schools. In public schools, this differentiation is not made but many activities are openly sex-linked in terms of eligibility for participation in certain high school activities, i.e. the competitive sports and social clubs. Other areas in the school curriculum that prescribe covert inclusion of the sexes are as follows:

Primarily Women	*Primarily Men*
Home Economics	Vocational Arts
Typing	Advanced Science Courses
	(Math in particular)
Physical Education Courses	Physical Education Courses
Family-Life Education	Family-Life Education

The distinct sex roles serve to foster the notion of a man-centered universe. The female sex is induced to serve the domestic needs of a household and share the status derived from her husband's occupation. What is significant is that women seem to be achieving a clearer self-identity and the opportunities to pursue their own status goals. It appears that in the near future social roles defined by sex will become blurred with the female sex making the greater transition in status and roles.

Peer socialization. The formation of groups, cliques and dyads become conspicuous in the latter years of a student's education. By being a member of these various social networks, the student can seek clarification of the social structure of the school and his immediate community. Certain kinds of questions like "Why is so-and-so popular?" and "What exists in reality" are asked and answered. What happens in the process is an amelioration of the social discrepancies that a student encounters.

Social identity is established by the number and status of clubs, groups and cliques that accept the individual student. The student dons a "social mask" and plays a role upon which feedback from the various social networks will serve as guides relative to the appropriateness of his behavior. The better he plays his role, the more social upward mobility; hence, more social prestige.

Isolated are those students who not only are not members of any particular group but also are members who refuse to fully participate in the "game theory" which is directed toward the winning of social acceptance. All kinds of suppositions are made in reference to their presumed inadequate social makeup.

Adolescents seem to have their own dominant patterns of behavior. It appears their lifestyle is definitive not only in terms of their manner of dress, speech, and music but also in differing ideas and values. The youth subculture is a reailty; whereas, such values as athletic prowess, popularity, and academic achievement permeate throughout their social structure, it seems that it is an oppositional mode in terms of the social forces that culminate in a generation gap which serves as the cohesive factor. Youth with their vivid cries of "tell it like it is," claim that the heart of the matter is the existence of social discrepancies contained in the value systems of the culture. Consequently, the schools are placed in the delicate position of resolving the conflict of what society expects of the student and what the student believes should be done. Often the problem becomes so intense that it is the school in the end who is blamed by both sides as being the contributor to cultural alienation.

CEREMONIES AND RITES

These are the adaptive mechanisms that facilitate the transition within the hierarchal social structure from one status to another and from one role to another. Ceremonies like commencements are held to formally recognize and prepare the students for their social transition. They also serve as a social reinforcer for everyone in attendance. An appeal to a sense of history, loyalty, and pride in one's culture highlights the program. Rites are generally confined to groups of people as opposed to a class of people. Rites which are utilized for initiation purposes convey social acceptance and the extension of the group to that particular student.

Adolescents and young adults in attendance of college often seem uncomfortable with the traditional format of ceremonies and rites. This is evidenced by their unique garb which is noncompliant to the traditional garb, their social defiance during the program to some of the norms and national policies of the culture and their refusal to accept awards and other achievements because of vast disagreement with the larger community. It is questionable whether the school can integrate the customs, beliefs, and values within a range of compatibility vis-à-vis ceremonies and rites.

TECHNOLOGY

Besides man's ability to use symbols, man's ability to invent and manipulate tools have set him apart from the rest of the primates. Historically, man has manufactured tools in an attempt to exercise control over his environment and to come to better grips with "reality." Thereby, he is setting in motion a process that would enable him to deal with the natural forces about him. This we call technology. Technology transcends that of men and machinery which Marshall McLuhan refers to as extensions of man. Technology is a process that brings to bear all the insights and resources that man can muster at any given time to deal with his natural environment.

Although there is a lag in the use of "hardware" and systems-oriented designs on the part of the schools as opposed to industry and the military, educators are moving rapidly to bridge the gap. Computerized instructional programs, multi-media equipment, functionally designed school-architecture and in general, the systems approach to education, are gradually becoming an integral part of the normal operation of schools. In retrospect, the school is not only trying to keep up with a rapidly changing technological society but also to prepare a more dynamic learning environment for students.

School behavior is greatly affected as the school becomes more involved in education technology. First of all, the traditional role of teaching is altered. Instead of being the transmitter of knowledge, the teacher is viewed as a resource guide. He is also able to give more individualized help when needed because his teaching role no longer harnesses him to be the focal point of attention. The social climate of classes that have access to educational technological services and equipment seem more relaxed and open.

Technology in the schools has considerable impact upon the students' social behavior. Students appear to develop a belief system which views man as the center of his universe. Nature can be controlled and dominated by man because nature is viewed as being basically mechanical and explicative relative to the laws of physics and chemistry.

In this mechanistic system of belief, man's social universe is perceived as a hierachal ordering. One's position in the hierarchy is secured through the social mechanisms of the culture, i.e. achievement, popularity, social contacts, etc.

To say this represents the general populous of school behavior is inaccurate. For the schools, unlike many other social systems, are directly tied to tradition. It is society that runs the schools as evidenced by the mode of financing and the powers the school board possesses. It is for this reason that schools in the American society serve as excellent case studies in ascertaining the cultural patterns that are brought to bear in the socialization process of the child.

THE SCHOOL AS THE PRINCIPAL AGENT OF SOCIAL TRANSMISSION

As discussed previously, the school has replaced the family in terms of assuming the responsibilities assigned to the socialization process of children.

The school has also replaced the Church as the ideological source. Documentations illustrate where traditionally the "destiny of the country lay in its Christian heritage," now the might of the country rests with its educational resources" and "knowledge is power." The school is not only responsible for the social adjustment and emotional well-being of the child but also for his ethical development. So often school authorities work hand-in-hand with juvenile authorities as well as family case workers. Often it is the school that initiates the machinery for specilized social services at the request of the family or where there is a clear cut breakdown on the part of the home to do so.

As one readily deduces, the onus of responsibility placed upon the schools are great. The school cannot continue its pursuit of quality education without the rest of society sharing in the burden of socializing the child. In some cases, the school is also charged with the responsibility of feeding and clothing needy children. As a result, the school cannot be all things to all men. Whenever certain social disruptions occur in society, somehow the public traces its social antecedents to the school.

CONCLUSION

To study the school is to study the cultural mode of life. It follows that much of the culture is learned through the schools. But not all cultures entrust this responsibility to the school. Such cultures as the Balinese and the Iatmuls transmit their customs from person to person. The family is entrusted with the major share of socializing the child.

A study of the school in the American society is not a study of the whole culture. It is a study of human behavior within a socio-cultural system which is in context made up of a myriad of social interaction in vivo, in natural setting, within the larger community. The cultural interplay between the community and the school is an on-going event with no conspicuous demarcation where the involvement of both begin and end in the educational process of the child. Dr. Walter Goldschmidt describes the role of education in terms of continuity of culture very aptly:

> Education, in sum, is the process by which both the obvious aspects of culture and its hidden minutiae are transmitted from one generation to another and passed on through time. It is partly a conscious and deliberate process, partly automatic or unconscious, both on the part of the teacher and the pupil. Education does not cause or create culture, for it is itself a part of culture: cultural patterns set the attitudes of education and training. Yet, insofar as each of us is a piece of our own culture, the educational process to which we have been subjected has created that part in us.[5]

[5]Walter Goldschmidt, *Exploring the Ways of Mankind* (New York: Holt, Rinehart and Winston, 1966).